HISTORY OF BIBLICAL INTERPRETATION

VOLUME 2: FROM LATE ANTIQUITY
TO THE END OF THE MIDDLE AGES

Society of Biblical Literature

Resources for Biblical Study

Susan Ackerman, Old Testament/Hebrew Bible Editor
Tom Thatcher, New Testament Editor

Number 61

History of Biblical Interpretation
Volume 2: From Late Antiquity to the End of the Middle Ages

HISTORY OF BIBLICAL INTERPRETATION

VOLUME 2: FROM LATE ANTIQUITY TO THE END OF THE MIDDLE AGES

By

Henning Graf Reventlow

Translated by

James O. Duke

Society of Biblical Literature
Atlanta

HISTORY OF BIBLICAL INTERPRETATION VOLUME 2: FROM LATE ANTIQUITY TO THE END OF THE MIDDLE AGES

Original title: *Epochen der Bibelauslegung Band II: Von der Spätantike bis zum Ausgang des Mittelalters*, by Henning Graf Reventlow, copyright © Verlag C.H. Beck oHG, Munich 1994. English translation produced under license from the publisher.

Library of Congress Cataloging-in-Publication Data

Reventlow, Henning, Graf.
   [Epochen der Bibelauslegung. English]
   History of biblical interpretation / by Henning Graf Reventlow
      p. cm. — (Society of Biblical Literature resources for biblical study ; no. 50, 61–63)
   Includes bibliographical references and indexes.
   ISBN-13: 978-1-58983-202-2 (paper binding, vol. 1 : alk. paper) — ISBN 978-1-58983-455-2 (paper binding, vol. 2 : alk. paper) — ISBN 978-1-58983-459-0 (paper binding, vol. 3 : alk. paper) — ISBN 978-1-58983-460-6 (paper binding, vol. 4 : alk. paper)
   1. Bible—Criticism, interpretation, etc.—History. I. Title.
   BS500.R4813 2009b V. 2
   220.609—dc22
                                                      2009045014

17 16 15 14 13 12 11 10 09   5 4 3 2 1
Printed in the United States of America on acid-free, recycled paper conforming to ANSI/NISO Z39.48-1992 (R1997) and ISO 9706:1994 standards for paper permanence.

Contents

Abbreviations

Primary Sources

Abr.	Ambrose, *De Abraham*
Acad.	Cicero, *Academicae quaestiones*
Apol. Hier.	Rufinus, *Apologia contra Hieronymum*
b.	Babylonian Talmud
Brev.	Bonaventure, *Breviloquium* (*Brief Discourse*)
Cain	Ambrose, *De Cain et Abel*
Cant.	Venerable Bede, *In Cantica canticorum*
Coll. Hex.	Bonaventure, *Collationes in Hexaemeron*
Comm. Apoc.	Rupert of Deutz, *Commentaria in Apocalypsim*
Comm. Joh.	John Scotus Eriugena, *Commentarius in Evangelium Johannis*; Rupert of Deutz, *Commentaria in Evangelium sancti Joannis*; Bonaventure, *Commentarius in Evangelium Johannis*
Comm. Luc.	Bonaventure, *Commentarius in Lucam*
Comm. sent.	Thomas Aquinas, *Commentaria in Libros Sententiarum*
Conc.	Joachim of Fiore, *Liber Concordiae Novi ac Veteris Testamenti* (*Book of the Harmonies of the Old and New Testaments*)
Congr.	Philo, *De congressu eruditionis gratia* (*On the Preliminary Studies*)
Conl.	John Cassian, *Conlationes patrum* (*The Conversations of the Fathers*)
Did.	Hugh of St. Victor, *Didascalion de studio legendi* (*Textbook on the Study of Reading*)
Div. praed.	John Scotus Eriugena, *De divina praedestinatione* (*On Divine Predestination*)
Dom. div.	John Wyclif, *De dominio divino*

Enarrat. Ps.	Ambrose, *Enarrationes in XII Psalmos davidicos*; Augustine, *Enarrationes in Psalmos* (*Enarrations on the Psalms*)
Ep. miss.	Gregory the Great, *Moralia in Job, Epistola missoria ad Leandrum*
Ep.	*Epistula(e)*
Etym.	Isodore of Seville, *Etymologiae* (*Etymologies*)
Exc.	Ambrose, *De excessu fratris sui Satyri*
Exp. Apoc.	Joachim of Fiore, *Expositio in Apocalypsim* (*Exposition of the Apocalypse of John*)
Exp. Luc.	Ambrose, *Expositio Evangelii secundum Lucam*
Exp. Ps. 118	Ambrose, *Expositio Psalmi CXVIII*
Expl. Apoc.	Venerable Bede, *Explanatio Apocalypseos*
Fasc. ziz.	*Fasciculi zizaniorum* (*Booklet about Weed*)
Fid. Grat.	Ambrose, *De fide ad Gratianum*
Gen. litt.	Augustine, *De Genesi ad litteram* (*On Genesis Literally Interpreted*)
Gen. Rab.	Genesis Rabbah
Glor. et hon.	Rupert of Deutz, *De gloria et honore filii hominis super Mattheum*
Glor. trin.	Rupert of Deutz, *De glorificatione trinitatis et processione Sancti Spiritus*
Hex.	Ambrose, *Hexaemeron libri sex* (*Six Days of Creation*)
Hist. eccl.	Venerable Bede, *Historia ecclesiastica gentis Anglorum* (*Church History of the English People*)
Hom. Ezech.	Gregory the Great, *Homiliae in Ezechielem*
Inst.	John Cassian, *De institutis coenobiorum*
Inter. Gen.	Alcuin, *Interrogationes et responsiones in Genesin*
Isaac	Ambrose, *De Isaac vel anima* (*Isaac, or The Soul*)
Jac.	Ambrose, *De Jacob et vita beata* (*Jacob and the Happy Life*)
Lect. Eph.	Thomas Aquinas, *Lectura super Epistolam ad Ephesios*
Lib. fig.	Joachim of Fiore, *Liber figurarum* (*Book of Figures*)
Moral.	Gregory the Great, *Moralia in Job* (*Magna moralia*)
LXX	Septuagint
Off.	Ambrose, *De officiis ministrorum*
Opif.	Ambrose, *De opificio mundi* (*On the Creation of the World*)
Parad.	Ambrose, *De paradiso* (*On Paradise*)

Patr.	Ambrose, *De benedictionibus patriarcharum* (*The Patriarchs*)
Periph.	John Scotus Eriugena, *Periphyseon*
Pesiq. Rab.	Pesiqta Rabbati
prooem.	prooemium
Psalt.	Joiachim of Fiore, *Psalterium decem chordarum* (*Psalter of Ten Strings*)
Quaest.	Isodore of Seville, *Quaestiones in Vetus Testamentum* (*Questions on the Old Testament*)
Quodl.	Thomas Aquinas, *Quodlibeta*
Retract.	Augustine, *Retractationum libri II* (*Retractions*); Venerable Bede, *Retractatio* (*Retractions*)
Ruf.	Jerome, *Adversus Rufinum* (*Apology against Rufinus*)
Sacr.	Ambrose, *De sacramentis* (*The Sacraments*); Hugh of St. Victor, *De sacramentis christianae fidei*
Sanct. trin.	Rupert of Deutz, *De sancta trinitate et operibus eius* (*On the Holy Trinity and Its Works*)
Sanh.	*Sanhedrin*
Script.	Hugh of St. Victor, *De scripturis et scriptoribus sacris* (*On the Holy Scriptures and Their Authors*)
Summa theol.	Thomas Aquinas, *Summa theologica*
Sup. Rom.	Thomas Aquinas, *Super Epistolam ad Romanos lectura*
Tract.	Joachim of Fiore, *Tractatus super quottuor Evangelia* (*Treatise on the Four Gospels*)
Ver.	Thomas Aquinas, *De veritate sacre scripture*; John Wyclif, *De veritate sacre scripture* (*On the Truth of the Holy Scriptures*)
Vict.	Rupert of Deutz, *De victoria verbi Dei*
Vita Ant.	Athanasius, *Vita Antonii* (*Life of Antony*)
y.	Jerusalem Talmud
Yebam.	Yebamot

Secondary Sources

ALKG	*Archiv für Litteratur- und Kirchengeschichte des Mittelalters*
BGBH	Beiträge zur Geschichte der biblischen Hermeneutik
BGPhMA	Beiträge zur Geschichte der Philosophie und Theologie des Mittelalters

BJRL	*Bulletin of the John Rylands University Library of Manchester*
CCCM	Corpus christianorum: Continuatio mediaevalis
CCSL	Corpus Christianorum: Series latina
CSEL	Corpus scriptorum ecclesiasticorum latinorum
FC	Fathers of the Church
MGH	Monumenta Germaniae historica
MGH, QG	Monumenta Germaniae historica, Quellen zur Geistesgeschichte des Mittelalters
MGWJ	*Monatsschrift für Geschichte und Wissenschaft des Judentums*
O.P.	*ordo praedicatorum*
PG	Patrologia graeca. Edited by Jacques-Paul Migne. 162 vols. Paris: Migne, 1857–1886.
PL	Patrologia latina. Edited by Jacques-Paul Migne. 217 vols. Paris: Migne, 1844–1864.
PTA	Papyrologische Texte und Abhandlungen
PTS	Patristische Texte und Studien
RGG	*Religion in Geschichte und Gegenwart.* Edited by Kurt Galling. 7 vols. 3rd ed. Tübingen: Mohr Siebeck, 1957–1965.
RThAM	*Recherches de theologie ancienne et medievale*
SBLWGRW	Society of Biblical Literature Writings from the Greco-Roman World
SC	Sources chrétiennes
SMRL	Studies in Medieval and Renaissance Latin
TAPS	Transactions of the American Philosophical Society
TRE	*Theologische Realenzyklopädie.* Edited by Gerhard Krause and Gerhard Müller. 36 vols. Berlin: de Gruyter, 1976–2004.
TThSt	Trierer Theologische Studien
TTS	Tübinger Theologische Studien
TRE	Theologische Realenzyklopädie
WdF	Wege der Forschung
ZKG	*Zeitschrift für Kirchengeschichte*

Introduction

With this book, the second of a planned multivolume series on the history of biblical interpretation is brought to the public. It spans roughly a thousand years, from late antiquity to the end of the Middle Ages. A clear line of demarcation is set neither at the start nor the end. Late antiquity and the Middle Ages can be differentiated from each other in various ways; in reality, the two overlap because the legacy of antiquity endured long beyond the end of the western Roman Empire (if this is where one draws a line). Everywhere in western Europe and North African until the Islamic invasion, the Latin language and the sciences of antiquity formed a cultural bond uniting secular and spiritual learning, court life—inasmuch as some, like Charlemagne, tried to promote culture at court—and clerical formation. Throughout the Middle Ages, monasticism continued a tradition that had begun in the setting of ancient Egypt but accepted more and more other cultural materials, too. To this extent, the Christian West can be spoken of as a cultural unity—without denying a great deal of diversity in it also. Since the pages that follow are concerned with the interpretation of the Bible, the Jewish contributions to the understanding of the Holy Scriptures are also to be remembered gratefully.

A clear turning point can no more be identified for the end of the period than for its start. Although the Renaissance is usually seen as the start of new epoch bringing the Middle Ages to their end, this is actually the case only in a limited sense. Many medieval ways of thinking were influential for far much longer. Nevertheless, it seemed wise to set a cutoff point at the fourteenth century. At the end of this period, new developments announce themselves that can await treatment in a later volume.

A full thousand years of the history of interpretation produced a body of literature too vast for even approximate coverage in the space available here. Thus in this volume, even more than in volume 1, only a selection of exemplars can be offered. This time the area the work covers is itself more and more limited to the West. This outcome is virtually a matter of course in as the work proceeds, because advances of knowledge in understanding the Bible took place chiefly in the western part of the former Roman Empire from the early Middle Ages on. But above all only a select circle of the large number of exegetes can be gathered into our field of vision.

Medieval biblical interpretation is in large measure a literature of tradition. Not originality, but the true preservation of the ways of understanding passed down from the fathers, was the highest goal of the teachers who offered instruction in the cathedral schools and monasteries and handed on the fruits of the readings of their predecessors in their lectures. Thus, with the passing of antiquity came as well, with few exceptions, the end of the succession of figures of the church fathers who worked highly independently and left their deep impress on later times.

Nevertheless, it is possible in the case of the Middle Ages to point out the dominant foci and methods of selected biblical interpreters and some of their most important commentaries. Despite how little is known of the biography of these exegetes in so many cases, the distinctiveness of their thought comes into view vividly in their works. When we learn something of the circumstances in which they lived, the conditions under which they wrote their works and taught their students, and the institutions in which they were active, we draw more closely to their understanding of the Bible, which at our first glance may often seem strange. Thus most of the chapters in this volume discuss a particular interpreter, selected mainly on the basis of which theologians can be considered especially representative of a specific type of biblical understanding. These are not always the best-known names; it was fascinating to deal at times as well with an interpreter who is mentioned more at the margin of customary handbooks.

This volume is not meant to be a handbook for specialists. It makes no claim to be encyclopedic in character. Such a goal is ever more difficult to achieve in any case. Thus, field specialists will discover numerous gaps and regard other authors or works more important than those treated here. Yet it seemed more important to show the large contexts in which biblical interpretation developed in the West. How one generation of exegetes stands on the shoulders of another, how knowledge that had been gained in earlier times had powerful ongoing effects, is one of the most important insights to be gained from the history of medieval biblical interpretation. The younger generations acknowledged their debt to the elders gratefully; some—like Augustine, Gregory the Great, or Jerome, in particular—are named time and again. These connections seem to be largely broken off in the modern age. It is therefore time to remember our predecessors in faith and their dealings with the Bible.

1

FAMOUS INTERPRETERS OF LATE ANTIQUITY

1.1. IT DEPENDS ON THE LITERAL SENSE: THEODORE OF MOPSUESTIA

Antioch (today Antakia), situated on the Orontes in northern Syria, was in the fourth century the third largest city of the Roman Empire and at the time experienced its flowering. For a time it was, along with Constantinople (built 324–330 C.E.), an economic and cultural center for all Asia Minor. Though the native language was Syriac, Greek remained as before the language of the cultured. The influence of Hellenistic culture remained unbroken since the city's founding around 300 B.C.E. by Seleucus I, a former general of Alexander the Great and the first ruler of the Seleucid Empire, although after 64 B.C.E. Antioch belonged to the Roman Empire as the capital of the province of Syria.

The first Christians had been in the city early on. There were probably missions first among the Jews (Acts 11:19); the original Jerusalem community sent Barnabas there (11:22–24); he then accompanied Paul from Tarsus to Antioch (11:25–26). There was already, it appears, a mission also to pagans at the time. The pillar apostles permitted Paul's Gentile mission (Gal 2:1–10; see also Acts 15) and upheld its legitimacy despite disputes with Jewish Christians (see Gal 2:11–14). Extensive mission activity developed from Antioch in the first century, to which at first Barnabas and Paul were chosen together (Acts 13:1–3) until they later separated and each undertook missions on his own initiative (15:36–41). The bishop of Antioch around the turn of the century was Ignatius, who suffered martyrdom in Rome shortly after 110. While journeying there, he wrote his well-known letters to churches in Asia. By his day a hierarchy with bishop, presbyters, and deacons had developed in the church.

During the next two centuries the Christian communities in Antioch underwent a varied history. Christians grew steadily in numbers under repeated persecutions; already in the fourth century the population was largely Christian. A fundamental change in Christianity's official status came in 324, when the emperor Constantine finally defeated his co-ruler in the East, Licinius, and united the whole eastern part of the empire and the West under his scepter. Constantine raised Christianity to the state religion. He did his utmost to glorify the new faith in Antioch, too, beginning with the construction of the Golden Cathedral, considered one of the largest and most splendid churches of the empire. In 325 "all Asia" was lodged under the patriarchate of Antioch. If, because of the changed political situation, the large mass of inhabitants now professed Christianity publicly, this did not always mean a change of life or inner attitude. This is shown by the sermons given in Antioch between 386 and 398 by the famous John who was later nicknamed Chrysostomos ("the golden-tongued") because of his eloquence.

There was also a radical solution: monasticism. It had spread from Egypt throughout Asia, and in Antioch also zealous young Christians renounced marriage and worldly careers and withdrew to ascetic lives, biblical study, and meditation in the surrounding wilderness. Although there were what strike us today as bizarre forms of self-mortification, such as being walled up in a cell or living on a pillar (both by Simeon Stylites, 390–459 and ca. 521–596), the hermits and monasteries radiated a strong impulse of faith, and they were above all places of theological work, too.

Antioch developed into the second center of Greek theology, in competition with Alexandria. We cannot in this context delve into the early church's confusing dogmatic disputes about Christology and the Trinity, which prompted a schism lasting for decades in Antioch (330–414). Much of this cannot even be adequately evaluated any longer, because each victorious party of the time destroyed the writings of the vanquished. They sought by this means to prevent the spread of their teachings, which we now know from accounts by opponents alone. But we are not concerned at all with the early church history of dogma, which handbooks present at length. The conflict over confessional statements that theologians of the first Christian centuries fought out with one another, the judgments that synods drafted about christological formulae, are only *one* side of theological work. There was an unbroken awareness that the Holy Scripture was the real foundation of Christian faith and Christian teaching; it, above all else, was to be understood. Hence it is no accident that many of the most significant theologians wrote numerous biblical commentaries, frequently dealing with both Testaments of the entire Bible book by book. Most of these writings likewise are apparently lost. The Antiochene theologians were especially unfortunate in this regard, since they were much later accused of heresy. Nevertheless, based on what survives or on commentaries recently constructed from citations and catena (collections of patristic citations arranged by biblical passages) by modern researchers, we can form for ourselves a good picture of the distinctive features of Antiochene exegesis.

The concern was first and foremost with the text of the Bible itself, that is, the Old Testament in Greek translation, the Septuagint. Origen had already made use of comparisons of other translations and the Hebraic original for the reproduction of a reliable text, the Hexapla, the sole exemplar of which lay in the library of Caesarea. Lucian (martyred in 312), working in Antioch from roughly 260 on, used this text and others in order to produce his own version of the Septuagint, which then spread across the entire East. For him, it was important to interpret the terms derived from Hebrew that violated classical Greek stylistic sensibility and to smooth over the crudest offenses against Greek syntax. Later Antiochenes then composed extensive commentary literature on both Testaments.

The distinctive features of the biblical interpretation carried on in Antioch first becomes understandable when we look at the educational system prevailing at the time among the Greek-speaking classes or the upper classes who understood this language, particularly in the East of the Roman Empire. Hellenistic culture lived by dealing with classical Greek literature and poetry. Homer played a central role in this (see *History*, 1:29–36). The *Iliad* and *Odyssey* were the reading materials on the basis of which a grammar teacher taught youngsters reading and writing. Thereafter a qualified teacher of the second level instructed them about figurative language and poetic literature. The mature student reached the highest level of education with the rhetorician, who, again by drawing upon classical literature, led him into the techniques and art of extemporaneous speech. For the most part the student remained with this teacher several years. High-state office-holders, nobles, and rich property owners allowed themselves to send their sons to the school of a famous rhetorician, often in a far-away city. After a few years, this schooling enabled the young people, having also gained sound morality, to assume positions similar to that of their fathers or (since fathers often died early) their uncles.

We are particularly well-informed about school conditions in Antioch. The famous rhetorician Libanius taught there from 354 until his death in 393. Students came to him from the most far-flung provinces, and he instructed them on the basis of the classical authors. His vast correspondence informs us in detail of his relations to his students and their fathers, who held influential posts. Schooling in rhetoric was the basic precondition for career progress, and classical education was expected for social status. In addition, strengthening the personality of his students was very much on Libanius's heart. Even Antioch's Christian citizens entrusted the education of their sons to him, although he remained a lifelong pagan. A series of later leading bishops and theologians such as Basil the Great, Gregory of Nazianzus, and John Chrysostom attended his school. Theodore of Mopsuetia is said to have been among them.

Theodore was born in Antioch in 352. If we can trust the church historian Socrates (*Hist. eccl.* 6.3), Theodore attended the school of Libanius after 366 and left in 370. He converted to Christianity in 368. In 370 or 371 he entered the *asketerion*, a sort of informal monastic community that Diodore of Tarsus, the founder of the Antiochene exegetical school, had established in Antioch for biblical study and ascetic living for young Christians who took seriously their faith and Christian ideals. Among others, the young John Chrysostom stayed there, too. Two of his writings to Theodore are preserved (*Ad Theodorum lapsum* [*Exhortation to Theodore after His Fall*]). Using fiery words, John ordered Theodore to return to the monastery community after Theodore had temporarily withdrawn with the intention of pursuing a legal education and marrying. Celibacy was one of the most important rules of monasticism. John's appeal was evidently successful, because Theodore resumed his biblical study and ascetic life, and Bishop Flavian of Antioch ordained him a priest around 383. In 392 he assumed the office of bishop of Mopsuestia in Cilicia, which he administered until his death in 428. In its condemnation of his teachings, the fifth ecumenical Council of Constantinople in 553 presumably did him an injustice, because during his lifetime he was considered a true defender of the Nicene confession against Arians and other heretics. Unfortunately, the result of the condemnation was that of his commentaries only that on the twelve Minor Prophets remains fully preserved in its Greek original, whereas the important commentary on the Psalms, for example, can be reconstructed only in part and from mainly Latin catena-fragments and fragmentary quotations in other ancient writers. Others, like Theodore's John commentary, are preserved only in Syriac translation. Yet the case is much the same with Origen's literary remains. Only a few fragments of Diodore's commentary works are known; from them, however, it emerges that his method was very similar to that of his student Theodore. Thus, it seems well-advised to learn about the Antiochene method of interpretation from Theodore's commentaries, especially since they are generally regarded as the high point of Antiochene exegesis.

The distinctive features of his interpretation can best be gathered from his Old Testament commentaries. Already the Psalms commentary, which is to be considered one of Theodore's relatively early works, reflects a special exegetical method. What is most striking there—because it represents an absolute exception among early church biblical interpreters—is that he engages in textual criticism for passages where the Septuagint text before him seems to be destroyed; that is, he tries to reconstruct the passage by comparison with other textual witnesses. Unfortunately, he rarely does so by referring to the Hebrew original text. (So on Ps 25 [24 in the LXX]:14–15: "And he makes known his covenant to them"—"In the Hebrew scrolls it reads: 'He will also communicate his testament to them.'" So, too, Symmachus reads: "And he will make his covenant known to them.") Since Theodore is not thought to have understood Hebrew, such reports are probably second-hand. References to other Greek translators are more frequent: Symmachus, as already above, is quoted most; Aquila and Theodotion, less frequently. Textual mistakes due to scribal errors that distorted the sense are noted (so in Ps 56 [55]:8, which is an error already coming from the Hebrew text: "You will *save* the godless on account of their offense," instead of *reject* [them]—in Greek only an additional s: *soseis* instead of *oseis*).

In addition to such text-critical measures, however, Theodore also discusses the linguistic form of the Septuagint text before him. He realizes, correctly, that its stylistic impurities as judged by the Greek sense of style are the result of translation from Hebrew. Since Hebrew has only two tenses, which are often carried over mechanically in the LXX, he decides on time changes (future for present and so on) in order to reconstruct a sequence of tenses corresponding to Greek grammar. When a statement about the future is made in a past tense, he speaks of an "exchange of times." He also recognizes other stylistic peculiarities coming from the Hebrew, such as the regular use of two verbs for a single action (dieresis) or variant meanings of a word unknown in Greek, such as the use of the same verb for "say," "think," and "feel." Other observations have to do with figurative uses of terms, such as the part for the whole (synecdoche: e.g., "soul," "flesh," "heart," "tongue" for the whole person, as in Ps 35 [34]:28) and the concrete for the abstract (metonymy: the "right hand" of God for help, his "arm" for power, and so forth). He also examines the rich metaphors and comparisons appearing in the Psalms. This careful reflection on unusual linguistic forms reflects the classical-philological schooling that Theodore now applies to biblical interpretation. Decisive here are the exact literal sense and the logical sequence of the statement—a standard that understandably enough raises special problems in the Psalms.

With regard to interpreting content, Theodore seems to identify for each psalm an overall meaning, a "hypothesis," that he set in advance of the actual interpretation. Here also he is following the rules of Greek secular hermeneutics. He accepts the titles subsequently prefixed to individual psalms—often becoming unintelligible headings in the Septuagint translation—only when they seem in keeping with the text that follows. But he shares the traditional view that considers David the author of all the psalms. His search for a historical occasion for each psalm—this, too, is a characteristic trait of Antiochene exegesis—leads him first to suppose this in David's life itself (as already had been done in some of the psalm headings). This works for a number of psalms relating, for example, to the persecution by Saul (Pss 11 [10]; 17 [16]; 36 [35]; 39 [38]; 64 [63]), the adultery with Bathsheba (Pss 6; 13 [12]; 38 [37]), the rebellion of Absalom (Pss 3; 22 [21]; 70 [69]), or the plot of Ahithophel (Ps 7). But another group of psalms clearly belong to a later period of Israel's history, thus in the time of Solomon (Ps 72 [71]), the siege of Jerusalem by Rezin and Pekah at the time of Ahaz (Ps 46 [45]; see also Isa 7) or that by Sennacherib at the time of Hezekiah (e.g., Pss 14 [13]; 52 [51]; 53 [52]; 54 [53]), many even in the Babylonian captivity (e.g., Pss 5; 23 [22]; 24 [23]; 26 [25]), the return from there (e.g., Pss 40 [39]; 65 [64]), and even in the Maccabean era (e.g., Pss 44 [43]; 47 [46]; 55–60 [54–59]). This, according to Theodore, is explained in that David, inspired by the Spirit of God, had prophetic visions in which he was transposed into future figures of history and could speak in their name, in this way announcing beforehand what was to occur centuries after him. "As regards Jeremiah, the blessed David prophesies by assuming his person [*prosopon*] and speaks in prophecy of what was appropriate that the latter would so speak of the matter according to the situation of things" (Hypothesis to Ps 34). Theodore thus deals with the problem that the psalms are not usually formulated as prophecies but as laments, petitions, praise, and thanks—a peculiar combination of exegesis of the literal sense, historical considerations (both results of Hellenistic-philosophical schooling), and the Christian doctrine of inspiration. A striking principle is that Theodore limits the fulfillment of such prophetic foresight to the people and history of Old Testament Israel from the Maccabean era to the end. In addition, with regard to Ps 16 [15]:10 ("You will not let your holy one experience corruption"), which according to Acts 13:35 Peter quotes about Jesus

Christ, Theodore denies that it is a direct prophetic foretelling of Christ. Everything, even the words of Jesus on the cross from Ps 22 [21]:2 ("My God, my God, why have you forsaken me?") or "into your hands I commend my Spirit" from Ps 31[30]:16, means only an accommodated usage that the pious of all ages gave to the prophetic words of psalms that had already been fulfilled. Only four psalms refer with little doubt directly to Christ: Ps 2, in which Christ reveals his kingly rule over the world to David after the resurrection; the triumph of the man Jesus raised by God in Ps 8; the king Christ and his bride, the church, in Ps 45 [44]; and, presumably, Ps 110 [109] also, although the comment on it is not preserved. These were psalms traditionally understood as christological, for which Theodore follows the customary interpretation.

This points to the fact that, in addition to historical prophecy of the literal sense and its fulfillment in human history, Theodore knows an additional level of sense for which the first is only preparatory. The Antiochene school calls it *theoria*, meaning, in the case of Christian understanding, the customary reference of the Old Testament to Christ. This, however, is shown only indirectly, not in the sense of direct foretelling or allegory. Theodore repeatedly polemicizes against the unfounded use of allegory (pursued by the Alexandrians). This becomes clearer when we turn our attention to Theodore's only fully preserved Old Testament commentary, that on the twelve Minor Prophets. This commentary is an early work of Theodore, like the Psalms commentary, and presumably arose not very long thereafter. The relatively large agreement of the two in basic approach and method goes along with the fact that Theodore in his overall view of Scripture shares the common view of the early church that regards Scripture as a whole as inspired and a unity. Scripture as a whole has a prophetic character. But Theodore also draws a boundary line: Proverbs and Ecclesiastes are "human teachings" that Solomon "himself wrote personally for the use of others, because he had not received the grace of prophecy but the gift of wisdom." For Job, Theodore holds that the narrative framework, which can lead to the emulation of pious Job, was filled in by the book's author, seeking fame with vain fables taken from the pagan cultural heritage. He also introduced the persons who converse with Job, the devil, who puts God to the test, and at the conclusion Elihu, "who says so much that is full of injustice against the righteous," so that the book as a whole deviates from the character of Holy Scripture (PG 66:697–98). Unworthy, too, is the way, right at the start (Job 3), that the author lets Job curse himself. Theodore therefore excludes the wisdom books from the Scriptures because they are not prophecy, and everything that is not historical is "pagan fables" and "fictions" (ibid.). Once again, the two levels toward which his thinking moves emerge here.

This is not the difficulty in the case of the prophetic books; they are prophetic in a direct sense, as even the Psalter can be. Theodore stresses ecstasy and visions as the means by which the prophets received a view of the future (on Nah 1:1; Sprenger 238,30–240,24; subsequent references to the Minor Prophets commentary are to this edition). He interprets the Minor Prophets from the outset as foretellings. But much as he did in the Psalms commentary, he limits the area of application of the predictions in historical-grammatical interpretation to the realm of Israel's history itself—which led later critics to accuse him of "Judaism." His John Commentary (see below) shows that the opposite is the case. Obviously, it has to do here also with a principle from Hellenistic hermeneutics going back as far as Aristarchus: Homer is to be explained from Homer. One must interpret a literary work out of itself, if one wants to introduce nothing from outside it. This principle certainly does not lighten the work of a Christian theologian for whom the customary direct interpretation of the Old Testament to Christ is taken for granted. But Theodore is a conscientious exegete. He tries to identify for each prophecy the historical setting to which it refers. That Scripture is a "true history of events" is important to him. Of help in this regard are, among other things, the titles of the prophetic books, which Theodore considers, unlike the titles of the Psalms, thoroughly credible. Thus in opposing the opinion that these prophets would not have prophesied around the time of King Uzziah, because there is no word against his crime (2 Chr 26:16), he cites the headings of Hosea, Isaiah, and Amos, in which the activity of the three prophets under this king is expressly confirmed (108,12–23). On Mic 1:15 (LXX), some maintain that the city of Lachish is mentioned because its inhabitants were the first in Judah to have killed a king, Amaziah. Against this, Theodore notes that, already before Amaziah, his father Joash (2 Kgs 12:21) and, as the text of 2 Kgs 14:19 clearly shows, Amaziah was murdered by the inhabitants not of Lachish but of Jerusalem. Therefore the four horns in Zech 1:21 cannot be the Assyrians, Babylonians, Medes, and Persians, as some interpreters claimed, because in Zechariah's day the Assyrians and Babylonians had been long punished, the Medes were disposed of by Cyrus, and the Persians did nothing evil to the Jews but even freed them from captivity (334,22–23.) Rather, the four horns are to be referred to the four corners of the world from which the different peoples will approach (333,7–10).

Theodore also allows close examination of historical circumstances in such passages to decide against the dominant view, where these contain dogmatically important information. As in the Psalms commentary, he excludes a direct foretelling of Christ in the Old Testament prophets. Thus especially for Zech 1:8, where other interpreters had seen in the "man" a reference to the Son of God. According to Theodore, this is impossible, because "none of those who (lived) before the appearance of the Lord Christ knew the Father and the Son" (325,3–4). "But since there was the designation of the Father and the Son in the Old Testament, in that God was called the universal Father because of the care for humans who were deemed worthy, and sons, those who were somewhat advanced in the appropriation of God, yet as I already said, no one then living knew of God as Father of the Son of God and the Son-God as the Son of God the Father" (325,6–11). Theodore decides on the question of the Holy Spirit in a similar way. He repeatedly emphasizes that the Old Testament prophets knew nothing of the Trinity (95,17–21; 210,28–30; 311,4–5, 16–18; 325,3–6, 10–11). When the Holy Spirit is spoken of in the Old Testament, it is not the Holy Spirit of the Christian Trinitarian creeds that is meant. Rather, the statement of Joel 2:18, "I will pour out my Spirit," means nothing other than "I will grant all," he says, "my abundant care" (95,15). The term "Spirit of God" in the Old Testament refers, as Theodore then explains, to God's grace, care, and disposition in general (95,20–21). He adduces additional examples of this and argues similarly on Hag 2:5, interpreting the statement "and my Spirit stands in your midst" as follows: "the 'my Spirit' refers to the grace (coming) from him [God]" (310,27–28).

Therefore, passages traditionally understood as messianic foretellings are related from the outset to events within the history of Old Testament Israel. Thus the promise in Mic 5:2 points, within the Old Testament itself, to Zerubbabel as the provisional fulfillment of Nathan's prophecy (here Theodore evidently thinks of Ps 89 [88]:30, 37, 38; see also Sprenger 213,14; 368,12) taking place with the return from exile (213,19–23). Zechariah 9:9–10 is another passage referring to Zerubbabel (367, 23–24).

On the whole, the proclamations of the prophets, at least at the outset, remain within the bounds of Old Testament history, which is summarized once more in the prologue to the Haggai commentary (303,8–305,8). It begins with the activity of the prophets Hosea, Joel, Amos, and Micah in the kingdom of the ten tribes in Samaria and Judah in Jerusalem, to which, in view of their multiple sins, is proclaimed the impending "punishment" by the Assyrians and the Babylonians, respectively, which then actually occurs. But they also announce the return of the people from captivity. Nahum announces the impending destruction of Nineveh by the Babylonians. Habakkuk and Zephaniah announce the impending punishment of the tribe of Judah, the only one remaining, and the inhabitants of Jerusalem because of their sins, by the Babylonians. Haggai summons those already returned from exile to the building of the temple, since God, who actually does not need the temple at all (Isa 66:1), wished the Judeans to do so. In this way they could conduct their worship to him appropriately for the time and improve their morals, so that in his time the Lord Jesus could appear from these people for the salvation of all. The last of the prophets, Malachi, announces that God will enter his temple and restore righteousness from the ingratitude of the people and the neglect of the priests; Elijah, his messenger, will prepare this coming. Theodore even sees the Maccabees already announced beforehand in several oracles of Zechariah and Malachi (Zech 11:11–14:21 [383–400]; Mal 3:3–4 [422]).

Of course, Theodore would not have been a Christian theologian if he had been unable to read the Old Testament as referring in a certain way to Jesus Christ (he regularly speaks of "the Lord Christ"). The truth "at hand" (see 368,3) that Theodore deals with in historical interpretation is indeed only (although also unavoidably) preparation for the real truth that first appears in a further step. Theodore seeks the transition in a finding that again receives its standard from classic rhetoric: prophetic statements are considered hyperbolic in reference to the Old Testament events they announce; they express more than is realized in these provisional fulfillments. We have already heard about Theodore's view of the inner Old Testament meaning of the outpouring of the spirit announced in Joel 3:1, but he is not content with this alone, especially because Peter quotes Joel 3:1–5 in the context of his proclamation of Christ in Acts 2:17–21. Theodore sees here a deeper significance behind the historical sense (the signs following the return of the people from exile). Since the law contains merely the shadow of coming things (an allusion to Heb 10:1) and so its fulfillments are only "all small," so in it "more is stated hyperbolically than the events contain." "The truth of what is said appeared, since it had the Lord Christ as its starting point, as altogether great and fruitful and in fact new, and surpassing what took place in the law" (96,14–24). The correctness of this view is confirmed also by the citation from Ps 16 [15] in Acts 2:27, 31: that God will not leave his soul in Hades and that his flesh will not see corruption, David says of himself "metaphorically and hyperbolically, because he was snatched from danger and decay. The truth of the matter points to the Lord Christ, because it was not the case that his soul was left in Hades but instead his body was restored by the resurrection, nor did his body suffer any sort of decay" (96,17–97).

But Theodore does not find this real truth very often. He deals with the announcement of salvation in Amos 9:11–12 similarly. Here, too, the provisional truth is the return of the people from the exile, but its true fulfillment is in the Lord Christ, on account of which James (Acts 15:13–18) quotes it as well (155,19–156,5). For Theodore there is likewise a reference to Christ in the promise in Mic 5:2 (see above) pointing within the Old Testament itself to Zerubbabel. This time it is supported not by a quotation from the New Testament but by reference back to Ps 89 [88], first citing verses 31–34 and then 30, 37, 38, then concluding that the latter verses cannot refer to David's descendants but to the kingdom of Lord Christ alone. The same holds for Zech 9:9–10, although "it is clear that this is said about Zerubbabel" (367,23–24) and not partly to Zerubbabel and partly to Christ, yet its real truth refers to Lord Christ, "since the law was only a shadow of everything relating to the Lord Christ" (see Heb 10:1; 367,30–31), to Christ, "who brings an end to the shadows of the law in all" (see Rom 10:4; 368,5). Scripture speaks here also in a hyperbolic way (368,2–3).

The method Theodore applies is the well-known typology. But the term "type" appears in Theodore only once, with regard to Jonah, "who represents in himself a type for what was to occur with Lord Christ" (174,17–18). Here Theodore refers to Matt 12:40 (172,16–19). It is characteristic of a type (*typos*) that it is at first an actual reality for its contemporaries, but its deeper meaning relates to a future event concealed in the prophecy that they have not experienced (definition in Theodore 170,4–8). But it seems obvious that Theodore limits the application of typology largely to cases in which the New Testament offers occasion for it.

For Theodore, however, Old Testament history as a whole reaches its goal in Christ.

> The prophets did not speak of this [the historical events] without any cause, but because God exercised his overall care for the people because of the expected Lord Christ, who was to come at this time for the common salvation of all. For his sake God set them apart from the peoples, distinguished them by circumcision, and provided that they would have a homeland, and by the ordinances of the law he instructed them, isolated at Mount Zion, in the worship of God they were to offer. Therefore when he appeared, the Lord Christ could make clear to all, in accord with the prophetic announcements and the corresponding governance of the people brought about from above, that he was not introducing salvation for all only recently but that this was long predetermined. (105,14–25)

Therefore, besides typological correspondences, there is also God's universal plan of salvation into which the history of the Old Testament people of God is incorporated.

Theodore knows of three periods within revelatory history. For the Old Testament period, it is necessary for God to be known as the creator of the world, indeed both the world in its entirety as well as humanity in particular. It can be shown nearly everywhere that Theodore is led to this knowledge by equivalent statements in the Old Testament. The only striking point is that he does not designate this history itself as an object or means of revelation. Yet something similar to it is to be found in his view of prophecy. The second period is ushered in particularly by the missionary command of Jesus in Matt 28:19, in which Christ taught us about the Trinity for the first time (311,11–14). The third stage is not reached until after Christ's ascension, when the Son's full divinity is made known to the disciples by the Holy Spirit. (Theodore refers to John 16:12–13; 326,10–11, 21–24.)

We have, then, reference to John's Gospel already in the commentary on the Minor Prophets. In his older age (possibly soon after 410), Theodore turned to the interpretation of this theologically significant Gospel. Although he is dealing with a New Testament book, we can detect a good many similarities to his Old Testament commentaries with respect to the methodological approach of his exegesis and his basic views. Theodore remained largely true to his position. On the other hand, he found himself challenged by the Gospel of John in a special way because it contains a wide range of theological, particularly christological, statements that Theodore was forced to evaluate. During the christological debates of his time, he held to a firmly dogmatic standpoint with which Johannine formulations were definitely not always in agreement. Since, on the other hand, the authority of this Gospel, as part of Holy Scripture, was for him beyond all doubt, it was necessary to interpret the texts in a sense compatible with his dogmatic view. In formulating matters this way, however, we must recall that the situation is being viewed from a modern standpoint and, as it were, from the outside. Theodore was—like countless biblical interpreters before and after him—understandably convinced that his dogmatics agreed with the Bible. The art of interpretation consisted in demonstrating this point from the text against those who think otherwise—"the heretics." An additional problem, specific to John, was due to this Gospel's placement alongside the Synoptic Evangelists Matthew, Mark, and Luke. For Theodore, like all his contemporaries, the biblical canon represented a unity, and there could be no sort of contradiction between its parts. Hence reconciliation of parallel traditions deviating from one another had to be found. This general problem applied to the Gospels in a special way.

Theodore set forth his principles of interpretation and the special problems of exegeting John's Gospel in the prologue of his commentary. (I cite the Latin transition of the Syriac edition of J.-M. Vosté, 1–7; comparisons are made to the pertinent Greek fragments in Devresse.) He first explains that he will discuss the simple passages only briefly and those of more difficulty at greater length, "so that when we explain words we do not ignore anything that is difficult for others and do not dwell on what is obvious to everyone simply by reading." "The task of the exegete, we believe, is to explain the words that are difficult to most others, while that of the preacher is to consider and speak about what is clear as well." Theodore also wants to express himself in brief, except "when we cannot make the explanation clear without using a lot of words—as is the case when we come to verses that are ruined by the tricks of heretics because of the sickness of their godlessness." "For it is also the task of the interpreter, especially one who interprets texts with precision, that he not only argues with authority but also refutes the view contrary to his words." The effects of these maxims make themselves known in the text of the commentary in that particularly those passages of christological significance but not always readily compatible with Theodore's christological theories are treated at length, while others are mentioned only briefly.

As to the origin of John's Gospel, Theodore states the view—unquestioned until the modern era—that its author was "the disciple whom Jesus loved," who is several times mentioned (John 13:23; 19:26; 20:2; 21:20). The Evangelist wrote this Gospel only after the other three Gospels had been written. "One finds the same and similar things described in those three Gospels," with apparently the only important difference to Theodore being that all three began their own Gospels differently. But there was no material contradiction, "because the one believed one had to write about the birth of our Lord in the flesh; … another began immediately with the baptism of John. Luke, however, began with the events relating to the birth of John, went on from there to the birth of our Lord, and also came himself to the baptism by John." The principle of the internal unity of the canon excluded true contradictions between the Gospels; thus Tatian had produced a harmony of the four Gospels, the *Diatessaron*, already in the second century. Above all, Theodore had to account for the existence of a fourth Gospel that deviated so considerably from the other three. According to his view—which he took, by the way, from Eusebius's *Ecclesiastical History* (3.24.6–13)—the other Gospels lay before the author when, at the request of the faithful in Asia because of his intimate relations with the Lord, he found himself ready to write his own Gospel. "They brought him the books of the Gospels in order to be apprised of his judgments about what was written in them. He praised the authors as very much in agreement with the truth. But they passed over quite a bit, he said, and indeed the miracles should be recounted without exception, but the doctrine in them was lacking in, as it were, completeness. Further, he added, while they reported on the coming of Christ in the flesh, his divinity should not have been passed over in silence." Theodore's chief interest in John's Gospel, as we see, is its christological statements, particularly those from which he thinks something about Christ's divinity can be derived. In so doing, he followed the creed of the Council of Nicaea (325), which, against the Arians, who regarded Jesus as a created being, had emphasized the Son's essential unity with the Father. As Theodore expressly says, it is its teaching that distinguishes the Gospel of John. It is Theodore the dogmatician who undertakes to interpret the Gospel; we detect this also in details at every step.

The program of the Evangelist (John) actually consisted in filling out the teaching missing in the other Gospels. "He thought he had to write about what the others had left out." He was concerned particularly with the discourses of Jesus and the miracles that the others had nearly all passed over. "But whenever he recalls a sign that they had already reported, he mentions it without question because of its special usefulness." The feeding of the five thousand in John 6 is one example, "because of the discourse associated with it, in which he [Jesus] speaks also of the mystery (of the Last Supper)." On the whole, the Gospel of John appears to be "a supplement (*complementum*) adding everything that was wished for and had been passed over by the others."

In addition, Theodore attests that John's Gospel took great care for the correct sequence of events and precise determinations of time and place, "because none of the others had bothered this." "That is to say, they reported many things that did not take place until later, and, vice versa, they narrated as later things that had occurred earlier." This astute observation and the view, which is more frequently advocated again today, that the chronology of John's Gospel may be on the whole more accurate than that of the Synoptics shows once again an interpreter who is amazingly progressive in many insights. Yet these differences do not disturb the harmony he presupposed; for example, with regard to the differing reports of the appearances of the Risen One, he says that the objections of "the intriguers" are unconvincing, because it suffices that the statements agree in essentials: "Since all proclaim the resurrection, cite the same day, and say that the women came to the grave first," while details that are due to human circumstances (such as that not all the Evangelists knew the Lord personally, not all the disciples were witnesses of the events because they had fled) are of no importance (Vosté, 244–45).

On the other hand, when dogmatic problems are touched on, his premises prevent him from a genuine understanding of the theological statements in John's Gospel. This applies to Christology in particular. One of the general premises characteristic of late Platonic thinking, which other Greek-educated theologians share as well, is Theodore's conviction that divinity—or, formulated in Johannine terms, the Word of God—is removed from the world, eternal and unchangeable. "That is, the nature of the Word of God did not assume the agony of the cross, nor will he encounter anything new soon after the passion" (Vosté, 199, on John 14:28). For it is "obvious that the divine cannot suffer" (Vosté, 51). Nor is motion within time and space conceivable of the eternal divine; that is, it would be a sign of great stupidity for anyone to claim that the divine "ascends" and "descends" (John 3:13). What sort of ascent and descent would this be for the one removed from the world, eternally, and for the one who is always in heaven and on earth?" (Vosté, 50)

After the definition of the Son as of the same essence with the Father had been set forth at Nicaea, the discussion among the theological schools went further into the relationship between the divine and the human in the person of Jesus. Theodore held to the view of the Antiochene school on this matter. According to it, the Word (the Logos) within the Trinity is of the same sort as God the Father, in accord with the formulation of the so-called Nicene (more precisely, the Niceno-Constantinopolitan) confession of faith still used today, "God from God, light from light, true God from true God." This Word, divine, unchanging, and incapable of suffering, assumed the man Jesus, and God's gracious act that came to completion in the resurrection of Jesus from death exalted him to the status of lordship. This is at the same time the event of the free-will choice of the man Jesus for the good, which was enabled by God's grace but took place nonetheless within the framework of human freedom. The Antiochenes, Theodore among them, laid great weight on the true humanity within the God-man person of the individual Jesus. But intellectual difficulties then arose here, too, because the inseparable unity of the divine and human in one person makes impossible statements about the man

Jesus that would mean a lower position of the Word of God with reference to the Father.

The effect of this, for Theodore, makes itself known in his John commentary, especially in the interpretation of the Gospel's christological statements. Thus at the statement in John 5:20, "for the Father loves the Son and shows him everything that he does, and will show him still greater works," Theodore states: "It is obvious that it is not in keeping with the words that precede it to take this literally, nor to refer it to the divinity itself. For what sort of things are these that the God-Word will see, shown him by the Father—he, who is the creator of all things visible and invisible, whose nature is higher than all else, he who himself equally does what the Father does, as he said above (in verse 19)?" (Vosté, 80). Theodore maintains that the Lord Jesus Christ assumed his human nature only for the sake of his hearers, the Jews, and "since indeed all things dwell in God by nature, but humans are ascribed all things according to series by God's unification to the Word," he wanted to dispel any doubt with respect to his person. Similarly, with regard to John 10:15, "just as the Father knows me, so I know the Father": "He says this about his human nature, as the context clearly shows. That is, inasmuch as I have a familial relation with the Father that does not end, I cannot become a stranger to him later either, since, indeed, the one who acknowledges I am the Word-Son by my unification with God recognizes him as Father." (Vosté, 145)

In the view of the Antiochene theologians, the Son is equal to the Father only with respect to his divine nature; with respect to his human nature, however, he is subordinate. He is Son by the assumption (adoption) of the man Jesus. The disciples do not learn of his divine nature until the gift of Spirit at Pentecost. As regards John 20:22–23, where the Risen One tells the disciples, "receive the Holy Spirit," Theodore comments: "He said this 'to receive' for 'you will receive it,' because if he had given the disciples the Spirit when he breathed on them, … it would have been superfluous to tell them later, at the time of his ascent to heaven, … to wait for the promised Spirit, and then, 'you will receive the power of the Holy Spirit' (Acts 1:8)" (Vosté, 254). At John 20:27, where Thomas addresses the Risen One as "my Lord and my God": "What? While Thomas had not previously believed that the Savior had risen from the dead, he now calls him Lord and God? This is unlikely." It would be an exclamation of surprise only because of the miracle. In addition to his christological principles, Theodore's view of the Bible overall plays a role here: such contradictions should never appear. But this model of thinking can be readily harmonized with only a portion of the statements Jesus makes about

himself in John's Gospel, namely, those in which he stresses his dependence on the Father, such as John 7:16–18 and 14:10b, 24b, 28b. Theodore
calls attention to these words beforehand, in his prologue: "For he [Jesus]
was accustomed to refer all his words and deeds to the Father, since he
expressly attested to this when he said that what he himself speaks and
does is not his own" (Vosté, 6).

But there are also words in which a distinction of the two natures in
Jesus hardly seems possible. Here Theodore is forced into a very complex
interpretation. So, on John 3:13: "And no one ascends to heaven except the
one who descends from heaven, the Son of Man." Obviously the "descending" and "ascending" here refers to one and the same person. The descent,
as we saw, cannot be said of the eternal Godhead. On the other hand, "but
when this is said of his human nature, which in fact rises from earth to
heaven (Acts 1:9), then this 'descending' does not apply to him; since he
is born of the seed of David, by no means does he descend from heaven."
The solution Theodore finds is that Jesus summarized his divine and
human nature for him (Vosté, 50) because what was said had exceeded
Nicodemus's ability to grasp it. He interprets John 16:28 similarly (Vosté,
217). In other cases he must reckon with vague ways of speaking, as in
John 3:16, where suffering seems linked to the divine nature (the "only
begotten Son" (Vosté, 51–52), or John 6:33, where the "bread that comes
down from heaven" seems to suggest the preexistence of Christ's body.
This too could only be meant figuratively (Vosté, 101–102).

As might be expected, the well-known statements in the prologue of
John's Gospel that are irreconcilable with Theodore's Christology pose the
greatest difficulties for him. He can avoid the discrepancies, evident even
to his eyes, only by tortured interpretations. On John 1:14a, "and the Word
became flesh," he remarks, "Word is used here in a very conspicuous way.
This, he [the Evangelist] says, is to be considered as becoming *as it were*
flesh. Since this could be actually the opinion of those who saw him—since
he was in his humanity so lowly and was believed by many to be only what
he appeared to be—he therefore adds, in order to explain 'the word was':
'and dwelt among us'; that is, he became flesh in the sense to the extent he
lived in our nature. Indeed, as the apostle said about us, we humans: 'We,
we who are in this tent, groan' (2 Cor 5:4), in that he called our bodies
a 'tent.'" This explanation, Theodore thinks, suffices against "opponents":
"they have argued 'has become' means 'has become changed into'; this can
to our point of view only be said by misunderstanding"(Vosté, 23).

It is obvious that Theodore was unable in this way to do justice to the
statements of the Evangelists. His christological theory remains overall

ambiguous. One must nevertheless appreciate that in resisting Arianism—which asserted the complete creaturehood of Jesus—he firmly held, from the "in the beginning" of John 1:1, the divinity of the "Word of God" (Logos) as the one who was before all creatures: "But when, as we have said, we realize from these words that he is the first cause, as it were the creator of all (things), the title 'only begotten (Son)' is ascribed him and to no one who has been created" (Vosté, 11). On the one hand, the worldview presupposition that the divine Being cannot be confined within boundaries created difficulties to think of a full incarnation of God. On the other hand, the full humanity of Jesus was necessary for humanity's salvation. On this matter, Theodore does not advance beyond the Antiochene theory of the assumption of the human Jesus by the God-Logos.

Even though dogmatics governs exegesis in this way, we should still not disdain the efforts Theodore made in a time when critical standards were lacking. Reflection on the Trinity is an admirable intellectual achievement of the ancient church, naturally by means of Greek thinking, because the Greek theologians were raised in it and hence sought to understand the mysteries of faith within this framework. Also worth noting is how carefully Theodore deals with the Johannine text and seeks confirmation for his christological theory from it, even if he could not reach an outcome convincing to us. As we can learn from the prologue to his commentary, Theodore took his mandate as a theologian responsible for correct doctrine very seriously; along with it, however, he frequently stressed that he wanted to interpret the text as accurately as possible.

Theodore flatly rejects allegorical explanation also in John's Gospel. Only where John himself speaks of fulfilled prophecy is Theodore ready to acknowledge it, as in the case of the quotation from Isa 53:1 in John 12:37. In another instance, John 19:28, he appropriately calls attention to the fact that Jesus had asked to drink, according to John, so that "the words of the prophet" would be fulfilled (Vosté, 242). We saw that for Theodore the Psalms, too, are prophecy (Ps 22:16 is alluded to). In some cases what is meant as prophecy in John is not even acknowledged as such. Thus on John 2:17 (quoting Ps 69:10), Theodore says: "Indeed, he said this not by way of prophecy but quoted it in passing, since he purified the temple" (Vosté, 42). Examples of typology are infrequent; John 3:14 is no more than paraphrased (Vosté, 51), because once again the text contains a typology. Other typological passages, in the passion history, are even completely passed over. This is altogether in keeping with the dislike of this way of consideration that Theodore has already shown in his exegesis of the prophetic books.

In one respect Theodore is highly time-bound: he identifies the opponents of Jesus, who in John are called "Jews" as a label meant only symbolically, with the Jews themselves, since he takes the label literally. This is obviously due not only to the fact that his way of interpretation is oriented to the literal sense but also to the continuing tensions that determined the relationship of the two faith communities thereafter.

It was Theodore's christological statements particularly that led to his posthumous condemnation by the Council of Constantinople in 553. In the development of Christian dogma, the christological dualism of the Antiochenes is certainly a level that has been surpassed. The Alexandrian view, which speaks of a reciprocal exchange of the divine and the human natures (*communicatio idiomatum*) in the person of Christ and preserved by this the unity of them, has gained acceptance. It is nevertheless a stroke of good fortune that the Syrian tradition (alongside some Greek fragments) passed down to us today in Theodore's commentary on John such a revealing example of his exegetical efforts. He remains one of the most significant interpreters of the Greek church fathers for whom there is once again increasing interest today.

1.2. The Deeper Sense Is Decisive: Didymus the Blind

It was in the middle of the Second World War. In a cliff wall in Tura, some ten kilometers south of Cairo, Egyptian workers were preparing a place for a planned munitions depot. While clearing a great cave under the rubble created by ancient quarrying, they came across papyrus pages piled up in a heap. The papyri came from books (codices) in Greek script from the sixth century, originally bound but later ripped apart. Before experts from the Egyptian Museum could rush there, workers had stashed the treasure and sold the manuscripts by packets and leaves to interested parties. It is no wonder, when one thinks of their worth compared to the meager wages of an Egyptian worker! The Egyptian Museum was able, nonetheless, to buy together the greatest part of the originally more than two thousand pages. It was also possible to make the scattered materials surfacing elsewhere accessible for research. Even so, some two hundred leaves still remain lost. Situated directly above the cave are ruins of the Arsenios monastery that Greek monks occupied from the fourth to perhaps the fifteenth centuries. The simplest explanation is that the texts came from there and were hidden in the caves at a time unknown to us. More detailed information is uncertain; various conjectures about the matter are of no further help.

The contents of the manuscripts are more important. It is indeed a matter of one of the most extensive and sensational papyrus finds. They included in particular, along with some of Origen's writings previously unknown or missing, numerous commentaries by this master's most important successor as leader of the Alexandrian catechetical school (founded around 180): Didymus the Blind (ca. 313–398). Prior to this discovery, very little had been known of these writings because the literary remains of Didymus had fallen victim to the same fate as those of Origen and Theodore of Mopsuetia. Since Didymus had openly admitted he was a follower of Origen who accepted Origen's doctrines of preexistence of the soul and the "restoration of all things" at the last judgment, he was finally condemned as heretical in 553 despite his otherwise orthodox position; afterward, his writings were largely destroyed. Now that the most important of his commentaries have resurfaced and gradually made available for research through scholarly editions, it is understood that Didymus was considered during his lifetime one of the most important biblical interpreters, whose lectures were frequented by numerous students and attracted visits of well-known theologians from afar. Jerome, for example, along with his spiritual companion Paula, went to hear his lectures, as did Rufinus, Palladius, Ambrose, and many others.

The career of Didymus passed outwardly quite uneventfully. Born in Alexandria, blind from the fourth or fifth year of his life, he joined presumably early on to the anchorites, the monks and settlers who lived outside the city gates in caves and monasteries in the desert. Whether he had a wife and children is unknown. We know little about his personal lot in life. Despite his blindness, he had acquired a wide education in the Hellenistic sense, especially a detailed knowledge of the Bible. In solitude, he was evidently able to avoid the fluctuating theological and church-political struggles that raged in the city and several times drove the patriarch Athanasius, leader of the orthodox party, into exile. Although Didymus engaged in polemics against Arians and other heretics, we know of no persecutions directed against him personally. But we also need not imagine his retreat to the desert as too severe: in his cell Didymus evidently had the assistance of individuals who read to him from the Bible and other writings as well as stenographers to whom he could dictate his own works. As for the rest, his vast memory helped him: he early on learned the Bible and many other works by heart and could quote from them in each suitable context.

The finds at Tura make the exegetical remains of Didymus known to us in two very different forms, which cannot really be called commentaries with equal right. As books meant for publication and conceived by Didymus himself, there are only the commentaries on Zechariah and Genesis as well as the commentary on Job. On the other hand, interpretations of the Psalms and Ecclesiastes (the Preacher) are actually lecture notes that grew out of the wide teaching of Didymus and were written down by participants or perhaps professional stenographers. Due to the inclusion of questions his hearers raised and the answers Didymus gave, they convey an unusually direct impression of the biblical lectures that brought him widespread fame. These lectures were evidently constructed in the school-fashion style of lectures on classical authors in Hellenistic grammar and rhetorical schools; they were probably delivered in a lecture hall where a larger number of hearers could gather. Unlike the Museum, the university where pagan philosophy was taught, the catechetical school apparently had no buildings of its own. Nevertheless, in a Christian academy like that led by Didymus, the personal relationship between student and teacher was close.

In his biblical interpretation, Didymus continued in the spirit of the interpretative tradition of the Alexandrian school founded by Origen. Didymus respected Origen with his whole heart, followed his theological premises and principles of interpretation, and developed them further in systematic form. But he was by no means slavishly dependent on him, advocating positions of his own as well. This brought with it his lively participation in the theological controversies of his time.

Since his commentaries were not published until recent times, they are still in many respects new frontiers in research. To date, only his Zechariah commentary and commentary on Psalms have gained somewhat wider attention. First involved was the clarification of the conceptuality in which Didymus formulated his interpretive principles, which served as a methodological framework for his understanding. Much of this will seem familiar to readers who have already followed the interpretation of Origen.

Didymus likewise proceeds first from the text of the Bible: its wording is the basis for all the senses to be derived from it. Therefore, he is anxious to offer, as the first step of his multilevel interpretation, his explanation of the wording of the passage in question. "According to what is said" is therefore a frequently recurring formula for which "according to what is in hand" can also appear, by which it is to recognized that here Didymus has to do with the written text lying before him. This literal interpretation frequently consists in nothing more than a somewhat detailed paraphrasing restatement of the wording, especially difficult passages, but without by this means always making them more understandable. In addition, the wording of a text first refers to facts and events within the framework of Old Testament history; "according to history" is the formula Didymus uses for this. Although he works on both with extreme care, literal understanding and history are only preparatory to real interpretation, which relates to the deeper sense ("according to anagogy") of the text. Didymus reaches this sense by employing the "allegorical" method, which finds a figurative meaning behind the wording. As a member of the Alexandrian school tradition and in Origen's succession, he is of the opinion that a deeper sense is to be assumed behind every biblical word.

This mode of interpretation is carried out with special consistency and schematically in sequential steps in the commentary of Genesis. This commentary is, to be sure, preserved for us only in fragments (of Gen 1–17) and is damaged and full of gaps especially at the beginning and end. But thanks to the efforts of the editor, its essential sections are now easily accessible and readable in the published edition. In order to learn about the method employed, we can select sections virtually at will.

Let us take the interpretation of Gen 4:1–2, the introductory verses of the narrative of Cain and Abel. Here Didymus first concerns himself with the interpretation of the literal sense. Thus he explains, by comparing various parallel passages (1 Sam 1:19; Gen 24:16; Luke 1:34), that the word "know" in the sentence "Adam knew Eve his wife" was a term for sexual relations, and "conceived" in the next statement, "and she conceived and gave birth to Cain," as occurring by human seed. But when Eve—in the Hebrew original a wordplay on the name Cain—explains, "I have gained a man through God," it is not denying that Adam and Eve are the bodily parents, but Eve means to say that everything is thus ordered and directed by God. Here Didymus refers to the parallel, Gen 40:8, where Joseph used the same phrase "through God" instead of "from God," which is actually meant. At the next sentence, "she afterward gave birth to Abel, Cain's brother," Didymus refers to a claim of Philo (not preserved to us) that Cain and Abel were twins. He leaves the judgment on that matter to the reader, "since it is also possible that they were born separately, at different times." The "book of the covenant," too (evidently an apocryphal Jewish text that Didymus quotes several times), in which one can even look up how large the age difference of the brothers was, supports this view.

After these remarks on the literal sense, Didymus moves on to the figurative meaning: "Now the educated will be aware of everything Philo has said about this in an allegorical way; nevertheless, it must be spoken of [here] to the extent possible." Even though Didymus does not mention

Philo very often by name, he assumes his readers know Philo's works—here, the text *De sacrificiis Abelis et Caini* (*On the Sacrifices of Abel and Cain*)—and he considers Philo's allegorical method indispensable, for from it comes a deeper understanding of the narrative of the first of the two brothers: "The soul, when it falls into error and sin, brings forth evil descendants, but when reason [*nous*] has again become sober and has a conversion, then it begins to set evil aside and give birth to acquiring virtue, which is to be praised. In short, since it increases in growth, it one day attains to perfection." What Didymus says here is nothing other than what Philo had said before. Even the idea of moral progress corresponds to Philo's ethically oriented philosophy.

Didymus knows how to gain an important sense even from information in the texts about the occupations of the two brothers and the sequence in which the two were named: "With respect to history," the prior mention of Abel's occupation as shepherd, reversing the sequence of the brothers' births, is important, because "Abel's (occupation) was more fine and honorable than that of Cain. For creatures with souls differ by nature from those without souls. Philo was right to say that those who want to govern others and themselves [as well] must be practiced in the shepherd's art." Here the transition from historical to allegorical interpretation is quick indeed; the historical interpretation is important only because from it can one can gain the other, deeper one, which is Didymus's sole concern.

As a rule, Didymus does not appeal to Philo explicitly, though Philo's method is in the background even when he does not do so. On the other hand, he absolutely sees the literal sense too as an important level of understanding for the text. Only rarely, when no historical sense seems present at all, does he completely give up on a literal interpretation, as for Zech 14:8–9a (Doutreleau 378,12–13)—that relates only to this passage! This is expressed, for example, in his explanation of the narrative of Sarah and Hagar (Gen 15), for which, through Paul's typological use of the two figures Sarah and Hagar in Gal 4:22–26, there was already a tradition of figurative interpretation from the New Testament on. In interpreting Gen 16:1–2, Didymus immediately recalls Paul but may not be content with Paul's interpretation: "The apostle, following the rule of allegory, saw the deeper significance of these two women in the two covenants. But since this also occurred in the content of the literal sense, this, too, is worthy of consideration." Didymus then explains that the "saints" (of the old covenant) did not marry for the sake of pleasure but for children, and that therefore they did not have relations with their wives who were nursing their children or pregnant. Sarah's praiseworthy behavior is the result: when she realized she could not have children, she refrained from relations with her husband Abraham—nothing of this is in the text—and instead gave him Hagar as a concubine. "This shows both abstinence and lack of jealousy on Sarah's part and an absence of passion [a Stoic ideal!] in Abraham, who agreed to this solution only at his wife's initiative and not at his own impulse, giving in only in order to bring children into the world."

Didymus concludes these observations by remarking: "Even the wording is therefore useful for what we have reflected on." As regards possible deeper meanings, he recalls Paul's use of the passage but also mentions the view of Philo, who saw in Sarah perfect virtue and philosophy, because she was a free woman (see esp. Philo, *Congr.* 1–9) who lived with her husband in accord with the laws. "Now virtue, too, lives with the wise in accord with the laws so that he brings forth divine descendants from her." To Philo, Hagar signifies preliminary practices; to Paul, the shadow.

That this combination of Paul and Philo is quite typical can be seen by looking at the intellectual makeup of the Alexandrian theologians, in whose thinking Greek philosophy, with its ethicizing allegorizing, seems to play a role nearly as large as Paul and the New Testament. The environing culture, still basically pagan, had an influence on Christianity and its understanding of the Bible that is not to be underestimated. As already in Philo's days, Hellenistic philosophy of mainly Neoplatonist character— taught in the Museum—was the foundation of education throughout the fourth century, even for educated Christians.

Nevertheless Didymus absolutely considers himself a theologian. This becomes clear, for example, in the introduction to book 3 of his Zechariah commentary (182,8–26; Doutreleau 614) in which he describes the spiritual interpretation of Scripture. According to this, God alone is the giver of all the truth contained in the biblical word: "God, who never deceives, who is the source and father of truth, never ceases to educate and teach those who decide to prepare room for the gifts of the Holy Spirit. Thus he gives a word of wisdom and a word of knowledge without hesitation to those who want to accept it." Didymus cites Jas 1:5–6, Prov 2:6, Ps 94 (93):12, and John 13:15 as scriptural proofs of this point. Characteristic of this selection and the content of the truth it describes is that Didymus views it as teaching and its effect as education leading to knowledge. As one proceeds, however, this goal can be attained only through prayer.

That Didymus takes a special interest in the book of Job goes along with the ethical orientation of his theology and piety. His commentary on this book was among those found in Tura. Compared to other commentaries, which, as manuscript notes by auditors, are written in often-disjointed style, the Job commentary, with its elegant Greek, represents a literary work from the very start. The commentary begins, appropriately, with a basic reflection (*hypothese*) in which Didymus goes into the essential contents of the book of Job (1:1–8:13). At the very outset he mentions as the most important point that Job sets forth "everything relating to God's judgments and how none of the evils humans encounter takes place without God's approval … and about endurance and disdain of inessential things [*adiaphora*] as well as the demonstration of (human) freedom to decide and instruction about various dogmas" (PTA 1,8–20). The question of justifying God for his activity (theodicy) with respect to a world pervaded by evils is itself a theme running through the biblical book of Job. But theodicy was a matter of concern as a philosophical problem in the Stoa, too. Didymus adopts Stoic answers to the problems when he states (93,25–30; on Job 4:1): "There are doubtless two reasons for the misfortunes that befall people: the one, the punishment of sins; the other, the steadfastness and probation of those in distress." Connected with this in Neoplatonism is the theory of a twofold manner of the soul's embodiment: one compulsory, serving as its punishment; and the other voluntary, serving the salvation of other souls. Didymus adopts this as well (56,20–28): "The human soul, which is immortal and not only has a nature other than the body but a divine [one], was joined with this [body] in various ways, either that it valued a communion of the body out of its own desire and longing or it was joined with it to be of use to those who need help." Hellenistic thought of varied ancestry, the differences of which Dionysius presumably did not know at all but presupposed as the popular philosophical worldview, flowed into his biblical interpretation. The idea of the preexistence of the soul, which Didymus also took over from Origen, one of the reasons for his later condemnation as a heretic, is formulated in this passage most clearly.

Didymus is encouraged to set the figure of Job before the eyes of the reader as "model of steadfastness" (58,28) "by which he [God] established for people a model and goal that they could view and imitate" (275,2–5; see also 212,9–11) by statements such as Job 1:1; 13:8, and especially 40:8, where the Septuagint version, deviating from the Hebrew text, has God himself declare, "Do you think that I have been of service to you for any other purpose than that you may appear righteous?" The hero of the book seems to be put forth as an exemplar of righteousness (see 35,27; 56,9; 286,26; 364,13). Scripture is understood as a source of "divine education"

(107,33; 276,8; see also the Zechariah commentary 179,15; 212,9; 307,12; 350,9). In so doing, of course, the tension between narrative framework and the dialogical sections of the book of Job is misunderstood, and thus also the book's true intention, which according to modern scholarly knowledge the book pursues in its final form: showing the failure of all attempts at wise calculations of human doings in view of the incomprehensibility of divine action. Didymus, by contrast, has an optimistic image of God and humanity: God as creator is good, and although all people—except for the "saints" who came to earth already sinless—are burdened by guilt as a result of original sin, as Didymus often stresses, they are able nonetheless to find the way to the good by education and standing the test. Against the Manichaeans, who begin with a principle of evil dualistically posited over against the principle of good, Didymus holds that not even the devil was created by God as the devil but as originally good, a fallen angel who out of envy sought to dissuade the heirs of heavenly citizenship from it. Yet those who are virtuous can successfully resist him (2,8–4,30). Evil is, in keeping with a Platonic pattern of thought, not a being in itself; it consists merely in a lack of good.

Now, our aim is not to write an essay on the dogmatic teachings of Didymus but to attend to the character of his biblical interpretation. Not even this can be proved comprehensively in a short chapter, let alone in a few examples. But it is absolutely necessary to take a look at the Psalms commentary, because it differs considerably from the other commentaries. We have already pointed out its character as a lecture copy. This requires another style—less artful but in keeping with personal and oral discourse. We gain a vivid impression of this famous theological teacher's lecturing, not least from the questions interposed by the listeners that are included in the text and that the teacher immediately answers. The Psalms commentary does not differ in method—unfortunately, a mere fragment is available to us, with the interpretation of Pss 20–44, following Septuagint numbering—from the other commentaries. Here, too, we find the division between the literal sense and the deeper sense that is the interpreter's chief interest. Yet Didymus goes to great efforts to do justice to the literal sense too. Thus at Ps 39 (40):7 he deals with the phrase he reads in some Septuagint manuscripts, "you have created a body for me," and comments, "in other (manuscripts) it reads 'but you have created ears for me'" (PTA 285,13). In one interpreter (whom as usual he does not name), he found, "You have transfixed my ears" (285,18). For each of these versions he derives a possible interpretation from the context of the psalm. One auditor then asks, "How do we understand this in the case of

Jesus?" Answer: "I said that allegorical interpretations do not tally completely with the original meanings" (285,19–20). A rather direct carryover of the psalm statement to Jesus is then made: "I told you that the soul of Jesus is not an immutable essence. It is the same in essence as other souls, and everything it has of goodness, it has from God's Logos [the Word became flesh in Jesus; see John 1:14]. Since it now also has good-hearing, it has it from the Savior (the Word)" (285,21–22). This statement is at the same time evidence of the peculiar Christology of Didymus, which we will discuss below.

Didymus often deals in the Psalms commentary with individual word meanings. For example, Ps 24 (25):17 reads, "the troubles of my heart have become vast." To this, Didymus first comments, "Not among all, I say, will the troubles become vast, but (only) in the one who bears them bravely." Paul's statement in 2 Cor 4:8, that "we stand in every trouble but not in hopelessness," serves as proof of this interpretation. "Those who understand the language of the Hebrews say that the phrase 'to stand in hopelessness,' when it occurs next to 'trouble,' means the following: to be troubled willfully, being cornered because one does not bear the troubles bravely" (e.g., Job 1:21; Acts 5:41). "But (it is so) even in the realm of visible (worldly) things: whoever struggles in expectation of a wreath and sees it lying before his eyes bears the blows bravely, rejoices that, although he is struck, he does not yield. Therefore, when the word 'trouble' is tied to 'hopelessness,' it means that one is not troubled in spirit but bears it bravely. When either of the two terms is found alone in Scripture, 'trouble' and 'hopelessness' mean the same thing" (e.g., Isa 30:6; PTA 87,17–29).

But grammatical questions also, such as context and punctuation, are important to Didymus for understanding the literal sense. Although reference to (biblical) history in the Psalms is not so frequent, it, too, can play a role, as in Ps 34 (35):13, "I humbled my soul by fasting," to which Didymus comments that fasting, when it occurred in history as in the fasting of the Ninevites (Jon 3:5–9) or the Jews (Esth 4:16), achieved a great deal: the Ninevites were preserved from destruction, and the Jews were saved from Haman (213,1–4).

Above all, however, the frequency with which Didymus interprets the Psalms christologically distinguishes his commentary on the Psalms from those on other biblical books. In so doing he is, of course, following another long-established Christian tradition of interpretation. The Psalter had long played a special role in the Christian understanding of the Old Testament. In the New Testament, the messianic psalms particularly, such as Pss 2 and 110, were interpreted in their direct reference to Christ and therefore gained special attention, but a psalm like Ps 22 as well, the application of which to the passion presumably went back to Jesus himself (Mark 15:34//Matt 27:46), had expanded the basis of interpretation considerably already in the second century. In so doing, two christological interpretive possibilities especially had developed: the one, which in the framework of a basic Trinitarian understanding identified the "Lord" to which numerous psalms in the Septuagint version were directed with Christ; the other, in which one referred the statements of the petitioners in the psalms—as David was generally considered its author—typologically to Jesus Christ. This "Christology from below" received extensive space in Didymus in the framework of his special christological approach in psalm interpretation. He also developed it in refuting opposing christological views that he combatted as false teachings, above all the Arians on the one side and the Apollinarians on the other.

The point of departure characteristic for Christology, and indeed in a Neoplatonically stamped interpretation as it was advocated by Alexandrians generally, was John 1:14: "The Word [Logos] became flesh." The problem facing every Christology is the relationship between the confession set down at Nicaea in the formula "true God from true God," which subordinated the Son to the Father within the Trinity, and the human being Jesus, on whom the reality of the cross-event depends. Athanasius (around 295–373) formulated his Christology against the Arians on the basis of John 1:14 and Phil 2:6–7 in terms of the assumption of the man Jesus by the preexistent Logos. But this definition left open much in determining the humanity of Jesus. Apollinarius of Laodicea (ca. 315–before 392) took another step: he, too, had spoken of the incarnation of the Logos, but he held to the divinity of the Logos (the flesh-becoming God) and in so doing so emphasized the one nature of Christ that he could not be considered a complete person endowed with human reason.

Didymus directed his own teaching about the human soul of Christ against this Apollinarian theory, but also against the Arians, who considered Jesus Christ as created but ascribed Christ's passion to the Logos, likewise created. He stresses the reality of the incarnation against the docetists, who assumed that the body was a mere appearance. This, in turn, is necessary so that the cross also is real. On Ps 23 (24):10, "Who is this king of glory," Didymus cites the opinion of "certain people" who understand "the Lord of glory who was crucified" (1 Cor 2:9) as "God's Logos" and then quotes an (otherwise unknown) syllogism of Apollinarius: "Christ is the king of glory. But Christ has been crucified. Therefore, the king of glory has been crucified." To this Didymus responds,

And these people fantasize. The cross is a reality; that is to say, it is the nailing down of a body: "They have pierced my hands and feet" (Ps 21 [22]:17). Anyone who claims that the Logos of God, who is incorporeal, has been crucified allegorizes the cross. But if the cross is allegorized, the resurrection has to be allegorized, too. But if the resurrection is allegorized, everything that took place is like a dream. (73,9–21)

But the full humanity of Jesus includes a human soul in a full sense, capable of human feeling and thinking. We already quoted the Psalms commentary on Ps 39 (40):7 (285,21–22), where Didymus stresses that the soul of Jesus is the same as that of all humans. He stresses the same point at Ps 36 (37):11, by reference to Matt 11:29, "I am gentle and humble of heart." "All the Old and New Testament writings speak of 'heart' for 'reason' [*nous*]" (referring to Isa 46:12; Ezek 11:19) "If he therefore has a heart and this heart has virtue, for he is gentle of heart and humble, then he has assumed a complete human being." As a human soul, the soul of Jesus is not unchangeable, like the divine. The incarnation is "transformation," as Didymus explains in his lengthy exegesis of this catchword in Ps 33 (34):2—under the presupposition of equating David-Jesus (184,31–185,31). This also means his capacity for genuine human feelings such as fear and anxiety. At eight places in his commentary (on Ps 21 [22]:15c; 33,28; on Ps 21[22]:21; 43,18; on Ps 34 [35]:17c: 221,33; on Ps 36 [37]:24a; 253,33; on Ps 37 [38]:6; 263,11; on Ps 38 [39]:12c; 279,26; on Ps 39 [40]:2b; 282,3; on Ps 40 [41]:6; 293,4, 6, 10), Didymus introduces for this capacity the term *propathie* (an idiosyncrasy): the phase of the beginning of an affect the succumbing to which would mean a real breakdown of the spirit (see esp. 252,26–35). It is inconceivable that Jesus would have broken down in his temptations (Mark 14:33//Matt 26:37; see 43,20; 222,10; 293,7), because then he would have fallen into sin. According to Heb 4:15, however, he was "tested in every respect as we are, yet without sin." Holding to this final point is, for Didymus, of decisive importance (see for this especially at Ps 34 [35]:17c; 221,1–226,17, where we also learn of a lengthy discussion of the problem with his hearers). The humanity of Jesus permits the interpreter to refer numerous statements in individual psalms to Jesus Christ, or at least allows this possibility alongside others. To be sure, this model of consideration does not stand up to modern knowledge about the original meaning of the psalms. But given the conditions of understanding and traditions of interpretation at the time, it allowed Didymus a Christology that not only took up essential New Testament statements but also gained an understanding of Jesus as "truly God and truly human" that more recent attempts at christological definition can hardly surpass.

It cannot be surprising that number symbolism (e.g., on the numbering of the psalms, 106,23–24; on individual numbers, 106,24–25) and other forms of allegorical interpretation play a role in the commentary. The total dominance of this allegory as seen in Origen, however, is avoided in Didymus by the concern for the full incarnation of Christ. Here, too, an anthropology that is more highly Aristotelian than Neoplatonist seems to play a role. In the philosophical syncretism of Hellenistic Alexandria, first one school and then another gained greater influence. Explicitly Stoic terminology is also frequently encountered in Didymus. In conclusion, it can be said that it is well worthwhile to deal with an interpreter such as Didymus more closely. His rediscovered commentaries opened up significant source materials for early church exegesis and theology.

1.3. A BIBLE FOR THE WEST: JEROME

Jerome—his full name was Eusebius Sophronius Hieronymus—was born in the small country town of Stridon on the border between Dalmatia and Pannonia (today Hungary.) The town's precise location is no longer ascertainable because it was completely destroyed during the age of migrations. Scholars debate the year of Jerome's birth. A decision for 331 instead of 347/348 supposed by most is recommended especially because in his letters Augustine, born in 354, treats Jerome as a much older senior. Hence Jerome would have been nearly ninety years old at his death in 420. His family was Christian and Latinized for a long time. Thus it was evidently a matter of course for his apparently well-to-do father Eusebius to send his son at the appropriate age (eleven to twelve years) to the best school possible, that of the famous teacher in Rome, Aelius Donatus. Jerome spent several years in this grammar school along with his young friend Bonosus from Dalmatia, Rufinus (another Greek theologian later particularly famous as the translator of Origen's work), and also possibly Pammachius, who, coming from a distinguished Roman family, was later to become Jerome's most faithful associate in Rome. The school program followed the Hellenistic model in grammar and stylistics especially in its study of texts by classical authors—only, as everywhere in the West, in Latin. Instead of Homer, Virgil, Terrence, Sallust as historian, and especially Cicero were the stylistic, historical, and philosophical models to aim at. Plautus, Horace, the Epicurean Lucretius, and others were added. Here Jerome laid the foundations for his outstanding linguistic skills, which later made him known as one of the most significant masters of Latin style. At the age of about fifteen or sixteen, students usually advanced to the rhetoric academy. There they learned public speaking, above all in preparation for an office in politics and administration. The rhetorical skills Jerome gained there are evident in his later writings at every point—though while the biting polemics or tendency to gross exaggeration is perhaps hardly to our liking, the inference to Jerome's character is not in any case justified. On the other hand, Jerome does not seem to have been very well informed about ancient philosophy, which was of little interest to him.

It is worth noting that a pagan rhetorical education was still a matter of course even for Christians in the fourth century. Christian schools were established only much later. The same was the case, we saw, in Antioch. Though Jerome along with his friends enjoyed the many sorts of worldly pleasures the capital of the world empire offered, he did not forget that he was a Christian. He reports how on Sundays he visited the catacombs with Christian friends to show respect for the apostles and early Christian martyrs interred there. In this time he was presumably baptized, too, as a young man, as was then customary. Yet he was also a devotee of classical literature and collected a considerable private library. Even later (374), when during a life-threatening illness he had a dream that the heavenly Judge accused him of being a follower not of Christ but Cicero (see *Ep.* 22), he could not separate himself from his books. Although he no longer touched them for years thereafter, the pagan writers and poets were nonetheless so familiar to him that he quoted them effortlessly by heart all his life.

We know little more about this period. Thus it is also unknown how long Jerome attended the rhetorical academy. He went to Trier (ca. 367) for a while with his friend Bonosus, apparently to pursue the official career path in the then imperial residence. There, however, his life took a decisive turn: he was grasped by the monastic ideal that was then sweeping across Gaul and the West from the East. The work of Athanasius celebrating the "life of Anthony," the Egyptian hermit (ca. 250–356), contributed greatly to its propagation. From then on Jerome was one of the most fanatical supporters of the ascetic way of life, converting to it also many distinguished ladies in particular.

Not much is known of the years that followed either; Jerome later mentions, among other things, stays in Stridon and Aquileia. There a group of young people, Rufinus among them, met together, dedicating themselves to biblical study and asceticism. Yet the group did not stay together long. Jerome soon went his own way. He set out for the East, probably as early as 372, and his journey of several months took him via Athens to Antioch. There he was a guest of the wealthy priest Evagrius. In Antioch he took systematic instruction in Greek, the language of the cultured throughout the East, which he previously had barely commanded. In addition, he heard the biblical lectures of Apollinarius of Laodicea, a representative of the Antiochene school. The inclusion of the literal sense in his later exegesis was something Jerome would have learned from this teacher. Yet his ascetic ideals soon regained control over him. Barely recovered from the serious illness during which he had the dream mentioned above, he abandoned his plans for a pilgrimage to Jerusalem and took up residence with the monks in the desert of Chalcis, not far from Antioch, where one of the numerous caves in the cliffs became his quarters. Although he shared the stinted life of the inhabitants, he had many comforts due to the friendship of Evagrius: books for study, especially biblical commentaries, were available to him, as were transcribers for copying manuscripts and stenographers for dictating his own writings. According to his own testimony (*Ep.* 125, ca. 411), he also began there something decisive: he took lessons in Hebrew from a Jewish convert to Christianity.

Jerome remained in the Chalcis desert only a few years. He left the monks, amid quarrels, as early as 376 or 377, because among other things they tried to draw him into the bitter-fought battle over Trinitarian formulas then raging everywhere. After stopovers in Antioch and Constantinople, he went on to Rome in 382. There he soon became so well known that Pope Damasus I (366–384) appointed him his secretary. The most important project he undertook at the Pope's prompting was a thorough revision and standardization of the numerous Latin biblical translations based on the Septuagint in current circulation. These had originated in various places of the Latin-speaking world for practical use in churches, frequently in careless language and with considerable deviations from one other. The New Testament was of primary concern to Damasus. Jerome began his work with the Gospels, which he completed. Whether he similarly revised the other New Testament writings is uncertain. He seems to have been unfamiliar with today's Vulgate texts of these books. Problems we know from modern revisions of Luther's Bible were not unfamiliar to Jerome in his efforts of revision; he often had to stick with a wording sanctified by long use even though it did not exactly match the original text, since changing it would hurt the feelings of readers.

In Rome, Jerome also gave biblical instruction and dedicated himself to the care of several distinguished Christian ladies, including the rich widows Marcella and Paula as well as Paula's daughter Eustochium. He

aroused them with enthusiasm for his ascetic ideal, but his zealous propa-
gandizing, along with his presumably legitimate criticism of the lifestyle of
the clergy and alleged "virgins" (see *Ep.* 21), gained him many enemies. He
wrote an attack against Helvidius, who had appealed to biblical witnesses
in defense of Christian marriage as an equally worthy way of life. After the
death of his patron Damasus (11 December 384), hostile attacks from all
sides made it impossible for him to remain in Rome any longer (see *Ep.*
45). Embittered, he left the city in 385 and sailed to Palestine, where Paula
and Eustochium also arrived. After a pilgrimage together through Palestine
and a visit to Egypt, the cradle of monasticism—in Alexandria, however,
Jerome also heard lectures by Didymus the Blind for several weeks—they
founded a monastery for men and women in Bethlehem, near the Church
of the Nativity. Living amid the original places of faith was for the group
the fulfillment of their highest ideals. There were, of course, practical cares
of many sorts, too, above all financial. Yet pious donors were always found,
ready to offer their fortunes in support of the monasteries, like Paula, who
at the outset gave her considerable wealth for their founding.

Jerome remained in Bethlehem the rest of his life. He dedicated himself to caring for the monks and nuns and his numerous visitors and
correspondents, but above all his extensive literary activity. In so doing
he benefited from the proximity of the Caesarea library, the rich treasures
of which he used time and again. He worked steadily into his final years
of life, during which illness increasingly limited his productive powers,
as did incidents such as the raid on the monasteries, both of which were
burned in 416 by savage gangs.

Biblical themes play a role in a good many of his letters, some of which
are designed as small tractates and intended not for their direct recipients
alone. Thus in *Ep.* 18A and 18B he wrote to Pope Damasus about Isa 6:1–9
and in so doing carefully compared the Septuagint edition to other Greek
translations. He also sent Damasus an interpretation of the parable of the
prodigal son (*Ep.* 21). "Nothing indeed, I think, could be a matter more
worthy of our conversation than to talk together about this writing," Damasus once wrote to his young friend. "I will ask, you may answer" (*Ep.* 35).
He then presents Jerome with various questions about patriarchal history,
which Jerome answers in *Ep.* 36. Other inquiries directed to him related to
the *diapsalma* (Hebrew *selah*) in the Septuagint Psalter (*Ep.* 8, to Marcella)
and young Samuel's service in the temple at Shiloh (1 Sam 2:18–19, 27–28;
Ep. 29, to Marcella) He even sent in 404 two Gothic women, Sumnia and
Fretela, a lengthy treatise on textual corruptions in the Septuagint Psalter
(*Ep.* 106). It is amazing that two women from the warlike German people

took interest in such specialized text-critical questions! Yet the correspondence shows that discussions of biblical problems played a significant role among cultured Christians of the time. Even in his early years Jerome was regarded a specialist in this area to whom people gladly turned for information. His reputation increased more and more over time, and even within his own lifetime he was considered one of the foremost authorities on biblical questions.

Jerome also frequently wrote his commentaries on biblical books at the request of friends. This accounts for the haphazard sequence in which they appeared. Shortly after arriving in Bethlehem, for example, he began a series of commentaries on Paul's letters by interpreting the letter to Philemon, the last and shortest, in order to be able to accede most easily to the persistent requests of Paula and Eustochium for an interpretation of Paul's letters. The irregular appearance of his series of commentaries on the Minor Prophets (Nahum, Micah, Zephaniah, Haggai, Habakkuk, Obadiah [first version lost] in 396; the rest—Zechariah, Malachi, Hosea, Joel, Amos, Obadiah [second version], Jonah—followed much later, in 406) went along, as he himself explains (Amos commentary, prologue to book 3), with his own evaluation of his abilities and requests that others made of him.

With respect to their contents, Jerome's earlier biblical commentaries are worth no special consideration. It has long been known that he copied the content of commentaries by older interpreters, especially Origen, in wide range. He had no qualms in this regard and did not mention the specific sources for his discussions. Yet here he was merely following the procedure customary at the time, because the idea of personal intellectual property did not emerge until the beginning of modernity. In general, Jerome says that he constantly read everything available to him in order to pluck as many blossoms as possible, so also Origen's commentaries, since he "interpreted the Scriptures well in many respects, explained obscurities in the prophecies, and revealed the greatest mysteries of the New as well as the Old Testament" (*Ep.* 61.2). The last phrase points to allegorical interpretation, which Jerome takes over from Origen in wide range in his commentaries. Even in his last commentary, on Jeremiah (begun ca. 414), he confirms his view of "the rules of commentaries," in which numerous opinions of different (authors) are presented, with or without mentioning the authors' names, so that the readers are left to judge what is best to choose (Jeremiah commentary, prologue, 3).

Jerome's special merit lies rather in his efforts on the Latin Bible. The first step was to attempt a thorough revision of the current Latin edition of the whole Old Testament. Jerome evidently busied himself with this in his first years in Bethlehem (386–392). He used the Septuagint as his basis, comparing it to other Greek translations and even the Hebrew text. For this, Origen's Hexapla in Caesarea was helpful to him, because it included a column in which Origen had reconstructed a critically revised text of the Septuagint with notations on its additions and omissions vis-à-vis the Hebrew version. Jerome began with a revision of the Psalter. This text had an unexpectedly rich future ahead of it. Introduced into Gaul (and hence called the Gallican Psalter), it gradually displaced the later version of the Psalms that Jerome translated from the original Hebrew text, becoming a component of the Vulgate and the Roman breviary that was not replaced by a modern translation until 1945. Modern editions of the Vulgate contain both versions. In addition, Jerome prepared revised versions of Job, 1 and 2 Chronicles, Proverbs, Ecclesiastes, and Song of Songs. Then he evidently broke off this work, the results of which could no longer satisfy him over time.

Meanwhile, Jerome made energetic efforts to improve his knowledge of Hebrew. As he reports (*Ep.* 84.3), he worked with a Jew named Baraninas as a teacher, who visited him at night out of fear of others of his faith. Among Christians, too, such contact with Jews was not uncontroversial. After Jerome's break with Rufinus (in 393, due to a dispute over Origen's orthodoxy), Rufinus attacked him (Rufinus, *Apol. Hier.* 2.12) for this and other reasons and in so doing polemically distorted the name Baraninas into Barabbas.

How far Jerome advanced in Hebrew learning, whether he mastered the language overall independently, is as disputed in research today as ever, although at present the dominant view is to put complete faith in Jerome's own statements. His accounts of how he took lessons from Jews or consulted with them on certain questions are too detailed to be simply shoved aside. Suspicion arose because many things that at first glance seem his own knowledge are demonstrably taken from the works of others, especially Origen's commentaries. Yet the quality of his translation of the Old Testament into Latin, of which we will hear more soon, can hardly be accounted for apart from knowledge of the original language. Such knowledge was virtually unique in Christian antiquity, for relations with the Jews were bad and rabbinic literature was unfamiliar and unintelligible to Christians. It must also be recalled that there were not yet any Hebrew grammars and dictionaries; they were not begun until the ninth century. Thus Jerome's efforts with the original language of the Hebrew Bible were a truly pioneering achievement.

Knowledge of Hebrew seemed to Jerome over time indispensable for an adequate understanding of the Old Testament text and its translation into Latin. "Just as the reliability of the ancient books [the Old Testament] is to be determined on the basis of the Hebrew volumes, so that of the New [Testament] demands the norm of Greek language" (*Ep.* 71.5). The weaknesses of the Septuagint made it, in his view, impossible to aim at a correct wording—although he made use of the Hexapla's other Greek translations that attempted a literal rendering of the original text and thereby a correction of the Septuagint text. His ever-increasing realization of the Septuagint's unreliability can be traced from his prologue to Isaiah, in which he still thought it was possible to produce an edition of the Septuagint corrected from other old translations, to the prologue to Jeremiah, where he referred to the Hebrew edition over against the "confused sequence of visions in Greek and Latin reproduction," and on to his remark in the prologue to Daniel that in this instance the church did not use the Septuagint but the Theodotion text because the Septuagint did not reproduce the Hebrew wording correctly. From then on he was to advocate again and again *hebraica veritas*, the "Hebraic truth," by which he had in view—something to be noted!—nothing other than the original Hebrew text. To make this the basis of the Latin version was revolutionary for the fourth century and not something undertaken without opposition, for faith in the inspiration of the Septuagint was universally widespread, reinforced by a thousand-year tradition. In several letters, even Augustine expressed concern about Jerome's plan to make the Hebrew texts instead of the Septuagint the basis of his edition (*Ep.* 28 = 56 in Jerome's correspondence, ca. 394/395; *Ep.* 71 = 104 in Jerome, 403). Augustine mentions, among other things, his fear that, if Jerome's translation gained widespread acceptance, it would cause a rift between the Western and Eastern church, because Greek-speaking Christians would hold to the Septuagint. He also tells about a riot that broke out in Oea (Tripoli) when the bishop there had read aloud from Jerome's translation of the book of Jonah a saying that included a word the congregation did not know. Jerome had rendered the plant that spread its shade over Jonah in 4:6 by "ivy" instead of "pumpkin." At this point in his Jonah commentary he explains at length why he chose this translation, considered sacrilegious in Rome as well: he wanted to designate a type of shade plant found in Palestine for which there was no corresponding word in Latin. One sees how he was concerned for a translation that included localized, even natural scientific, observations. He sought advice from rabbinic specialists on questions of fact as well. We find his final judgment on the Septuagint in the prologue to his translation of the books of Chronicles (see also prologue to Job). Here he admits that his translation would indeed be unnecessary if we still had the Septuagint in its original, pure version, on which the faith of the developing church was founded. But the differing versions then in circulation—that of Hesychius in Egypt, that of Lucian from Constantinople to Antioch, and a "middle" version in Palestine—show that the ancient, authentic tradition is lost. In addition, Jerome refers to the Old Testament quotations in the New Testament that are not derived from the Septuagint but are similar to those found only in the original text of the Old Testament. One would have to turn back there, "from where the Lord also speaks and the disciples draw examples." The assumption of an original inspiration of the Septuagint is found only here, perhaps as a concession to his two Roman friends to whom he dedicated the book. On the other hand, Jerome is quite willing to acknowledge the legitimacy of using the Septuagint in the church, "partly because it is the first and was in use before Christ's coming, partly because the apostles used it whenever it does not deviate from the Hebrew (texts)" (*Ep.* 57.11). But he is no longer prepared to believe the pious legend of the Septuagint's origin (see *History*, 1:19):

> I do not know who was first responsible for the lie about the seventy separate cells in Alexandria in which (the translators) are alleged to have produced together an identical text, since Aristeas and Josephus at a much later time gave no such reports but tell us that they translated, not prophesied, in a single hall. For it is one thing to be a prophet and another a translator: in the one case, the Spirit foretells future things; in the other, knowledge and fluent style reproduces what the translator understands. (*Ruf.* 2.25)

In returning to "Hebrew truth," Jerome also has an apologetic purpose. Thus in the foreword to his *Psalms according to the Hebrews* he relates how Sofronius, to whom the translation is dedicated, was ridiculed by a Jew when he produced scriptural proofs for the Lord from the Septuagint Psalter and the Jew objected that these were not present at all in the Hebrew edition. Therefore the demand on him for a new translation from the original text is justified, "because it is one thing to read the Psalms in communities of people who believe in Christ and another to respond to crafty Jews with respect to particular words." Similarly in the foreword to Isaiah: from even among those who now constantly tear him to pieces because of his translation, he would be repaid in the future by the one "who is aware that I struggled to learn a foreign language so that the Jews might no longer attack the church for the incorrectness of its

Scriptures." In future controversies with Jews, the Christians would now be able to refer to a text that was without doubt correct but nonetheless plainly spoke of Christ's coming (see also the foreword to Joshua).

The turn to "Hebraic truth" also had implications for Jerome's view of the limits of the canon. During his early, "precritical" period, quotations are found from deuterocanonical (apocryphal) writings such as the Wisdom of Solomon, Sirach, Tobit, and 2 Maccabees, as well as the additions to Daniel (Song of the Three Young Men [Dan 3:51–90 LXX], Susanna [Dan 13 LXX], Bel and the Dragon [Dan 14 LXX]) found only in the Septuagint. From the New Testament he quotes Hebrews frequently, although its inclusion in the canon was disputed in the Latin church. But we come across an explicit restriction to a narrow canon corresponding to the twenty-two (twenty-four) books of the Hebrew Bible in the foreword to Samuel–Kings (which Jerome called "helmeted," that is, for his preemptory defense against attacks he expected, and the prologue becoming known by that term). After specifically listing the books he translated from Hebrew, he explicitly says, "anything other than these must be set aside as apocryphal." As such he mentions the Wisdom of Solomon, Sirach, Judith, Tobit, and the Shepherd of Hermas (!). He adds that he found a Hebrew text of 1 Maccabees but only a Greek one of 2 Maccabees. It remains unclear in this case whether Jerome considers the availability of a Hebrew version to speak in favor of including 1 Maccabees in the canon. Generally, however, this is obviously the standard he uses for canonicity. Even the sequence of the books follows the Hebrew Bible. It is quite otherwise in *Ep.* 53 (to Paulina, 394). There the scope of the canon is the same, but the twelve Minor Prophets are placed at the front of the prophetic canon, and Daniel is included among the prophets, after Ezekiel. Here the influence of the Septuagint canon makes itself noticeable. By the way, the Luther Bible contains a similar mixed sequence of the books.

Jerome's stance toward the canon is worth noting because the position he takes is singular in the ancient church. Luther was the first to adopt a similar position, interestingly, likewise out of philological-humanistic interests. To be sure, Jerome's preference for "Hebraic truth" had no direct influence on the church's canon, and he himself translated Tobit and Judith, well aware that the two did not belong to the Hebrew canon (see the prologues to the two books)—and he did not even omit the additions to Esther and Daniel.

Jerome began the great work of translating the original text into Latin around 390 and completed it around 406. In so doing he did not follow the sequence of the books in the canon but once again the wishes of others or considerations of difficulty instead. Since the "helmeted" prologue to Samuel–Kings speaks of the whole Bible, he ought to have begun with these books. As one can easily see by comparing, for example, the two versions of Psalms (the "Gallican" from the Septuagint and that "according to the Hebrew"), the new translation was incomparably better than any before it. But his text was not acknowledged to be "universally accepted" (Vulgate) throughout the Western church until the ninth century. Besides the Old Testament books, the older revision of the Gospels came from Jerome's pen; the translators of the other New Testament writings are unknown.

At the same time, Jerome also took a new initiative in his commentary on the Old Testament. He first of all issued a trilogy of technical handbooks. By drawing upon older word lists going back to the third century, he compiled a listing of Hebrew names (*Onomasticon*) that were then explained etymologically, judged according to recent knowledge mostly false, often fantastic and correct only in small part. There followed a revised translation of the *Onomasticon* by Eusebius of Caesarea (from around 300), a list of Palestinian place names with brief topical and historical information to which Jerome added little new. Of greatest significance is the third work, *Hebrew Questions in the Book of Genesis* (*Quaestionum hebraicarum liber in Genesim*). Here Jerome discusses selected variants in the customary Latin texts (derived from the Septuagint) with respect to word meanings and geographical and historical facts for the first time critically on the basis of the Hebrew original text, which he also regularly compared with the old translations of Aquila, Symmachus, and Theodotion. It is also noteworthy that he is so exclusively concerned with the literal sense, which he frequently tries to correct, that he completely disregards allegorical interpretation. In terms of method, this was an entirely new form of interpretation: an exclusively historical-philological commentary. That in so doing Jerome drew a large part of the explanations from the *Antiquitates Judaicae* (*Jewish Antiquities*) of the Jewish historian Flavius Josephus (37/38–after 100 c.e.) is in keeping with his customary way of working, as is the fact that he mentions Josephus by name only when he occasionally polemicizes against him. In addition, he takes up an entire body of haggadic material, the edifying tales that his Jewish consultants told him.

Jerome had planned to explicate the entire Old Testament in this way, but he did not carry out its implementation. Instead, he began a new series of commentaries, beginning with five of the twelve Minor Prophets (Nahum, Micah, Zephaniah, Haggai, Habakkuk). Here, too, following his discovery of "Hebraic truth," he developed a new method that may seem to a modern observer ambiguous but was shaped by the special situation: he sets his own translation of the Hebrew original alongside the usual Latin translation of the Septuagint (wherever they deviated considerably from one other) and comments on each separately. In fact, he must have fought hard for recognition of his new translation (which became widely accepted centuries after his death). The traditional text was the usual basis for "spiritual," that is, predominantly allegorical and typological, interpretation. Here Jerome took over many statements from Origen's commentaries, while going back on the basis of the original text to contemporary rabbinic interpretation for questions of the text and the historical background. But he firmly rejected Jewish statements of faith such as the view that the Messiah would not come until the final days and then Jerusalem would be rebuilt and rule over all peoples (on Mic 4:11–13; 5:7–14; Zeph 2:12–15), then the Holy Scriptures would be taken from Christians and given to the Jews (on Mic 7:8–13).

That he still remained, as ever, an adherent of spiritual or "mystical" modes of interpretation we can see, among other places, in the interpretation of Ps 45 he gives in a letter from the year 397 (*Ep. 65*, to Principia). What historical-critical research today characterizes as a song on the occasion of a king's marriage, Jerome relates to Christ and his bride, the church.

After a longer interval, Jerome then commented in 406 on the remaining Minor Prophets: Zechariah, Malachi, Hosea, Joel, Amos, Obadiah, Jonah. These commentaries are likewise constructed and revised using contemporary rabbinic exegesis for "historical" interpretation. For "spiritual" interpretation they use largely available Christian interpretations.

The Daniel commentary (written 407), with which Jerome began his interpretation of the Major Prophets, is especially characteristic of his way of dealing with an Old Testament book. Here he does not offer a double translation because, as he remarks, the church was not using the Septuagint translation anyway, but that of Theodotion, which in Jerome's judgment largely corresponded to the Hebrew text. With regard to the book's historical origin, he has to deal with the special factor that the Neoplatonist Porphyry (third century) stated (in chapter 12 of his book *Against the Christians*, preserved today only in fragments) the remarkable insight that the events described there actually related to the time of Antiochus IV and the Maccabees and that the book was not written by the prophet Daniel but by a contemporary of Antiochus who did not prophesy the future but described contemporary events. Over against this

Jerome sets the Christian view, which he shares, that "none of the prophets wrote of Christ so openly" (prologue to Daniel commentary). On the
other hand, Jerome cannot dismiss Porphyry's (correct!) knowledge that
the final battle described in Daniel relates to the age of Antiochus. His
solution is similar to the approach of Theodore of Mopsuetia: the sixth-
century prophet (of whom the book of Daniel professes to speak) foretold
first on the level of history the events at the time of Antiochus, but these
are merely a foreshadowing (*typos*) of the end-time Christ-event to which
the real, spiritual sense of Daniel's book refers. This is conveyed in the
usual, allegorical way, as when Jerome equates the "stone that was cut
from the mountain not by human hands" (Dan 2:45) with the "Lord and
Savior who is come from his mother's body without sexual relations and
human seeds." Yet he no longer followed Origen's views without reservation, having turned against the master he esteemed most as a translator
due to the conflict over certain of Origen's teachings as heretical, which
Epiphanius of Salamis, Origen's fanatical opponent, brought to Jerusalem
in 393. For example, he rejected as false exegesis Origen's understanding
(without stating his name!) of Dan 3:95–96 LXX that Nebuchadnezzar is
a type of the devil and his conversion a proof that the devil himself will
eventually be converted and preach repentance.

Jerome's most comprehensive commentary, the eighteen books on
Isaiah (written 408–410), which was to be followed only by the one on
Ezekiel and the one, incomplete, on Jeremiah, still shows the distinctive
features of his way of working, in which he mixed historical-philological
interests with allegorical interpretation. In the case of this book in particular, the implications of the presupposition—first refuted by modern
critical research—that the entire book came from a single prophet were
especially weighty. In the prologue, Jerome says he wanted to "interpret
it in such a way that I teach him not only as a prophet but as an evangelist and apostle as well." Following the commandment in John 5:39:
"Seek in the Scriptures," (which played a central role in christological
interpretation of the Old Testament), he sees the most important goal of
all exegesis of this book to be its reference to Christ. "Therefore everything is to be understood in accord with the truth of history in a spiritual
way, thus Judea and Jerusalem, Babylon and the Philistines ... are to be
understood such that we seek everything in the sense (of the word) and
for all this the apostle Paul may become a true architect laying the foundation, that is, none other except Christ Jesus" (see 1 Cor 3:11). Jerome,
however, also grants an amount of space, out of balance with this, to his
historical-philological interests. Hence he inserts the strictly historical

interpretation of the visions in Isa 13–23 (already finished in 397) as book 5 but then follows it with a detailed allegorical interpretation in books 6 and 7. He staunchly defends the Septuagint reading of Isa 7:14, "A virgin will become pregnant," against "a young woman will become pregnant" in other translations. Yet the level of historical facts remains of fundamental significance to him: "We also say that while we do not condemn tropological [figurative] understanding, the spiritual interpretation must follow the sequence of the history" (book 5, on Isa 13:19). In book 5 (on Isa 17:7–8), he can even comment critically against those who regard this word fulfilled in Christ: "The interpreter's intention is pious indeed, but not one found in the sequence of history." Yet when we compare the interpretation of these same two verses in book 7, we find there a figurative interpretation with no recognizable connection at all to the historical background of this word.

It is striking how fiercely Jerome polemicizes against the Jews in this commentary: against their ignorance of Scripture and their blindness (Isa 1:30; 27:12; 42:18–19) and against their moral weaknesses (on Isa 2:7; 3:3; 45:19; 66:17). Jerome finds the fate of Jerusalem (in 70 and 135 c.e.) wrought by the Romans under Titus and Hadrian proclaimed in various passages in Isaiah (see, e.g., 1:7; 2:11; 3:5; 5:15; 29:1–8). The destruction of the temple by the Romans will last to the end of the world (on Isa 1:12); they have fought as God's army against the Jews, who persist in blasphemy (on Isa 59:1–61:8). This seems incompatible with Jerome's close relationships with various Jews, but it lies on another level: it is a theological judgment, and a traditional one at that. We already found in Justin's *Apology* the view that the destruction of Jerusalem by the Romans and the expulsion of the Jews is a sign of their rejection by God. But, living so close to Jerusalem, Jerome also had the ravages of that time so often before his eyes that they will have made a special impression on him.

Besides Jews, Jerome also turns against various heretics, such as the "semi-Jews" who interpret Isa 62:10–12 in the sense of the end time when, after the full number of the pagans are saved, Israel will return to the Lord (see Rom 11:25–26). Or on Isa 65:13: "All this, the chiliasts [believers in the millennial kingdom] think will be fulfilled in a thousand years, since they think the kingdom of God is eating and drinking and do not understand what is written: 'Do not labor for the food that perishes but for the bread of life and of truth'" (John 6:27). At Isa 64:4 he polemicizes against the gnostics who—otherwise than in the case of the apostle Paul's legitimate allusion to this word (see 1 Cor 2:9)—would have confused numerous women, especially in Spain and Lusitania

(Portugal), by their citation of Isa 64:4 in the apocryphal writings the Ascension of Isaiah (11.34) and the Apocalypse of Elijah (fragment) and many similar statements. Irenaeus would have written against them. At Isa 65:4–5, Jerome again attacks Marcion, along with gnostics like Valentinus and the Arian Eunomius. For Jerome, as customary in the early church, a commentary on a biblical book has dogmatic, polemical, and apologetic purposes. But we find also in the Isaiah commentary a wealth of text-critical investigations in which he draws upon various translations at his disposal in a comprehensive way. This is not without interest even for modern exegesis.

That the Isaiah commentary as a whole is highly dependent on older commentaries comes as no surprise, since we saw much the same in his earlier commentaries as well. Even after Jerome had publicly renounced Origen's dogmatic errors, he continued to draw upon Origen's commentaries extensively, along with commentaries by other Christian interpreters as well as contemporary Jewish exegesis to the extent they were available to him. He is usually called an eclectic; the term is certainly apt.

Nonetheless, Jerome deserves the reputation accorded him as one of the great teachers of the church. His great biblical translation alone, even if nothing else, would have gained him this, because he granted the Western church for the first time a reliable text that was incomparably closer to the original text than the old translations based on the Septuagint. In fact, it became the Vulgate, in general use and, after Trent, the official Bible of one of the great Christian confessional churches. It remained unsurpassed for over a millennium, until Luther for quite similar motives but under far more favorable conditions once again took the same path. The irony of the history is that in Luther's time the Vulgate embodied the rigid church tradition in much the same way as the Septuagint had once done for Jerome and which he sought to replace by a new Holy Scripture created from the original truth.

1.4. An Interpreter with the Shepherd's Staff: Ambrose of Milan

Ambrose was presumably born in 339 in Trier, the son of a commander-in-chief of the praetorians for Gaul in a family belonging to the Roman city nobility and for a long time Christian. After the early death of his father, his mother returned with three children to Rome. Ambrose's older sister Marcellina received the veil of the God-dedicated virgins in 353. His brother Uranius Satyrus, likewise unmarried, served until his death in 373 as Ambrose's most trusted helper in Milan.

After Ambrose gained a basic humanistic, rhetorical, and legal education in Trier and Rome, he entered in keeping with family tradition high-state service. After briefly serving as an advocate in the law court of the prefect in Sirmium (close to Belgrade), he became an adviser to Sextus Petronius Probus, then resident commander-in-chief of the praetorians of Italy, Illyria, and North Africa, and by his patronage became around 370 consul (governor) of the provinces of Liguria and Aemilia, with his official seat in Milan.

Due to the decline of Rome, Milan had developed in the fourth century into the most significant city of Italy. It was the residential capital and the administrative seat of the empire, as well as one of the most important dioceses. But Milan was also where one of the most significant internal church battles of the century, that between Arians and Catholics (adherents of the Nicene Creed), was fought out. Although the Nicenes held most of the episcopal seats in Italy, the Arian Bishop Auxentius resided in Milan. Emperor Valentinian I (363–375), who ruled the Western empire, was neutral in confessional questions and did not interfere in church politics. Yet Arianism, in part because it was the confession of the Gothic soldiers, had no slight influence at court. The battle between the Arians and Catholics was not yet decided.

Since he came from a Christian family and secular education was in pagan hands, Ambrose presumably received instruction in the basic teachings of Christianity from a theologian. Since the custom at the time was to receive baptism, as an unrepeatable purification of all sins, late in life, if possible on one's deathbed, he had not yet been baptized in the fall of 373, when Bishop Auxentius died. A fierce conflict over the succession broke out between the Arians and Catholics among the people assembled in the cathedral for the election. Fearing a public riot, Ambrose rushed, in his official function as governor, into the church and spoke some calming words to the agitated masses. According to the legend passed down by his biographer Paulinus (*Vita Ambrosii* 6), at this moment a child is supposed to have called out "Ambrose Bishop!" and the crowd, forgetting the conflict, joined the call in unison, "Ambrose, Bishop." As an unbaptized layperson, Ambrose at first sought to decline this calling, but when the approval of Valentinian, staying in Trier, reached him, he did not resist any longer. His baptism at the hand of a Catholic bishop and ordination as bishop soon followed. Hence Ambrose unexpectedly found himself with responsibility for one of the most important episcopal seats of the Western kingdom. By celebrating the homecoming of the bones of Dionysius, his last orthodox predecessor, from Cappadocian exile, Ambrose symbolically displayed his resolve to serve the Catholic cause, although he worked as well for reconciliation within his community by leaving Arian priests in office.

Otherwise Ambrose developed into an ever-resolute champion of the Nicene Creed. Valentinian I died in 375; his young son Gratian became emperor in the West. Ambrose had to try to win him over to his church-political goals. Gratian's stepmother, Justina, leaned toward the Arians; hence resistance in the court was to be anticipated. One anti-Arian success came with the selection of an adherent of orthodoxy to the bishop's chair in Sirmium; another was the dismissal of the Arian Bishop Leontius of Salona.

In 378 the Goths launched a dreadful invasion of the Balkans. The Roman army of the East was crushed at Adrianople (Edirne); Valens, emperor of the East, was slain. Gratian, for a brief time the sole ruler, moved the court from Sirmium to Milan for security reasons. This gave Ambrose the opportunity to increase his influence over the young emperor even by the impress of his personality. The emperor had issued in Sirmium an edict of tolerance granting equal rights to all confessions (except extremist directions) in 378. It was replaced in 379 by a new order forbidding all heresies. In the same year came the first clash with Justina and the Arians whom she protected. At Justina's recommendation, the emperor granted the Arians in Milan the use of a basilica. Ambrose succeeded in getting this measure revoked. The Arians were largely in retreat in Italy and the other Western provinces at the time; in the Danube provinces they had, as always, a considerable following. In 381 Ambrose was finally successful in having a council convened, at Aquileia, from which the Oriental bishops with Arian leanings were excluded. The council turned into a tribunal for the few Illyrian Arians in attendance: they were condemned. In the same year Emperor Theodosius I (the Great), ruling in the East from 379, convened at Constantinople a council that confirmed the Nicene Creed in a slightly altered form (Niceno-Constantinopolitan creed). With this, victory over Arianism was complete. The emperor Gratian also laid aside the title of *pontifex maximus* and had the altar of the goddess Victory, the symbol of the Senators who still held to paganism, removed from the Roman curia. By this action the rest of Roman paganism was dealt its death blow.

Gratian's death in 383 led to the takeover of the entire West by his half-brother Valentinian II, who, still underage, was the nominal ruler from 375 on under the guardianship of his mother Justina. Conflict then arose when Justina sought to put a small basilica in Milan at the disposal of Gothic auxiliary troops for Arian worship. When Ambrose was summoned for trial before the imperial consistory, the people rioted outside the palace. The emperor's mother had to abandon her plan. The following year the court tried to compensate for the setback by issuing an edict of toleration that guaranteed the Arians equal rights and permission to hold their own assemblies. Ambrose described what happened in a letter to his sister Marcellina (*Ep.* 20). One of the larger basilicas was expropriated for the Arians; the news reached Ambrose during Psalm Sunday worship. Thereupon Ambrose set out in a letter to the emperor his reasons (*Ep.* 21) for refusing to appear before the court of arbitration assigned to settle the case and went personally into the threatened church. Troops encircled it. Yet the faithful, enthusiastic followers of Ambrose held out in the church while their bishop celebrated the Holy Week worship services. Hymns were composed, psalm singing encouraged the community to stick it out, and at last, when the soldiers who had surrounded the church went over to Ambrose, the siege was broken. The most important principle Ambrose defended against the emperor with firmness was the church's freedom from the state: "The palaces belong to the emperor, the houses of God to the bishop" (*Ep.* 20.19). But this did not mean that the state should remain religiously neutral: when the Roman Senate petitioned for the restoration of the statue of Victory, Ambrose immediately protested in two letters to the emperor (*Ep.* 17 and 18). The state, in his view, is obliged as well to uphold the supremacy of Christian truth and the Catholic church that propounds it and to resist heretics and pagans.

Also famous is Emperor Theodosius's penance in 390, which Ambrose imposed on him in a handwritten letter (*Ep.* 51) after the emperor ordered a bloodbath in Thessalonica and then was too late in rescinding it. After Gratian's death in 383, General Maximus in Trier had established himself Augustus of the Western provinces. Summoned by Valentinian II in 387 to help against a barbarian invasion, he seized the area for himself; meanwhile the court, residing in Aquileia, fled toward Thessalonica to Theodosius. Theodosius thereupon undertook the next year a military campaign against Maximus, who was defeated and then murdered by his own troops. The emperor's penance took place thereafter in his three-year stay in Milan, during which he developed a heartfelt relationship with Ambrose; he appeared in the church for a time without the imperial insignia, until, after making public confession of his sin, he was readmitted to the sacrament.

Space is lacking here to go into the political turmoil any further. Valentinian II died in Vienna in 392, Theodosius in Milan in 395, and for each Ambrose delivered a eulogy preserved for us. Ambrose had no ties at all to Honorius, the incompetent, still hardly grown younger son and successor of Theodosius in the West, and his competent but high-handed commander-in-chief and guard, the Vandal Stilicho. During the last two years of his life, Ambrose completely dedicated himself to his community. His death on 4 April 397 after a lengthy illness is described by his secretary and biographer Paulinus in edifying detail.

Despite the varied church-political tasks that fell to Ambrose as the bishop of Milan, the residential city, and the metropolitan of a church province, he took his obligations as pastor and preacher of his community seriously. "Not the grace of the prophets, not the virtue of the Evangelists, not the prudence of the shepherd, but only the effort for and understanding with regard to the divine Scriptures, which the apostle (Paul) counts among the duties of the saints, do I hope to attain," he once wrote (*Off.* 1.1.3). Since these duties fell to him suddenly and without his foresight or preparatory education, he had to learn them on his own by doing them. Of aid to him in this regard, of course, was his linguistic and rhetorical schooling, which supported his natural eloquence and enabled him to read Greek sources fluently in the original. Despite voluminous Latin literature, Greek was as always the language of a superior culture; the most significant theological works particularly were written in Greek. One should also consider that Jerome did not begun his translation of the Old Testament until shortly before the death of Ambrose and that the Vulgate came into universal use only much later. Ambrose is therefore one of the most important witnesses to the old Latin translation, which he used in various regional forms of the text. But on occasion he also explicitly drew from the Septuagint, which he valued especially not only as the church-approved version but also because, in his view, its content was clear and free of contradictions (see *Exp. Ps. 118* 9.13). In his Psalms commentary he used Aquila and Symmachus, too, and on occasion compared the wording of the three Greek translations. A copy of the Hexapla may have been available to him. On the other hand, he was a profound connoisseur of Virgil; this knowledge made him capable of a heightened poetic understanding of the Psalms.

Ambrose did not develop a theory of hermeneutics. His interpretation was altogether in the service of practice. Further, in keeping with the custom of the time, he had no misgivings about drawing widely on the works available to him. Of the theologians, he prized Origen in particular highly and Basil the Great, but also Eusebius of Caesarea, Hippolytus, Didymus, and Athanasius. Of Jewish authors, he used Philo in particular, but he knew the writings of Josephus as well. By his education he was also familiar with the traditions of Greek philosophy, especially Platonism and Neoplatonism, but also the teachings of Aristotle, Epicureans, and Stoics. Hellenistic popular philosophy had long before led to a mixture of all the systems, in any case. Naturally, Ambrose knew Cicero, who as the authority on classical Roman education gathered his teachings together from all the philosophers. To the extent Ambrose took up their teachings, he did so not as an end in itself but in service to the sole aim of concern to him: proclaiming the biblical message. He was firmly convinced in any case that pagan philosophy owed its wisdom not to itself but exclusively to the Bible: "For the wise of the world also drew from our laws, for they could not derive this in the teachings of humans, if they had not been able to draw from that heavenly wellspring of divine law" (*Exc.* 1.42.1–9)

Besides engagement as a prince of the church to which his position and his theological commitments obligated him, Ambrose was above all else a bishop, the shepherd of his community. Foremost among the tasks of this office were pastoral care and, related to it, preaching above all—along with administrative, judicial, and executive functions (see *Off.* 1.1–4). Preaching was part of eucharistic worship, and since celebrating the Eucharist was the bishop's duty, preaching regularly fell to him. It is not by accident that Ambrose engaged in biblical interpretation primarily in preaching. Most of the commentaries we have from him, such as the commentary on Ps 118 (119) and the Luke commentary in particular, are in reality nothing other than reworked sermons. The Luke commentary is by no means a verse-by-verse interpretation of the entire Gospel, only of selected parts; in addition, sections of Luke's Gospel were compared in detail to parallels in Matthew's Gospel. However, the edifying aim of the exposition shines through everywhere.

Ambrose was a famous preacher. A legend told by his biographer Paulinus (*Vita* 3.2–4) recalls that, when Ambrose as a child was sleeping with his mouth open in the cradle, a swarm of bees came and landed on his face and mouth. But the swarm just as quickly rose again and disappeared from view. Since the bees were said to be prophetic gifts, their visit meant that the discourses of Ambrose would be as sweet as honey and their ascent to heaven that Ambrose would direct people's minds to heaven.

Something of the character of Ambrose's biblical interpretation is already suggested by this picture. Limitless esteem of the Bible is the indisputable presupposition of his interpretation. Accepting the well-known statement of 2 Tim 3:16, Ambrose can say that "all divine Scripture breathes the grace of God" (*Exp. Ps. 118* 1.4). In the Scripture one can meet God himself: "God, too, walks in paradise (Gen 3:8) when I read the divine Scriptures. The paradise is the book of Genesis, in which the virtues of the patriarchs germinate aloft; the paradise is Deuteronomy, in which the commands of the law blossom; the paradise is the gospel in which the tree of life brings good fruits" (*Ep.* 49/33.3). Ambrose knows of several images for the Scripture's identification with the word of God. Comparison with the bread shows the close connection of Eucharist and the proclaimed word: "Heavenly bread namely is the word of God" (*Exp. Luc.* 6.63). Or the speeches about Jesus with several breads that multiply in the mouth of the preacher (*Exp. Luc.* 6.86). Indeed, the biblical traditions are, like the church, the body of Christ (*Exp. Luc.* 6.33.). The image of milk (see already 1 Cor 3:2; Heb 5:12–13; 1 Pet 2:2) represents education: "He called the two Testaments breasts—and breasts truly, for the Son, after he had nourished us with a spiritual milk, taught (us) and so offered God" (*Patr.* 51). Expressed here at the same time is moral interpretation, which plays an important role in Ambrose, as in his predecessors: "There are also (interpreters) who suppose that the clear commands of the Lord coming from his divine mouth have been shared with us like milk, by which we are nourished to come to eat heavenly bread" (*Patr.* 25). The image of wine and divine intoxication leads Ambrose to the level of mystical (or spiritual) interpretation: "There is also a power more fierce than that of the word, like that of wine. A good intoxication that leads to a reaching out of the spirit for better and joyous things, that our spirit forgets its troubles and is refreshed by the wine of joyfulness" (*Exp. Ps. 118* 24). Ambrose's heavy dependence on the Greek exegetes he considers his models makes itself felt in his emphasis on these two sorts of interpretation—among the philosophers, especially Philo. But it is also to be noted that the literal sense, as historical sense, is of no interest to him. It comes into effect only when it can be interpreted directly morally. Exegesis is directed solely by pastoral concern.

That Ambrose drew on Philo followed as a matter of course for his interpretation of the Old Testament, which is a priority to him, because Philo was known as the classic of allegorical exegesis. (Of the New Testament books, only his commentary based on his sermons on Luke's Gospel is preserved.) Besides, for Ambrose there were many points of contact with Philo with respect to the moral aim of interpretation, and the spiritualizing tendency of allegory was common to both.

But Ambrose distanced himself from Philo explicitly in one place and implicitly in many others. He once mentions him by name: "Philo, however, remained within moral things because, due to his Jewish outlook, he did not understand spiritual things" (*Parad.* 4.25). Ambrose separated himself from Judaism as decisively as from heresies (and combated them with equal church-political rigor). He understands by "spiritual things" the truths of Christian faith, and extracting them is the real goal of his biblical interpretation. Even ethics is subordinate to it, because the moral directions to be drawn from the Bible are rules for the new life the Christian has gained through the saving work of Jesus Christ and participation in the sacraments. But for "spiritual" interpretation, he uses the allegorical method freely, as is natural for his time. He can also freely draw from Philo's work anything that seems of use to him for his own work.

Such support was understandably welcome, especially during his early years in office as bishop, when he was thrust unprepared into the diverse duties of a bishop: "I began, when I was cast from the courts of justice and the honors of administration into the priestly office, to teach you about things I myself had not learned." (*Off.* 1.4)

Relatively early in his career Ambrose occupied himself with the interpretation of Genesis, in part in sermons and in part in works designed for publication. The first work of this sort is *On Paradise*. In it Ambrose pursued the intention of debating with objections that evidently rationalism active even in his community was accustomed to raise against the biblical story of paradise in Gen 2–3. These objections had attained classical formulation in *The Syllogisms* (not preserved), a work by Apelles, a student of Marcion. It is astonishing to see that this work of the second century was still known in the fourth and worthy of refutation, especially since the Marcionite sect was already extinct in Ambrose's time. Yet the rationalism of antiquity was still virulent, and its criticism of the Bible was a cause of disturbance for the community that Ambrose thought had to be urgently confronted.

He used for this purpose the schema of "questions and answers" that Christian authors had taken over from Aristotle's philosophy and exegesis of Homer. He first named three questions that Apelles and other rationalists in his succession put to the biblical narrative of paradise: (1) How could the tree of life seem more potent for life than God's breath of life? (2) "If God did not create humanity perfect and each person attains the perfection of virtue by his or her own efforts, does it not seem, then, that humanity has provided for itself more than God has given it?" (3) "If humans had not tasted death, they could by no means know what they had not tasted. Therefore, if they had not tasted, they did not know (it), and if they did not know (it), they could not fear it. It was therefore futile for God to set out death as a deterrence that humans did not fear" (*Parad.*

5.28) Other objections are: (4) "It is not always bad not to obey a law. If the law is good, obedience is honorable; but if the law is bad, not to obey it is useful. But the tree that leads to knowledge of good and evil is good, since indeed even God knows good and evil.... The one who forbids it to humanity seems not to forbid it justly" (*Parad.* 6.30); (5) "Another question: Whoever does not know good and evil is no different than a child. But the child has no guilt before a just judge, for a just director of the world would never hold a child responsible for not knowing Good and evil" (*Parad.* 6.31). (6) "Whoever does not know good and evil does also not know that it is evil not to obey the law and also does not know the good that it means to obey the law. Since one does not know it, one deserves forgiveness, not condemnation" (*Parad.* 6.32). Similar to the second question mentioned above is the following: (7) "Why did death strike Adam, by the nature of such a tree or by God? If we attribute it to the nature of the tree, the fruit of this divine power, but if he knew it and nonetheless commanded what he knew would not be obeyed, then is this not a matter of God prescribing something superfluous? God does nothing superfluous. Therefore, the Scripture is not from God" (*Parad.* 8.38). The ninth question moves in this same direction (*Parad.* 8.40). It is uncertain if a tenth Apelles-quotation still followed.

The objections of Apelles may seem naïve to a modern reader; to Ambrose, they seemed dangerous. He answered them first on their own level, "so that they do not mislead simple minds by perverse interpretation" (*Parad.* 5.28) Thus as regards, say, the problem that the first man could fear death even though he did not know it, Ambrose points to the animals, which have an innate fear of their natural enemies. "How much more [likely], then, would the first humans, who were fully endowed with reason, have a natural idea that death would have to be avoided" (*Parad.* 6.29). He also recalls Eve's answer to the serpent's question about God's commandment not to eat of the tree of knowledge; Eve repeats it with the words, "Do not eat of it and do not touch it, lest you die" (Gen 3:3; *Parad.* 12.56): "There is nothing wrong with the commandment, but in restating it," for to avoid evil, it is altogether necessary to know it. To learn this knowledge, it would be important to touch the tree of knowledge—which is still significantly different from eating of its fruit! All these answers seem to him only moderately convincing, so he switches finally to another level, making use of the allegorical method Philo used for interpreting the primeval history. The occasion for this is the realization that, despite all of the reasons he gave on the basis of the literal sense, skeptics would not be satisfied why the devil (in the form of a serpent) had to be in paradise.

The allusion to Philo, without mentioning his name, is quite clear: "There was one prior to us who maintained that man's transgression was due to pleasure and sensuality in that he accepted the image of pleasure in the figure of a serpent, defined the senses of the soul and the spirit in terms of the figure of the woman, and explained the spirit of transgression in terms of history as the deception of the senses" (*Parad.* 2.10). Thus in an entire block of his essay Ambrose came to interpret the events in paradise as occurrences within the interior of the soul, completely in the way customary to Philo, and by this means set aside temptations by rationalistic skepticism.

We find, then, a strong apologetic impulse already in this earliest writing of Ambrose: the bishop is concerned to protect his community from temptations by rational objections to the Bible and to put in the hands of its members arguments they can use against late disciples of Apelles who still use his writing. The impression gained this way is confirmed by other writings.

One well-known example is the beginning of the work that arose from sermons on the first creation account (Gen 1), which bears the Greek title *Hexaemeron libri sex* (*Six Days of Creation*). Ambrose begins with a section (*Hex.* 1.1) in which he sets forth the irreconcilable contradictions of the philosophers with regard to their views of the origin of the world. In so doing, he presumably went back to Aristotle's work *On Philosophy.* Over against the philosophers, who cannot agree among themselves whether matter is eternal, whether or not the world as a whole is God and hence should be worshiped as such, or perhaps only its parts, which are specific divinities, he counterposes the first sentence of the Bible, in which he presupposes with all contemporaries that Moses was the author of the creation history and that he preceded the pagan philosophers by centuries.

> Therefore, Moses, who foresaw in the Holy Spirit that this would be the errors of humanity, spoke at the start of his discourse in this way, "in the beginning God created heaven and earth," because he included the beginning of things, the creator of the world, and the creation of matter. By this, you should understand that God was before the beginning of the world or he himself is the beginning of all things. Just as in the Gospel the Son of God answered those who asked "who are you? Why do I speak to you at all? (John 8:25) and that he had given all things their beginning and that he was the creator of the world. He says also nicely "created in the beginning" in order to express the inconceivable quickness of the work, since he explained the outcome of the completed action earlier than the discovery of its beginning. (*Hex.* 1.2.5)

With this sentence Ambrose was apparently combating the view of the gnostics in particular, who considered matter to be eternal and uncreated and thus God as merely the "fashioner of matter," from which he was able to create his works not according to his will but only in accord with a preestablished model (1.2.5). A praise of Moses follows (1.2.6) in which Ambrose—evidently picking up on a statement in Acts (7:22)—points out that at the instigation of Pharaoh's daughter Moses had been "educated in all the wisdom of the Egyptians." But he then also recalls Moses' return for the liberation of his people and his activity as a prophet to whom God spoke face to face (Deut 14:10) and as God's emissary to Pharaoh (Exod 4:12). Ambrose even mentions the name Moses, which Exod 2:10 connects to "water," in order to use it for another attack on philosophy: it does not mean that everything consists of water, as the Greek natural philosopher Thales had surmised. For Ambrose, the conflict between philosophy and theology is decided in advance by the authority of the Bible, by the personal authority God granted Moses, and by the fact that Moses preceded the pagan philosophers by centuries.

Paganism was already largely in retreat in Ambrose's day, but the battle between paganism and Christianity was not yet finally concluded. Therefore, this apologetic front had, for him, pastoral and evangelistic urgency, which he addressed with these discussions. In so doing, he thereby gave the starting signal for many later discussions.

Another example is *Jacob and the Happy Life*. This essay evidently owes its present form to the binding together of several sermons. Although this structure is thus first the product of redactional work, the well-conceived plan behind it can be recognized. Ambrose begins with a philosophical essay on the rule of reason over the passions (1.1.1–1.2.8). His source here is the book of 4 Maccabees, a first-century Jewish-Hellenistic text (early on, falsely attributed to Josephus) that elucidates (4 Macc 5:1–17:6) the validity of this Stoic proposition (see 1:1–12) by specific reference to the examples of Eleazar's martyrdom as well as the seven brothers and their mother (see 2 Macc 6:18–7:42). Ambrose recapitulates its contents, at times in his own words, and adduces from the Old Testament several examples of the benefits of moderation: David, who abstained from the water from Bethlehem brought to him under danger (2 Sam 23:15–17; *Jac.* 1.1.3); Jacob, who through his moderation received the birthright of Esau (Gen 25:29–34); Joseph's refusal to have sex with Potiphar's wife (Gen 39:7–20; *Jac.* 1.2.6); Jacob's rebuke of his sons Simeon and Levi because of their blood revenge on the Shechemites (Gen 34:30; *Jac.* 1.3.7); and Adam and Eve's desire for the forbidden fruit in paradise (Gen 3:1–7; *Jac.* 1.3.8).

The book of 4 Maccabees is an interesting Jewish attempt to demonstrate the superiority of the laws of Moses as a basis of ethics against the background of the principles of ancient ethics. Even Ambrose, it seems, shares these principles when right at the outset (*Jac.* 1.1.1) he repeats the general philosophical principles "virtue is teachable" and "the spirit eager for reason precedes the virtues; [he[bridles the passions." Reason is said to be the mistress of the passions several other times in this introductory piece, which seems like a didactic piece of pagan-ethical anthropology.

At first glance, even more amazing is the fact that attached to this, without a lengthy transition, is a free exegesis of Rom 5:13–8:39, the core of the Pauline message (*Jac.* 1.3.10–1.6.26). But the intent of this juxtaposition is to correct the pagan image of humanity Ambrose seemed at first to follow uncritically: thus it emerges from Rom 7:24–25 that humans are not free to follow the law, for the human spirit is subject to the flesh, "if one does not have Christ's guidance." "Hence we must try hard to attain to the grace of God." That is, "there has come the Lord Jesus, who fixed our passions to his cross, so that sins should be forgiven" (1.5.17) The entire Christian doctrine of salvation then follows, concluding with the appeal to the listener (the style of the original sermon now becomes altogether clear) to take up the cross of Christ in discipleship and proceed through all afflictions to the goal. "In these we are preserved; in them is the happy life, even if it is flooded over by many dangers" (1.7.27) A typically Stoic proposition can then follow without further ado: "that is to say, the wise person is not broken by pains of the body nor destroyed by difficulties but remains happy even in times of difficulty" (1.7.28). Ambrose did it: he is able to meet his goal of admonishing his community ethically, while at the same time preserving the Christian approach that understands God's laws as rules of living for those saved by Christ.

In the following section (1.7.28–1.8.39), then, is a description, once again in a rational spirit, of the wise man whose life passes happily because he follows reason. Here, a life of prudence and conscientiousness is antithetically set over against living according to the flesh, to bodily pleasure, "for indeed the happiness of life consists not in the pleasure of the body but in the conscience free of every slip of sin" (1.7.28). Fully expressed here once again is philosophical ethics, as advocated by the Stoics Seneca and Cicero or the Neoplatonist Plotinus, although Ambrose illustrates them by several examples from the Old Testament (Hezekiah, Jeremiah, Daniel, the three men in the fiery oven; 1.8.36).

The second book then contains, as a collection of examples for the advocated ideal, an exegesis of the life of Jacob (2.1.1–2.9.42), who led a happy life because he had a pure conscience—what a contrast to the depiction of Jacob's character in the Old Testament itself!—and a description of the martyrdom of the Maccabees (2.10.43–2.12.58). Each was originally a separate sermon, which Ambrose revised and put to use for the new purpose.

Yet he remained true to his pastoral concern even in this crafted writing. The essay is intended to teach Christians how to lead happy, that is, moral, lives. It is the bishop's task to lead them to this path. It is astonishing in this regard how far the principles of ancient-pagan morality come into effect with respect to content. For instance, the antithesis of body and spirit, the engine of the ascetic movement in the early church, plays an important role—still completely in its philosophical context. The role of reason is also ambiguous: in *On Paradise* Ambrose sought to refute rationalist skepticism, but here he grants reason a central place. He fiercely battled Arianism, a decidedly rationalistic form of Christianity, but orthodoxy, too, whose churchly representative he is, is bound in ancient intellectuality by numerous roots. Thus even biblical exegesis can be put into its service in large measure.

In developing his principles of interpretation, however, Ambrose seeks his own line, which illustrates the combination of antiquity and Christianity in his thinking in a distinctive way. We find his principles on this stated at the beginning of his two larger commentaries, the interpretation of Ps 118 (119) and the commentary on Luke. The beginning of the psalm, "Happy are those who live blamelessly, who walk in the law of the Lord. Happy are those who keep his testimonies, who seek him from their whole heart," occasions Ambrose, to call attention to the—in his eyes remarkable—sequence of the psalmist's statements.

> What beautiful order, how full of learning and grace. He did not first say "keep the decrees—this could be suggested in keeping with the wording—but first "Happy are those who live blamelessly." That is, living is to be sought before learning. A good life has grace even without learning, [but] learning has no perfection without grace.... Therefore, the struggle of living is first to practice correct morality. When we have once done this, we can then turn to our studies, to attain to knowledge in its order and way. Moral things are first; the mystical, the second. (*Exp. Ps. 118* 1.2)

In addition to these two levels of sense on which Ambrose bases his interpretation of Scripture, he mentions a third also, "things of nature." In each case he finds these elements predominant in the three books ascribed to Solomon: in Proverbs, the moral; the nature-related in Ecclesiastes; and the mystical in the Song of Songs (*Exp. Ps. 118* 1.3). In his subsequent exposition (1.5–7) Ambrose explains the meaning of "moral"—for us easily understandable—and "mystical," which relates to religious things, "where the divine mysteries are then revealed to him and he dresses the resurrection of the Lord, tastes the thanksgiving for the passion, and sees the communities of the righteous ones" (1.5.7). What "things of nature" are is not explained. The prologue to the Luke commentary, however, is of additional aid in this regard. Here Ambrose recalls at the beginning (*Exp. Luc.* prol. 2) the tradition (going back to Plato and Aristotle and picked up by Cicero) of the tripartite division of philosophy: physics, ethics, logic (*naturalis, moralis, rationalis*). Ambrose finds these three sorts of philosophy reflected in the descriptions of Isaac's three wells as well: the well of vision (Gen 24:62), of spacious room (26:22), and of the oath (26:33)—an idea he had spun out even further in *Isaac, or The Soul* 20–29.

It is interesting to see how Ambrose Christianizes the division of secular philosophy. Cicero had defined it as follows: "The threefold way of philosophizing was therefore already accepted by Plato: one regarding the conduct of life and morality; the other, nature and hidden things; the third, the way of discussion and judging what is true, false, correct, and wrong in discourse [and] what is consistent and [what is] contradictory" (*Acad.* 1.19) Ambrose, on the other hand, defines the three sorts of thinking in connection to Isaac's wells: "The rational (wisdom) is the well of vision, because reason sharpens the glance of the spirit and purifies the sight of the soul. The well of spacious room is ethical, in that, after the foreigners in whose image the vices of the body are represented were removed, Isaac found the water of the living spirit. The third well (is that) of the oath, that is, natural wisdom, which understands what is beyond nature or in nature" (*Exp. Luc.* prol. 2). Here the task of rational thought is revised from the function of formal logic into the task of purifying the spirit in preparation for contemplation, and physics becomes metaphysics, "for what is confirmed and as it were sworn with God as witness embraces divine things, too, because the Lord of nature is called upon as witness of faithfulness" (prol. 2). Here again reference to the three books of Solomon follows, only somewhat more openly:

> He [Solomon] wrote about rational and ethical things in Proverbs, about natural [things] in Ecclesiastes, for "vanity of vanities, and all is vanity" (Eccl 1:2) in everything that is in the world, for "the creature was made subject to transience" (Rom 8:20); [and] as regards moral and ratio-

nal things in the Song of Songs: Because love for the heavenly Word is poured out into our soul and the holy mind is as it were united in company with the rational (spiritual), wondrous mysteries are disclosed.

Ambrose believes these various features are found in the Gospels, too. "Natural wisdom" (metaphysics is meant) is found in the Gospel of John. "For no one, I dare say, has seen the majesty of God with such humble wisdom. He has risen above the clouds, above the heavenly powers, above the angels in order to discover the work that was at the beginning, and the Word with God" (John 1:1; *Exp. Luc.* prol. 3) Matthew is the moralist who teaches the rules of life; this is evident especially in view of the Sermon on the Mount. Mark, on the other hand, is described as "rational," evidently in the sense of the word usage explained above, for here Ambrose refers to the beginning of the Gospel (1:2–8) where John the Baptist is spoken of, "so that he [Mark], moved to admiration [of the Baptist], teaches that one must attain happiness by humility, celibacy, and faith, as that saint John the Baptist rose with each step, his clothes, his food, his message" (*Exp. Luc.* prol. 1.3) The catchword "faith" is to be stressed, for paradoxically faith replaces the formal logic that has its place among the philosophers, to which one reaches by right reason (*ratio*) as the goal of these preparations and the precondition for deeper knowledge. In a later sermon, the interpretation of Ps 36 (37), Ambrose can also carry the three aspects over to the Pentateuch: "All Scripture is either natural or mystical or moral: nature in Genesis, which expresses how heaven, seas, lands were made; mystical in Leviticus, in which the mystery of the priesthood is conceived; moral in Deuteronomy, in which human life is formed according to the instruction of the law" (*Enarrat. Ps.* 36.1) Ambrose believes all three levels of understanding are found in the Gospel of Luke, notwithstanding the fact that he calls this Gospel "historical" because Luke "described the deeds of the Lord in great fullness of detail." (*Exp. Luc.* prol. 1). But the same holds for the other Gospels also and for Scripture itself, for these three aspects basically direct Ambrose's biblical interpretation.

By which method these aspects of interpretation are won here does not play a decisive role, because in, for example, Ps 118 (119) or the Sermon on the Mount the literal sense leads readily to a moral interpretation. But elsewhere allegory can be used as an aid in order to reach an understanding that is in Ambrose's view adequate.

In so doing, how powerfully the aspect of spiritual ascent of the soul is decisive—here the unbroken influence of Origen is noticeable even in Ambrose—is especially clear in the fourth chapter of *Isaac, or The Soul,* in which, along with mention of Isaac's wells (*Isaac* 4.20–22) and the three books of Solomon (4.23), the interpretation of verses from the Song of Songs plays a special role. The chapter begins with an interpretation of Song 1:4, "the king led me into his chamber." To this, Ambrose says, "each blessed soul penetrates to the interior, for it raises itself from the body, further distances itself from all things, and explores and seeks that divinity within itself as if it could then reach it" (*Isaac* 4.11) Purification, moral action, and mystical knowledge—these are the steps along the path leading the believer to God. Although this schema from philosophy has replaced Origen's hermeneutical conceptuality, his influence on Ambrose with regard to the goal of interpretation remains central. But Ambrose has evidently adapted his presentation for his pastoral concern. Besides the threefold schema, a fourfold scheme can also be recognized; the soul's union with God, already successful, is endangered by fleshly temptations (4.13), and self-knowledge (4.15) alone leads to reformation, to control of the desires (4.16), to discipleship, and thereby to perfection.

The point of departure for the relationship of the Old Testament to the New is for Ambrose the conviction of the unity of the two Testaments. Their unity is based on the fact that God is their founder (*Ep.* 74.1): "It is settled to believe that the two Testaments have one author" (*Parad.* 8.38). This author can be identified with Christ: "Because it is said that 'all things are made through him' (John 1:3), he is described as the founder of both the New as well as the Old Testament, so that the Manichaeans have no place for temptation" (*Fid. Grat.* 1.8.57). Against the sectaries of many sorts who deny the Old Testament's authority, Ambrose holds firmly to the unity of the Scripture. This unity, however, is also based within Scripture itself by the New Testament. Ambrose comments, for example, on the word of Jesus in Luke 4:27, where Jesus comes to speak of the Syrian Naaman (2 Kgs 5:14) in connection with his own healings: "It is shown that the Lord's action corresponds to the ancient Scriptures" (*Exp. Luc.* 4.49). But more than this, "drink Christ, so that you drink his speech: his speech is the Old, his speech is the New Testament" (*Enarrat. Ps.* 1.33). Set against the background of Trinitarian thought, the basic assumption that the whole Bible is the Word of God leads to a christological interpretation of the Old Testament. The triune God speaks in the whole Bible: "Here Christ speaks, there the Father, there the Spirit to the Father. This is not a contradiction but correspondence. What the one speaks, the three speak, because it is the one voice of the Trinity" (*Exp. Luc.* 10.12). But it holds particularly: "It is Christ who spoke, both in the Prophets as well as the Gospel" (*Fid. Grat.* 2.37). Nevertheless, there is an order of priority between the Old and New Testaments: "The first is the law, the second the gospel; nonetheless, fear is less than grace" (*Exp. Luc.* 5.31). Herein God's educational aim toward humanity is expressed: "The law follows nature in many so as to call us to the search for righteousness by the fact that natural desires are experienced more strongly" (8.1). Hence, there is also a sequential order in which the Testaments are to be heard: "Drink of the Old Testament first, so that you can drink of the New Testament as well. If you do not drink of the first, you will not be able to drink of the second. Drink of the first in order to slacken your thirst; drink of the second so that you drink your full in drinking. In the Old Testament there is remorse; in the New, joy" (*Enarrat. Ps.* 1.33).

There is, in the image of drinking, a recollection of the Eucharist around which the bishop's thinking circles. Here again the concern is for the spiritual education of Christians in which the law, identified with the Old Testament, and the gospel, equated with the New, are steps that should be taken in this sequence. Ambrose also deals with this theme, which already plays a role in Paul, in several letters. Thus in *Ep.* 74 he elucidates Gal 3:24 on the "law as a taskmaster to Christ" and in *Ep.* 75 the adjoining statement, Gal 3:10, that "those who rely on the works of the law are under a curse." For him, the decisive thing is that, since Christ has come, the law is removed for Christians by the gospel. On this he comments, against the claim of the Jews to the Old Testament, by appeal to Heb 9:17 (stating that a testament first comes in effect with the death of the testator), that they are indeed heirs, but without an inheritance (*Ep.* 75).

The contrast between the Testaments is also illustrated by the counter-positioning of the two brothers; here again Ambrose uses traditional models. An important motive in this regard is the aim of demonstrating that salvation has been transferred from the Jews to the pagans and so also to the (pagan-Christian) church. Paul earlier had viewed Isaac and Ishmael and their mothers Sarah and Hagar as types of the two Testaments and people (see Rom 9:8–9; Gal 4:21–31). In his last work, the exposition of Ps 43 (44), Ambrose takes up this image anew, which he used many times before (see *Abr.* 1.4.28; 2.10.72; *Ep.* 72), understanding the two women as the two Testaments and their sons as the two peoples, Christians and Jews. The Testament of Mount Sinai—Ambrose interprets the name as "his measure," that is, the Mosaic law, or as "his wage"; the Jews preferred to be justified by the works of the law than through grace—gave the Jews birth into servitude. Sarah, on the other hand, is the Jerusalem from above, which gave birth to the peoples from the nations who believe in Christ. Likewise also in the cases of the sons: Ishmael was "born according to the flesh because he interpreted the divine Scripture according to the flesh and the letter, not according to the Spirit. But those who are the free are born according to the promise" (*Enarrat. Ps.* 43.57). At the conclusion of this section Ambrose appeals explicitly to Paul: "This is thus the solution, since what the Jew disregarded was resolved by the faith of the pagans, which was instilled into the hearts of the nations by the teacher Paul." In contrast to Paul, however, the antithesis is intensified into a basic repudiation of the Jews, whom Ambrose names in the same breath as the heretics, "whose [Sarah's] maid is the synagogue or every heresy, which does not free the slaves" (*Abr.* 2.72).

Even in the pairs of brothers Cain and Abel (*Cain* 1.2.5), Ephraim and Manasseh (*Patr.* 1.2–4; *Exp. Ps. 118* 14.31–23; *Enarrat. Ps.* 43.18) as well as Perez and Zarah, the sons of Tamar and Judas (Gen 38:27, 30—a lengthy essay on this in the Luke commentary (*Exp. Luc.* 3.17–29)—Ambrose makes clear the relationship of the Testaments, placing in the foreground the contrast of law and gospel that is reflected as well in the two peoples, the Jews and Christians (from pagans). But Ambrose also knows of the hope of an ultimate conversion of the Jews that will make possible a free service of the gospel among all peoples (see *Ep.* 77.6-7). He can accept Paul's statement (Rom 11:25–26): "But once the full number of the pagans [Gentiles] has entered in (to salvation), all Israel will be saved" (*Enarrat. Ps.* 61.29). In his final work, the explanation of Ps 43 (44), he combines the image of the multiple marriage also with the relationship of the Testaments. The Jewish people (the synagogue) are tied to the law (*nomos* in the masculine) like a husband, "but it is tied by chains to the bodily (material) law, not the spiritual, that is, to the Jewish rite of the law, because it does not know the mysteries of a legitimate marriage. But when the law is dead, that is, the bodily (material) interpretation of the law, then the people marry, after as it were the first man is dead, the second man who is raised from the dead. It is the gospel that is the head of this woman (*Enarrat. Ps.* 43.62). Here, too, Paul stands in the background; Ambrose quotes Rom 7:2–4 literally immediately afterward. He continues, "Therefore the first man is the law [the Old Testament]; later the marriage of the second man occurs, that is, the mysteries of the gospel, for the two Testaments are, as it were, two marriages. The one marriage is the Old Testament, which is dissolved after the death of the first man. Therefore this woman for whom the law is dead can rightly enter into a new marriage, that is, the New Testament." The outcome of this for the community that Ambrose is directly addressing is that it, too, is dead to the law;that is, it can leave material interpretation when it has access to the gospel. Finally—and this should also be noted by those in modern times who criticize Ambrose as anti-Jew—he has like Paul a pastoral concern: he is concerned to safeguard his community from what is in his view a false position that assumes the literal applicability of the Old Testament law for Christians. He evidently saw this as a present danger, and these remarks dictated on his deathbed are his testament in this regard.

The extent to which Ambrose draws on the theology of Paul is worthy of note. Characteristic of this is, among other things, that he can view Paul as the innkeeper to whom the good Samaritan entrusted the care for the one fallen among robbers. "The good distributor, who even dispenses something extra! Good distributor Paul, whose sermons and letters as it were overflow from the knowledge he had received!" (*Exp. Luc.* 82). If one looks closely, Ambrose has taken in an astonishingly large amount of Pauline theology.

Naturally, Ambrose also speaks of Old Testament promise and New Testament fulfillment. "The law has the task of pre-proclaiming Christ" (*Exp. Ps. 118* 16.39). "The whole content of the Old Testament law was merely a model of the future" (*Exp. Luc.* 2.56). He is familiar, like all the church fathers, with the traditional proofs from Scripture: Melchizedek (Gen 14:18–20; Heb 7:1–19) as a type of Christ (*Ep.* 63.49) or the passage on the virgin birth (Isa 7:14; see also, e.g., *Cain* 1.10; *Exp. Luc.* 2.4–15, 18, 78; 8.10). He saw David especially, whom he considered the author of all the psalms (as was customary in the early church), the prophet who proclaimed Jesus in a clear way. "What others proclaimed by riddles seems to him to have been promised in complete openness and without concealment: that the Lord Jesus would be born from his seed" (reference to Ps 131 [132]:11). "In the Psalms, therefore, Jesus is not only born to us but also takes on himself the saving passion of the body, rests, arises, ascends to heaven, sits at the right hand of the Father. That which no one had suspected that anyone would speak, this prophet alone proclaims, and later the Lord himself proclaims it in the gospel" (*Enarrat. Ps.* 1.8), The last expression recalls at the same time the idea, documented in Ambrose elsewhere as well, that the Old Testament (= law) was locked away until Christ opened it. "It is a well-known mystery that the law was not strong enough to convince the peoples and call the nations or that it was indeed shut up until the coming of Christ, who presented us the prophetic oracles that presented the testimonies of the ancient Scripture and, as it were, opened the mouth of the law so that the call of faith reached into the whole world" (*Abr.* 2.74) Only then, that is, for Christians, is the Old Testament really understandable. For this reason, it is not set aside but takes on new worth; this is especially important for Ambrose, who chooses the texts with a fondness of the Old Testament, understood in a Christian way, for his sermons.

The worth of the Old Testament is also expressed in the threefold schema of salvation history that is special to Ambrose with respect to the Bible. Instead of the two-part schema, which he already used frequently, in which the Old Testament as "law" (a term for the Testament as a whole, as well as for the literal, fleshly interpretation of the Jews) is set over against the New Testament as gospel, he can also use a division of salvation history in which the Old Testament falls into two periods. An apologetic purpose is among the motives that may again have played a role in this.

The argument that pagan philosophy must have taken its teachings from Moses because they were much more recent and Moses had learned the wisdom of ancient Egypt was already current in Jewish apologetics (thus Philo, among others). This argument from greater antiquity was taken over by Christianity and became important for the battle with classical antiquity, which appealed to its philosophers and poets in order to highlight their greater worth over against newly emergent Oriental sects— as Christianity was depicted by Celsus and other defenders of paganism. But Christians also contested Judaism's claim to the Old Testament by trying to demonstrate that Christianity was even earlier than Judaism. Jews appeal to Moses as the mediator of the Torah; Christians have witnesses to their faith older than Moses! This is the point Ambrose stresses in his commentary on Luke in connection with mention of Tamar's two sons, Perez and Zarah. For Ambrose, the fact that the one brother, Perez, stretched his hand from the mother's body first but that Zerah was then the first to came out (Gen 38:28–30) had a deeper meaning:

> Why did the one stretch out his hand from the mother's body and the other came out of the birth canal first if it were not that here the life of the peoples is described by the mystery of the twins, the one according to the law, the other according to faith, the one according to the letter, the other according to grace? That is to say, grace is earlier than the law, faith earlier than the letter. Therefore, the type of grace stretches out his hand first, since indeed the act of grace precedes, as in Job, Melchizedek, Abraham, Isaac, Jacob, who lived by faith without the law; Abraham believed, and it was reckoned as righteousness to him. (*Exp. Luc.* 3.212; see Gen 15:6)

One readily recalls that Paul had already called upon this statement (Rom 4:3; Gal 3:6). Ambrose follows Paul here again but turns his arguments in another direction. For Ambrose, the sequence of appearance of those before Moses who were justified before God without the law—including Job as a pious man of the former age who lived outside of Israel—has the result that faith based on grace alone has priority in any case because of its greater age, "because the holy patriarchs who were free from the chains of its regulations gleamed with a freedom and grace of the gospel similar to ours." It is worth noting that Ambrose does not exclude the Jews, who are symbolized by the younger brother: "The two ways of life (exist) in accord with God. For those who fought a God-fearing and pious fight in accord with the law of Moses are not without grace and honor. But the fruit of piety is earlier in the originators than in the heirs" (*Exp. Luc.* 3.22),

In this three-part historical schema, observance of the law has, "so to say, been pushed aside like a veil, and the way of living of the original fathers seems in a certain way unbroken" (3.22). Again there is a recollection of Paul (Rom 5:20; see also Gal 3:19), which Ambrose has developed systematically. In his view, everything depends, as he states at another place, on the fact "that the mysteries of the Christians are older than those of the Jews and the mysteries of the faith of the Christians are more divine than those of the Jews" (*Sacr.* 4.10). The patriarchs become precursors and types of Christians:

> The school of piety in keeping with the gospel is first, because we believe by the cross and the blood of Christ, whose day Abraham saw and rejoiced [see John 8:56], whose grace, which is represented in the type of the church, Noah sensed beforehand in spiritual knowledge, whose self-representation in the sacrifice of Isaac is not denied [see Gen 22:10], whom Jacob, since he conquered, worshiped [see Gen 32:25], the red color of whose garments Isaiah saw [see Isa 63:2]—for even the lives of the prophets took place in accord with the gospel. (*Exp. Luc.* 3.23).

This tripartite division of salvation history appears in other places. Thus Ambrose says, when explaining the parable of the fig tree (on Luke 13:7), that the term of three years mentioned there has symbolic meaning, because Christ also has a threefold coming.

> He came to Abraham, he came to Moses, he came to Mary; that is, he came in signs, he came in the law, he came in the body. We recognize his coming by the gifts of his grace: there is purification, there sanctification, here justification. Circumcision purified, the law sanctified, grace justified: one in all, and all in one. For no one can be purified apart from fear of the Lord. No one is worthy of accepting the law apart from puri-

fication of sin; no one attains grace apart from knowledge of the law. (*Exp. Luc.* 7.166).

Thus salvation becomes clear in the three periods: the age of the patriarchs, that of the law of Moses, and that after the coming of the Lord. But it is no unified development but, so to speak, a return to the beginning, for the grace of Christ was already present in the lives of the patriarchs.

Incidentally, beside this threefold division separating the Old Testament into two periods, Ambrose also knows of the (Platonic) threefold division of salvation history that we encounter in Origen with the catchwords "shadow, image, truth." According to this, history moves from shadow through image to truth. "The shadow (is found) in the law [Old Testament], the image in the gospel, the truth in heavenly things [the eschatological time of salvation]" (*Off.* 1.238; see also *Exc.* 2.109).

As important as a correct understanding of the Old Testament was to Ambrose—already in respect to Marcionite inclinations within his community—his central concern was preaching the gospel that came in Jesus Christ. He understands its significance to be above all the forgiveness of sins. "The church is already justified in a way greater than the law; that is, the law did not know of forgiveness of sins at all; the law does not have the mystery by which secret things are purified; therefore, what is less in the law comes to completion in the gospel" (*Exp. Luc.* 6.23). The second half of this statement must be noted, because Ambrose definitely knew of the sinfulness of the inadvertently committed trespasses foreseen in Lev 5:16. What he has in view is baptism, which is the sole means for the actual forgiveness of sins that the law (Old Testament) merely pre-announces. Stated differently, everything depends on actually participating in Christ, which becomes possible only after his coming in the flesh. This becomes clear, for example, in the interpretation of the story of the rich man (Luke 18:18–26), which Ambrose offered on various occasions. In his sermon on Ps 1, now contained in his commentary on Ps 118 (119), he makes it clear that Jesus, with his demand to the rich man who confesses to have fulfilled all the law, "Sell all that you own and give it to the poor ... and come, follow me" (Luke 18:23), intended "that the Lord would become his share, the Lord, not gold, not possessions, but the true God" (*Exp. Ps. 118* 9). This interpretation is developed further in the Luke commentary: to the address by the rich one "good master" and Jesus' rebuke, "why do you call me good? No one is good but God alone" (Luke 18:18–19), Ambrose remarks: "A crafty question and therefore an outstanding answer! For that arch-tempter who should have called him the good God calls him a good master" (*Exp. Luc.* 8.65). On this, he refers to Ps 115 (116):11, "everyone is a liar," as well as Ps 13 (14):3, "there is no one who does good, not even one," and makes clear that by his address the rich man accepted Jesus as only partially for God and in so doing denied his divinity, "for God is perfect good, humans only partly." "For this reason the Lord (says): Who do you call me, whom you deny as God, good? Why do you call me good when indeed no one is good but God alone? Therefore he does not dispute that he is good, but designates himself as God; for who is good except the one who is full of goodness?" The rich man's failing is that he cannot recognize Jesus as the highest good for which it is worth surrendering all one's worldly goods.

The Christocentric interpretation of the Bible in Ambrose's case shows itself especially clearly in this example, but also in the way he can interpret the double command of love in Luke 10:27. The combination of the two laws in Deut 6:5 and Lev 19:18 is directed against those "who attend to law-giving, indeed keep the words of the law, (but) do not know the power of the law, because in the beginning the law proclaimed the Father as well as the Son and announced the mystery of the Lord's incarnation in that it stated 'love the Lord your God' and 'love your neighbor as yourself.' But someone who did not know his neighbor because he did not believe in Christ answered, 'Who, then, is my neighbor?'" (*Exp. Luc.* 70.69–70). Jesus Christ is the neighbor of the parable in a special sense, because he is the incarnate Son. Shortly afterward the good Samaritan of the following parable is described in a "spiritual" interpretation with an allusion to John 3:13 as the "Samaritan ... in concealment ... who is come down, who characterizes our neighbor by having taken suffering with us upon himself and by sharing mercy with us has become our neighbor" (*Exp. Luc.* 7.74).

Instances of dogmatically oriented exegesis in Ambrose could be easily multiplied. This goes along with the fact that he considered himself a champion of Catholic (Nicene) doctrine and sought each time to establish it biblically, for the Bible is, for him, an infallible source of truth: "Follow the Scriptures, so that you might not err" (*Exp. Luc.* 2.12). This sort of interpretation is therefore encountered especially in works dealing with dogmatic themes. Ambrose is the author of a series of such works. In them he expresses also the areas he feels himself responsible for as bishop for his community. An example is, say, the book *The Sacraments*, which arose from six Easter-week sermons Ambrose gave to the newly baptized and were presumably not meant for publication. Rather, they were written down by a stenographer and not published until after Ambrose's death. We can cite his explanation of the words of institution Mark 14:22, 24 as an illustration: "You say perhaps, 'This is my ordinary bread.' But this bread is bread before the words of institution. When the consecration occurs, it turns from bread to the body of Christ … because everything that is said afterward is said by the priest: thanksgiving to God (is made); the prayer is offered interceding for the people, for the kings, for all the others. At the point in the sequence that a sacrament worthy of reverence occurs, the preacher does not use his own words but the words of Christ. There the Word of Christ effects this sacrament" (*Sacr.* 4.14). A more lengthy section follows in which Ambrose refers to the fact that it is by the word of the Lord that all creation is made (4.15). Hence the doctrine of creation is unfolded Christocentrically. The quoted section also shows, however, that for Ambrose word and sacrament are closely bound to one other: "The divine sacraments are a good pasture; the words of the heavenly Scriptures are a good pasture, by the daily reading of which we are nourished, in which we are refreshed and find refuge" (*Exp. Ps. 118* 14.2).

From the style it becomes clear that here one has to do with another sort of interpretation: it is a component of catechesis, as it is offered to baptismal candidates and the newly baptized. With respect to content, it can be ascertained that Catholic sacramental doctrine is already firmly developed, in this case the doctrine of the change of the elements in the Eucharist.

The various ways in which Ambrose deals with the Bible correspond closely to the tasks he had to fulfill as bishop of one of the most important communities of the West. For him, biblical interpretation was not an end but the foundation of his pastoral activity, whether as preacher, pastor, or catechist. Ambrose stands before us as an example of episcopal-pastoral biblical practice as it was exercised in countless communities. He is certainly a prominent example, an influential prince of the church. But as shepherd of his community, he was still only one bishop among others. The significance of the Bible for the bishop's preaching practice in Milan was similar to that elsewhere. The fact that its authority was in this way determinative for the life of the community, for the ethics and dogmatic teachings that gained acceptance in it, shows the early church's emphatic biblical orientation. Even in its "early Catholic" period it remained a church of the word. Ambrose had an important part in that.

1.5. Monastic Life with the Bible: John Cassian

We have already heard about Egyptian monasticism in passing, in connection with Didymus the Blind and Jerome. Egypt was the cradle of monasticism. In the second half of the third century, individual Christians began to retreat to the desert and live there in caves as anchorites. They pursued their goal of avoiding the world and worldly influences they considered ruinous for salvation by rigorous asceticism that can be characterized by the catchwords *poverty*, *chastity*, and *obedience* as the basic rules of monastic life. The ideal was to return to original Christian simplicity in which the basically body-hating, dualistic tenor of the time played an important motivating role. Sexual temptations in particular afflicted the ascetics in the deserts. They felt themselves constantly surrounded by demons whose sensual temptations and apparitions they had to combat. The temptations of Anthony are the best known, becoming a popular theme in Christian art. Anthony (ca. 250–356)—whose biography, legendary in part but at core historical, was written shortly after his death by Athanasius—is credited as the real father of monasticism. By gathering eremites together into colonies, he created the beginnings of a communal form of life that Pachomius (d. 348) further developed into a truly organized monastic life (coenobites).

The monastic life (for monks and nuns, often in adjoining cloisters) later spread from Egypt to the varied provinces of the empire, though its land of origins long remained exemplary. The first monastic rules with directions for the life conduct of monks (and nuns) in every detail go back to Pachomius. Originally written in Coptic, they became known in the West as well through a Latin translation from Origen's pen. Other literary testimonies that transmit the thought-world of the Egyptian monks to us are the "Sayings of the Fathers" (Apothegmata Patrum) and the spiritual writings of Evagrius Ponticus (346–399), in which the inner stance of Origenist monasticism becomes visible. The soul's ascent leading from moral purification and the dissolution of all earthly ties to the vision of the eternal, as Origen had taught it, was foundational for all the external and internal forms of life in this form of monasticism. One sees them in Cassian as well (as a statement of Abbot Moyses, *Conl.* 1) in the description of the goal as the "kingdom of God" and the way to it as "purity of the heart," for which the word "love" is also used. They survived in their basic traits and were transplanted from Egypt into the West, when the anti-Origenist persecution of 399/400 coming from Alexandria brought Origenist monasticism to an end.

The Bible played an important role in the monk's life. Most that we know of the matter is from the writings of John Cassian (ca. 360–after 432), who learned about Egyptian monks and their life with his own eyes and reported on it from a wider temporal and spatial perspective. Cassian, who presumably came from today's region of Dobruja, lived for some years with his countryman and friend Germanus in a cloister in Bethlehem before the two of them set off, around 392, on a visit to the monks in Egypt. From the brief informational trip they originally planned, there developed a longer stay that lasted until the flight of the Origenist monks from Egypt. Cassian went first to Patriarch John Chrysostom in Constantinople, regarded as a champion of the Origenists, and was ordained a deacon (against his will) by him. But after John's expulsion in 403, Cassian had to flee again, this time to Rome, where he became friends with the later Pope Leo I. His last, and ultimate, sphere of activity was Marseilles. There he founded the monastery of St. Victor and at the same time a women's cloister. These were among the first monasteries in Gaul.

Cassian's writings contributed substantially to making known the traditions of the Egyptian eremites and monks in the West and extending their monastic rules to the Latin church. The significance of his influence on the rule of Benedict of Nursia (at the start of the sixth century), authoritative for Western monasticism, cannot be overemphasized. Of particular interest to us are his works about monasticism: *De Institutis coenobiorum (On the Rules of Monks)*, written between 419 and 436, and *Conlationes patrum (The Conversations of the Fathers)*, originating in 425–429. The first-named work has three parts: three books on monastic clothing, prayers, and psalm singing; one book of monastic rules; and eight books on the most important sins and their overcoming. The *Conlationes* grew out of conversations Cassian and his friend Germanus had with famous abbots and monastic theologians during their stay in Egypt. The dialogue form, in which reminiscences of conversations carried on long ago are intermingled with Cassian's own thoughts, corresponds to an ancient literary convention. Even the questions, most of which Cassian has Germanus ask, serve to make Germanus more a mouthpiece of the author's own reflections. For all that, we can trust that Cassian reproduces in essentials the Egyptian monastic traditions as he encountered them during his stay, for he was deeply influenced by them and sought to make them the basis of life in his own monastery in Gaul. The figures of the teachers he met there are likewise historical and presumably described truthfully, though we should not overinterpret their statements as the views of each individual.

Although the dealings of the Egyptian monks with the Bible is not the sole or at first glance even the central theme, we can still learn a lot from Cassian about the role of the Scripture in monastic living and daily life of the monk. There was sufficient occasion for him to speak of it, and if the Bible is not discussed more frequently, it is evidently because Holy Scripture was a natural companion of the monks.

One problem of monastic life was the varied education of monks. The early Egyptian anchorites were rather rough and uncultured; many could not read or write. Not even Anthony received any schooling (Athanasius, *Vita Ant.* 72–73) and was speaking only vernacular Coptic, so that he had to communicate with Greek speaking visitors by a translator (72, 74, 77). But he could read the Bible in Coptic (see *Vita Ant.* 75) and was much admired for his biblical knowledge. Efforts to remedy illiteracy were made early on. Pachomius had already prescribed in his rule:

> When an uneducated person enters the cloister..., someone will give him twenty psalms or two letters of the apostle (Paul) or another piece of another writing, and if he does not know letters (cannot read), someone who can teach him and who is assigned to him should go to him at the first, third, and sixth hours, and he (the novice) should stand before him and learn eagerly. Later he should write the elements [of speech]: syllables, verbs, and nouns. He should be forced to read even if he may not want to. There should not be anyone in the monastery who is not learning to read and holds some Scripture in his hands. (rule 77)

On the other hand, there were highly educated monks, like the Abbot Joseph, for instance, who came from a leading family of his home city Thmuis (*Conl.* 16.1), the Abbot Moses (*Conl.* 1), and indeed Cassian himself. In a conversation with Abbot Nesteros (*Conl.* 14), he once explicitly expressed his concern that his pagan literary education, which led him to think of lewd poetic songs, fables, or trivial war histories while he was in the midst of praying or psalm singing, might pose a difficult obstacle to salvation (14.12). Nesteros answered that he need only devote equal zeal and perseverance to the study of the Bible, for this would drive away the disturbing thoughts completely (14.13).

As already indicated, every monk evidently had a text (codex) of the Bible in his cell. Some guarded it so zealously that they would not let anyone else read or touch it even fleetingly (*Conl.* 1.6). This behavior was criticized, and rightly so. Manuscripts were rare and quite valuable at the time, yet they did not belong to the monk, for whom even personal possession was forbidden (see John Cassian, *Inst.* 4.13), and as we know from various rules, they were collected and locked up each evening. Neverthe-less, an alleged theft of a codex from the cell of a monk by another (the later famous Abbot Paphnutius) led to a sensational incident that Cassian reports to us in *Conl.* 18. Copying manuscripts was already a regular occupation of the monks in the ancient monasteries. The language of the codices was usually Greek. From where Cassian knew of Hebrew manu-scripts as well (*Conl.* 8.10; *Inst.* 12.31) is uncertain.

In addition to washing, fasting, and prayer, dealing with the Holy Scriptures was part of the ascetic exercises of the monks, and it was given a large place in daily living. "Meditation," the term frequently used for this, evidently had a more specific meaning than in today's usage: it meant reading aloud from Scripture or even reciting it by memory, alone or together with others. In the rule of Pachomius it is ordered to "meditate on something from the Scriptures" on the way to the liturgical celebration (rule 3) and likewise on returning to the cell (rule 28). Like-wise, the monk should accompany various forms of handwork with the recitation of scriptural words: for instance, knocking on the cell wall as a sign for lunch (rule 36); the sharing of sweets after meals (rule 37); the common departure for fieldwork (rule 59); and the work itself (rule 60). There should also be communal psalm singing and recitation of Scripture, while, say, baking bread (rule 116). Cassian says of the Egyptian monks that "in their cells they constantly dedicated themselves to work in the way that meditation on the Psalms and other Scriptures never altogether ceases" (*Inst.* 3.2).

In addition to these dealings with the Bible on an individual basis, there was already in Egypt the custom of the assembly for prayer sev-eral times during the day and the night (although a regulation of specific hours [*horae*] is not found in Cassian). On this occasion twelve psalms were sung in common, followed by a reading from the Old and New Tes-taments (see *Inst.* 2–3). According to the statement of Abbot Moses, this intensive recitation and hearing of biblical texts was of great use. Indeed, the human spirit could not prevent the unexpected arousal of ideas, but "it is in large measure up to us that to improve the quality of our thought and develop it either in a holy and spiritual or in an earthly and fleshly way. That is to say, the frequent reading and constant mediation on the Scriptures are practiced precisely so that an occasion for spiri-tual memory is offered us, and the frequent singing of psalms, so that constant repentance is facilitated in us" (*Conl.* 1.17). According to Cas-sian, participation in such a common gathering and the opportunity for hearing the Bible offered there can suffice in any event for the spiritual progress of the illiterate among the monks, who must have always been present despite all these efforts at instruction. "It is known that no one is completely excluded from perfection of the heart because of ignorance of letters, nor can lack of education stand in the way of understanding purity of the heart and soul" (*Conl.* 10.14).

This constant exercise must have led the monks, as a matter of course, to come to know the Bible mostly by heart. The rule of Pachomius (rule 59) explicitly directs that monks should learn large parts of the Scriptures by heart. Even Cassian lets it be known, in all humility, that he knew the Bible by heart (*Conl.* 14.1). This is achieved by constant repetition.

The monks, however, to be sure, sought a deeper knowledge of the Bible beyond being able to memorize it. In keeping with the basic approach already described, Abbot Nesteros took as his starting point the basic division of all knowledge into two areas: "The first, practical, . . . which is completed in the improvement of morals and the purification of vices; the another, the theoretical, which consists in the consideration of divine things and the knowledge of the most holy thoughts" (*Conl.* 14.1). Theoretical knowledge deals with the Bible. Following Origen's model, Cassian knows here two sorts of interpretation, "historical interpretation and spiritual understanding." He distinguishes three types of spiritual understanding: Tropology (moral meaning), allegory (figurative) meaning, and anagogy (relating to "the more spiritual mysteries extending to those more sublime and more sacred heavenly hidden things" (*Conl.* 14.8). For Nesteros, however, the practical side, i.e., the moral preparation for theoretical knowledge, is first off more important: "Therefore persist in careful reading . . . and hurry with all zeal to understand perfectly the current, i.e., ethical, discipline first off. For without it, what we called theoretical purity cannot be reached either." For this, practical deeds are required. "That is to say, it is not in reaching understanding by meditating on the law but by the fruit of action that they sing with the psalmist, "I have understood it of your laws" (Ps 119:104, Septuagint; *Conl.* 14.9). Understanding also presupposes constant humility of the heart: "An impure spirit cannot possibly gain the gift of spiritual knowledge." Nesteros warns in particular against considering a talent for discussion and rhetorical skills as spiritual knowledge, and against the pride and ambition that can spring from would-be learning. Knowledge of the Bible can only be gained by memorizing its wording. "Therefore the sequence of the sacred Scriptures must be diligently entrusted to memory and repeated without ceasing." There is hope that anything that is unclear will be understood later by an inspiration, "so that when we rest and are as it were plunged in the stupor of sleep, the understanding of the most secret obscure meanings of which we did not have the remotest notion while awake, is revealed to us" (*Conl.* 14.10). Prayer in particular can also open a way to understanding the Scriptures. Thus Theodore once persevered in prayer for seven days and nights until the solution to a difficult question became clear to him through divine revelation (*Inst.* 5.33).

Only an equivalent moral preparation can lead to true knowledge of Scripture. So for Nesteros also the objection that Germanus poses is brushed aside: if purity of heart is the precondition for understanding Scripture correctly, how can it be that "many Jews and heretics, or even Catholics who are entangled in various vices, having reached such perfect knowledge of the Scripture, boast of the greatness of their spiritual learning while a countless number of saintly men, whose hearts are cleansed of every spot of sin, are content with the piety of simple faith and do not know the mysteries of deeper knowledge?" (*Conl.* 14.15). It is clear to Nesteros "that men of this sort have experience only in disputing and preparation for eloquence [but] in other respects are unable to penetrate to the very heart of Scripture and the mysteries of spiritual meanings" (*Conl.* 14.16). Jeremiah 5:21 is quoted in support of this statement. Once again a basic skepticism about the usefulness of profane education is expressed: "This true and spiritual knowledge is indeed so far from that of worldly learning, which is soiled by the filth of fleshly sins, that we know how it sometimes flourishes in admirable fashion among men without eloquence and nearly illiterate" (14.16). There is explicit warning against declaiming to impure people the knowledge to be gained by laborious spiritual experience out of thirst for glory (14.17). One should share it instead with penitent sinners in order to comfort them with it.

Cassian's striking warning against the use of biblical commentaries is obviously in keeping with these principles. Cassian is surely reporting his own view also as a statement by Abbot Theodore: "A monk who wishes to gain knowledge of the Scriptures does not need to put his efforts into books of commentaries at all, but instead direct all the diligence of the spirit and inclination of the heart to the purification of fleshly sins, for as soon as these are driven away [and] the veil of desires is removed, the eyes of the heart will view the mysteries of the Scriptures in a natural way." When sins are set aside, "the reading of Holy Scripture itself will reach so far as to consider true knowledge alone and have no need of the institution of commentators, just as the bodily eyes have no need of instruction for seeing if only they are free of any cataract and the darkness of blindness" (*Inst.* 5.34).

It must be pointed out that the principle set down here, stated as a strict prohibition against reading commentaries, to some extent played a role hardly conducive for biblical science in monastic life of later centuries. Augustine expressly opposed it in the prologue (esp. prol. 7) of his hermeneutics (*De doctrina christiana*). On the other hand, it is worth noting that Benedict's *Rule* absolutely approved of commentaries, even if only a specified selection. It states (rule 9): "For readings in the night watches, one may take the books of the Old and New Testaments believed to be from God, but also interpretations that are written by acknowledged and orthodox Catholic fathers." Nevertheless, there was something like biblical research among the Egyptian monks, too. *Inst.* 12.27 seems to speak of a presentation (a catechesis) in which a listener is lacking in the necessary concentration and attentiveness. According to the rule of Pachomius, the monastic leader would present catechesis of this sort, along with questions about the Bible, several times each week. The *conlatio*, or conversation, of two or three participants, one of whom is an experienced teacher, is passed on to us in the course of Cassian's reports. Not everyone was permitted to participate; the special permission of those to be interviewed was required. (*Conl.* 1.1) But it was also possible for the participants in such a presentation to discuss their controversial views afterwards. Thus Abbot Joseph reports of his youth: "I recall from that time when my youth still suggested that I take up the companionship of books that would give us insight into both moral training and the Holy Scriptures so that we considered nothing more true, nothing more reasonable, than these. But then when we met together and started to present our opinions, there were many things that, after having gone through the common testing, were first termed false and dangerous by one or another [of us] and then soon declared by common judgment to be vain and reprobate" (*Conl.* 16.10). But then the fathers' authority was once again decisive: "This had been inspired by the devil beforehand and had shone with such light that it would easily have caused discord if we had not been held back from any quarrels by a command from the fathers that was heeded like a divine judgment." On the other hand, there is the view of Abbot Serenus (*Conl.* 8.4), who with regard to obscure passages holds the opinion that the Holy Spirit placed them in the Scriptures so readers would put their efforts into them and open up their sense by proofs and conjectures. Such passages might be thoroughly discussed and differing opinions about them might be offered without doing faith any harm. However, everyone should express his or her view about them temperately and not declare them to be finally proved. A decision could finally be made only by "plain testimonies of the Scriptures" (*Conl.* 8.5). The principle that Scripture can only be interpreted by Scripture is certainly typical of the monastic way of interpretation.

According to monastic tradition as Cassian formulated it, knowledge of Scripture is primarily moral-spiritual in character. The ideal of the scripturally informed monk is perhaps represented by Abbot Theodore, whom Cassian notes was preeminent in supreme holiness and knowledge not only in daily living but in knowledge of the Scriptures as well, which he acquired not so much by studies of readings as by purity of heart alone, especially since he himself was able to understand and speak hardly even a few words of the Greek language (*Inst.* 5.33). This approach to the Bible is of a different character than the scriptural study of the great theologians of antiquity who approached the Bible by way of the scholarship of the day. It differs as well from interpretation that is oriented toward preaching, as we saw it, for example, in the case of Ambrose, a church bishop. In the end, it fostered the spiritual edification of the individual's own soul. On the other hand, here the goal of dealing with the Scriptures daily was that of an intimacy with the biblical text of an intensity such as has hardly been attained ever again, apart from parallels in Judaism. In admirable consistency these fathers devoted themselves under very harsh living conditions in a hostile environment to Christian living tied to Scripture. In so doing they created a model that was to have ongoing effects across the centuries.

1.6. The Bible and the Thought of Antiquity: Augustine

Augustine was the most significant theologian of late antiquity. His influence has deeply marked Western theology to the present. His works stand not only chronologically at the end of the ancient world—when he died, the Vandals were at the gates of his city and the entire West sank into the turmoil of the era of migrations—but in his thought he combined the diverse currents of ancient culture and the Christian tradition into an impressive synthesis and in so doing created the foundations for further theological development in the West as a whole. When we consider in what follows his contribution to the interpretation of the Bible, we attend to only a selection—and, indeed, not the most important—of his manifold works. Yet the fact that Augustine was the first Western theologian to develop a systematically organized theory of interpreting the Bible—a biblical hermeneutics—lifts him above the group of interpreters considered thus far in this area.

Augustine was born on 13 November 354 in Thagaste in Roman North Africa. He completed the customary school education before he began, at the age of sixteen, the study of rhetoric in Carthage. At eighteen, Cicero's *Hortensius* fell into his hands; under its influence he decided henceforth to seek after true wisdom alone. In the further course of his studies he acquired a comprehensive knowledge of ancient philosophy and the other liberal arts. But through his Christian mother Monica he also stood early on close to the church and was at least a catechumen. He never got Christian ideas out of his mind completely. Still, he led an unbridled life that he deeply regretted later. Thus, he had a son, Adeodatus, by a woman with whom he lived outside of marriage. For nine years (373–382) he presented himself as a "hearer" in the then-widespread sect (for a time it presented a threat to the Great Church) of the Manichaeans, which combined in its system, which the modern observer finds abstruse, Persian-dualistic (absolute antithesis of good and evil, light and darkness), gnostic-Marcionite (denial of the Old Testament), and Christian elements. Yet Manichaean teachings could not satisfy his restless quest for truth. When the Manichaean Bishop Faustus came to Carthage, where Augustine then taught grammar and rhetoric, he himself appeared too uneducated to be able to answer the inquisitive young man's critical questions. But Augustine did not complete his external break with Manichaeism at the time. In 383 he received official appointment as master of rhetoric of the city of Milan.

Augustine's stay in Milan was decisive for his later inward and external development. His encounter with Ambrose, especially the impact of his sermons, brought about a gradual turn toward Catholic Christianity—but still not a quick decision. True, Augustine soon broke with Manichaeism and resumed his catechumenate, but he fell into an internal crisis. Here his readings of some Neoplatonist writings (probably Plotinus and Porphyry especially) were at first helpful to him in the summer of 384. From then on Neoplatonist thinking remained a basic motive of Augustine that, as we will see, became essential for his understanding of the Bible.

In an earlier attempt, before he turned away from the apparently rational system of the Manichaeans, Augustine did not deal with the Bible very well. He did not want to believe the "letter" of the Bible solely on the authority of the church. Its content seemed irreconcilable with the knowledge he had gained from his education, and its linguistic forms were in diametric opposition to the rules of classical rhetoric. It was first in Milan that the Holy Scripture came to play a key role in his "conversion." Augustine's concern, like that of other committed Christians of the day, was choosing between an ordinary life with a career and family and the ascetic ideal of renouncing marriage and property. Augustine's mother had already arranged a marriage engagement for him, and he held a respected worldly position; he vacillated over his decision. Tales of the conversion of the rhetorician Marius Victorinus and the life of the hermit Antony intensified his inner struggle. In the eighth book of his *Confessions*, his life confessions he directed to God, Augustine describes the moment in the summer of 386 when, while in the garden of his home, he heard the voice of a child from a neighboring house: "Take and read!" (*Conf.* 8.12.29). He understands this as the voice of God, opens a volume containing Paul's epistles, and comes upon the passage Rom 13:13–14. All uncertainty vanishes; he knows he is destined for the ascetic life.

Soon thereafter Augustine announced his resignation from his office as rhetorician. He was baptized on Easter night, 387. Then he returned via Rome and Carthage to Thagaste, where he spent the next period in seclusion. Monica had died in Ostia before the departure. While staying a while in the city of Hippo not far from Thagaste, he was (at the wish of Bishop Valerius) chosen for the priesthood by the acclamation of the people during a worship service he attended (probably in 390). As a priest, he was commissioned by his bishop to do preaching, but he continued the writing he had already begun as well. Works against various heresies—Manichaeans and Donatists (a schismatic movement widespread in North Africa that upheld the ideal of the martyrs' church purity)—fall in this period, along with various works on the Bible. A monastery was built in which Augustine lived with like-minded associates. He was later ordained at the request of Valerius first as co-bishop, then after Valerius's death (probably 396) sole bishop, of Hippo. He administered this office until his death in 430. During this period he increasingly became, along with Bishop Aurelius of Carthage, the spiritual leader of the African church. He led the battle against the Donatists, who for a time threatened to outstrip the Catholics in numbers and influence in Africa, by means of his numerous writings but also by increased reliance on state prosecutorial measures and many synods that made decisions against them. Although his great work *Contra Faustum* (*Against Faustus*) was written during his early years in Hippo, the battle against the Manichaeans receded into the background. Of utmost importance for Augustine's theology was the debate with Pelagius and his followers. Fleeing the Visigoths, who conquered and plundered Rome in 410, Pelagius traveled to Hippo and Carthage, where he met Augustine, then went on to Palestine. He advocated a pure Sermon on the Mount Christianity that taught the gospel, understood as the intensification of the law, and the God-given freedom of the human will. Human beings are by nature capable of the good; they are able to fulfill the law, so sin is a free act. Augustine, on the other hand, realized from his reading of Paul's epistles that all human good will is dependent on God's grace. In this way, the great theme of Augustinianism, which later moved Luther as well, was first sounded. Over the years thereafter until the end of his life, Augustine wrote numerous anti-Pelagian works in which original sin and sinful desire (*concupiscence*) are central themes. He also took a significant part in several synods (the last in Carthage in 418) that condemned Pelagianism.

During Augustine's last years the great church teacher continued to engage in disputes with Arianism, which had come to Africa with Germanic mercenaries. Their arrival had itself announced the end of Roman rule: the Vandals crossed the Strait of Gibraltar in 429 and conquered the entire province step by step. In the summer of 430 they began the siege of Hippo, which was to last over a year. Augustine did not live to see the city's capture and destruction; he died on 28 August 430.

Augustine mainly left writings on dogmatics. His profound reflections on the city of God (*De civitate Dei*), the Trinity (*De trinitate*), predestination, original sin, and grace have shaped later discussion of the great themes of theology to the present day. Augustinianism is in this sense a basic structure of Western theology. It is in keeping with the systematic approach of his thinking that Augustine distinguishes himself less by the special features of his biblical interpretation—he largely follows the tradition of the fathers in his way of interpreting Scripture—than by writing his own treatise on understanding the Bible. It is, aside from that of Tyconius, the first comprehensive Latin hermeneutics in the history of Christian theology.

But this work *De doctrina christiana* (*On Christian Doctrine*, perhaps best translated as "On Christian Scholarship") had an even more comprehensive goal: it was evidently meant to be a kind of basic textbook on everything a Christian theologian needed to know and preach. The supposition that it was written at the request of Bishop Aurelius for training his priests has much to commend it, though it cannot be proved in the strict sense. But the preacher's tasks require above all else sound rules for how to deal with the Bible.

For some reason still unknown, Augustine, who had begun the work in the early years of his bishopric (395–397), did not bring it to completion right away. When toward the end of his life he looked over his earlier works in his *Retractiones* (*Retractions*) and corrected what seemed to him to have been untenable, he came to speak of *De doctrina christiana* (*Retr.* 2.4) also. He would have broken off writing the book at the time in the middle of book 3 (after 3.3.35), adding its conclusion (including book 4) only quite recently (426 or 427). In fact, between the two parts can be seen a clear advance in Augustine's dealings with the Bible.

The extent to which Augustine was influenced by Neoplatonist thought is much disputed in Augustine research. The deep impression his readings of Neoplatonist writings had made on him is undeniable, and the conceptuality typical of this philosophical school plays an important role in his terminology. Basic to the Neoplatonist worldview was the distinction between the visible and the intelligible world. The goal of knowledge, the attainment of which is the supreme destiny of the human soul (*anima*) is the vision of the Most High, the One. This, however, is removed from all time; it is eternal and unchangeable. Everything earthly is a mere obstacle along the way; the task is to set aside temporal things as quickly as possible.

The extent to which Augustine follows the Neoplatonist worldview is best picked up from a specific text. *De doctrina christiana* is informative in this regard, for its treatment of the Bible as a collection of witnesses constitutive of Christian faith makes it evident how far the stamp of Neoplatonic thought or at least Neoplatonist terminology extended. The systematic design of the work is immediately recognizable from its organization. Augustine intends to deal in book 1 with the "things" and in book 2 with the "signs" (see 1.2.2.6), which can be objects of hermeneutical discussion. The "things" (or immediately evident objects; see 1.2.2.4) are divided into two areas. The first section, running from 1.5.5 to 21.19, sets forth what faith's object is. Here Augustine begins with a Trinitarian formula, "Thus the things to be enjoyed are Father, Son and Holy Spirit and precisely these Trinity" (5.59). In accepting the church's Trinitarian confession, Augustine consciously places himself within the Christian tradition. By the term "to enjoy," however, he makes use of a typically Platonic expression. For Platonists the vision of the eternal is the highest fulfillment. But the distinctiveness of his thought emerges in the definition Augustine gives before using this word: "'to enjoy' is, namely, to cling in love to something for its own sake" (1.4.4). "Love" is a catchword central to his theology, in which the pure intellectuality of Neoplatonist thinking is overcome. In describing the triune God (5.5), Augustine once again takes up Platonist statements, such as God is ineffable (6.6), and Christian statements, "And yet God wanted, although nothing more worthy can be said of him … to delight in our words to his praise." Then philosophical thoughts follow again: God is the highest good (7.7) beyond all visible and intelligible natures; God is the life, immutable, and wisdom itself (8.8).

Yet it is the case that all humans have theoretical knowledge of everything to be found in God, described as the highest good. "No one is so impudent and tasteless as to say, 'How do you know a life that is consistently wise is preferable to a changeable one?'" Yet people do not actually live in accord with this knowledge: "People are driven away from their native land by, as it were, contrary winds of evil customs, pursuing things lower and less worthy than what they acknowledge is better and more excellent" (9.9).

Here the transition from the intellectual to the moral view becomes clear, and with it what is in Augustine's view specifically Christian. "Therefore the spirit must be purified so that it is in a position both to see that light and cling to what is seen. That is, we will not be locally moved toward him who is everywhere present except by sound study and sound morals" (10.10).

The second article can be joined to this: in the incarnation of wisdom itself, in Christ, we are given an exemplar for living. To the proud, it is foolish and weak (11.11). This prompts quoting 1 Cor 1:25 and 1:21 above all, to which this section (12.11–12) leads.

In due course—in the article on the Holy Spirit, who is mentioned only briefly (15.14)—the church to which Christ handed over the power of the keys (see Matt. 16:19) is discussed: "That, whoever does not believe that his sins are forgiven in the church, they will not remitted to him, but whoever believes and, improved, turns away from them is saved in the bosom of this church by this very faith and reprimand" (18.17). After a few remarks about "last things" (death, resurrection, and eternal life, 19.18), Augustine ends this section with a concluding remark in which he once again refers to the distinction between "to enjoy" and "to use": "In all these things, only those we called eternal and unchanging are to be enjoyed; the others, however, are to be used so that we can attain to the enjoyment of the former" (22.20). Now here, to be sure, an *aporia* remains, for this eternal, immutable one can be God only in the philosophical sense, while Christ and the church can merely be means to be used. But this contradicts the Trinitarian reference, in which in keeping with Christian faith both must be incorporated.

It is also important to recognize the aim Augustine is pursuing in the second part of the first book. This second section likewise is built up around a biblical quotation: the double love command (Matt 23:37–40; 26.27; see also 22.21). The problem here for Augustine is that of a contradition with the Platonic goal, which knows of enjoying only the one, God, the highest good. He resolves it by seeing the love of neighbor as included in love of God, even in the sense that one would have to bring the neighbor also to the love of God (22.21). We can pass over the other problems that are discussed.

All in all, this section of the book leads to a meditation, prompted by the double love commandment, that Christianly identifies the Platonic definition of the highest goal of wisdom—enjoyment of the highest Good—with God. As a meditative text, however, the love command leads Augustine to a characteristic expression of this definition: by the catchword "love," the purely intellectual reference of philosophy becomes an ethical-personal relationship. The theology of Augustine himself emerges.

At this point an unanswered question presents itself: What role, then, can Holy Scripture play for Augustine? Despite all the differentiations vis-à-vis Platonism, his newly defined construal of the ultimate goal still remains close to Neoplatonist thought. Moreover, this modified model is close to a timeless thinking. The definition of God as transcendent and unchanging corresponds to a typical rational ontology. Love of God and neighbor, which Augustine elevates to the key of the Holy Scripture, takes place in the interior of each individual, and the church as the means of salvation works through the ages as an institution that is in principle unchanging. From this, how can one come to appreciate the Bible as a historical document of the revelation of God?

As we have seen, Augustine had organized his discussions around two biblical quotations. To him the Bible was, like the confession of faith, given as the inheritance of the church, its practical use apparently a matter of course. It was far more difficult, given his presuppositions, to establish its necessity in theory as well.

In fact, we read, "The person who relies on faith, hope, and love [see 1 Cor 13:13; to this, 37.41] and tenaciously holds to them does not need the Scriptures, not even to teach others. Thus, many live by these three (principles) even in solitude without books" (39.43; see also his *Enarrat. Ps.* 119:6, "The justified and saints enjoy the word of God without reading, without letters"). Augustine has in view here the example of the hermits dispersed at the time even in North Africa: many could neither read nor write. Yet the Bible is useful nevertheless, though only in the sense of "custom." It assists in making known the commandments of the love of God and the neighbor. It is "so that we would know and can know these [commandments] that by divine providence the whole temporal provision [*dispensatio*] for our salvation has occurred, which we should use not so to speak as an enduring love and amusement but as one temporary way, of as it were vehicles or some other sort of instrument, or, in order to say it more suitably, that we love that by which we are transported for the sake of that to which we are transported" (35.39).

With these brief remarks, Augustine refers to a theme that he expressed frequently and that assumes a central place in his thinking. In Augustine's terminology, the phrase "temporal provision" means God's historically mediated activity in its entirety. Earthly history, embracing the history of the Old Testament people of Israel and with them the witnesses of the Old Testament, is a means by which God accommodates to the situation of human beings placed in the world of sense and thereby grants them access to the intelligible world. At the center of this temporal action is the incarnation of Jesus. Jesus in his form adapted to human weakness is at the same time a sign (*sacramentum*) that points to invisible divine truth, as well as the bringer of salvation in that by his exemplary humility he saves humans from their pride (see *Conf.* 7.18.24). In so doing, however, the transience of all earthly events and its referential-character to eternal truth, including the Bible as a means of salvation, remain. For Augustine, nothing more can be claimed of the Bible's role than this. He even has a quite narrow canon within the canon: "So that all may know that the goal of the law is love, with pure hearts and good conscience and unfeigned faith [see 1 Tim 1:5], he will, in that the entire understanding of the divine Scriptures relates to these three things, assuredly enter upon the treatment of these writings" (40.44) The Bible, therefore, is seen as a textbook on ethics: Emphasis falls on the catchword "commandments" (see also 22.20; 26.57–58; 30.31). By this means a course is set that is regulative for treating the question of interpretation thereafter, even if other viewpoints are added later. But Scripture, so that it can be a textbook of ethics, is also a textbook of faith's doctrines: "But faith will waver if the authority of the divine Scriptures is weakened. Moreover, if faith wavers, love itself will disappear, too. For one cannot love something that one does not believe exists" (37.41).

Against this background Augustine develops in book 2 his much-studied doctrine of signs. He begins with the remark that in book 1 he wrote of the things that one attends to only for "what they are, not also whether they refer to something other outside themselves." But in the case of signs one must attend not only to "what they are but in addition that they are signs, that is, what they refer to." Augustine was evidently not original in his use of the term *sign*. The closest approximation to his usage is found in Stoic logic and semantics, with which Augustine was obviously familiar. His definition of a sign is: "a thing that, in addition to the impression it makes on the senses, brings forth from itself something else for consideration" (2.1.1) One distinction that follows (1.2) is important, that between natural and given signs. Augustine mentions natural signs at the very start; examples are tracks that animals leave behind on the ground, the smoke that announces an unseen fire, trumpets that give soldiers important signals. The last example is itself no longer fortunate, because Augustine defines natural signs as those "that without will and any sort of intention indicate that something else outside themselves is to be known, such as smoke that indicates fire" (1.2) But natural signs are of no importance to the subsequent train of thought; Augustine explicitly states he mentioned them only for systematic reasons.

Given signs are of greater importance; they are "those that living beings of various sorts share with one another in order to show, as best they can, each movement of their spirit, their perceptions, or their insights" (2.3). This involves a process of transmission: "We have no reason to designate (anything), that is, to give a sign, other than to retrieve what the one who gives the sign carries in his spirit and transmit it into the spirit of another" (2.3). The significance of this process then becomes clear when one turns to Augustine's dialogue *De magistro (On the Teacher)*. There the basic idea is that signs and their transmission in the human spirit cannot call forth anything new; the things we recognize by receiving signs must be already present in the spirit and retrieved from it by memory.

"Some of the signs people give each other are directed to the eyes, but most of them (are directed) to the ears. Words in particular are superior to other signs, because they can be reproduced with words, but not vice versa" (3.4). "But since they immediately pass away after they have struck the air, and remain only as long as they sound, signs for these words are made by letters." According to Augustine, the fact that these signs are not common to all peoples is the result of human hubris, to which the story of the tower of Babel (Gen 11) gives witness (4.5).

With this, the basis is found for the discussions to follow, containing an introduction to dealing with the Bible (5.6–17.26). It was for this reason, says Augustine, that the Bible, having originally arisen in one language, had to be translated into the differing languages current among the peoples and interpreted (5.6). Here, first come warnings of the difficulties of interpretation, because the Scriptures can easily lead to mistaken interpretations. But this is willed by God "in order to restrain pride by effort and protect the understanding from weariness, because what is easy to investigate seems most cheap." Here Augustine sees the role of images (e.g., Song 4:2, where the members of the church purified by Christ are meant), which makes many things that can only be described in a long-winded way evident in an accessible way (6.7). The idea of a pedagogical intention in the Bible, though not directly stated, is evidently in the background.

> Now no one doubts that something is known preferably by parables and that what is sought with some effort is preferred to be found. Whoever does not find what he is seeking is plagued by hunger, but someone who does not have to inquire because it is obvious is often overcome by weariness. Hence the Holy Spirit formed the Holy Scriptures in such an admirable and advantageous way that he met the hunger with easily understandable passages but chased away the weariness with more obscure [passages]. (6.8)

Taken together, however, the Bible contains all that is necessary to be known: "Nearly nothing can be learned from the obscure passages that cannot be found stated with full clarity elsewhere" (6.8).

We also learn in passing that for Augustine the Holy Spirit is the real author of the Bible. But he can mention as well "the reflections and the wills of those who wrote it (the divine Scripture)." One learns from them "the will of God" in keeping with what we believe men of such a sort spoke" (5.6). The later theory of verbal inspiration, which makes the authors of the biblical writings instruments without any will of their own, is in the case of Augustine obviously not yet in view.

The subsequent discussions (7.9–11) again make it clear that the Bible does not hold the highest place in Augustine's theological thinking. He sets before the Christian and Bible reader a seven-step schema by which to ascend to wisdom as the highest step. He requires the Bible only for the three first steps: (1) fear of God, which leads to knowledge of the will of God and fear of death; (2) agreement with the Scripture, "to the extent we understand how much it reveals our errors, to the extent we do not understand it, that we would rather think and believe that what is written is better and more true, even if it is hidden, than what we could learn on our own"; (3) knowledge of the part of the reader of the Holy Scripture, the center of which is the double love command, that one is far off from the love demanded there. "For then that fear, with which one thinks of God's judgment, and that piety with which one cannot do other than to believe and obey the authority of the holy books, compels one to mourn for oneself." By this grief one is led to beg for comfort from God and, receiving it, reach the fourth level: the courage in which one hungers and thirsts for righteousness (see Matt 5:6). By this suffering one turns away from all the death-bringing comforts of transitory things and toward love of eternal things, namely, the unchanging unity and Trinity therein. The remaining levels, then, are: (5) compassion, in which one is purified of lower appetites and trained in the love of the neighbor; (6) love of the enemy and purification of "the eyes of the heart," that one prefers not even the neighbor, as well as oneself, to the truth; and, (7) as the highest level, wisdom. In this schema of ascent of the soul, with wisdom as the highest level, we recognize the Platonic model, though the Christian theme of repentance and the role of the Bible are inserted into it.

Returning to the third step, Augustine deals with biblical study in the stricter sense of the term. He recommends first reading all the Scriptures, beginning with the canonical books. Since the biblical canon, as still today, is not uncontested, he advises following as much as possible the authority of the Catholic churches, "among which there are certainly those who hold apostolic chairs and were deserving of receiving their epistles." It is worth noting that nothing is said of any special status for the chair of Rome. The books acknowledged by all the Catholic churches should be preferred. In the case of those that are not acknowledged by all, one is to prefer those acknowledged by most of the churches and the most important. These books, too, are equally authoritative (8.12). Augustine follows these recommendations with a precise listing of all the biblical writings.

Reading the Bible should therefore be the starting point, the goal being to learn it by heart and by this means to know it, even if one does not yet understand it. The next step is to study everything that can be understood easily. "Among these are all the things that maintain the faith and the moral life, namely, hope, and love." The more obscure statements are then to be interpreted on the basis of those that are easier to understand. "In so doing, memory is of greatest help" (9.14).

At this point (10.15) Augustine returns once again to his theory of signs. He distinguishes between two sorts of signs: literal and figurative. A literal sign is, for example, the name "ox" for a sort of animal. "They are called literal when they are used to name things for which they are established." "Figurative (signs) are when the things that we name with literal words are themselves used to name something other," such as the quotation of Deut 25:4 in 1 Tim 5:18, where the "ox" means the apostle. Signs that are unknown are also to be distinguished from ambiguous signs. Augustine considers knowledge of Hebrew and Greek necessary for understanding the unknown signs (i.e., words) in the Bible, but he later lets it be known (16.23) that he does not command Hebrew himself and is therefore dependent on the aid of existing word-interpretations. In fact, in Augustine's day readers of the Latin Bible had to cope with an "enormous diversity of Latin translators" (11.16). Even comparisons of various handwritten manuscripts can be helpful, and in this regard Augustine reveals a tendency toward harmonization, because from various renderings of Isa 58:7 and 7:9 he is able in each case to put them into meaningful statements in themselves (11.17). Here it becomes clear that he is concerned less with penetrating to the original text than with extracting from the Bible as many edifying statements as possible. But he is also aware of plainly mistaken translations that need to be corrected (12.18). The original text must be the control. Many phrases that are stylistically offensive to inherited Latin are due to carrying over the original text all too literally. This would not be bad for ordinary matters, but readers who are weaker in faith might take offense at something they falsely imagine for themselves due to their knowledge of language. Thus, for example, Augustine recommends a more simple, loose translation (13.20) for 1 Cor 1:25a. In the case of a foreign language, unknown words and forms of speech—two types of unknown signs—can be learned from people who speak it; with practice, one can memorize Latin or, in the case of the Bible, find out by comparing various manuscripts (14.21).

Among the translations, Augustine grants the old Latin priority, "for it is more reliable with respect to its wording, connected with the clarity of the sense." Of the Greek translations, the Septuagint—here Augustine refers to it in terms of its legendary origin—is to be preferred, "because even when something different is found in the Hebrew exemplars than what it reproduces, it is, I believe, in accord with the divine providence that took place by them (the seventy translators)" (15.22).

According to Augustine, misunderstandings of biblical statements are due to various causes. These include misjudging figurative usages of animals, stones, and plants whose nature is unknown, such as the snake. To illustrate the point, however, Augustine cites two typically allegorizing examples, for Jesus' saying "be wise like serpents" (Matt 10:16) is interpreted by associating "head" to Christ as the head of the church, for which we are to sacrifice our body in times of persecution. The fact that serpents shed their skin is an occasion to recall the apostle's admonition to put off the old person and to put on the new (Eph 4:22, 24; Col 3:9–10). More evident is the reference that the phrase "cleanse me with hyssop" (Ps 51:9) is to be understood only by knowing about the cleansing power that hyssop exerts on the lungs. Augustine dedicates one entire section (41.25) to the figurative (and "mystical") meaning of numbers in the Bible, such as the forty-year fasts of Moses, Elijah, and Jesus, the number three, and others. Even ignorance of the significance of biblical musical instruments is harmful (16.26)!

At this point Augustine breaks off his practically oriented discussions of biblical interpretation and its sources of error. What follows is a longer section—evidently conceived as an interpretation of Rom 1:21–23 (see 18.28)—about human knowledge and human culture. It fills up the remainder of book 2. Here Augustine distinguishes the things to be known into two sorts: "One, those things that humans establish; the other, those that they notice were already completed and established by God" (19.29). The former encompasses the entire domain of superstition and idol worship, which Augustine dwells on a long time. The second falls into the two subdivisions of sensory and intellectual objects of perception; the various sciences, such as history, dialectics, logic, rhetoric, mathematics, and philosophy, are listed here. These sciences, Augustine emphasizes, are all established by God, not invented by humans. In themselves, then, they are likewise a path possibly leading to wisdom. Christians can make use of them all, like the silver and golden objects and clothing that Israel carried away from Egypt (Exod 3:21–22; 12:35–36. But—and with this Augustine concludes this book—no one can depart from Egypt and be saved without the Passover sacrifice, which is the cross of Christ (41.62). Pertinent here is the word of Paul, "knowledge puffs up, but love builds up" (1 Cor 8:1, quoted in 41.62). Only when the sciences, in themselves given by God, are put to correct Christian use, that is, directed by love, are they helpful. Under this banner, there is no cultural pessimism at all!

From one phrase near the end of these discussions (41.62), it emerges that they, too, are directed to "the student of the divine Scriptures" who is beginning to enter upon his or her studies. This background becomes clear again and again in various remarks. Augustine's wide scope shows that he considers this undertaking against a conceivably wide horizon. At the beginning of book 3 (1.1) he remarks in retrospect that the knowledge of things is necessary along with knowledge of language in order to understand figurative forms of speech, so that the interpreter avoids mistaking the significance and nature of things that are associated (as image) because of their similarity" (see also 2.16.24). To gain this knowledge, the sciences given by God—which are to be strictly separated from superstition and idol worship established by humans—are necessary.

In book 3 Augustine goes into the ambiguities in the Scriptures (mainly in the Old Testament). Ambiguities can arise at times by words used in their literal senses and at times by using them in figurative (allegorical) senses. Ambiguities have to do only with complete sentences, which Augustine therefore discusses. Words used in the literal senses cause fewer difficulties (1.1–4.8), Here, when dealing with doubtful punctuation, emphases in oral presentation, and the like, the main concern is to attend to the context and above all the rule of faith (*regula fidei*), which gathers together Scripture's clear statements. Augustine first comes to the main topic—but with it the real difficulties as well, as he immediately remarks (5.9)—when he then deals with words used figuratively. Here also his concern has to do, in keeping with what was said in book 1, with the relationship of "things" to signs. But this time the signs stand for figures that first represent what is really meant. Here a danger immediately arises: "For from the very outset you should avoid taking figurative ways of speaking literally." Augustine sets his reflections on these problems under the motto "the letter kills, but the Spirit gives life" (2 Cor 3:6). This Pauline text is indeed one of his favorite quotations; he quotes it literally more than forty times in his work, and allusions to it are more frequent still. Allegorical interpretation is his real goal. Clinging to the letter is "wretched servitude of the spirit, and it cannot lift up the eye of understanding above bodily nature in order to take in the eternal light" (5.9). "That is to say, anyone who honors something that is a sign without knowing what it signifies is the sign's bondservant" (9.13). Now, by this, Old Testament signs would actually have to lose their value, because ancient Israel could not understand their meaning until the coming of Christ. Augustine resolves this difficulty with the remark, "Although they paid attention to the signs of spiritual things instead of the things themselves, without knowing to what they referred, yet it was peculiar to them that they served with this servitude the one God of all things whom they did not see" (6.10). The Gal 3:24 passage about the law as a "taskmaster" for Christ serves as a scriptural proof. Of course, no genuinely historical consideration is being offered here. The special position of the Old Testament era by its reference to the one God and creator not only saves the Old Testament but also leads to a distinction between the Israelites of that day and all the pagans honoring self-made images as gods (6.11) and relating them, as signs, to created things, as well as the Jews at the time of Jesus who "stubbornly clung to" signs (such as the Sabbath and sacrifices, 5.9) "and therefore, when the time of revelation concerning them had come, could not tolerate the Lord who despised these things" (6.10). But Augustine takes yet another step: he also knows of Old Testament figures who, though living under signs in a time of servitude, were spiritual and free nevertheless. They are the patriarchs and prophets who already knew the meaning of the signs (as pointing to Christ; 9.13).

Christian freedom liberated the Israelites who converted to Christianity in that by the interpretation of the signs it raised them to the things themselves. It liberated the converted pagans from their useless signs and instructed them in the understanding of the spiritual sense of useful (biblical) signs, without placing them any longer in servitude to them (8.12).

Augustine can now proceed from these presuppositions to the second main part of book 3, an introduction to the distinction between allegorical and literal discourse (10.14–24.34). Finding precise rules for this was important, on the one hand, to avoid a total allegorization of the Bible that might simply interpret away any demands annoying to the reader (10.15) and, on the other hand, to prevent taking morally offensive texts literally and therefore rejecting the Old Testament itself. The scandalous conduct of the patriarchs and even the Old Testament God himself in the eyes of many contemporaries frequently gave cause—and still does to this day!—for such a rejection. Here Augustine lays down the principle, already mentioned in book 1, as a material norm for deciding between allegorical or literal understanding: "In figural ways of speaking, a helpful rule is to reflect on what is read with careful consideration for as long as it takes until the interpretation leads to the rule of love. But when the rule of love can be heard right away in the actual wording, a figural way of speaking should not be assumed" (15.23). Scripture's clear moral instructions are to be taken in their literal sense, not allegorized. The antithesis of love and desire is the criterion for judging each and every statement in the Bible. "I call love a spiritual movement of enjoying God for his own sake and for the sake of self and the neighbor. Desire, however, is a spiritual movement of (enjoying) oneself and the neighbor and any other body not for the sake of God" (10.16)

On the basis of this viewpoint on morality and the content of faith, already developed in book 1, one can make a judgment whether each biblical statement is meant figuratively or not. "You should recognize anything in the Word of God that cannot be related either to moral decency or the truth of faith in its actual wording as figurative" (10.14)

But a rash condemnation of unfamiliar morals is to be warned against. "Since the human race is prone to judge sins not in terms of the desire itself but rather in terms of familiarity, in the main each person considers blameworthy only those things that others of one's locale and time are accustomed to blaming and condemning, and approves and praises only that which the custom of those with whom one lives permits." But for this reason it is at times the case that commands or prohibitions of the Bible that deviate from the custom of the hearers, though in principle acknowledged as binding, are interpreted as figurative ways of speaking. Here the principle applies by analogy: "But Scripture neither commands anything other than love nor designates as sin anything other than desire, and in this way teaches people morality" (10.15)

This criterion leads to judgments about offensive statements of another sort as well: "Whatever is always read as hard and so to speak wild in the action and speech of the person of God or his saints serves to destroy the realm of desire" (11.17). Here Augustine cites Rom 2:5–9; such statements should be understood literally, yet the statement in Jer 1:10, serving the same purpose, is meant figuratively. But when words and deeds that seem virtually outrageous are presented as though God or people commended as holy, they should be taken figuratively. The substantive background for this is that "what is in the main outrageous in others is, in the case of the divine or a prophetic person, the sign of a great matter" (11.17.). This is not an irresolvable paradox in terms of pure logic. In such cases "their mysteries are to be opened up for nourishing love" (12.18). For example, the foot-washing by the woman in John 12:13 is usually a waste to be condemned, but here a sign of the good reputation "that everyone who follows the footsteps of Jesus by works of a good life will have" (12.18.).

That the patriarchs had several wives was of use for the increase of their descendants and was therefore not forbidden. Likewise, wearing togas and long-sleeved tunics was an outrage among the ancient Romans; now it is by no means that any longer for the nobles (12.20). Amid all the diversity of morals the golden rule is indeed still of value—but convincing only to a few—as a standard for good and evil (14.22). If a biblical word seems to command an outrageous action or forbid something compassionate, it should be taken figuratively (e.g., John 6:54). Romans 12:20 seems to link good and evil deeds together; therefore, speaking of the "burning coals" that are heaped on the head of the enemy means only "a burning lament of repentance by which the person's pride is healed" (16.24).

Another norm is whether an action was done out of pleasure (*libido*) or duty (*officium*), even if other rules now apply. "That is, there is much that was undertaken as obligations at the time that cannot be done without pleasure" (22.32) Augustine thinks that the patriarchs would only have lived with their wives without pleasure for the sake of descendants; indeed, they would have immediately castrated themselves for the sake of the kingdom of heaven (see Matt 19:12) if they had lived after the coming of the Lord (18.27). Here we see that because of certain principles—that it is inconceivable that the Bible would ascribe immoral behavior as such to holy men—Augustine considers a literal interpretation of certain statements impossible. King David. too, who was himself severely punished for the one adultery he committed (2 Sam 12:5), is cited as an example of restraint in dealings with his wives, for clinging to his son Absalom and mourning his death (2 Sam 18:33–19:1), even though he had seized his harem (2 Sam 16:21–22; 21.31). But Solomon, who "lost by fleshly love the wisdom he had gained by spiritual love" (21.31), is rebuked for his polygamy.

At the conclusion of these discussions, Augustine gives attention to a new problem, the treatment of which he was not to complete until thirty years later. It has to do with the relationship between ambiguous signs and the "things" they signify. With regard to figurative ways of speaking, "one will find that the words it consists of are taken either from other similar things or from things standing in some proximity to each another" (25.35). Those that are similar to one another can be classified as (1) oppositions (e.g., leaven in Matt 16:6, 11; 13:33; lions in Rev 5:5; 1 Pet 5:8; snake in Matt 10:16; 13:33; bread in John 6:51; Prov 9:17); (2) mere differences (water in Rev 17:15; 19:6; John 7:38); and (3) multiples. The more obscure passages are to be interpreted by those that are clear (26.37). Here Augustine applies the rule of the internal noncontradiction of all Scripture, which he had become much more clear about in his maturity than in his younger years, when his interest was solely in the deeper sense of every passage. In so doing, he is, certainly, merely taking up what was long a matter of course in the church's understanding of Scripture. For borderline cases when two or several meanings can be shown from different passages and so all of them would have to be true, one should try nonetheless to ascertain the sense the author intended. If this is concealed, it is not even bad "if something can be shown by other passages in the Holy Scriptures as in accord with the truth." Even if the author was not aware of it, at least the Holy Spirit who directed his pen was. But perhaps it was the Spirit's own intention that a passage should have several meanings, which then have to be considered alongside each other as divine (27.38)? But if the sense of an expression cannot be found at all by comparison with other scriptural passages, but only still by rational considerations, this one absolutely should be advocated, even though the author did not intend it (18.39). These are problems that are still of concern in modern hermeneutics.

Augustine concludes book 3 with a look at the rules of Tyconius. Tyconius, a Donatist layman (died ca. 400), had written *Liber regularum* (*Book of Rules*) from which Augustine cites extensively (3.30.42–37.56). The rules of Tyconius were evidently of value because he established a number of content-based viewpoints that would then have to be the "things" by which to interpret the Holy Scriptures. Augustine explicitly states that in referring to Tyconius he was pursuing pedagogical aims: "I have found it necessary to say this so that students will read the book itself because it is very helpful in understanding the Scriptures and hence do not hope from it something it does not have" (30.43). The rules of Tyconius are useful so that "we can understand almost everything we found obscure in the law, that is, in the biblical books, on the basis of these well-known (rules), if we draw from them (30.43). They are important above all by their references to material connections between individual "things" to which interpretation can refer. Thus the first rule (see 31.44) connects the head, Christ, and his body, the church. The second (see 32.45) speaks of the "two-part body of Christ," the true and the mixed church. The third rule, "On Promises and Law," is likewise of dogmatic content in character, while the others are of a more technical sort. Thus the fourth rule deals with individual exemplars and genre (see 34.47). Often the Bible says something about a specific city (e.g., Jerusalem or Babylon) or an individual person (e.g., Solomon) that applies to all peoples or humanity as a whole. The fifth rule, "On Times," deals with the numbering of days, years, and so on. Reckonings according to the model "the part for the whole" (synecdoche in the rules of Greek rhetoricians) should be distinguished from true numbers the Bible gives for a whole. An example of the former is the reckoning of the three-day stay of Christ in the underworld (Matt 12:40), in which parts of nights and days counted as a full unit. Examples of the latter are, among others, the number 144,000 (12 x 1,200) for the totality of the saints (Rev 7:4; 35.50–51). The sixth rule (see 36.52) deals with recapitulation: things are not always reported in chronological order, and instead earlier events are on occasion recalled. The seventh, once again a content-based rule, "On the Devil and His Body" (see 37.55), parallels the first: when the Bible speaks of the devil, one should note whether what is meant is his head, the person of the devil, or his body, the godless, who are in any case included in the church as a mixed body (cf. rule 2).

Although Augustine does not agree with the rules of Tyconius completely, they seemed to him important enough to place them at the conclusion of book 3. Book 4 then offers a theory of preaching. For Augustine, understanding Scripture and proclaiming what is understood belong together (s 1.1.1= 4.1.1). Here the pastoral intent of his handbook once again becomes clear. His discussions about understanding the Bible correctly are thus not to be read apart from the background that they are of use for sermon preparation for preaching. This is of central interest to Augustine as church theologian and bishop.

Much in Augustine's handbook of biblical interpretation will strike today's reader as strange. Indeed, judged by today's knowledge, the Neoplatonist and other ancient models of thinking are the least suitable basis for an adequate understanding of the Bible. In this, one sees what a strange impression the Holy Scriptures must have made on educated people in classical antiquity. Augustine tried to bridge this gap by his theory of signs. The outcome is worth our attention, because Augustine addressed problems that are of significance even today. Remaining of importance in the present is, in particular, the insight Augustine speaks of several times, that words are signs, and written words are signs of signs, which by their fixation as text leave behind their previous, original context and so also their author's intention; thus everything depends on grasping the "thing" standing behind the sign. Various modern systems, such as structuralism, are in their own way concerned with questions arising from this. That understanding the Bible and preaching rely upon one another, a matter so important to Augustine, Luther later made a central theme of his theology. Augustine refers technical considerations of all sorts, which modern interpreters must also attend to. Thus he would have earned a lasting reputation by this work alone.

It has often been noted that Augustine's own biblical interpretation did not reflect his hermeneutical theory. An exact implementation is in fact nowhere to be found, although allegorical interpretation predominates in most of Augustine's commentaries and sermons. Some of these commentaries proceed rather atomistically: Augustine considers the individual phrases of the text in sequence and offers for each of them a figurative interpretation without regard for the larger context. His annotations on the book of Job (*Adnotationum in Job liber I*) is an example of this. Quite often exegesis of this sort is largely a paraphrase of the text, as is the case, for example, in one portion of his interpretations of the Psalms (*Enarrationes in Psalmos*), Augustine's most comprehensive, quite disorganized work. His interpretation of John's Gospel (*In Evangelium Johannis tractatus*), based in part on sermons, is in the main allegorical, as is suggested by this Gospel's predominantly spiritual character, in keeping with early church tradition. But even when Augustine raises attentiveness to the literal sense into as it were a program, as in his Genesis commentary "according to the letter" (*De Genesi ad litteram*), we do not find what is expected but a mode of consideration that is partly allegorizing but in any case using the wording for wide-reaching, often fantastic speculations. Included, however, among his works on the Bible is one work of apologetics (*De consensu evangelistarum*); in it he proves, like Tatian and other Greek theologians before him, the agreement of the contents of all four Gospels against pagan criticism. Distinctive is Augustine's interpretation of the Sermon on the Mount in Matthew (*De sermone Domini in monte*, originating early, around 394), which he views as perfect guidance on all the commandments applicable to the Christian life (1.1.1). Already here we meet the seven-step schema of the soul's ascent to wisdom as the highest perfection (1.3), which Augustine finds expressed in the Beatitudes (reduced to seven; Matt 5:3–12; 1.1.3–2.9). This seven-step schema, which to him (by appeal to Isa 11:2–3) "seems to express a sevenfold activity of the Holy Spirit" as well (1.4.11), serves for him also as a measure by which to divide the Sermon of the Mount overall into seven sections. It reappears likewise in the seven petitions of the Our Father (see esp. 2.11.38): "That is, it seems to me that the number seven in these petitions corresponds to the seven in number from which the entire sermon proceeds." But the only thing that is striking about this commentary is its constructive attempt at an overall division, not its underlying approach, which combines the Neoplatonist schema of ascent with ethical intent. Yet of course it was written before his encounter with Pelagius, which was fundamentally to change Augustine's theological understanding.

Much more could be said about Augustine's commentaries, which influenced later Christian interpretation of the Bible in the West in manifold ways. There is not space to do so here. Therefore, this brief view may suffice at this point.

2

Mediators between Antiquity and the Middle Ages

2.1. A Roman on the Chair of St. Peter: Gregory the Great

The Italy of around 540, where Gregory was born in Rome, had entered
one of the darkest epochs of its history. The decline of the ancient imperial
capital city, which had been visible to the whole world even in Augustine's
lifetime with its capture and sacking by the Visigoth King Alaric in 410, had
continued relentlessly during the later confusion of the age of migrations
of peoples. The authority of the empire—its center having already shifted
to Byzantium in the fourth century—collapsed throughout the West under
the assault by the German peoples. Paradoxically, there had been a Roman
renaissance during the reign of the Ostrogoth King Theodoric the Great
(489–526), because he governed his Roman, Catholic subjects—in distinction to the Arian Goths—in the name of the emperor according to Roman
laws by native officials and felt bound to Roman culture. After his death,
however, his kingdom collapsed quite quickly, falling to the assault of the
Byzantine troops of Emperor Justinian (sole ruler, 527–565). Justinian's
ambition was to restore the empire to its ancient size. His success in this
regard was considerable: North Africa was torn from the Vandals, parts of
Spain from the Visigoths, and in 554, after decades-long battles against the
Ostrogoths, all Italy was reconquered. The triumph lasted, however, only a
few years after Justinian's reign. The Lombards invaded Italy from the north
in 568, and since hardly any resistance could be mounted against them,
they took over large parts of north Italy. In 579 they laid siege, though
without success, to Rome. Milan had become the imperial residential city
instead of Rome long before, when Ambrose was bishop there. Theodoric
the Great had resided in Ravenna, and from there the Byzantine governor,
later called exarch, ruled the areas of Italy remaining to the emperor.

The murder, sacking, and plundering by the troops of various warring
parties had devastated the land. The tax system became intolerably severe

because of corrupt officials who, lining their own pockets, exploited the populace. Crop failures or the theft of foodstuffs by soldiers left without pay led to famines. Then came the plagues, which raged in periodically repeated waves, carrying off up to a third of the inhabitants. Rome, too, was struck by most of these plagues, although Sicily, its corn-chamber, continued to supply grain. It was besieged three times by Byzantine troops. Diseases raged. Many nobles had emigrated to Byzantium. Buildings stood empty or in decay; there was neither funding nor interest for maintaining them. Proud Rome was a mere shadow of itself.

This was the world, this the city, Gregory was born into. He came from a well-to-do, large landholding family that owned a palace on the Caelian Hill and held influential posts in the state and church. In Felix I (483–492) it had even supplied a pope. Gregory's father Gordianus was an official in the papal administration. After his death, Gregory's mother lived piously in a cell; several of his aunts also led the lives of nuns in their own houses.

Gregory received the customary early school education. He did not, however, learn Greek there or even later in Constantinople. In 573, while holding a state office (precisely which is uncertain), he made the decision to give it up and become a monk himself. This way of life was still very popular. Founding a monastery dedicated to Saint Andrew within the family palace on the Caelian Hill, Gregory lived there with other monks under the direction of an abbot from then on. This time came to its end around 578, when the pope (Benedict I or Pelagius II) entrusted him with an important office in the Roman church and had him ordained deacon. At the time, the deacon was still a high-ranking office in the hierarchy. When, soon after, Pelagius II (579–590) sent him to the imperial court in Constantinople with the important post of apostolic nuncio (*apokrisiarius*), he took a number of "brothers" with him and lived with them there in a monastic community. Gregory was recalled to Rome in 586, where he resumed his duties as deacon in the Lateran, then the seat of the curia, but continued to live in the Andrew monastery he had founded.

The winter of 589–590 was marked by catastrophes. The worst was a flooding of the Tiber that destroyed the papal warehouses; famine followed, then plague. Pope Pelagius II succumbed to it in February 590. Gregory was elected his successor by clergy, nobles, and the people. Against his own will, he found himself entrusted, in especially difficult circumstances, with a task that meant the end of his monastic tranquility. In the absence of state authority, Rome's bishop was largely responsible for the well-being of the entire city, including its political and economic interests. Since the exarch in Ravenna cared only about defending his own residence, the Lombard danger had to be averted by money and diplomacy; even the city's grain supply imposed an ever-heavier burden on the church. Gregory cared for these tasks just as he coped with the church's internal tasks. These included maintaining discipline and justice in the church as well as administering the church's properties, reform of the liturgy, and relations with other bishops in Italy and Sicily. In order to raise the level of the church's officeholders, Gregory strengthened the pope's rights to participate in the selection of bishops. He described the ideal bishop in a book of his own, the *Regula pastoralis* (*The Pastoral Rule*). The bishop was to lead the community and uphold discipline by exemplary life conduct and teaching and preaching. So Gregory understood his own office, too. It is characteristic of him to surround himself with monks as advisers, even in his papal court. A pope and a curia from the monastic ranks—this was the design he sought to bring about over the long run, though he failed because the party of secular clergy later got their candidates through again. In his wide-ranging correspondence Gregory sought also to influence church affairs in other provinces, such as in Africa, where he attempted, though with little success, to combat the Donatists by appealing to state authorities and local bishops.

His engagement in missions, however, was of crucial significance for the church's overall development. It is not well-known that missions to pagans were still necessary within Italy itself, because many farmers in the rural areas especially remained unconverted devotees of the ancient cults. Gregory sought to promote further Christianizing in other provinces of the empire and in Gaul as well. Of greatest import, however, was his mission to the Anglo-Saxons, for which he dispatched in 597 forty monks under the direction of Augustine, the abbot of his Andrew monastery, to the kingdom of Kent, with Canterbury its capital city. The conversion of King Aethelbert, followed by thousands of baptisms, laid the cornerstone for the gradual conversion of all England to Christianity. Canterbury remains the metropolitan church of England to this day.

It is not to be forgotten that Gregory wrested these important achievements from a constitution susceptible to frequent illness. Because severe gout supervened on stomach disorders and recurrent bouts of fever, he had to spend the last years of his pontificate mostly in bed, rising only for his worship duties. Although isolated instances of thoughtless severity toward his fellow brothers are handed down, humility emerges as Gregory's basic character trait. His withdrawal from the world to the monastery was due to a heartfelt sense of his own sinfulness, which he expressed in various places.

His work with the book of Job also had to do with this inward attitude. Study of the Bible was one of a monk's chief duties; Gregory pursued it intensively from his entry into the monastery and continued it undiminished during his stay in Constantinople. There arose his chief work that will occupy us more closely in what follows, the *Moralia in Job* (also called *Magna moralia*). Gregory himself explains the circumstances of its origin in some detail in the dedication to Bishop Leander of Seville, whom he had met at court as an ambassador of the Visigoth church in Spain. There he reports (*Ep. miss.* 1, 1:2,43–50 Adriaen) how his fellow brothers and even Leander urged him to interpret the book of Job for them. He did so originally in the form of oral lectures. Gregory completed only the first part while in Constantinople; he later developed this part and the rest in writing into a voluminous work of thirty-five books.

The dedicatory letter contains revealing remarks of Gregory's about the ideas that moved him in his work with the book of Job. There he first looks back to the beginning of his conversion, how he had confided to his friend Leander at the time in Constantinople, "when I confided to your ears alone everything I did not like about myself and how I pushed off the grace of conversion long and far and after I was already influenced by heavenly longings, I considered it better to clothe myself in worldly robes. That is to say, although I had already been made aware that I should seek eternity through love, in-rooted habit had overcome me and I did not change my outward way of life" (*Ep. miss.* 1, 1:1,4ff.). Gregory follows a simple, traditional model in his ideal of life and piety. It was necessary, in view of the coming end—a feeling that was intensified for a patriotic Roman like Gregory by the sight of this historically adorned metropolis now everywhere in the visible decay—to turn away from the world and toward the eternal. The contemplative vision of the heavenly, which for Christians was the hope of the future world as well, but in other respects already a Platonist ideal, could be realized fully only by living in seclusion as a monk. Gregory complained vigorously in what follows that he was denied such a life over the long run. Instead, obedience to the church required him time and again to follow the call to activity in the public sphere, "in the service of the holy altar" (*Ep. miss.* 1, 1:2,21, 24)—which throughout the various leadership tasks up to the highest office of shepherd brought with it "that I was driven to and fro by the constant push of worldly affairs." Yet he hoped by his writings above all to overcome the tension between the way of life he yearned for and the one he was compelled to take. But Gregory also had a quite personal connection to the figure of Job, in that he recognized in Job his own sufferings: "Perhaps it was a decision of divine providence that I, as one struck down, interpreted the stricken Job, and because of my own afflictions I would better understand the spirit of the afflicted (one)" (*Ep. miss.* 5, 1:6,195–197)

In the construction of his Job commentary, Gregory is largely bound by tradition. But the methodical division into various levels of interpretation visible there is also in keeping with the wishes of his first listeners in the small monastic community of the Constantinople nuncio. They had asked, "not only that I interpret the words of history by allegorical meanings, but apply those allegorical meanings to the practice of morals" (*Ep. miss.* 5, 1:2,47–50). They also wanted additional prooftexts for each *topos* and to have them interpreted.

The commentary is in fact arranged in accord with this design, which came into use since Origen's time and Gregory took over from tradition (see also *Ep. miss.* 2, 1:3,86–89; *Ep. miss.* 3, 1:4,106–114). Its main emphasis, in keeping with Gregory's practical intentions, was on the moral or even tropological level. But always in the background was the aim of leading readers along the path of turning away from the transitory world and toward the heavenly goal. Technically, the commentary proceeds in accord with the ancient way of interpretation: it is a verse-by-verse exegesis that gives no attention at all to any larger context, not even the structure of the book of Job as a whole. This becomes serious when Gregory does not take into account the variance between the book's narrative framework in Job 1–2, where Job is depicted as the righteous sufferer enduring all his sufferings with endless patience, and the dialogues, in which he finally rebels against God openly and has to be put back in his place by God. But only the Job figure of the narrative framework is suitable as an exemplar in the sense wished for. Here Gregory can enter into the literal sense right away, beginning with Job 1:1–4 (*Moral.* 1.1–10.14, 1:24,1–31,19). The righteous Job here can lay claim to be exemplary in all his conduct.

Adherence to the traditional method has the effect, however, that Gregory stops at this point and then interprets the same verse at the allegorical level: "The sequence of interpretation now requires us to repeat the beginning and open up the mystery of allegorical meanings" (*Moral.* 1.10.14, 1:31,5–17). That the allegorical interpretation of the figure of Job has to mean Jesus Christ is self-evident to Gregory. He explicitly says so in the foreword: the righteous in the Old Testament from Abel to Job are like stars in the heaven, which preillumined the true morning star (*Moral.* pref. 6.13, 1:18,1–29, 23). "All the elect, having lived righteously, preceded him [Christ] and announced him by prophecy in deeds and words. For there was none of the righteous who would not have lived as messenger by being a figure [*typus*] of him" (*Moral.* pref. 6.14, 1:19,14–26). Hence Gregory works for a second time through the first verse of the book of Job. Indeed, here allegorical meanings are not merely references to Jesus Christ, like the symbolically interpreted names in Job 1:1 (Job = the mourner, Uz = the reconciler; *Moral.* 1.11,15, 1:31,1–17) or with respect to Job's daily offering in Job 1:5, "since indeed the Savior sacrificed for us a full offering without interruption (*Moral.* 1.24.32, 1:42,2–43,3). They refer to the apostles also: the seven sons of Job (1:2) are said to herald the apostles, who "manfully stepped forward [to preach]," because seven is the number of perfection. Furthermore, the number seven tends toward the higher number of perfection, twelve (*Moral.* 1.14.19, 1:33,14ff.), and also the believers hearing the sermon together. (This is the meaning of Job's three daughters in 1:2; they stand for the three estates in the church: the pastors, the celibates, and the married; they also stand for the three exemplars of righteousness mentioned in Ezek 14:20: Noah, the pastors; Daniel, the celibate; Job, the married; see *Moral.*1.14.20, 1:19,38–20,43). In concluding, Gregory once again summarizes the wide range of applicability this has (see already *Moral.* pref. 6.14, 1:19,38–20,43): "That by the person of saintly Job the Lord is announced, that by him the head and the body is signified, that is, Christ and the church" (*Moral.* 1.24.33, 1:43,9–11).

Moral interpretation, which concludes this methodical process, leads to a third, new, initiative toward Job 1:1. Here the interpreter's heart beats in a special way, for he comes to describe the path and goal he has in mind for his own life, too. At the very start of this section, Gregory characterizes the two large groups into which all humanity is divided. There are, first, those "who neglect their lives and in part strive for transitory things and in part remain unaware of eternal things, or if they are aware, scorn them. They do not ever lift the eyes of the spirit to the light of truth, toward what they were created for; in no way do they direct the peak of their longings to the vision of the eternal homeland" (*Moral.* 1.25.34; 1:43,5–7, 9–12) Over against them are the elect, who "regard everything transitory as nothing and strive toward what they are created for. And since nothing except God suffices for the satisfaction of their spirits, wearied by the toil of inquiry, [they] find rest in the hope of their creator and the vision of him, longing to be included among the citizens above" (*Moral.* 1.25.34, 1:43,15–44,19). Of paramount concern, then, is the spiritual-contemplative way of life often called "mystical," though this term does not really fit. But moral action belongs here as well. For this Gregory develops a principle from the literal application of the statement of Job 1:1: Job was "simple and honest, God-fearing, and turned away from evil." "Whoever longs for the eternal fatherland lives without question simply and honestly. Simple in the good he does (here) below, upright in the highest things he feels inwardly" (*Moral.* 1.26.36, 1:44,2–45,5). But elsewhere Gregory can use the allegorical method for moral interpretation in abundance. Here it truly comes to full development for the first time: thus Job's seven sons (Job 1:2) signify the seven virtues of the Holy Spirit in us; according to Isa 11:2–3, which Gregory invokes here, these are "the spirit of wisdom and of understanding, the spirit of counsel and steadfastness, the spirit of knowledge and of piety, [and] the Spirit of the fear of God" (*Moral.* 1.27.38, 1:45,6–8). Even the statement about the three thousand camels Job owned (1:3) can be interpreted in similar fashion: "Since we preserve the truth of history, we can present what we have learned in a bodily way in a corresponding spiritual way" (*Moral.* 1.28.39, 1:46, 2–4). Here, then, a wide palette of interpretative possibilities emerges; even the ritual standards of priestly purification regulations, that camels chew the cud but their hooves are not divided (see Lev 11:4–5; Deut 14:7), are included among them. This means, then, that, even while one is caring solely for earthly things (not keeping distance from them = the hooves not divided), it is nevertheless by carrying out one's earthly affairs rightly that the sure hope of heavenly things is held to = chew the cud (*Moral.* 1.28.40, 1:46,14ff.).

Though Gregory's handling of the text in his Job commentary is, in keeping with ancient custom, atomistic, and individual expressions are interpreted without regard for their context, the commentary is by no means without any systematic organization. One feature is how its method and content are strictly divided into three steps: interpretation of the literal sense = history; then that of the typological sense = reference to Christ and the church; and, finally, as the crown, the moral (tropological) sense, which attempts to disclose the spiritual and moral aspects of Christian conduct in the text, mostly by allegorical methods. Gregory keeps these three steps clearly distinct from one another. After treating a delimited text-group in the first way or the second way, he starts over and examines the previously treated text again from the second or third viewpoint. He often signals these transitions by introductory remarks. So, for example, in returning for his third treatment of Job 1:1–5, he states, "Since we have heard from history what we should admire [and] have learned what we should believe with respect to the head (Christ), we want now to consider what we should hold to with regard to the conduct of our bodily living" (*Moral.* 1.25.33, 1:43,14–16) But he later abandons this strict schema; from book 4 on it is no longer discernible. The commentary can also be seen to become more brief toward the end, no longer hammering out every conceivable aspect of interpretation in equal detail.

There are also systematic viewpoints running through the work. Thus it is already noted in the foreword that Job's friends, "who, while giving advice, scold, represent the figures of heretics who, in the guise of advice-giving, engage in the business of seduction" (*Moral.* pref. 6.15, 1:20,57–59). On occasion (as in Job 2:11; *Moral.* 3.22.42, 1:142,5–9) Gregory returns to the point; for him the crucial passage (!) is Job 13:4, where Job calls the friends (in the Vulgate edition) "fabricators of lies and admirers of false teachings" (see *Moral.* 11.23.34, 2:606,1ff.; the passage is also cited at Job 2:11; see *Moral.* 3.22.42, 1:142,9–11). With Job 42:8, however, he is convinced that repenting and returning to the Catholic Church remain open to heretics, as numerous cases show, "when the almighty God frequently incorporated them into the body of the holy church by the knowledge of truth (*Moral.* 35.8.11,3:178,12–14). Yet a strict systematic organization, typical of ancient works, is nowhere evident.

There is no mistaking that Gregory drew on Origen for the allegorical method and the goal of interpretation of leading readers along the path from the visible world to the vision of the heavenly world. Finding literal carryovers is difficult; the approach was to an extent common property at the time, and it was also in accord especially with the monastic ideal that Gregory, like many others, pursued. Augustine's strong influence is also detectable. The eternal and heavenly over against the earthly-bodily (a Platonist legacy) as well as the Christian awareness of living in a transitory world are determinative of his basic stance (Gregory speaks of the "present world" as that of sin but also as transitory, the end of which is near; see *Ep. miss.* 1; 1:1,10, 2,27–28). Incidentally, Augustine had opposed the sense of the end time at the fall of Rome (410). One detects the Roman in Gregory's moral concerns, altogether apart from his practical-political activities on behalf of the well-being of the city and its citizens. Gregory seeks to understand the Holy Scripture as the basis for the daily life of every Christian citizen no less than for that of monks, priests, and statesmen. This becomes clear in his letters as well, in which he not infrequently speaks of the Bible; in his dedicatory letter to Leander he uses the graphic image of the Bible as a river that is at once "shallow and deep," in which the sheep wades and the elephant swims" (*Ep. miss.* 4, 1:6,177–178).

Besides the *Moralia*, his chief work, Gregory also published two collections of sermons: the forty *Homilies on the Gospels* (delivered 591–592, published in 593) and 220 *Homilies on Ezekiel* (delivered 592–593, published 601–602). He attempted to fulfill a bishop's chief task, congregational preaching, at least at the beginning when his health still permitted it. For many reasons, it did not gain as central a place for him as it did for, say, Ambrose of Milan.

It is no wonder that Gregory's *Moralia* in particular was widely influential during the following centuries in the Latin Middle Ages. His official position contributed to this, in that he vigorously strengthened the influence of the Roman bishop as he knew it. But it was the character of the book especially that commended it for practical use in dioceses and monasteries. This was already evident during his lifetime. His great modesty, an essential character trait that sprang from his humility, was the cause of his anger upon learning that Bishop John of Syracuse had read from his writings at table with strangers; he should read instead, Gregory advised, from the works of the ancient church fathers. (*Ep.* 7.9, CCSL 140:458,14–19). He reacted similarly when he heard that Archbishop Marinianus of Ravenna had read from his Job commentary in public worship, "for this work is not universally understandable (popular), and in uncultured ears it creates an obstacle rather than progress (*Ep.* 12.6, CCSL 140A:975,47–49). This did not prevent this very work from gaining immense circulation in subsequent centuries, as we see from the large number of manuscripts that survive and the fact that the title is missing in hardly even one of the ancient monastic library catalogues known to us. In addition, Gregory, and his *Moralia* in particular, is extolled in numerous statements of medieval exegetes as a great model, a source to draw from time and again.

One can absolutely recognize traits of originality in Gregory's writings. For the history of biblical exegesis, however, he was important above all as a mediator. His Job commentary transmitted to theologians and biblical interpreters in the West, in handbook form, an extract from the exegesis of the church fathers, insofar as it was available in the Latin language. Ignorance of the Greek language largely cut off the Latin Middle Ages from the heritage of the Greek church fathers. Origen in particular was lost—the translations by Rufinus notwithstanding—because of his condemnation as a heretic. Augustine was influential, especially through his theology. Gregory had taken up the legacy of Jerome, too, relying predominately on his Vulgate as his basic text. Hence it was Gregory who, as the last of the church fathers and the scion of ancient Rome, passed along the tradition of the early church to the new epoch. His preeminent authority was such that he might virtually be called the father of medieval biblical exegesis. His works exercised a great degree of influence over the following millennium.

2.2. A COLLECTOR OF ANTIQUITY'S HERITAGE: ISIDORE OF SEVILLE

Isidore of Seville was a younger brother of the Leander whom Gregory the Great had met during his stay in Constantinople, and he followed Gregory to the bishop's chair of his native city. He held the shepherd's office from 599 until his death in 636. The scarcity of sources permits hardly any other information about the years before. We know only that, after the early death of his parents, who emigrated, fled, or were driven from Cartagena, Leander raised him along with his siblings Fulgentius (later bishop of Écija [Astigi]) and Florentina (later a nun). He must have received a good school education, although whether in a monastery or in the bishop's city school we cannot say. If the rule requiring candidates for episcopal ordination to be at least forty years of age was then in force in Spain, Isidore's birth can be placed shortly before 560.

The Visigoths ruled most of Spain in Isidore's time. The empire they had founded there near the end of the fifth century lasted until the Moors conquered it in 711. The reconquest the Byzantines attempted under Justinian I extended no farther than the southwest coastal area, with Cartagena as the capital city. King Leowigild (568–586) had retaken these areas again, subjected the Suevians in Galicia, and threw the Franks back to the northern border, bringing all Spain under Visigoth rule. But meanwhile in the way of internal unity was the fact that the Goths adhered to the Arian faith, which denied the divinity of Christ, while the Romanized native population professed Catholicism. Leowigild's attempt to convert them to Arianism by force came to nothing. Instead, his son and successor Reccared crossed over to the Catholic Church in 587, followed by nearly all the Gothic people. The subsequent all-Spanish synod held in the capital city in 589 sealed state-church union.

Under the Visigoth kings, Spain in the seventh century again enjoyed internal and external peace following a long period of invasions, wars, and destructions. The unity of the faith permitted a quick assimilation of the two elements of the population, in which the Goths even gave up their language in favor of the Roman vernacular. Roman culture had survived astonishingly well in some parts of the country, among them the province of Baetica. Seville was the capital city of this province; its bishop was metropolitan over a number of suffragan bishops. Although Seville was not the king's residential city, Isidore had significant influence on the current rulers, especially the pious kings Sisebut (612–621) and Suintila (621–631), by virtue of his personal authority As successors of the emperor, both claimed rights of oversight over church affairs but relied on the expertise of church leaders. Also important is Isidore's role in various councils, especially the all-Spanish Council of Toledo (633), on which as the longest-serving metropolitan he impressed his stamp widely. Important decisions for regulating the life of the Spanish-Visigoth church were made there.

Yet it is not because of his official influence as a prince of the church that posterity remembers Isidore. It is instead due above all to his distinctive role in transmitting the heritage of antiquity and the early church to the Latin Middle Ages. The most important witness for this is his *Etymologiae* (*Etymologies*), a collection of all the natural and social-scientific knowledge of antiquity in handbook form. It was completed in 630 but first equipped with chapter divisions by Isidore's student Braulio. In this work Isidore drew upon his uncommonly large library, which included not a few works since lost, the content of which is known only through him. By a special stroke of luck, we know some things about this library because its titles are preserved for us in verse forms he had placed at the entrances to its sections. Original to him is his initiative in deriving the word meanings of important terms. These are, of course, hardly tenable in terms of modern knowledge, yet this is not of concern. What is decisive is, instead, that in his encyclopedic collection Isidore has preserved an immense store of knowledge. Copies of the *Etymologiae* and other of Isidore's works circulating throughout western Europe during the Middle Ages served as sources of information for numerous readers.

The wide-ranging character of the *Etymologiae* can be seen in that one of its books (book 6, "On Books and Church Offices") includes several chapters about the Bible. Here the Scriptures of the Old and New Testaments are listed (ch. 1, PL 82:229–30), their authors reported on, and the names of the books explained in Greek, Hebrew, and Latin (ch. 2, PL 82:230–35). One chapter tells about the canons (rules) for analyzing the Synoptic passages in the Gospels, those occurring four times, three times, two times, and once (ch. 15, PL 82:242). Another chapter has to do with biblical translators (ch. 4, PL 82:236). These discussions, however, are colorfully mixed in with others reporting on libraries (ch. 3, PL 82:235f–36), who first brought books to Rome (ch. 5, PL 82:236–37), who wrote the most (ch. 7, PL 82:237), and what types of Scriptures there are (ch. 8, PL 82:237–39). Pagan (Varro, Didymus Chalkenteros) and Christian (Origen, Jerome) authors are distinguished but compared in terms of their literary output. Chapters 9–12 (PL 82:239–41) are technical in character, dealing with writing materials such as papyrus and parchment and with book production. Christian, including biblical-related, knowledge could be incorporated fully into the overall scope of education, as required for a bishop to carry out his commission in an early medieval cultural center of Roman stamp. But this educational ideal was already established in the church schools. From Isidore's discussions, one detects that he conceived them in their presently concise formulation above all for instructional purposes.

The works Isidore dedicated to biblical interpretation in the strict sense also make clear that his intention was preeminently that of passing along to the younger generation the treasury of exegetical knowledge of the fathers up to Gregory the Great. Any claim to special originality is altogether foreign to him. In *Quaestiones in Vetus Testamentum* (*Questions on the Old Testament*), which can best be called a commentary, Isidore makes it clear right away in the foreword: for the sake of "not only students but scrupulous readers as well," he has there, "with the aid of divine grace," as he says, "sought out and woven together in brief format what was said figuratively or took place and is full of mystical mysteries in it (the sacred history), and in so doing we have collected statements of the early church fathers, gathered as it were like flowers from different meadows, summarized in brief some things of the many, while adding to or even partly changing many others." (*Quaest.* pref. 2, PL 83:207). In fact, one can recognize in the work a string of selections from the works of all the interpreters of the Bible available in Latin to Isidore, who cites them by name: "In drawing these figures from the mystical treasures of the wise, we have gathered them together in a brief compendium in such a form that the reader will not read our discussions but read those of the ancients again. For what I say, they say, and my voice is their tongue. They are taken from the authors Origen, Victorinus, Ambrose, Fulgentius, Cassian, and Gregory, the particularly eloquent (author) of our time" (*Quaest.* pref. 5, PL 83:209).

These discussions clearly reflect the transition to a new epoch. Instead of the originality and creativity we encountered in the most important biblical interpreters of the era of the church fathers, here a conscious traditionalism emerges in which the chief concern is to preserve the exegetical heritage from the first centuries of church history as fully as possible. In essence, new viewpoints are no longer produced; we also find in the case of Isidore's treatment of Genesis the well-known verse-by-verse interpretation that is concerned with the spiritual and moral sense. The other parts of the work, in which he deals with the other books of the Pentateuch, Joshua, Ruth, 1 and 2 Samuel, 1 and 2 Kings, Ezra, and Maccabees, become ever more brief and summary. The very busy bishop obviously had no time for additional elaboration.

In Isidore's other writings dealing with biblical themes, the author's pedagogical intentions emerge even more clearly. The work *De ortu et obitu patrum* (*On the Origin and Passing of the Fathers*) considers sixty-four major figures of the Old Testament, with particular attention to their typological significance, as well as twenty-two persons from the New Testament. Similar to it is *Allegoriae quaedam sacrae scripturae* (*Some Allegories of Holy Scripture*). The two books of *De fide catholica contra Judaeos* (*On the Catholic Faith against the Jews*) are likewise concerned to identify typological correspondences between the Testaments. The same is true of the tractate (rediscovered only a few years ago) *Isaiae testimonia de Christo domino* (*Isaiah's Testimonies to Christ, the Lord*); its anti-Jewish polemics are traditional. A distinctive work is the *Liber numerorum* (*The Book of Numbers appearing in the Holy Scriptures*), which lists the numbers used in the Bible and examines them for their symbolic and typological significance. Also designed for instruction about the Bible is *In libros Veteris ac Novi Testamenti prooemia* (*Prefaces to the Books of the Old and New Testament*), containing brief synopses of the contents of each book.

Isidore's place in the history of biblical interpretation may seem quite insignificant to today's observer, but if we consider the effects his work had, the perspective changes. Along with his *Etymologiae* and *De natura rerum* (*On the Nature of Things*), which summarize the knowledge of ancient natural science, his exegetical works also (his *Quaestiones* above all) gained wide distribution, as evident from the large number of medieval manuscripts dispersed throughout western Europe as well as from quotations of Isidore by later biblical interpreters throughout the Middle Ages. If we can hardly ascribe to him the fame due an original author in terms of modern standards, that of an unequaled mediator of ancient culture and early church tradition is all the more certain. That this came about by a route leading outward from the former Roman border province of Spain—from there, Isidore's manuscripts migrated to Ireland and back to the continent—distinguishes the unusual situation. There was precisely here, during the dark centuries when the old structures of Europe were in decline, an island of order made possible by the symbiosis of Romanism and Germanism based on a common faith. Here a decisive role fell to the church and one of its highest office holders, if he knew how to use it. In this way Isidore enters worthily into the chain of outstanding bishops who did not succumb to the daily burdens of their official duties but went beyond them to make a contribution to the development of the Christian culture of the West. The blending of ancient and Christian heritage characteristic of this development is the result of the activity of men like

Isidore, who did not let the treasures of ancient culture simply pass away with paganism but preserved what they deemed of value in it under the sign of the cross for their contemporaries and posterity.

2.3. A Learned Monastic Brother in the Northland: Venerable Bede

Christianity had already reached Britain, one of the most remote provinces of the empire, under Roman rule. In the fourth century there were already stone church buildings (some converted from pagan temples), an episcopal church organization, and a largely Christianized population. Toward the end of the Roman era, Christianity was even pressing beyond the empire's boundaries, toward Ireland. Then everything changed. The legions were withdrawn from Britain in 497 because of an urgent need in Italy, leaving the former province on its own. Local Roman-Celtic tribal rulers managed to hold on for a time, but around the middle of the sixth century there was an uprising throughout the east part of the former province by the Jutes, Angles, and Saxons, whom the Romans had first settled as auxiliary troops. From across the sea they received continuous additions of adventurers out for booty who sailed from northern Germany in light boats, conquered cities, and gradually settled down as farmers on the land along the river courses still covered by thick woods and impenetrable swamps. They established seven independent pagan kingdoms and destroyed in their territory, while British (Celtic) Christian kingdoms in the West were able, after fluctuating battles, to hold on. The long-lasting animosity between the two population groups impeded Christian missions from the West into the Anglo-Saxon areas. A turnaround came, first in Kent, only in 597, with the initiative from Rome in the sending of Augustine and his companions. The Christianizing of the Anglo-Saxon kingdoms came, although not without setbacks, relatively swiftly. The mission from Ireland played a role in the northernmost of the kingdoms, Northumbria, the land north of the Humber, temporarily divided into two parts: Bernicia and Deira. A distinctive form of church government prevailed there. Unlike elsewhere, not bishops but abbots of monasteries had oversight of monastic holdings; the bishops required for ordinations were subject to the abbots as monks. In addition, there were differences over the date of Easter between the British and Irish churches, on the one hand, and the Anglo-Saxon church evangelized by Rome, on the other. Oswald, the king of Northumbria, had had to live for years in exile in Ireland, where he converted to Christianity. Being able to return home as king in 635, he traveled to the important Irish monastic center on the island of Iona and there received support from Aidan, who founded a monastery by the Irish model on the island of Lindisfarne, off the north coast of Northumbria. Lindisfarne became the center of church life in the land because of the learning, exemplary piety, and missionary zeal of its monks. From there Aidan (d. 651) and his students undertook missions as wandering preachers throughout Northumbria, and later (after 656) to other Anglo-Saxon kingdoms as well. The synod of Whitby (near York, formerly Streaneshalch), to which King Oswald invited representatives of the Irish and "Romans" in his kingdom around the end of 663, became important. Oswald himself kept the Irish date for Easter, his wife, a princess from Kent, and his son, the Roman date—which Wilfrith, originally educated at Lindisfarne but later, in Canterbury, won over to Roman usage, supported forcefully. He got the king to accept the Roman date, and his grandees then followed. Most of the Irish at Lindisfarne then returned to their homeland. Thus the foundation was put in place for a unified English church order in harmony with the Great Church. It was completed by the activity of Theodore of Tarsus, a Greek from Asia Minor, who as archbishop of Canterbury (669–690) established the new order of the Anglo-Saxon church in fifteen bishoprics with clear allegiance to Rome.

In 674, hardly fifty years after the Christianization of Northumbria, the boy Bede, about seven years old, was given by his parents to the abbot of the Wearmouth monastery (in the vicinity of today's Newcastle) as an oblate (certain students turned over for later monastic life). The abbot, the monastery's founder and first abbot, was Benedict Biscop (d. 689/690), who in 681 founded the neighboring twin monastery of Jarrow where Bede spent his entire life as a monk. In his history of the abbeys of Wearmouth and Jarrow, Bede gratefully memorialized the two first abbots Benedict and Ceolfrith (690–716) as his honored teachers. Both were of distinguished lineage and well-educated. Benedict Biscop in particular had on several trips to Rome provided for the rich equipment of his monastery with liturgical vestments, objects, and, above all, books. Ceolfrith enlarged the library considerably, and hence Bede could have at his disposal one of the most significant collections of books in the north.

Outwardly, Bede's life presents no special events. He became a deacon at the age of nineteen and was ordained to the priesthood at thirty, but he apparently never assumed a leading position in his monastery. Nothing is known of longer trips away (except visits in York and Lindisfarne). Thus outwardly his entire work life was spent quietly, filled with the duties of a monk, which, according to the rule Benedict Biscop compiled from models of several sorts, included above all worship tasks: liturgical songs and prayers, as well as handworks for the support of the monastery, benevolence to the needy, and hospitality to strangers. Bede was entrusted, it seems, with instructional tasks in particular, presumably in a monastery-owned school. From this activity came directly the production of textbooks and indirectly a rich authorship, on which Bede's extraordinary fame was based. This fame, arising soon after his death in 735, is evident from the large number of copies of his work in circulation throughout the Middle Ages, especially on the continent. Modern judgments regard his book, *Historia ecclesiastica gentis Anglorum* (*Church History of the English People*), which he completed in 731, as by far his most important work. Yet Bede himself and his medieval readers judge the matter otherwise. In the short sketch of his life he inserted in the concluding chapter of his church history (*Hist. eccl.* 5.24, 357 Plummer), he explicitly emphasizes: "I have devoted all my efforts to reflections on the Scriptures," and when he then provides a (not complete) list of his works, he does not arrange them chronologically but in terms of their importance, in so doing beginning with biblical commentaries.

Bede is doubtless to be viewed within the tradition of the Alexandrian school of biblical interpretation. If, as one surmises based on several of Bede's own remarks, Theodore of Tarsus and his companion Abbot Hadrian at Canterbury followed the Antiochene line of stressing the literal sense in their oral teachings, then Bede's highly allegorical interpretations—such as his interpretation of the tabernacle, its equipment, and the clothing of the priests (*De tabernaculo*, CCSL 119A:1–139) or the temple of Solomon (*De templo*, CCSL 119A:141–234)—show that he returned to the preference of the Latin fathers for figurative, spiritual interpretation. In so doing he laid the foundations for all the medieval exegesis continuing in that direction. It is no wonder that he interpreted the Song of Songs altogether allegorically (*In cantica Canticorum*, CCSL 119B:165–375), for this was in line with Jewish and Christian tradition of interpretation overall. In this commentary, he first offers a brief refutation of the (unpreserved) heretical commentary on the Song of Songs by Julius of Acclanum (ca. 454), at its conclusion (book 6), a collection of Gregory the Great's scattered statements on the Song of Songs, drawing on Gregory's *Moralia* on Job in particular. His own interpretation (books 1–5) follows tradition in equating the "bride" in the Song of Songs with the church or the believing soul. His emphasis falls entirely on the interpretation as church. At several passages, Bede's personal opinion clearly emerges, as when he refers to the community of the two churches of the elect before and after

Christ (*Cant.* 1, CCSL 119B:190,20–25; 1.1.3, 119B:193,36–194,164; 5.7.13, 119B:337,823–40) and, without explicit reference to Rom 11:26–32 but evidently accepting Pauline ideas, to the expected end of a "reconciliation of both peoples, church and synagogue, "in Christ." (*Cant.* 4.7.1; CCSL 119B:317,85). Here, too, Bede explicitly emphasized that he "followed the footsteps of the fathers" (*Cant.* foreword, CCSL 119B:180,503). But something of his own very personal interests becomes clear in the remark that follows: readers should not regard his effort to offer more detailed explanations "about the nature of trees or aromatic plants" of the Orient "based on what I learned from the books of the ancients" to be superfluous. "I did this not out of arrogance but to remedy for myself and those with me the inexperience that we, far outside the world—that is, born and raised on an island of the ocean—have of events in the most original parts of the earth, I mean Arabia, India, Judea, and Egypt, by no means other than the writings of those in a position to know."

On the other hand, it has been pointed out that Bede interpreted the Old Testament historical texts in particular: Genesis (*In Genesim*; CCSL 118A), 1 Samuel (*In primam parten Samuelis*, CCSL 119:1–287), the books of Kings (*In regum librum XXX quaestiones*, CCSL 119:289–322), Ezra and Nehemiah (CCSL 119A:235–392). Such an emphasis can be seen even in the New Testament, as, say, his interpretation of Acts (*Expositio Actuum Apostolorum et retractatio*) and two Synoptic Gospels, Luke and Mark *(In Lucae evangelium expositio*, CCSL 120:1–425; *In Marci evangelium expositio*, 120:427–648; John is omitted).

Yet figurative, "spiritual" interpretations are by no means missing in these commentaries either. A church teacher such as Bede took it for granted that the most important goal of biblical interpretation was the edification of hearers and readers; he repeatedly expressed himself in this sense. Thus in the foreword to the Samuel commentary:

> We will zealously strive, to the best of the powers of our limited understanding, to imitate this learned writer who brought forth something both new and old from treasure [see Matt 13:52]. For if we care only for bringing forth something old from the treasure, that is, pursue only the figures of the letter in the Jewish way, what can we learn as readers or hearers of consoling spiritual teaching amid the daily sins of corruption, the increasing troubles of the times, the countless errors of this life?

The allegorical method was already available by tradition for this purpose. In all the humility characteristic of a monk, Bede understood himself as a transmitter of tradition: "From the time I received the priesthood until in my fifty-ninth year of life, I have been concerned to make brief notations on the Holy Scriptures according to my own needs and those with me from the works of the venerable fathers or even to add something to express the sense (meant by them) and their interpretation" (*Hist. eccl.* 5.24, 357 Plummer). The intention guiding Bede in this activity was pedagogical. He considered it his duty to open up to the understanding of his barely educated pupils the biblical writings, which were certainly foreign to them, by using treasures from the tradition of the fathers and terms they could easily grasp—Northumberland, remember, was Christianized only a half century before, and Latin was no longer a living language there! Critical editions of his works appearing in recent times make it possible for the first time, based on Bede's quotations, to know with greater accuracy which writings Bede has drawn from. He originally provided for making the author of each quotation known by means of sigla in the margins of the handwritten manuscripts of his works. Later copyists for the most part ignored these. He used the four great Latin fathers most often— Augustine, Jerome, Ambrose, and Gregory—but many others as well, to the extent they were available in his library. Not originality, but the transmission of such solid knowledge, was what was important to him.

When we understand Bede as a schoolmaster, yet another aspect of his interpretation becomes understandable: his interest in the facts of history, geography, biography, or natural science, which is evident time and again in his commentaries and leads him to turn his attention once again to the literal sense. In this regard he resembles Jerome, from whom he drew much—say, the Latin explanation of Hebrew and Greek names of persons, topographical knowledge of biblical place names, and so on— and above all Isidore, whom he certainly knew and drew upon a great deal. Besides them, however, he preferred to go back to the ancient originals. Bede was already the schoolmaster in his earliest treatises, *De arte metrica* (*On the Art of Meter*), *De schematibus et tropis* (*On [Rhetorical] Figures and Tropes*), and *On Orthography*. Here he repeated the materials covered in the ancient trivium, the three basic fields of philology, which was the foundation of the seven liberal arts. The four fields of knowledge (in antiquity, arithmetic, geometry, music, and astrology) built on this, which together with the first three philological skills formed the seven liberal arts and, in keeping with Christian tradition, found service in the higher goal of biblical interpretation. Among these works is *De natura rerum* (*On the Nature of Things*), a brief description of the cosmos that was taken, along with its title, from Isidore but supplemented by Pliny's natural history. It is not at all to be understood as an end in and of itself.

Historical and geographical knowledge serve the same purpose. Thus Bede attaches as an appendix to his interpretation of 1 Samuel a list of place names collected "from the works of the blessed priests Jerome and Flavius Josephus" (CCSL 119:273). A list of regions and places in Acts (*Nomina regionum atque locorum de Actibus Apostolorum,* CCSL 121:165–78) is likewise a commentary appendix. But whether Bede read Josephus in the Greek original is disputed, since Latin editions were also available. At the request of others, he also elucidates specifically historical and other factual questions, as in the thirty questions on the books of Kings (see above).

The two commentaries on Acts, now combined in a modern edition (Laistner, repr., CCSL 121; quoted according to the first edition), are actually separated by decades. In his *Retractatio* (*Retractions*), the aged Bede once again picks up the work of his youth in keeping with the example of the "excellent teacher Augustine" (foreword, 93 Laistner), subjecting it to thorough-going critique. The most striking feature of this revision is that Bede now has at his disposal an entire series of various Latin manuscripts (old Latin, in addition to the Vulgate) and those with the Greek original (the exemplar he mostly used is preserved in Oxford) and by this means compares various readings in order to reconstruct the original text. Bede systematically carries forward the textual criticism practiced on the Bible since Origen. When, for example, the meaning is unclear in the Latin text of Acts 1:1 (Does it read "with the women and Mary, the mother of Jesus and her brothers" or "his brothers"? The Latin knows only one pronoun *eius,* which is used for both genders.) a glance at the Greek text helps, "where not "her" (*autes*) but "his" (*autou*) is written, which with them is without any doubt a pronoun of the masculine gender (*Retract.,* 96 Laistner). For the sense it is important: "That is to say, Saint Luke wanted to tell his readers that the Lord's brothers shared in faith in him at this time, whereas before his passion it was said, 'for not even his brothers believed in him'" (John 7:5). Similar, though purely technical, is his remark on Acts 2:3, "And there appeared to them divided tongues like fire." According to Bede, it had to do in the case of fire with a genitive: "in Greek, that is, it reads *pyros,* not *pyr.* This distinction would emerge more easily if it were stated with an additional word such as burning fire or streaming fire" (98 Laistner). A comparison of several Latin manuscripts as well as Greek texts of various books is found in a remark on Acts 2:34, a passage from Peter's Pentecost speech with a quotation from Ps 110, "David is not raised to heaven, but he himself says, 'the Lord said to my lord, sit at my right hand.'" To this Bede remarks, "some manuscripts have 'the Lord

says,' but the Greek exemplars in this book (Acts) and in the Psalter have
'the Lord said'" (*Retract.*, 104 Laistner).

In the foreword to the *Retractatio*, Bede explicitly points out that, in
contrast to the first commentary of long ago, he wanted to give consideration to the variants in the Greek original, which he judges to be more
trustworthy than the Latin edition. "For I dare not presume that the Greek
exemplar should have been falsified." He calls upon his readers to read this
"for the sake of education," although without correcting his text "except
when it is found to be so interpreted by chance in the Latin manuscript of
his edition." For this point he appeals to Jerome, who likewise presented
"Hebrew truth" but did not want to change the Latin edition correspondingly (*Retract.* pref., 93 Laistner). Here an intriguing conflict becomes
clear: that between a scholar interested in the most original text and a
conservative churchman who does not want to introduce any confusion
in the community by different editions of the text.

The two commentaries on Acts are an example of where Bede's particular interests lay in another respect, too. He writes out lengthy passages
in his earlier commentary, the *Expositio*, from his sources but then comes
to a point when he has personal questions. For example, at Acts 2:5, where
"Jews from every people under heaven" are said to be present at the Pentecost miracle in Jerusalem, "I find it appropriate to ask, Who are these
Jews from their captivity?" Since the captivity in Egypt and that in Babylon are long past and those under the Romans (after 70 c.e.) had not yet
begun, for Bede it can only be that under Antiochus (IV, in the Maccabean
era; *Expositio Actuum Apostolicum*, 16 Laistner). Although this is also in
error—the existence of a widespread Jewish Diaspora through antiquity as
a whole is long known—the remark demonstrates Bede's personal concern
about historical questions to which traditional literature gave no answer.

Interest of another sort altogether is evident in the structure of the
Genesis commentary. It is striking that this commentary ends with Gen
21:9–10, the expulsion of Hagar and Ishmael. The break-off at precisely
this point does not seem to be accidental but consciously planned. Bede
divides his work into four books, each concluding at a prominent point:
book 1, creation and fall; book 2, up to the end of the flood and the Noah
narratives in Gen 9; book 3, to the meeting of Abraham and Melchizedek in Gen 14; and book 4, to the separation of Isaac and Ishmael. The
intention seems to be symbolic: in accepting Gal 4:22–5:2, where Paul
discusses Hagar, the handmaiden, and Sarah, the free, along with their
respective sons, as types for the antithesis between law and promise, the
two Testaments, and the two Jerusalems (the temporal and the one "from

above"), Bede sought to read the primeval history and patriarchal history as a whole as referring to the two periods of salvation history. Although in particulars much material is drawn from the Genesis commentaries of Augustine, Jerome, and Ambrose as well as other patristic literature, Bede introduces a line altogether his very own into his interpretation by a method that today would be called a "canonical approach." The commentary did not arise all at once by any means. Book 1, the Hexaemeron (the creation in seven days) is a compendium by the young teacher, a brief collection of important statements from Augustine's Genesis commentary. The other books are from the pen of the mature exegete. Here Abraham in particular obtains his status as the exemplary new man, blessed and thereby chosen by God, in whom all the elect are incorporated as sons. At the same time he is the type of Christ. Here Bede's increasing devotional concern is shown.

How much questions of method occupied Bede, one also sees in that in the dedicatory letter to his interpretation of the Apocalypse of John (*Expl. Apoc.*; PL 93:131–32), he discusses the seven rules of Tyconius (which he read in Augustine). He thinks that the fifth rule (about tenses) is applicable to the symbolic value of numbers, too—yet another matter of concern characteristic of him. The seven rules of Tyconius are correlated with the seven sections into which Bede divides the Apocalypse as a whole. His interpretation of the Apocalypse seems compatible with this view, inasmuch as the number seven plays an important role as a symbolic number in the work itself, beginning with the seven open letters to the seven communities in Asia Minor (Rev 2–3), to the book with the seven seals (Rev 5–8), the seven angels with the seven trumpets (Rev 8–11), the seven angels with the bowls of wrath (Rev 15–16), and on to the seven heads of the beast (Rev 17). The fact that Bede again relies on the rules of Tyconius reveals his dual interest: on the one hand, to highlight the spiritual meaning of Scripture everywhere (particularly with reference to Christ and his church); on the other, to make use of the technical principles that ancient hermeneutics provided him.

If significance for the history of interpretation is defined in terms of the position an exegete takes in the transmitting the method and content of exegetical knowledge of the Bible, Bede deserves to be named with the greats. In his exposed setting at the edge of Europe, living among a people scarcely converted to Christian civilization, he preserved the heritage of biblical understanding from antiquity and the ancient church and fashioned it in a form that was congruent with medieval thinking and could be appropriated by the theological elites of peoples who had recently settled within and outside the boundaries of the former empire. The strong demand for his commentaries in later centuries demonstrates how important Bede's life work was in this respect. In addition, learning something more about his quite personal way, his faith, and his thought is not without appeal to later successors. In all humility, however, he always considered himself a student of the "ancients," and the only correct way to be a teacher, he thought, was by learning from them.

2.4. A Theologian in Charlemagne's Service: Alcuin

A few years before Bede's death (in recent opinion, around 730), a theologian of greater significance was born in Northumbria, near York: Alcuin. His influence far surpassed Bede's in terms of both his sphere of activity and his extraordinary social position, though Bede was doubtless the more able theological thinker. Alcuin, like Bede, was evidently already early dedicated for church service by his parents, who belonged to a distinguished family. He soon came to the cathedral school of York, which at the time had an outstanding reputation under the oversight of Egbert (in 732 the bishop and in 735 the archbishop of York). Egbert, a member of the ruling king's house and a student of Bede, sought in the cathedral school—whose actual leader and hence Alcuin's teacher was Aelbert, who became Egbert's successor as archbishop in 766—not only to produce a generation of better-educated clergy but also to raise the overall level of education in the land by offering liberal arts instruction to the sons of the nobility. Both aims were urgently necessary, because pagan immorality (e.g., alcoholism, extravagance, violence) was still rampant in England and found even in monasteries. Moreover, illiteracy was widespread even among the leading classes. The school of York was very successful in its battle against ignorance. Its fame was due to its excellent teachers but above all its distinctive library that Aelbert collected from all over, particularly Rome. Students soon streamed there from other parts of England, too, and even from the continent. York became the most famous educational center of the north.

Instruction in the secular and theological sciences was incorporated in a communal spiritual life (*vita communis*) for teachers and students. Although the school was not a monastery and no vows were required, the customary daily course included prayers of the hours, common worship, and common meals along with the school hours. Discipline was strict, as customary in the Middle Ages, yet encouragement was not lacking: the archbishop provided everyone an example by his personal participation in worship, kneeling together with them for prayer. He was also always ready in his cell to offer anyone who asked counsel about the mysteries of the Holy Scriptures; interpretation was oral teaching conveying knowledge and edification.

Alcuin grew up in these surroundings. When he became older, he learned a great deal from Aelbert, his real theological teacher, who instructed him in the church's doctrine and history, the writings of the fathers, and above all biblical exegesis. But natural sciences, especially astronomy, also interested him, particularly the zodiac and astronomical time calculations. He wanted to put this knowledge to use in understanding the Bible.

On the whole, we know little of this time, but evidently Alcuin was already a famous teacher when Aelbert became archbishop. Perhaps by this time he had been ordained deacon, too; he apparently never became a priest. Like Egbert before, Aelbert withdrew from his office in 778 in order to spend the rest of his life (he died 780) as a monk. Of his two best-known students he designated Eanbald as his successor (Eanbald I, archbishop 780–796). Alcuin became director of the school and library.

The change in the archbishop's chair brought a decisive turn in Alcuin's life as well. He traveled to Rome in 780 in order to ask Pope Hadrian I (772–795) for the *pallium* (a liturgical armband) for Eanbald as a symbol of his archiepiscopal rank. On his return journey, he met with Charlemagne in Parma in spring 781. Charles, who already knew the famous schoolman from an earlier meeting, immediately called upon him to enter his service as director of the palace school. Charles had set as his goal to unite his realm, formed from many tribes, into a Christian imperium. To this end, he would have to lead the Franks, unruly under Merovingian rule, as well as the newly converted Saxons, to the foundation of a Christian-stamped education. By a series of decrees he sought to reform and organize the educational system (which was in the hands of monasteries and bishops) in order gradually to raise the level of nobles and clergy. Among others things, Latin was to be taught in all the schools. He sought to make his own court a center of education and surrounded it with famous scholars and theologians. The seven liberal arts were taught in the court school; besides them, and building on them, was theology as the crown of science. Charles personally also had a burning interest in classic education, in questions of natural science, and he himself led the synods of the realm and took part in the conversations of the scholars at his court. As was the custom in the Middle Ages, the court retinue constantly traveled around the entire realm, from palatinate to palatinate in times of peace. Not until late did Charles, after 800 the emperor of a renewed (west Roman) realm, finally settled in Aachen, where he also found his final resting place.

Alcuin remained in the Frankish Empire thereafter, never returning to his homeland except for brief visits. Due to the confused political situation in Northumberland at the time, he declined the call to become Eanbald's successor as archbishop of York. At the court of Charles he had gained a position of trust as teacher, adviser, and friend of the king. He played a decisive role in Charles's educational politics.

We have in a small writing of Alcuin a revealing testimony to this role as well as to the understanding of science at the basis of the educational program he directed. He placed it, in the form of a dialogue between a teacher and two students starting their study with him, at the beginning of the three textbooks he wrote on the three basic fields of grammar, rhetoric (including the theory of virtue), and dialectics. This little book—its present title, *De vera philosophia* (*On True Philosophy*), perhaps not coming from Alcuin himself—clearly shows (PL 101:849–54) that study of the seven liberal arts is for Alcuin part of a comprehensive educational path that is to lead the learner step by step to wisdom. For this, not only the illumination of the Logos is necessary (John 1:9; PL 101:850A); the goal of wisdom cannot lie in earthly goods, which are transient. Wisdom itself is eternal, as is the soul (852 B). In order to reach it, one must advance step by step "until the feathers of the virtues by which to fly to the higher vision of pure air gradually grow" (853A). Solomon's proverb (Prov 9:1) of the house that wisdom built on seven pillars is a model for this way: just as it is with divine wisdom, "which built itself a house in the body and conquered it by the seven gifts of the Holy Spirit," or as it is with the church as the house of God, so also it is with the wisdom built on the pillars of the seven liberal arts (853B–C). Yet all these sciences by which students can become "teachers of our holy and catholic faith and its defenders in public disputes over heresy" are merely steps to the true goal that Alcuin sets at the end: they contribute to a process of development "until a more perfected maturity and a firmer sense of understanding reaches the heights of the Holy Scriptures" (854A).

That last statement is crucial. Alcuin's whole ideal of education and so also the controlling goal of the Carolingian reform is directed to the study of the Bible as the highest form of wisdom. The reason for this is not only that the course of study in the church schools serves first and foremost the education of clergy. It is, rather, the understanding of science itself that is crucial: certainly ancient knowledge in all its fullness (as it was known at the time) is taken up into instruction, but from the outset its signature is to be of service to theology, the highest science. Further, theology is identical to biblical science; all of its content comes from the Bible.

Alcuin felt it his responsibility to extend this form of education throughout the Frankish kingdom at large. This involved not only personal exchanges with scholars at the court and the royal family; he was also concerned in his wide-ranging correspondence with the education of the clergy throughout the entire land, as well as with questions such as the conversion of the defeated Saxons and Avars (included here is a catechetical work). He offered advice to numerous correspondents, admonished time and again, answered religious questions. Such a large number of these letters are preserved that they constitute an important source for Alcuin's world of thought. The letters are strikingly uniform in content. We learn virtually nothing about Alcuin's personal life from them; their contents are in the main admonitions regarding spiritual themes. Setting *caritas* (love) at the head is in keeping with the Augustinian tradition. *Caritas* means a spiritual quality, a form of piety. Humility, unanimity (*concordia*), sobriety are its presuppositions—how often the reality seemed otherwise! Emphasis lay chiefly on morality. Alcuin never tires of admonishing his former students to pious conduct or calling upon influential church leaders to attend to the exercise of official discipline in monasteries and among the secular clergy. The church hierarchy, and with it monks and, in new-won areas, missionaries, is the leading class in society. Yet Alcuin is also interested in educating the laity, as his *Laienbrevier* written for Count Wido under the title *On Virtues and Vices* (PL 101:613–38) shows. The fact that in a few works he entered into the then-current dogmatic dispute with Felix of Urgel and Elipand of Toledo over so-called adoptionism, which held that Jesus was first adopted as Son at his baptism, is mentioned only in passing.

Meanwhile, Alcuin was over sixty years old; the burden of instruction and itinerant court life weighed on him ever more heavily, so he requested his release. In 796 Charlemagne appointed him the abbot of the abbey of St. Martin in Tours. This was the most significant monastery in the land, with wide-dispersed properties and about two hundred slaves. Not until 801 could Alcuin, weakened by age and illness, turn over the numerous administrative tasks burdening him to younger hands. But here again his chief interest was the abbey's monastic school. The fame of its new abbot soon brought it a great upswing. Students from all around were sent to Tours for further education. Hrabanus, whom Alcuin gave the nickname "Maurus," was one of his most famous students. His abbot had sent him from Fulda, to which he later returned.

Yet it was precisely Alcuin's years in Tours, until his death in 804, that were the most fruitful for his literary output. One major task Charlemagne gave him was the revision of the Latin Bible. Alcuin was able to send him a finished exemplar for the imperial coronation in Rome in December 800. It represented an edition of the Vulgate purified of many errors that had made their way into biblical manuscripts during Merovingian times; the Vulgate had gained acceptance as the authoritative form of the text, although older Latin texts were used locally. The revision was penned in the so-called Carolingian miniscule, an improved handwriting script developed earlier at the court school, which was much more clearly readable. Unfortunately, the original of the Alcuin Bible no longer survives, apart from early copies. Alcuin was not the only one who worked on an improved biblical text: the work of his friend, Archbishop Theodulf of Orleans, was even equipped with a text-critical apparatus. Yet Alcuin's version gained acceptance because of its author's high authority; it had a lasting effect on today's Vulgate text. Alcuin also completed a revision of the biblical readings in the worship lectionary. Another witness to the interest in biblical study for Carolingian education reform is the *Clavis scripturae* (*Key to the Scripture*), a sort of systematically organized biblical encyclopedia that was most often appended to manuscripts of the Theodulf Bible.

Alcuin probably wrote most of his biblical commentaries in Tours, where his most significant dogmatic work, *On Faith in the Holy and Undivided Trinity* (completed 802), arose. Commentaries on a series of psalms, the Song of Songs, Ecclesiastes, and some Pauline epistles are preserved. Two of the commentaries especially are to be highlighted: the commentary on Genesis; and that on the Gospel of John. The relatively brief Genesis commentary, which according to its cover letter Alcuin sent his student Sigulf (PL 100:515–16 = 122–23 Dümmler), is in the form of questions and answers. For the most part, it contains discussions of historical problems that Alcuin took over largely from Jerome's Genesis commentary but summarized in pedagogically brief fashion. This skill at simplification was an essential key to Alcuin's wide and enduring influence: his reworkings made the complex exegetical heritage of the fathers accessible to his contemporaries and successors.

Alcuin sets out his views on Gen 49, the patriarch's blessing, at special length. By way of introduction, he answers the methodological question whether the statements of blessing, where Jacob tells his sons at the very start (Gen 49:1) that he wants to announce to them what "will occur in the final days," were to be understood "historically or allegorically." To this, Alcuin says, "both (are to be understood): history and allegory. History as regards the division of the promised land that must be allotted to his descendants. Likewise, allegory [= typological meaning] about Christ and the church that will take place in the end times. But the foundation in history must be laid first, so that the roof of allegory can be built more suitably on the first-established structure" (PL 100:559). Allegorical-typological interpretation, which was by tradition common for Gen 49 in particular, comes into play throughout the interpretations that follow, with the *Moralia in Job* of Gregory the Great as the model. Even so, the statement of principle as cited above leaves the impression that the literal sense is not unimportant to Alcuin as a biblical teacher.

The commentary on John's Gospel completed in 801 is somewhat different in character. Alcuin dedicated it to Gisela, Charlemagne's sister and abbess of the monastery of Chelles in Paris, and Rotrud, the daughter of Charlemagne, who lived in the monastery. These two noblewomen had expressed in a letter to Alcuin their earnest desire for an interpretation of the Gospel suited to their level of understanding: "To be sure, we have the interpretations of this Gospel, fashioned in edifying speech, by the famous teacher Augustine, but they are in places so obscure and adorned with great embellishment that it would not be good for little people such as we are, with such limited capacities of understanding, to delve into them (*Ep.* 196, 323–25, esp. 324 Dümmler). Here, too, the appeal was to Alcuin's ability to simplify the complex patristic tradition in terms appropriate for the capabilities of his contemporaries. Alcuin welcomed the request, because John's Gospel was especially dear to him. Thus he once writes to a former student, the English monk Calvin: "Write the Gospel in your heart and sing the Gospel frequently in place of the psalms, most often [the Gospel according to] John in which the higher mysteries are to be read" (*Ep.* 209, 346–49, esp. 349 Dümmler). Alcuin wrote this letter while he was already at work on his commentary, as he noted, "from the books of the fathers" (ibid.) Here, too, the pedagogical intention guiding him is to put a useful and intelligible handbook into the hands of his readers, male and female:the noblewomen were interested in an edifying interpretation. Yet John's Gospel was also a special love of Alcuin's personally, for like all his contemporaries he valued it for its profound spiritual statements.

In the dedicatory letter to Gisela and Rotrud he stresses once again that "of the authors of the Gospels, Saint John is by far preeminent in the depths of divine mysteries" (*Ep.* 213, 354–57, 354 Dümmler = PL 100:741). In short, the commentary certainly did not turn out as Alcuin meant it according to his letter to Calvin; it ended up a comprehensive exegetical work instead. This also goes along with the fact that Alcuin as usual engages in verse-by-verse exegesis. Comparing Alcuin's discussions with those of his originals in Bede, Gregory the Great, Ambrose, and above all Augustine's John commentary (Alcuin explicitly names his sources in his dedicatory letter; *Ep.* 213, 357 Dümmler = PL 100:744), we can clearly perceive a tightening up and systematic reworking of the materials that represents Alcuin's independent achievement. Among other things, one preference of his own that emerges is number symbolism, which involves him in arithmetic as well. Even the overall organizational division of the commentary into seven books follows such a viewpoint. Alcuin remarks in his dedicatory letter: "Thus I have also brought the entire work to its end with the number of seven books because I hope the sevenfold grace of the Spirit will inspire your hearts" (*Ep.* 213, 357 Dümmler = PL 100:744). We find an interpretation of the number "seven" as a number of perfection in Alcuin's Genesis commentary, where he writes about God's rest after the creation on the seventh day (Gen 2:2): "When you divide the number seven into one and six, the first two numbers will become perfection; the number one is perfect by its very nature and power; the number six, however, is perfect as the first in artful computation; it is constituted by its parts, because one, two, and three make six" (*Inter. Gen.* 42, PL 100:520). For Alcuin, number sequences are no mere pastime: concealed behind them is a deeper significance.

There is no real point to go into details of the commentary in other respects, since it literally reproduces discussions in the form of more or less lengthy excerpts from his sources. This, as we saw, is not because of his inability to formulate matters on his own, but it is an explicit program. Such a procedure was obviously the only one possible under the circumstances. The plan of Charlemagne, the scholars and theologians he took into his service, and the church leaders in the Frankish kingdom overall with which he collaborated was to educate the clergy and the laity and build from the combination of classical tradition and church tradition the educational foundation for a class of leaders capable of assuming state and church functions at every level. Beginning at nearly point zero, this undertaking could come to fruition only over the long term. For the reign of a single ruler, the program was virtually utopian, and it was only partly successful. Most of the scholars left the court soon after Charles died; even his library was spread to the winds. Creative intellectual achievements could not be expected in such a situation. Hence the widespread label "Carolingian renaissance" is scarcely appropriate for this period. It means a lot when there is a reconnection with a long-decayed tradition, and treasures of the past reworked in equivalent forms are brought to life once again. Herein lies Alcuin's merit, too. His lasting influence is not based all that much on the products of his literary activity. His influence was first and foremost on his students, who assumed important positions in two spheres of activity: England and the Frankish realm. His letters were means of maintaining contact with them and influencing them.

Something more remains to be said about one of Alcuin's students, Hrabanus Maurus, who has already been mentioned. He received his nickname from Alcuin and kept it his entire life, a sign of how much he valued his teacher. His career was similar to Alcuin's. He was first a monk in Fulda (born around 780 and probably given over to the monastery as a child). He was educated in monastic schools, first at Fulda and then Tours. Returning to Fulda, he became a teacher at the monastic school there, then its director, and finally, in 822, the abbot of the monastery. He had to relinquish this office in 842 because of a conflict of loyalty with Ludwig the German (king of the East Franks, 840–875), but in 847 Ludwig appointed him archbishop of Mainz, where he died in 856.

With Hrabanus we arrive at the period decisive for the formation of the European nation-states. With the Treaty of Verdun in 843, which divided the realm among the three sons of Louis the Pious (814–840), the last to rule over the entire realm, the Frankish Empire was divided into three states: the West Franks; the East Franks; and between them Lotharingia. With this began developments leading to their own, distinct cultural regions and over time separate vernacular languages. The modern European nations gradually emerged from the mix of peoples of Germanic, Roman, and Slavic stamp who lived together in these parts of the realm. The unity of Europe—reaching to frontier areas such as Spain, which was under Islamic rule but still had a significant Christian minority—was maintained by its common Catholic faith, reinforced by an overarching hierarchical church structure, with the pope in Rome as overlord. Here, of course, occasions arose for repeated conflicts between papacy and secular rulers that could not be brought to smooth harmony.

Hrabanus became the most important mediator of the educational tradition for the eastern area of the former Frankish realm from which the medieval "Holy Roman Empire of the German Nation" would develop. It is, of course, not to be thought of in terms of the standards of modern national consciousness, which did not emerge until the nineteenth century. It was above all Latin, as the language of the church, clergy, and also the scholars, who were able to communicate in this language across every border, that made possible the formation of a common European culture lasting almost to the twentieth century.

One can discern, nevertheless, the developments of local character that eventually led to separate cultures. Hrabanus was important in the German area especially, although he was read throughout Europe, as the presence of his works in libraries shows. Posterity called him the first *praeceptor Germaniae* ("teacher of Germany"). He was a many-sided scholar who, like Isidore, Bede, and Alcuin, was at home in every area of knowledge. But for him, too, theology was the crown of science, and theology meant above all else biblical exegesis. In attempting to gather together the totality of knowledge about the Bible to be found in the ancient interpreters, he wrote commentaries on nearly every book of the Bible, compiling them in the customary way and dealing with both the literal and the allegorical senses. These commentaries, written with a pastoral aim because he was a man of the church, were the basis for his fame among his contemporaries and over the centuries to follow. Some modern critics fault him for a lack of originality, but they misunderstand both the situation and the goal of his efforts to preserve the exegetical heritage of the fathers for his time.

2.5. AUTHORITY AND LOGICAL THINKING: JOHN SCOTUS ERIUGENA

What was the authority of the Bible in deciding questions of theological teaching, and how was this authority handled in the Carolingian era? This problem will be taken up in the section that follows.

The Anglo-Saxon tradition after Bede, its center having shifted to the Carolingian Empire with Alcuin and his school, had developed a fixed method for dealing with the Bible. It was applied in all cases where it was necessary to resolve a theological issue and, as occasion required, to defend against opposing views. In this regard, two principles formed the incontestable presupposition no one ever doubted: (1) the Bible is the highest authority, so anything that can be proved by biblical statements is thereby demonstrated as true, as there is no arguing against the Bible; (2) the interpretations of the Fathers are obligatory for understanding the Bible; thus, in order to prove that a theological statement is true, it is necessary first to set forth the pertinent biblical passages; then statements supportive of the understanding to be demonstrated have to be gathered from patristic literature, especially the works of theologians who enjoyed greatest respect. This dual proof of authority is so compelling that no further argumentation is necessary.

An example of a proof carried out in strict accord with this method is the work—passed down under Alcuin's name, but not appearing until a few years after his death—*De processione Spiritus sancti* (*On the Procession of the Holy Spirit*, PL 101:63–84). The work comes from the discussion that flared up again at the beginning of the ninth century between the Eastern church, which took as its starting point the Niceno-Constantino-politan creedal formula stating that the Holy Spirit proceeded from the Father, and the Western tradition, which, shaped by Augustine, taught the procession of the Spirit from the Father and the Son (*filioque*). As to be expected, the work represented the standpoint of the Latin church. In order to prove that (1) the Holy Spirit proceeded from the Father and the Son; (2) the Holy Ghost is the Spirit of the Father and the Son; and (3) the Holy Spirit was sent by the Father and the Son, the treatise follows the same course in each of its three chapters. First, pertinent passages from the Holy Scripture and then statements of the fathers confirming the dogmatic proposition under concern are presented, whereby it is to be assumed that the author made use of collections of passages (*catena*) available at hand. The presupposition—unstated, evidently because it was taken for granted—is that this listing produces an adequate proof of the truth of the proposition under concern.

Compared to this traditional way of proceeding, a new method developed by John Scotus Eriugena represented a decisive advance. His self-chosen nickname, "born in Ireland," refers to his descent from this land, from which many scholars of the time (in flight from Viking invasions) emigrated to the Frankish Empire. We first meet him around 845 at the court of Charles the Bald, king of the western Frankish Empire (840–877; after 875, emperor), where he was a teacher of the seven liberal arts but was also of service to the king as a theological advisor. Since Charles the Bald, the last Carolingian of significance, moved his court around the land constantly, instruction took place at different places. One important place of Eriugena's activity was Laon, where he met Martin, who taught at the cathedral school there. The two together furnished the ancient handbook on the seven liberal arts by Martianus Capella (beginning of the fifth century) with extensive glossing and interpreted its pagan-myth-ological narrative framework (the muses descend from the heavens as matchmakers and reascend with philology as the bride) allegorically as an all-embracing cosmology. But above all he taught his students to make use of logic as the most important instrument for coping with intellectual problems, making the syllogism—a conclusion (*conclusio*) is drawn from two given propositions (premises)—the central method. Ancient logic, of course, had been known beforehand within the framework of the trivium (the three basic linguistic sciences), but it had been treated in isolation and not yet used to resolve theological questions. Here Eriugena brought about a decisive change.

He was first able to employ the new method around 850, when Charles the Bald and Archbishop Hincmar of Reims asked him to proffer his formal opinion on the so-called controversy over predestination with the Saxon Gottschalk (of Orbais; ca. 806/808–866/870). Gottschalk had advocated a strict double predestination in several works. Adopting and sharpening Augustine's doctrine of predestination, he had concluded from the postulate of God's immutability that God had determined one part of humanity for perdition from the beginning, since he foreknew their sins and their consequent condemnation at the last judgment. The elect, then, can come to know they belong to the elect (destined in advance) only by their own moral actions. Here Gottschalk anticipated a standpoint that would later play a role once again in the classical Reformed doctrine of predestination from Beza on. Eriugena defended current church teaching against this position. This teaching, too, of course, is aware of the fall of Adam and the loss of knowledge of the way to salvation it caused, but it puts emphasis on the possibility offered to at least part of humanity to be baptized in Jesus and then as members of the church to be led back by it to true wisdom. It involves knowing where human fortune truly lies and deciding for it by regained freedom. This fends off the fatalism of Gottschalk's doctrine.

Eriugena was thus to defend nothing more than the customary view. But he was not satisfied with the likewise customary proof from authority by which a doctrine is considered true if it can be supported by Holy Scripture and the texts of the fathers. In a lengthy reflection on method prefaced to his opinion *De divina praedestinatione* (*Div. praed.* 1, 5–9 Madec), he called attention to the fact, by appealing to Augustine's statement in *De vera religione* 5 that philosophy (= science) and true religion are one, that questions of religion also would have to be settled by logical means of human rational conclusions, by logical disputation. Thus, the rules of the art of disputation would have to be used. Here Eriugena names four operations of problem-solving, designated by Greek terms: analyzing; defining; proving; and tracing operations (*Div. praed.* 6, 19–27 Madec). As for the heretical doctrine of predestination he is opposing, two things are to be said: "This extremely irrational and horrid madness is first refuted by divine authority and then annihilated by the rules of true reason" (*Div. praed.* 9, 105–7 Madec).

After this reflection on method, Eriugena indeed begins the process of demonstration by recourse to the authority of Scripture but limits this to two brief passages from the Psalms (25:10; 101:1; *Div. praed.* 9, 107–9 Madec). The longer discussions lead to the conclusions that Gottschalk's doctrine of predestination is itself logically contradictory (chs. 2–3) and therefore cannot be true—the principle of noncontradiction is the norm here—and, positively expressed, that human freedom of the will can be harmonized with divine predetermination (chs. 4–8). The proof from authority (chs. 9–15) then follows, in which Eriugena appeals to texts of the fathers (especially Augustine) in support of his argument. In so doing the presupposition is—explicitly stated elsewhere (*Periph.* 1.69; PL 122:513B–C)—that the authority of the fathers agrees with rationally ascertained truth. The proof from authority is therefore not given up, but it is clearly downgraded in significance.

Yet this pioneering innovation of method, in which Eriugena anticipates the modes of argumentation of later scholasticism, was unable to gain immediate acceptance during the Carolingian epoch. Eriugena's position provoked several formal counteropinions that, among other things, rejected the application of logical argumentation to matters of faith. Two synods (Valencia, 855; Langres, 859), formally confirmed this judgment.

Eriugena himself, however, put his method to work in scriptural interpretation, too. We have, in addition to sermons on John's Prologue, lengthy fragments of his commentary on John's Gospel (on 1:11–29; 3:1–4:28a; 6:5–14) in which his special view is expressed clearly. His John commentary is in many respects altogether traditional. Like every commentary of the time, it offers a verse-by-verse interpretation. Eriugena also draws abundantly on the tradition of interpretation. One peculiarity, however, is that he also includes the Greek fathers. He knew especially well—besides Augustine, of whom he made frequent use in his John commentary and other writings—the literature wrongly ascribed to the Dionysius Areopagita mentioned in Acts 17:17–34 but actually from the fifth–sixth century. At the king's order, he later prepared a revised edition of this literature. Carolingian scholars held the writings of Pseudo-Dionysius in high esteem. They are strongly stamped by Neoplatonism; Neoplatonist influences on Eriugena deriving from them but also in keeping with Augustine are unmistakable. One consequence is a striking proximity to Origen. Eriugena likewise translated the works of the Byzantine theologian Maximus the Confessor (580–662) and probably those of Basil the Great (329–379), and by means of his knowledge of Greek, though imperfect, he could read Greek fathers such as Gregory of Nyssa in their original texts.

Eriugena reached back to Pseudo-Dionysius for his view that the way of salvation for humanity is set out in three stages: purification; illumination; and completion (*Comm. Joh.* 4.7.52–54, SC 180:316,52–318,54; 6.2, 180:330,21–24). Three laws correspond to these stages: the law of Moses, which was nothing other than law; the law of grace that Jesus Christ brought; and the third law, which is the pure vision of truth in the hereafter (interpretation of John 1:17; *Comm. Joh.* 1.24, SC 180:112,36–114,56). To these, three priesthoods are correlated: that of the Old Testament, consisting only of obscure symbols; that of the New Testament, in part still formulated in obscure symbols but in part illumined by the light of knowledge; and that of the future life, where there are no longer symbols but pure truth rules alone. Eriugena usually distinguishes two senses of Scripture: the literal or historical sense and the spiritual sense. By this distinction, the literal sense is by no means devalued; whenever it narrates historical events, it is necessary preparation for the spiritual sense. Here the relationship between figure (*typos*) and spiritual significance (*antitypus*) governs, as in the traditional example of the bronze serpent (Num 21:6–9) as a type of the cross of Christ (*Comm. Joh.* 3.5; SC 180:228,62–65). What is original, however, is Eriugena's observation that there are statements that even in their literal sense do not refer to any historical facts; one must therefore distinguish between "mysteries" (*mysteria*) and "symbols." "Mysteries in the strict sense are those that are passed down as allegory both as occurrences and as narrated. What is strictly speaking called 'symbol' is another form; these are called allegory of what is said, not of what happened" (*Comm. Joh.* 6.5; SC 180:352,31–34, 44–48). Here Eriugena refers to the parables of the New Testament (180:354,58ff.) along with other examples. In making this distinction he was certainly aided by his knowledge of ancient rhetoric, where these were familiar forms of speech.

Several traits characterizing the advance in method that we found in Eriugena's formal opinion on predestination stand out here as well against the backdrop of traditional hermeneutics of John's commentary. One such trait is the characterization of the human soul's three powers of knowing. (Eriugena sees in them a correspondence to the divine Trinity.) According to Eriugena, the soul (*anima*) is divided into spirit (*animus*), reason (*ratio*), and the inward sense (*sensus interior*). The spirit (or intellect) is directed toward the vision of God around which it constantly circles, "and what the spirit grasps from this sublime vision, it passes over to reason, which entrusts it to memory." Reason deals with the causes of created things and knowledge about them; the inward sense rules the vegetative life of the body and is led by the body's five senses (*Comm. Joh.* 4.5, SC 180:304,26–306,39). In the traditional ascent of the soul (at root Neoplatonically conceived) a countermoving moment enters in inasmuch as reason takes on an important mediating function between the contemplative vision (which is, as ever, considered the highest goal, as in Origen) and memory. Nothing is retained in memory that has not passed critical examination by reason beforehand.

There is also a second movement, that from faith to understanding. Behind the relationship of the two terms is a long history of interpretation that is shaped by Augustine especially and goes back to the Septuagint version of Isaiah 7:9, "if you do not believe, you will not understand." For Eriugena, the two are closely connected and faith without understanding is not sufficient for the salvation of the soul (*Periph.* 2.20) in any case. He discusses this relationship several times in his John commentary. When a "symbol" such as the statement "you shall not boil a kid in its mother's milk" (Exod 23:19; 34:26) comes before the eyes or is presented to the ears of "fleshly" people, they merely believe that a deeper sense dwells within it, although they cannot grasp it. "The whole is grasped by those who understand spiritual things in a spiritual way" (*Comm. Joh.* 6.6, SC 180:362,68–364,76). The example of Nicodemus (John 3:4–7) makes it clear: it is not enough for Nicodemus to believe in Jesus; if he does not understand the deeper sense of baptism ("by water and the Spirit"), he cannot, according to the word of Jesus, enter the kingdom of God (*Comm. Joh.* 3.2, SC 180:208,20–25). "We received the grace by which we believe in him and the truth by which we understand him" (*Comm. Joh.* 1.24, SC 180:110, 20–112, 22; on John 1:17).

According to Eriugena, however, there are two sources of knowledge: nature and Scripture. He comes to speak of this point in his allegorical interpretation of John 1:27, the Baptist's statement about Christ's shoelaces. The shoes of Christ have left a double imprint, on the wording of Scripture and on the forms of the visible world, for Christ became incarnate in both, in the visible world and the Scriptures. "To untie Christ's shoelaces" means, figuratively, to get to the bottom of the mysteries of both (*Comm. Joh.* 1.29, SC 180:154,50–156,71).

This idea is also in the background of Eriugena's major work, the *Periphyseon* (*De divisione naturae*) in five books, an attempt at an all-embracing description of the totality of reality. Such attempts were not new. We have already seen how Isidore in his *Etymologiae* (*Etymologies*) had undertaken an inventory of the totality of inherited knowledge of his time. Isidore, however, set profane knowledge and biblical studies alongside each other additively and, although he considered the latter the highest form of scholarship, entered into the Bible only briefly. By contrast, Hrabanus who, sharing the presupposition of every Carolingian scholar that all the knowledge to be gained from nature had already been discovered in antiquity, tried to encompass the totality of truth contained in the Bible by interpreting all its books. Eriugena took a third path: he was of the opinion that the truth about the totality of reality (*natura*, understood in the comprehensive sense, as encompassing God and the world) can be drawn from the Bible only by interpreting it in a scientific way. But as support for this he did not take as a basis the whole Bible but only Gen 1–3. One important reason he did so was his recognition—which did not fully make its effects known again until many centuries later!—that these chapters are not reports about historical events but have to do with a mythic presentation. The prophet Moses, the author, had clothed his statements about reality in the schema of a six-day work merely for pedagogical reasons: "For he was not able to narrate at one and at the same time what God was able to create at one and the same time" (*Periph.* 3.31; PL 122:708C = 3:230,4–5 Sheldon-Williams) By taking this mode of presentation into account, however, one can learn the totality of Christian truth from the creation story. But in order to conceive it as truth in the philosophical sense, it has to be recast into the form that results from using logic and its rules.

The voluminous presentation, composed in keeping with the taste of the times as a dialogue between a teacher and a student, combines a logical-discursive process and exegesis of biblical statements in a way never before tried. Eriugena first (book 1) lays the epistemological foundations for producing a description of reality. Reality as a whole can be analyzed by connecting two possible principles of division—"creating," that which creates (*quae creat*), and "being created," that which is created (*quae creatur*)—into four groups. (1) God is the reality that "creates and is not created." (2) The reasons God creates certain things at a certain time are "creating and becoming created" reality. (3) The things that arise in time and space are "becoming created and not creating" reality. (4) God himself is, after the end of time and space, the reality that is "neither creating nor created," for all things will be completed in him. A second, overarching principle of division distinguishes between that which is "something that is determinate" (*ea quae sunt*) and that which is "something that is not determinate" (*ea quae non sunt*). These formulations express that one can always only formulate what one can state about reality, not what it ultimately is and hence not what truth is but only what is apparent. Also to be understood in this sense, then, is Eriugena's application of the ten Aristotelian categories within which reality can be grasped. Eriugena divides them into two classes: categories of condition (substance, quantity, position, place); and those of movement (quality, relation, state, time, action, affection). Taken together, they categorize the totality of all created things.

But what can be said about the nature of God? For this, reference to the Holy Scripture is necessary. The categories of acting and suffering cannot be applied to God. Since they express a movement with a beginning and an end, they are not applicable to God. God is, considered in his nature, without beginning and end and so, too, without movement. With this Eriugena concludes, as ancient logic did elsewhere, with the concept of God of Greek metaphysics. But he is convinced that Holy Scripture expresses the truth about God. Those who seek this truth must follow the authority of the Bible, but since Scripture makes statements about God that are applicable only to created things, these statements must have been meant figuratively. They must therefore be interpreted allegorically. Thus the allegorical method of interpretation is founded methodologically and metaphysically.

Book 2 turns to the grounds of origin (*primordiales causae*) of reality. Each created thing can be recognized as the individualized expression of a perfection—of absolute good, of absolute vitality, and so on—and strive to actualize it in life. It is noteworthy that Eriugena, having arrived at this point, begins with the interpretation of Scripture and thereafter (2.15) derives his every other statement—not only about the grounds of origin but everything else that follows—solely by exegesis of Gen 1–3. The allegorical method, which elevates figurative understanding to a principle, enables him to do so.

Thus with regard to the first sentence of the Bible, "In the beginning God created heaven and earth" (Gen 1:1), Eriugena says: "When I reflect on the interpretations of many interpreters, nothing seems to me more acceptable and nothing more probable than that by these words of Holy Scripture, 'heaven and earth,' we should understand the grounds of origin of all creation, and indeed that the grounds of origin of intelligible and heavenly beings are designated by the term 'heaven,' while the grounds of origin of visible things by the term 'earth' (PL122:546A–B = 2:48,32–50,3 Sheldon-Williams). The statements that follow are handled in this way as well. The sentence "The earth was formless and empty, and darkness was over the deep" (Gen 1:2) refers to the fact that the causes of origin were inconceivable to us before the created things had come forth from them

(PL 122:548A–552C = 2:52,36–62,23 Sheldon-Williams). The next phrase, "and the spirit of God hovered over the waters," means that God created, as it were, at the beginning the foundation and principles of all the natures coming from him, and his Spirit (not by spatial elevation but by the transcendence of knowledge) hovered over them (PL 122:553 = 2:62,33–36 Sheldon-Williams).

For Eriugena, the first words of the Bible, previously quoted, offer at the same time a systematic place for the doctrine of the Trinity (2.20–22): "In the beginning God created heaven and earth," that is, the Father by the name God, his Word by the name "beginning," and a little later the Holy Spirit, where he says "the Spirit of God hovers" (PL 122:555C = 2:68,32–35 Sheldon-Williams). Not the first article alone but the doctrine of the Trinity in its entirety is anchored in the doctrine of creation. With this comes a dogmatically crucial decision that endures, even though its methodological basis is no longer convincing today. Christian doctrine has undeviatingly maintained that the divine Trinity is indivisible, though there have been repeated efforts to isolate one person or the other, the Father as Creator, Christ, or the Spirit.

We need refer to book 3 only briefly. In it Eriugena shows that God also makes himself known to humanity in the lawful regularities (*rationes aeternae*) of created things. While chapters 5–23 discuss the theoretical foundation for this, chapters 24–40 move on to the exegesis of the biblical statements about this, namely, to a discussion of the first through the fifth days of creation. What is important here is that it deals at each point with considerations for understanding creation as a whole, and the temporal sequence of days and works of creation is purely due to narrative causes. Eriugena does not discuss the sixth day of creation at this point because he intends to devote the following book to the doctrine of humanity it contains.

The leading idea of the discussions filling these final two books (books 4 and 5) is Platonizing: the whole creation returns to its creator by and in humanity. In this connection an anthropology (doctrine of humanity) is developed first. It contains several basic statements. (1) Humanity is the embodiment of creation; this is based on the account of the creation of the land animals (fifth day of creation: Gen 1:24–25; *Periph.* 4.3–10). (2) Humanity is the image of God (4.11–14; Gen 1:26–27). (3) In order to prove the third aspect, Eriugena turns to the narrative of paradise in Gen 2–3. Here one should keep in mind that the knowledge that this chapter is of different ancestry than chapter 1 is modern; previously, the entire creation history was understood as a unity. As the third point, Eriugena speaks of the human's dual nature. On the one hand, human beings are perfect, sin-free, and therefore happy. This Eriugena draws from the description of paradise (4.15–18). On the other hand, they are imperfect and sinners. The narrative of the events in paradise (4.19–26) shows this.

Finally, in book 5, Eriugena discusses the return of creation to its creator. He sets out from a biblical text (5.1–2) as the basis of his discussion right at the start. A modern reader would not expect that the text chosen here would be that of the expulsion from paradise (Gen 3:22–24). Eriugena's distinctive interpretation here turns on a single Latin word. After man ate from the tree of knowledge and came to know what good and evil is, God expelled him from the garden with the words: "But now, so that [*ne*] he will *not* stretch out his hand and take and eat of the tree of life and live eternally." The sense and context seem clear, and Eriugena is aware of the customary view "that man was expelled from paradise so that he could not take from the tree of life and live eternally" (PL 122:861A), but he rejects it. Instead, he chooses another rendering for *ne*. In his view, it expresses a question of doubt on the part of God, who considers it altogether possible that man might return to his perfected nature even after his expulsion from paradise: "He [God] says, that is, 'perhaps he will indeed stretch out his hand and eat and live in eternity.' [It is] as if he said, 'that he perhaps would not stretch out his hand and take and eat of the tree of life and live eternally!' It is as if he said, 'Therefore no one should complain about the downfall of man and grieve over his fall from paradise, for the hope of returning is not completely taken away from him. Perhaps [*ne*] he will stretch out his hand, that is, to practice in the virtues in order to learn good conduct, and eat the food of pure contemplation, by the power of which he will live eternally" (PL 122:862D.)

The goal, pregiven with respect to its content, is a characteristically Greek-idealistic anthropology, and here it directs the exegesis as well, as is typical of allegorical interpretation.

With respect to the content of his views, Eriugena by no means strays from preestablished tradition. He supports his views, even at many places in this work, in the usual way by the writings of the fathers familiar to him. His theology does not distinguish itself at all by originality and profundity. It is instead his new methodological initiative that is pioneering, although not immediately. Since he devised a system for the development of theological statements by means of Aristotelian logic as well as reading the Bible by allegorical interpretation, and in so doing joined these two ways together, he inaugurated a new era that was in large measure determined by the juxtaposition and interaction of these two methods. It is therefore not wrong to call him the first scholastic biblical interpreter.

3
Bible and Theology in the Middle Ages

3.1. Ways of Preserving Tradition: Catena and Gloss

The *catena* tradition comes from the heritage of the Eastern church. Its beginnings, according to the manuscripts preserved to us, are to be set in the sixth century. At that time efforts to fashion catenae were begun in order to facilitate the work of those who made use of commentaries for elucidating biblical statements by providing them an overview of the interpretations of the best known fathers. Catena means "chain," the term indicating that quotations of the fathers on a given passage are arranged one after another like pearls on a necklace. Its user can immediately find the most important interpretations of a biblical passage (*lemma*) alongside one other. The term itself, however, was not attached to commentaries of this sort until relatively late (the early fourteenth century).

The catena tradition is largely anonymous. The titles of some old handwritten manuscripts, however, attribute catenae to Procopius (ca. 475–528), who lived in Gaza at the beginning of the fifth century. Perhaps he is the inventor of this method. Another fashioner of catenae, living considerably later, is Nicetas of Herakleia, who was the director of the patriarch's school in Constantinople before becoming the city's metropolitan (he is mentioned as such in 1117). Catenae, then, were composed for instructional purposes and related to theological education. We recall Bede, Alcuin, and other Western church teachers who likewise took care to make current exegetical knowledge accessible to their students in the context of schooling and writings arising from it. Hence we are not wrong in calling catenae textbooks.

The historian of interpretation views the existence of the catena tradition with mixed feelings. On the one hand, one result of this system was that quite a few commentaries, available in their entirety to the authors who made the catenae, were not passed on thereafter and hence lost. Financial factors were certainly involved as well, for producing handwritten copies of entire books was expensive, and smaller libraries were unable to afford purchasing all the commentaries. In addition, the catena includes only selections from the commentaries of the best-known theologians. On the other hand, the availability of catenae makes it possible to reconstruct, at least in part, works since lost. Further, catenae included not only the fathers of the early centuries who were then canonical but more recent works as well—and on occasion even those of heretics, when certain particular points of their interpretations seemed important to the catena's authors. From references in the catena to authors we know, we can learn something about the probable dating of a certain catena as well.

Catenae were also later prepared in the West, at first as translations of Greek sources. The tradition continued into the era after the invention of book printing. Under the title "the golden chain" (*catena aurea*), works of this sort were still being printed in the eighteenth century. These were a concern to Roman Catholic theologians in particular, who appealed to the ancient tradition transmitted in the catena against the Reformation teachings. Editions of catenae issued by the Jesuits, for example, frequently contain an introduction directed against Reformation teaching. But these are later developments taking us beyond the period we are considering.

One can therefore speak of catenae in a wider sense—this use of the term occurs frequently—when citations of the fathers are arranged in chain-like fashion in biblical commentaries, as they became customary in the West. This method is connected with the process of glossing, which we discuss in the next section.

Glossing is another form for transmitting tradition. The Greek Word *glossa* had originally meant "tongue, language"; as a technical term, it meant "commentary." *Glossa ordinaria*, the customary term today, is not attested until the fourteenth century. From the word *glossa* for "language" developed its distinctive meaning as the name for a biblical commentary of a quite particular sort. Its invention was attributed in the Middle Ages to Anselm von Laon (d. 1117), a theologian at the cathedral school at Laon that we know of from discussing Eriugena. Anselm, and his brother Ralph (d. 1131/1133) thereafter, led this school from around 1080 and made it widely famous. The false claim, arising in the sixteenth century, that its inventor was Walafried Strabo, the abbot of Reichenau and a student of Rabanus Maurus (d. 849), was not demonstrated to be erroneous until recent times.

Judgments about the origination of the process, however, are more differentiated today. Biblical manuscripts were glossed as early as the Carolingian age, although the glosses did not yet display their later systematic form. This was apparently developed for the first time in Laon. Anselm's activity, however, was not that of an isolated individual. Glosses on the Psalms, John's Gospel, and the Pauline epistles came from Anselm himself. His brother Ralph commented on the Gospel of Matthew. Anselm's student or co-worker, the master Gilbert Universalis (or Porretanus, de la Porrée; born in Poitiers, where he was bishop from 1142 to his death in 1154) worked on the Pentateuch, the Prophets, Lamentations, and apparently the books of Joshua to 2 Kings as well. Glosses on the Psalms and the Pauline writings were especially popular and hence revised many times. Anselm's commentary, the "Small Glossator," was revised first by Gilbert (the "Middle Glossator") and then once more by Peter Lombard (the "Great Glossator"). On the other hand, some parts of the Bible, the prophetic books, for example, were greatly neglected.

The origin of the glosses in schooling can still be clearly seen. A glossed biblical book contains—in its ultimate, finished form, which came about, however, only after a lengthy development—two sorts of glosses: the interlinear and the marginal. The interlinear gloss is inserted between the lines of the biblical texts written with wide line spacing and offers merely brief explanatory catchwords. Often found here also are grammatical elucidations, notes on different readings or the outline of the sense, and paraphrases of the text. Various expressions are also elucidated. Included here, for example, are etymological interpretations of Hebrew names— these are certainly not based on direct contact with contemporary Jews but are all traditional, taken from Jerome. By this means, the elementary teacher (*baccalaureus biblicus*) at the cathedral school had the resources ready that he needed for his initial process of explicating a biblical text to the students. Genuine scholarship itself began only with marginalia or marginal glosses. Here commentaries by the fathers and more recent theologians such as Bede or Rabanus Maurus were collected on the biblical passage in question, about which the master could then inform his hearers. This knowledge alone was what was important, not the teacher's personal opinion. But Gilbert Universalis incorporated into these glossing his own glosses, too. In the *Liber pancrisis*, the teachings of masters (*magistralia*) were collected along with the statements of the fathers. The intention is therefore much the same as that of the catena tradition—only the system is different.

We have cause to admire the great scholarship seen in this system of schooling and the knowledge of masters such as Anselm. But many contemporaries could view matters otherwise. We get an interesting behind-the-scenes glimpse from a report by Abelard (1079–1142) of his experience during his stay at the school of Laon; it appears in his well-known autobiography entitled *Historia calamitatum* (*History of Calamities*, though this title does not come from Abelard himself). Abelard describes his teacher very negatively: "I then went to this old man who had made a name more on long experience than intellect and memory. Anyone with an uncertainty who went to discuss a question with him left with even more uncertainty. He was indeed admirable in the eyes of his auditors, but a nothing with respect to what one asked him" (*Historia calamitatum*, 68 Monfrin). This was certainly a biased and exaggerated criticism and completely at odds with the judgments of others, who praise the master's great erudition. Even so, it well shows the weakness that went along with such a system of merely transmitting tradition. In protest, then, Abelard decided on interpreting the prophet Ezekiel—on whom there were no commentaries and who was considered especially difficult to understand—without any auxiliary resources. An especially obscure passage was chosen as the test case. Abelard passed this test brilliantly in front of a large audience. Anselm then, quite understandably, forbade any continuation.

Sometime after 1200, the previously still-disunited tradition of glosses was brought into a standard form. This took place in Paris, where, as we saw, Peter Lombard (d. 1160) expanded yet again the glosses of Anselm and Gilbert on the Psalter and the Pauline letters during his teaching activity there (1154–1159). It was also during this period that the existing episcopal schools there began the development leading, around 1200, to Europe's oldest university. Both Gilbert and Peter still wrote their commentaries as continuous texts. After each biblical passage in running context came its interpretation, with the listing of available interpretations. It was during this era also that lecturers began commenting on the Bible including its glosses—a gloss on the gloss! The arrangement into interlinear and maginal glosses (*glossator*) became fixed only later.

Research into glosses involves great difficulties because there is still no text-critical edition. True, there are older printings, but the most readily accessible—the edition of Migne (PL 113–114), reproducing the Douai printing of 1617—omits the interlinear gloss and hence cannot convey a correct impression of the work. The full riches of tradition stored in such a work can only appreciated by laying eyes on an old handwritten manuscript that reveals the painstaking care the authors took, within artful economy of space, to preserve both the biblical text itself and the commentary on it over the course of the church's history, which they considered a unity (whole). The recent reproduction of an earlier printing facilitates access to this, but the preparation of a new edition in the series Corpus Christianorum Continuatio Mediaevalis is a promise for the near future.

3.2. The Beginnings of Scholasticism: Sentences and Questions

Theological teaching more highly detached from the Bible developed only gradually from *lectio divina*, which was by ancient understanding biblical study embracing the totality of theological knowledge and hence the sole object of theological study. We can still trace the origins of this development very well in the school of Laon. Anselm of Laon was not the first to formulate sentences (*sententiae*), that is, theological doctrinal statements, but one can study its beginnings from exegetical lectures especially well in his work. It is also in Anselm that for the first time such dogmatic statements appear detached from biblical interpretation, and some time passed before it gained influence in larger measure. The sentence is closely connected with the question (*quaestio*): in the course of elucidating a biblical statement, a discussion might ensue, giving rise to a question (*quaestio*) that the master then answered in an excursus. These longer presentations on a theological topic then tended to become quasi-independent, to detach themselves more and more from their original function of explaining a biblical statement. These excurses were probably not included in toto in written commentaries; additional oral instruction on Anselm's part is to be expected. So, by way of example, with reference to Paul's sentence in Romans "the law intervened" (5:20), the question of the significance of the law arose, and Anselm pursued it in more lengthy presentations. In so doing he came to speak of Rom 7:7–24 as well. Here he again set about working through the particular statements in this section, as was his custom.

Then, over the course of time, there was a tendency for this element to become independent. The difficulty of obtaining the necessary books, the considerable cost of manuscripts, the vast range of the many works of the fathers that made it difficult to distinguish what was important from what was not—all these extrinsic factors had already led relatively early to the production of *florilegia* (collections of excerpts) from the writings of individual church fathers such as Augustine or Gregory the Great. Peter Lombard (ca. 1100–1160), who taught at the cathedral school of Paris after his studies in Italy and Reims, gained great fame (ca.

1100–1160). He was selected archbishop of Paris in 1159 but died after only one year in office. Between 1148 and 1152 he wrote four books of sentences that set forth a systematically arranged summary of dogmatic knowledge as a whole. These served thereafter as a textbook on dogmatics, which was becoming a distinct field of study that followed the study of the liberal arts and biblical study. A parallel development was the increasing independence of the questions, which resulted in the formation of a distinctive method of disputation on theological problems. Contributing to this was the juxtaposition of apparently contradictory sentences to one another and their harmonization, originally coming from canon law but presented in exemplary fashion in Abelard's work *Sic et Non* (*Yes and No*).

The era of early scholasticism is also characterized by the writing once again of more comprehensive theological works of a systematic sort that were not directly connected with biblical commentary. Special significance is ascribed to the work of Anselm of Canterbury (1033–1109) in this regard. He, like Peter Lombard, came from Lombardy and contributed to theological education, especially during his work as the prior, later abbot, of the Benedictine abbey in Bec in Normandy and director of the monastic school there. He became archbishop of Canterbury in 1093. Of his works, the *Monologion* (*Soliloquy*), the *Proslogion* (*Address*), and *Cur Deus homo?* (*Why God Became Man*) are especially important. Already in the *Monologion*, in which the soul speaks to itself about God, his nature, and, his work, the ontological relation between God and the soul, not the Bible, is the basis of the possibility for this reflection. This is the case even more for the *Proslogion*, in which Anselm lays out his scholarly program. The famous motto *fides quaerens intellectum* ("faith *seeking* understanding") shows that reason, not the Scripture, establishes the standard for assessing theological knowledge. Then, in his most famous book, it is the dialectical method that Anselm puts to use in order to answer the question of the reason for God's incarnation.

None of this means that the Bible loses its role as *sacra pagina*, as the central witness to revelation, during the era of early scholasticism. It does, however, lose the monopoly position it had at the beginning. The disputation, which deals with answering questions, gains a place of its own in theological education alongside biblical study, and the production of dogmatic works gains importance as an achievement of its own alongside the production of commentaries. This goes along as well with the higher evaluation of the role of *ratio*, which we can observe from Eriugena on. It is not that there is any denial of the significance of authority, the Bible, and the tradition of interpretation bound up with it; even the new form of theological endeavor saw itself as nothing other than an additional way of establishing this authority and with it the foundation of faith. Anselm of Canterbury's principle *fides quaerens intellectum* captures this stance quite aptly.

Because these developments can be widely observed during the first half of the twelfth century, the period has been referred to as a "renaissance of the twelfth century." Other phenomena of the time that seem to suggest such a characterization can be added, such as the renewed interest in the tradition of antiquity. Today, however, greater caution is exercised in applying slogans of this sort. The Carolingian epoch, too, as we saw, has been called a "renaissance." There the term is somewhat more appropriate, since in fact a more complete intellectual renewal came about in the Carolingian Empire. This is hardly the case for the twelfth century in this way. Still, the renewal during this period is not to be ignored.

Again, the system of schooling was really where these intellectual movements found their place—apart from various impulses of other sorts entirely that developed at the same time in the courts, such as love poetry and the troubadours. But the system of schooling was not unified. There was an essential distinction between the monastic schools that flowered in the eleventh century especially and the cathedral schools under the oversight of bishops. Over time, the monastic schools developed predominately as guardians of tradition, while the cathedral schools opened themselves to forward-looking developments. This also went along with the prominent personalities who worked at these institutions and exercised their influence there.

Yet it is significant that crucial intellectual developments in the field of theology took place in twelfth-century France. Here it was Paris, the residence of the Capetians and the center of their kingdom, that gained ever-increasing authority. Here various schools coexisted alongside one another and as competitors, further inflaming theological strife between the leaders of these schools, apart from the material differences they argued over.

3.3. DIALECTICS AND EXEGESIS: ABELARD

This becomes especially clear in the career of the theological thinker to whom we now turn. We have already encountered him with a witness to his personal autobiography in which he gave a description—very subjective and personal and not free of competitive envy—of his teacher at the time, Anselm of Laon. Anselm of Laon was a generation older than Abelard; the critical distance he took toward his teacher clearly marks the altered intellectual situation overall.

Abelard led a restless life of which quite a few dates are only very imperfectly handed down to us. The most important source is his *Historia Calamitatum* (*History of Calamities*) supplemented by letters—his correspondence with Heloise, the authenticity of which, however, is not altogether uncontested—and information we gather from his other works and writings against him by opponents. The son of a knight, Abelard (technically Abaelard; the double vowel in his name is to be spoken separately) was born in Brittany in 1079 in Le Pallet (Palais) and hence nicknamed *Palatinus*. His father, who was not uneducated, cared for the education of his sons. Abelard, even as a young man taken by the love of scholarship, renounced his rights as the eldest son and devoted himself to itinerancy as a student of the liberal arts (*artes liberales*). He first made philosophy (dialectics) his primary concern. He gained direct familiarity with the main positions of the founders of the two schools of thought in the then-emerging dispute over universals. Roscelin of Compiègne, who led a school in Loches, taught so-called nominalism, which held that universal concepts are nothing more than arbitrarily established signs without objective reality. William of Champeaux, a teacher of dialectics Abelard heard at the Notre Dame cathedral school in Paris around 1100, advocated so-called realism: only universal ideas of things are real; individual objects are merely individual embodiments of their idea. Already here Abelard's desire for controversy was evident. He fell out with William, left Paris, and worked on his own thereafter as a teacher of dialectics in Melun and Corbeil. After a while, a serious illness compelled him to give up this activity and spend some time at home. After his recovery in 1108, he returned to Paris and resumed his study with William, this time in rhetoric and at his new locale, the monastery of St. Victor. More will be said about this institution's significance later. Again conflict emerged, because Abelard, who was his teacher's intellectual superior, pressed him to modify his view of *realia*. Abelard had to sidestep in the meantime to Melun but returned after a while and founded on Mount St. Geneviève on the left bank of the Seine in Paris—still an isolated, wooded area at the time—an institution with its own well-attended school. Students from all around flocked to him in droves because of his stirring way of teaching. William, who had been absent for a time, now returned, and the conflict soon flared anew.

The decisive turn in Abelard's career seems to have been occasioned by the decision of his parents to enter a monastery. He now decided on the study of theology. Since Anselm of Laon was the most famous teacher of his day, Abelard went to him in Laon. We have already heard about what happened there. Not even Anselm could satisfy Abelard's demands.

Abelard went again to Paris, where he completed his commentary on Ezekiel and once again began to teach. His life then took another turn with his acquaintance with Heloise. He came to meet this highly educated, young (seventeen-year-old) girl as her tutor, at her uncle's, a canon named Fulbert, and soon fell in love with her. He met with her secretly. By the time Fulbert became aware of the situation, Heloise was already pregnant. Abelard took her to his sister, where a son, Astralabius, came into the world. A secret marriage, which Fulbert was supposed to keep secret, then followed. When Fulbert broke the secrecy, Heloise denied the marriage. She had not really wanted it because of her love for Abelard: as a married man, Abelard would have had to give up his career as a theologian. Fulbert avenged himself cruelly; he had Abelard castrated by hired knights in a nighttime surprise attack.

Abelard then entered the well-known monastery of St. Denis in Paris; Heloise, at her own request, became a nun in the Argenteuil monastery, and later its prioress. But neither in St. Denis nor later as abbot of the monastery of St. Gildas-de-Rhys in Brittany (after 1125/26) did Abelard find his longed-for peace. His love of controversy and his ethical rigorism led him again and again into conflict with his own monastic brothers. For a time he moved back to the environs of Nogent on the Seine and there built a chapel that he dedicated to the Paraclete (see John 14:16, 26; 16:13). He bequeathed this property to Heloise and her nuns in 1128–1129, when they were driven from Argenteuil. Around 1135/1136 he returned to Paris, where he resumed his teaching activity in philosophy and theology. During this time he also wrote his major theological and exegetical works. Increasingly, however, he had to struggle against attacks by his theological enemies during this time.

This struggle certainly had various causes, the combination of which is not easy to figure out. In it two imposing personalities particularly stood over against one another. The spokesman of the opposing party was Bernard of Clairvaux (1090–1153), reformer of monasticism in the framework of the Cistercian order and representative of a traditional theology oriented to meditation on Scripture and personal experience of the divine Spirit. Abelard had much in common with him: he, too, was passionately interested in the reform of the monastic way of life and had risked conflict with the occupants of the monastery where he lived. Yet unlike Bernard, he highly valued the role of reason, of dialectics, for the solution of theological problems and on this basis had an altogether different relationship toward to Holy Scripture, too.

The struggle began when William of St. Thierry (ca. 1085–1148), a friend of Bernard and like him a Cistercian and an advocate of an anti-rationalist, mystically colored theology, got his hands on Abelard's chief work, *Theologia scholarium*, along with the *Liber sententiarum* (*Book of Sentences*), a work by one of Abelard's students that William falsely attributed to Abelard. William thereupon collected thirteen doctrines he considered dubious into a polemical work that he sent to Bernard of Clairvaux and the bishop of Chartres. Bernard then did all he could to bring about Abelard's condemnation. Among other things he preached a sermon against him to the students in Paris and wrote letters to the pope and several cardinals. At the Synod of Sens (1140) he gained a condemnation of nineteen of Abelard's teachings, having won the bishops over to his side on the evening before the opening session. Shortly after, the pope too (Innocent II, 1130–1143) condemned Abelard personally as a heretic. This judgment, however, was later set aside due to the intervention of the abbot of Cluny, Peter the Venerable, with whom Abelard had found refuge on his journey to Rome, where he sought a personal audience with the Pope. Peter also succeeded in reconciling Abelard and Bernard. In 1142 Abelard died peacefully in an adjoining monastery belonging to Cluny.

Among Abelard's works are two biblical commentaries he wrote during his final time of teaching in Paris: *Expositio in hexaemeron* (*Commentary on the Creation Narrative*); and a commentary on Romans. Since the latter is especially indicative of his personalized style of interpretation, it is worthwhile to look into it further. Itself of immediate significance is the contrast between this commentary and the commentaries of the school of Laon, not so much with respect to method—differences here are only slight—as rather with respect to the amount of personalized theological views.

As regards method, one can say that Abelard, like his contemporaries, distinguishes a threefold sense of Scripture: historical; moral; and mystical (allegorical). The latter embraces the typological and the anagogical (related to end-time fulfillment) sense. But these three modes of interpretation appear only in the Old Testament commentary on the primeval history. The Epistle to the Romans is largely interpreted literally. This is in keeping with tradition, for a Pauline letter is by its very intention—and this basically could apply to Paul himself as well—an interpretation of Scripture and cannot be raised yet again to a meta-level. In the case of passages where Abelard comes to speak retrospectively of Old Testament events, the typological (figurative) meaning is quite frequent: thus Christ is the "figured Isaac" (CCCM 11:152,977, at Rom 4:24); the material temple of Old Testament Israel is a figure of the "spiritual temple," of the "body of Christ" (11:92,528–533), and so on. There is nothing striking about these traditional interpretations. More noteworthy is the extent to which Abelard incorporates into his commentary excurses in which he discusses basic theological questions. To be sure, we saw that this method was already in use in the school of Laon, but in Abelard the excurses are more frequent and comprehensive. One can thereby recognize his special interest in formulating questions of this sort. He is, as becomes clear here, first and foremost a systematician. In the excurses he comes to speak of basic issues, some of which he discussed in his dogmatic writings and some of which he promises to deal with in the future—but he does not in fact always get to it—but others of which to no small extent he discusses only in the framework of his commentary on the Epistle to the Romans. Hence a fair amount of Abelard's systematic-theological thought can be reconstructed from this commentary.

Especially striking to today's observer is that, despite his basically literal interpretation, Abelard misses so much of Paul's basic theological approach. This is shown in an especially striking way in Abelard's treatment of the Pauline doctrines of justification and reconciliation. Looking first at his comments on Rom 1:17, we find the term "God's righteousness" immediately rendered by the formulation "his righteous recompense" and indeed "among the elect to glory but the godless to punishment" (11:65,624–625). Reading a bit further, we find at the phrase "from faith in faith": "This means that he [God] leads us from *faith* in [= the sure expectation of] punishments to *faith* in rewards" (11:65,630–631).

Whereas the word spoken here is, at it seems, an ethics of merit, Abelard takes up in the great *quaestio*, which is attached to the treatment of Rom 3:24–26 but has in view the entire section 3:21–26, a position on the problem of justification in a somewhat different way (11:113,124–118,270). Here Abelard first refers back to the view, evidently taught in the school of Laon, that what is meant by salvation is that Christ has freed humanity from the devil's power. For this, a mere command of God—this results from a series of other considerations —that had given humanity over to the devil only for a term of punishment would have sufficed. "But why was it necessary that the Son of God, in that he assumed flesh, so often (and) so long endured fasts, abuses, scourging, spitting, and finally the most harsh and shameful death, and took upon himself the cross with its slaughter?" (11:116,205–209). Why, it must be asked above all, was the death of an innocent necessary for the forgiveness of the sins of many guilty? Could God not do this more simply?

Abelard's answer to these questions is as follows: "But it seems to us, we are justified in the blood of Christ and reconciled with God through the singular grace he shows us, in that his Son assumed our nature and in it taught us by word and example and remained steadfast until death closely bound to it, so that for his sake true love does not shrink from enduring anything more" (11:117,242–248). "The justified becomes one, that is, *an all-embracing lover of God*, after the passion of Christ rather than before, because a perfect good deed kindles love more comprehensively than one (merely) hoped for" (11:118,253–255). Abelard summarizes, "Thus our salvation is that highest love (awakened) by the passion of Christ, which frees us not only from servitude to sins but grants us the true freedom of children of God, so that we fulfill everything less out of fear than out of love for the one who shows us a grace so great that, by his own testimony [see John 15:13], none greater can be found" (11:118,256–261). The catchword "love" is reminiscent of Augustine, in whom it occupies such a central place. In a long excursus (11:201,469–204,594; in connection with Rom 7:13), Abelard extols love (*caritas*) as the fulfillment of the law and in so doing explicitly cites Augustine for whose thought this term is central. It must be said, nonetheless, that Abelard has taken over nothing of the doctrine of grace in Augustine, who had understood Paul's message as nobody else. On the contrary, Abelard's moralism comes closer to the teaching of Augustine's great counterpart, Pelagius—just as Abelard's contemporary opponents accused him. A true salvation by the sacrifice of Christ is not really necessary; his view, although formulated in a refined way, is that the earthly Jesus (to put the matter in a modern formulation) was the exemplar by which the inwardly overwhelmed Christian is now in a position to lead a life similarly defined by love.

Some of Paul's teaching is retained, though only apparently. Included here is the statement, in the interpretation of Rom 3:22, that believers have justification (= love) in the soul, not in their works (11:112,71–73), and further that Jews and pagans are justified in the same way (11:112,74–89). Yet inasmuch as all these statements are set in the context of an interpretive principle, they take on a changed sense over against Paul's intention. The real concern has to do with the exemplarism of the patient suffering of Christ. This is underscored yet again by the fact that Abelard stresses that "the ancient fathers were kindled by this love, too, although in lesser degree." Thus, as Abelard presents *justificatio* in his commentary on Romans, he offers it already in the most refined form it reached in him.

In the somewhat earlier dogmatic work *Theologia christiana* (4.60–63; CCCM 12:290–93), the sending of Christ is interpreted in more simple form as a pedagogical undertaking: Christ is the "flesh-become-wisdom of God" (12:291,882, 292,891), and "this wisdom became flesh precisely so that knowledge of true wisdom could dwell in us by illumination" (12:292,895–896). All of the Lord's actions in the flesh (during his earthly life) had an "educational purpose" (12:292,912–913).

Since, in Abelard's understanding, guilt and punishment as well as freedom from both are allotted by God individually, he cannot do anything with the dogma of original sin at all. He states his position on the problem in a lengthy *quaestio* on Rom 5:19 (CCCM 11:163,336–175,732). Guilt, according to Abelard, cannot be inherited, because it, like merit, depends on each individual's free judgment. Hence humanity did not inherit guilt from Adam and Eve, only its result, punishment. This punishment involves the bodily and eternal death of descendants of the original parents, but God can remit it to individuals. This takes place through the sacrament of baptism. But this gives rise to another question: Why is it that immortality, too, is not restored to humanity? Abelard's answer is, "As I believe, this punishment of a bodily, transitory death remains so that we will strive less for the sake of this temporal life, more readily perceive that it has an end, and love all the more that which is truly blessed and has no end" (11:175,726–729).

The views of Abelard described here go together with his underlying moral rationalism. In this regard, of course, he is not alone but can be compared to many predecessors and successors. The basis of this rationalism is found in his Romans commentary as early as the treatment of Rom 1:19–20 (11:67,689–71,817). There Abelard comments, in connection to Paul's remark that God's invisible nature could be recognized in his works from the beginning of the world, that this was already possible for pagans by "natural law" (*lex naturalis*): "through the reason he had given, that is, natural law" (11:67,702–703). What is revealed to the world about God's nature by the written law (Holy Scripture) had been already made known to humanity beforehand by natural reason (11:67,707–710) Many testimonies to the Trinity are, it seems, to be found in the pagan philosophers (11:67,710–68,715). For Abelard the rationalist, a double natural knowledge of God is also possible: from the works of creation, according to Paul; and from God-given natural reason. The two modes of knowledge work together. In the case of the mystery of the Trinity, the unity in the Trinity and how the three persons relate to one another can, according to Abelard, be illustrated by earthly likenesses. The brass and the statue of brass are the same substance and yet differ in their attributes. "And although brass and the brass statue are the same with respect to their essence, nevertheless the statue is out of brass, not the brass out of the statue. So, too, in the divine Trinity: although there is the same substance of three persons..., the three persons, however, are distinct with respect to their attributes" (11:70,806–810, on Rom 1:20). By daring to make such comparisons, Abelard incited critics to fierce criticism. But the situation is otherwise with regard to the incarnation of God in Jesus Christ. "The mystery of the incarnation could by no means be grasped by human reason from the visible works of God's like the power of God and his wisdom and goodness from things they saw were easily perceived" (11:68,725–728).

Abelard's view of the Old Testament can best be gathered from his comments on the Mosaic law, the *lex scripta*. Abelard stresses along with tradition that the circumcision law applied only to Isaac and his descendants (11:87,379–386) On Rom 3:20 it is remarked that circumcision, sacrifice, and Sabbath observance are figural instructions that do not justify one before God if they are fulfilled "fleshly" (*carnaliter*), not "spiritually" (*spiritualiter*) (11:111,33–40). But they must be fulfilled so long as the law "lives," that is, so long as its fulfillment is prescribed by God (11:188,23–27, on Rom 7:1).

Also contained in the law, however, are moral instructions, such as the commandments of love of God and neighbor, which reiterate natural law. But as Abelard explains in his lengthy *quaestio* on Rom 7:6 (11:190,126–196,301), they do not reach this, since "neighbor" meant only those belonging to the people of Israel. Abelard then discusses the question why this law had only earthy promises and not that of eternal life as well. The answer is: since the law (according to Heb 7:19 and Matt 5:27; 5:20) also includes imperfect laws, a perfect reward could not be granted for adherence to it. Striving for earthly things could not attain anything perfect.

But how—here a new question arises—could the Old Testament law not lead to life, when the love of God and neighbor it prescribed suffices for salvation? Here again reference is made that by "neighbor" the Old Testament law understood only one's countryman or friend. The command of love of enemy is missing. Here, however, Abelard encounters a difficulty with the word of Jesus to the rich young man (Matt 19:17–19) whom Jesus promises life if he keeps the commandments. This corresponds to the answer the scribes give to the question about the double command of love (Luke 10:28). This word is set in context with the parable of the good Samaritan. Abelard resolves the difficulty by an allegorical interpretation of the parable: "That Samaritan who proved merciful to the injured one is

Christ, who was truly a good neighbor to the Jews." If, therefore, the rich young man loved his neighbor at this time, Christ was also included, and this gained him a claim on eternal life (11:192,179–187).

Abelard's commentary on the Letter to the Romans is considered all in all something new in that Abelard, for the first time in an age of traditionalism, again undertakes a completely individually colored interpretation of Scripture. One also finds in this commentary that at many passages Abelard adduces quotations from ancient and recent interpreters in support of his argument. Yet he still develops this argument altogether independently and systematically. The discussion discloses that Abelard's true theological interest is that of a systematician. This is connected with his schooling in dialectics and his lifelong teaching in this field. *Quaestiones* in the form of lengthy excursuses clearly assume a central place in his commentary, but the principle of verse-by-verse exegesis is retained. Therefore, the placement of the *quaestiones* is determined by the given context within which a question is raised. In his genuinely systematic works, particularly his often-revised *Theologia*, Abelard treated the same themes many times in ways ordered by the areas of study. The juxtaposition of biblical commentaries and systematic presentations indicates the influence of tradition; in this respect, Abelard stands at the turn of a new period when the separation of the two methods was to emerge more clearly. The highly embattled position he worked in throughout his lifetime did not prevent him from gaining large influence thereafter. He had numerous students, some of whom wrote books of sentences of their own. His own writings were much read. He became a pioneer, especially because of his method. Besides the method of *Sic et Non*, which he had not invented but popularized, there was above all the *quaestio*—the disputation on a question of systematic significance—that gained currency in schooling because of his influence and ultimately gained a position of dominance.

Incidentally, it was Abelard who applied the term *theologia* to rational speculation about *doctrina sacra* (sacred doctrine or dogmatics).

3.4. Monastic Scriptural Interpretation: Rupert of Deutz

Still too little noted in the history of the biblical understanding is the significance of a Benedictine monk who lived at the flowering of the school of Laon but dealt with the Bible in a completely different way. He is Rupert, at the end of his life abbot of the monastery of Deutz on the bank of the Rhine across from Cologne (ca. 1076–1129). He is, along with and before Bernard of Clairvaux, who was a few years younger, one of the most significant representatives of monastic biblical understanding. In presenting here the biblical interpretation of Rupert rather than Bernard, who ordinarily receives a great deal of attention, we intend in part to do somewhat greater justice to his true significance. Bernard's sphere of influence was larger because of his position in the Cistercian order; that of Rupert was far more limited. Nevertheless, it is worthwhile to concern ourselves with his work. That his influence was not slight we can see from the relatively large number of manuscripts of his works still extant, despite the fact that the immense size of his major work restricted its circulation a great deal.

Further details about Rupert's birth date and ancestry are lacking, but it is to be assumed that he came from the region of Lüttich, where in keeping with the custom of the times he was accepted into the St. Laurent monastery as a *puer oblatus* (a child brought by his parents to a monastery). He was ordained a priest, perhaps around 1108, by Bishop Othbert of Lüttich. His life would have been spent as uneventfully as Bede's and he would have never left his monastery during his lifetime if a quarrel between his abbot Berengar and the then newly ordained Bishop Othbert had not driven him and his abbot into a three-year exile at Evergnicourt near Reims (1092–1095), before he could again return to St. Laurent. The two great Benedictine abbeys of Lüttich, St. Jacob and St. Laurent, had adopted the sweeping reforms that, proceeding from Cluny in the eleventh century, had led the Benedictines back to ancient monastic ideals and eliminated many abuses. They also owned well-provisioned libraries and were important intellectual centers in lower Lotharingia. Hence the conditions for inquisitive young monks to study were very favorable. After his exile (during which he had written *Carmina de sancto Laurentio*, a dramatic-liturgical poem on the monastery's patron saint), he resumed his studies and, receiving his license to teach even before ordination to the priesthood, he gathered around himself many students because of his biblical knowledge. After his ordination, between 1108 and 1111, he wrote, at first only anonymously, his first book dedicated to liturgy: *De divinis officiis (On Divine Services)*. This work was one of many prompted near the end of the eleventh and the early twelfth centuries by the monastic and liturgical reforms of Cluny supported by the popes. The Bible played a significant role in the monastic orders purified of abuses: it was the basis for the prayer and readings during the seven hours prescribed by the rule and for the celebration of the Mass as the highpoint of each day. Rupert sought in his work to set forth the meaning of the liturgy, the propers of the festivals throughout the year, and the regulations for the formation of the liturgy on the basis of the biblical texts that were used. As a monk, Rupert lived with the Bible daily, learning its texts by heart. Benedictines were also accustomed to meditating on Holy Scripture and forming their whole life by it. Rupert went beyond what was customary when he completely equates monastic life in its entirety with meditation on the Scriptures. He praises "the lustrous signs of the contemplative life, which are: listening to the word of God; going over it again and against; [and] presenting the mysteries of the divine writings orally as well as writing them with the stylus" (*Comm. Apoc.* 6.10, PL 169:1014D–1015A). Also distinguishing his position from what was otherwise customary is that he considers preaching and written commentary as well as meditation on Scriptures to be distinct tasks. Time after time one sees that the Scriptures were second nature to Rupert. When we look over his works as a whole, we find that the largest portion of them are biblical commentaries. Rupert was always especially proud of them, and on three occasions (1125, 1126, and 1128) he made lists of them, with hardly any mention of his polemical works so well-known today. It was also new that Rupert wrote commentaries on the entire Bible; his predecessors had been content with interpreting individual books, although many, such as Bede and Hrabanus Maurus, had treated nearly all the biblical books over time. On the other hand, Rupert was no longer willing to rely on the sheer authority of the fathers for resolving theological questions—in his day a near revolutionary novelty. For Rupert, too, the tradition of the fathers played an important role; like other medieval theologians, he repeatedly cites Augustine and Gregory the Great, along with Ambrose, Jerome, Cassian, Benedict of Nursia, and Hilary. Nevertheless, he often stresses that even the fathers were to be tested by the Scriptures, and he dares to express his own judgments over against theirs. In so doing he provoked protests from many of his contemporaries, who accused him of setting his own new view against the approved ancient one, as we learn from Rupert's letters to Abbot Kuno of Siegburg and Archbishop Friedrich of Cologne from the years around 1117. For his biblical interpretation, Rupert could reach back into the monastic library for all the usual commentaries of the fathers, but he was proud when he succeeded in gaining an insight beyond the fathers. He once confessed that he was thankful that "truly God opened his book to me, that is, the Holy Scriptures, and I have said something better than many expressions of the holy fathers whose memory is rightly famed in the holy church" (*Glor. et hon.*, CCCM 29:373,381–383; see also the prologue to the interpretation of John's apocalypse, PL 169:825–828).

His independent stance, however, was not without its consequences for him. On some disputed questions—he had denied, for example, that

Judas had been among the disciples with Jesus at the Last Supper—he aroused public contradiction (by the scholastic Alger of Lüttich particularly) and engaged in fierce debates.

While he was still at work drafting his response, which ended in the composition of a comprehensive commentary on John's Gospel, a new incident occurred. A fellow monk had returned from a term of study in Laon and had reported (mistakenly) the teaching there to be that "God wills that evil occurs; he even willed Adam's sin." This prompted Rupert to a rejoinder in a study *De voluntate Dei* (*On the Will of God*) and thereafter *De omnipotentia Dei* (*On God's Omnipotence*). In these he stresses, as the testimony of Scripture and reason, that on the contrary God hates and condemns evil. Only Scripture, not the teaching of a famous master, could serve as his guiding principle. The long-lasting conflict with his fellow monks that followed forced him, presumably in 1116, to leave his monastery and go to Michaelsberg Abbey in Siegburg. This monastery had undergone its own reform and developed into a scholarly center under the leadership of Abbot Kuno II. There Rupert completed in 1117 his monumental theological work *On the Trinity* (*De trinitate*), which must occupy us still more closely. He was meanwhile forced to defend himself once again against accusations against him in his old St. Laurent monastery by making a personal visit to Laon, where Anselm had just died. He then returned to Siegburg until, probably in 1120/1121, he was chosen abbot of the St. Heribert monastery in Deutz. There he wrote, besides many other works, including commentaries on the Song of Songs and Matthew's Gospel, the *Annulus sive dialogus inter Christianum et Judaeum*, a presentation cast in the form of a dialogue but in reality a polemical work advocating the Christian standpoint in understanding Holy Scripture over against the Jewish. Its form is that of a disputation in which not only the Scriptures but also reason are argued. A former Jew, Hermannus, later admits to having been converted by Rupert. Even in Deutz, Rupert had to withstand many battles, politically with his neighbors, the archbishop Friedrich of Cologne and the count of Berg, and theologically with his old opponents. In 1128 he survived a fire in Deutz that barely spared the monastery. He also began his last work, *De meditatio mortis* (*On Meditating on Death*), which he was unable to complete before his passing on 4 March 1129.

Rupert's major work, *De sancta trinitate et operibus eius* (*On the Holy Trinity and Its Works*), to which we now turn, has been justly called the most significant overview of salvation-history since Augustine's work on the city of God (*De civitate Dei*). It is at the same time Rupert's most comprehensive work. Due to its vast size, it could not be assembled into a single handwritten manuscript at the time of its origin; instead, its forty-two books filled up six volumes, which apparently only a single library (that of the Prüfening Abbey at Regensburg) was able to purchase in toto. Fortunately, there is now a modern critical edition (CCCM 21–24; hereafter cited by volume).

The work's most important distinctive characteristic is that in it Rupert offers a complete depiction of salvation history from the creation to the end of the world by means of an exegesis working its way through the whole Bible step by step from the First Book of Moses to the Apocalypse of John.

Rupert elucidates in a brief foreword (21:125–27) the principles that directed him. Though humans along their earthly way cannot possibly view the splendor of the triune God, they can do so at least in part by consideration of his works (see also *Vict.* 1.3, 7 Haacke). He divides salvation history, which is inextricably embedded in world history, in terms of the most overarching schema set by the leading themes, into three periods: the works of the Father; the works of the Son; and the works of the Holy Spirit. The first period extends "from the origin of the first light to the fall of the first humans," the second "from the fall of the first man to the passion of the second man, Jesus Christ, the Son of God," and the third "to the end of world-time, that is, the universal resurrection of the dead" (*Sanct. trin.* prol., 21:126,53–57). He must, of course, defend himself against the obvious reproach that he intends to split apart the action of the triune God. He therefore emphasizes: "Obviously, the inseparable Trinity acts inseparably as one God. However, as there is in each of them individually—that is, the Father and the Son and the Holy Spirit—the uniqueness of a person so also is the action of each with regard to the completion of the world to be considered: that of the creation by the Father, the salvation by the Son, and the renewal of creation by the Holy Spirit is each his own work. Finally, since the Father does all things through the Son and the Holy Spirit broods over the waters [see Gen 1:2], each of other two persons indeed work together with the one acting" (21:126,59–66).

A second important principle, which he expressed at another place, is that Holy Scripture is the treasure trove containing "everything God has done from the beginning of creation to the present" (*Glor. trin.* 1.4, PL 169:17). Since the Bible is the only reliable report of God's works, its literal sense must be taken seriously in every instance. But the spiritual sense is especially important to Rupert, which he often distinguishes as a whole from the literal, even though he is familiar with the seven rules of interpretation of Tyconius (through Augustine) as well as with Gregory the Great's threefold distinction of literal, allegorical, and tropological (moral) senses.

Rupert's intention is to trace the work of the triune God through all the books of Scripture. But he could do this only by cutting back on the expansive style he started with as he went along (nine books on Genesis, four on Exodus, two each on Leviticus–Deuteronomy, one each on Joshua and Judges/Ruth, and so on). It is clear from the interpretation as a whole that Rupert has in view nothing less than a *summa* of every statement possible about God and his work. That he thought the only way he could do this was by a running biblical commentary is characteristic of the monastic stamp of his theology. In the monastic context, the old form of doing theology, as distinct from the disputations in cathedral schools, still ruled. Rupert's theology is in a strict sense Scripture-bound; to say so is to say something essential about it. But this does not mean that reason plays no role in his work; it is integrated into the process of exegesis only as an instrument.

The sequence of themes treated corresponds largely to that in contemporary works on the sentences. Rupert begins his commentary by starting immediately with a Trinitarian interpretation of the cosmos. He connects the initial words of the creation account, "in the beginning God created heaven and earth," and the statement of Gen 2:1, "So heaven and earth have been made and their entire ornament [*ornatus*]." By this means he gains a threefold division and can come to the conclusion "that the heaven is truly created by the person of the Father, but the earth by the person of the Son, and the ornament of both is made ... by the very person of the Spirit" (21:129,23–26). For heaven is, like the Father, incorporeal, as is his ornament, the angels. The Son was to assume earthly substance in accord with the will of the Father, but the fact that the Holy Spirit is the ornament of heaven and earth is derived from Gen 1:2: "the Spirit of God brooded over the waters."

The interpretation of Gen 1:1 that follows comes to a dogmatic resolution as well. Of concern here are the words "in the beginning," in Latin, *in principio*. To this Rupert refers to the passage John 8:25, where Jesus says "Why do I speak at you at all?" This term "at all," in Greek *ten archen*, is reproduced in Latin as *principium*. According to Rupert, Jesus points to the word himself at this Johannine passage. Thereafter when it states "in the beginning," it means, in keeping with the allegorical interpretation of the passage familiar to Rupert, that the creation of the world occurred in Christ. The mediatorial role of the Son in creation, one of the most important of the affirmations of the doctrine of the Trinity, can therefore be found in its biblical formulation. This is a way of making the point other than the way that is customary, gained from the mediation of wisdom in creation in accord with Prov 8:22–31.

One of the next questions Rupert broaches had emerged long ago from Augustine's interpretation of Genesis and was passed down in the *Glossa ordinaria*. Why does it say that "God created heaven and earth" and not, as in subsequent statements, "God said, 'Let there be heaven and earth'" (*Sanct. trin.*, In Genesim 1.4; 21:131,112ff.)? Two of the three answers Rupert gives to this question correspond to formal propositional logic: (1) since *principium* means, according to what was just said, the Word, that is, the Son of God (John 1:1), it would have been superfluous to have said, "God said in a Word..."; (2) and God could not say "let there be" because in the beginning there was still nothing there, therefore no one to whom it could have been said. This is precisely the sort of argumentation customary in disputations by masters in the schools. The second answer, however, has in addition significance as regards important content. That is, here Rupert refers back to the view found in Augustine that there would have already had to be a formless matter that was given form by the "let there be" of the Son (Augustine, *Gen. litt.* 1.3–4; CSEL 28:7–8). In the third place, Rupert rejects the opinion of the "philosophers" that God created only the various forms, while matter, the *hyle*, is equally eternal with God.

One statement of importance to Rupert—to which we have already alluded several times—is also made in Gen 1:2: "and the Spirit of God brooded over the waters" (In Genesim 1.8; 21:134,225ff.). He compares this image with the hen by whose brooding warmth the egg is hatched. The Spirit has brooded not only over the waters but over the dry land as well; it is the love and goodness of God by which he has connected the creation to himself. Thus the concurrence of the entire Trinity is found in creation.

On the other hand, there are also passages where Rupert prefers a literal understanding of the events of creation. Thus for Gen 1:22–25, where he rejects the spiritual understanding of the "waters of the firmament" as angels and argues for simple water, although in a primitive state, in order to solve the physical problem (21:151–54).

In the case of paradise, which others interpreted allegorically, he stresses that it is a matter of a localizable garden with real trees, and he tries to identify its precise location by drawing upon ancient authors (In Genesim 2.2.24–25, 29; 21:212–14, 219–21).

The work of Christ occupies the large middle section of Rupert's work. He finds it, by adopting traditional typological and allegorical ways of interpretation, prefigured in the figures and mysteries of the Old Testament. He divides the age of the Son's activity into seven periods, as Augustine and Bede had done. In the first period, from Adam to Noah, Christ was prefigured only by deeds; in the second, from Noah to Abraham, by deeds and words; in the third, from Abraham to David, by direct promises. The rebuilding of the temple destroyed at the time of the Babylonian exile and shortly afterward prefigured the new priest (Jesus Christ), who is announced in Zechariah. With this begins the fifth age, lasting to the incarnation of Christ. The incarnation begins the sixth age, which still continues. These six ages correspond to the six stages of creation (In Genesim 3.34ff., 21:276–280).

It is striking, yet typical for the time, that Rupert looks for Christ's activity in the Old Testament above all; he dedicates only a single book to the four Gospels (book 33, 23:1781–1822). There is hardly any concern for the earthly activity of Jesus; of more importance is the allegorical-typological level, that is, the spiritual meaning of Scriptures, with which interpretation was completely preoccupied within the tradition stemming from Origen.

Also characteristic of the distinctiveness of Rupert's interpretation of Scriptures is how he understands the role of reason as a means for knowing the truth of Scripture. He objects to the use of reason in the scholastic theology of Paris and Laon for trying to conceive the divine mystery of salvation rationally by its customary dialectics. The notice in 1 Sam 6:19 in which God punished the people of Beth-shemesh because they looked into the ark of Yahweh offers him the opportunity to criticize churchmen "who dared to delve into the Scriptures for the mysteries of divinity not out of love of learning but out of ambition and curiosity, and have become chief heretics, because God has decided that the proud will not be permitted to gain knowledge of truth" (Sanct. trin. 22, CCCM 22:1223). No one will belong to those called the children of God who does not receive and accept it as grace from the blood of Christ, and "those who are puffed up and bristling with ambition may realize that, although they seem to know as much as they want and as much as they can, they still cannot attain to knowledge of this name" (Comm. Apoc. 2.2, PL 169:881). For this, renewal by the Holy Spirit is necessary, who "precisely through this renewal by his touch completes the one who knows about this matter and is a scholar" (2.2). But in Rupert's view, the Holy Spirit and reason are not antithetical; on the contrary, as he states in his commentary on John 1:4–5 and 1:9 (CCCM 9:14–18, 22–23), the inherent reason in each person by creation is then led to true knowledge only when it is illumined by the Holy Spirit and indeed by the true light who is Jesus Christ. But given this assumption, it is a tool with which an absolutely rationally worked out and impartial interpretation of the Scriptures can be undertaken.

In addition to his major work on the works of the Trinity, Rupert also wrote an entire series of other biblical commentaries. His commentary on John's Gospel has received particular attention. After Augustine's John commentary, which Rupert made use of in many ways while still maintaining his inward freedom from it, Rupert's was the first independent commentary on this Gospel, which had to be fascinating to an interpreter like Rupert because of its theological profundity. This commentary is fully connected to his major work on the works of the Trinity, in that that here also meditation on the triune God, Jesus as the Son of God, the incarnation, and the works of the Holy Spirit are at the center of consideration. The tradition of "spiritual scriptural reading," as it was the custom in medieval monasticism, is reflected everywhere in these pages. The goal of interpretation, as Rupert writes already in the foreword, had to be to "grasp with the whole heart, to desire with the whole soul, and above all … to love the witnesses of the Scriptures about the Son of God" (CCCM 9:6). Like the merchant in search of the precious pearl (Matt 13:45), the reader of the Gospel must "sell everything in order to be able to acquire this one pearl. Every speck of the dust of fleshly desires has to be rubbed out of the eyes of the heart of those who seek learning in the school of Christ from Holy Scripture" (CCCM 9:6) Asceticism and meditative concentration are preconditions for such an understanding that has as its goal more than rational explanation, namely, life with the Scriptures. Precisely this means for Rupert knowledge in the full sense. That the path to this goal proceeds in steps (*Comm. Joh.* 1.33, CCCM 9:72–73) is reminiscent of Origen—in whose indirect succession Rupert stands, although his direct models are to be found in the line of interpreters the church approved.

How the interpretation of John's Gospel is concretely formed comes into view in Rupert's discussion of the encounter of Jesus with the Samaritan women at the well (in his excerpt of John 4:7–15, CCCM 9:196–202). The woman, after she received the water from Jesus, is for Rupert the image for the church (formed of non-Jews), to which the living water is sent, that is, the grace of the Holy Spirit, which streams from the eternal Godhead into the souls of humans, which can then with this [grace] stream back to its origins, to eternal life. "But before it streams there, it becomes a fountain within the one who drinks it, pouring out streams of wisdom and knowledge" into the heart (CCCM 9:211). But before the woman receives the water, she is the image of "the thirsting and drooling pagan peoples, left in unreason to wager on the teaching of the philosophy of this world." Here Rupert mentions Stoics, Epicureans, Platonists, and those of other philosophical schools, all of whom hold that "their schools proclaim the way to true and highest happiness" (CCCM 9:196).

That it is the Gospel of John particularly that invites interpretation of this sort is understandable, inasmuch as in it stylistic means of deeper meaning and creative misunderstandings are formative elements. But Rupert is accustomed to deal with a multiple sense of Scripture elsewhere as well. His commentary on the Song of Songs is thus worth attention, because in contrast to customary Christian interpretation, he does not see it speaking allegorically of the relation between Christ and the church but as pointing to Mary. Yet what has now been said may suffice for a satisfactory account of the distinctive features of his interpretation. Rupert has been called a mediating theologian because, standing on the crest of a new age, he sought to reconcile the old ways with new interests.

It is not insignificant that some of Rupert's writings, his John commentary in particular, appeared in print in the age of the Reformation. The Reformers appreciated him as an author who anchored all theology in Holy Scripture itself and repudiated a disputatious scholasticism that constructed its systems in separation from scriptural interpretation. Indeed, standing in this monastic tradition of living with the Scriptures was the Reformer Luther himself, who adapted this heritage himself for a new age of the church. At the same time, it must be said that these theologians were separated by a good deal more than temporal distance. Rupert deserves our attention, nevertheless. His memory has unjustly fallen into oblivion in modern research for a long time.

3.5. History and Deeper Sense: Hugh of St. Victor

We encountered the schools of Paris earlier when we traced Abelard's career. He himself had studied for a time at the cathedral school and founded his own school on Mount St. Genevieve. Secular canons lived there; later, after the monastery's reform under the influence of Pope Eugenius II (1145–1153), regular canons. After Abelard, Alberich and Robert von Melun taught there, both representatives of the dialectical school tradition that Abelard founded. At the turn of the twelfth century we can see an increasing significance of the schools in and around Paris. Previously, places in the provinces such as Laon, Chartres, or Melun were the most

significant centers of education, but with the strengthening of the Cape-
tian dynasty—its most significant rulers were Louis VI (1108–1137) and
Louis VII (1137–1180)—the significance of the metropolis increased considerably. The most important educational institution was the cathedral
school on the Ile de France, where William of Champeaux (d. 1121/1122),
then archdeacon at Notre Dame, taught from around 1095 to 1108.
Another school arose, like St. Genevieve, on the left bank of the Seine,
with the foundation of the monastery of St. Victor in 1108. Its founder
was William of Champeaux, who then taught there from 1108 to 1113
until he became the bishop of Châlon-sur-Marne. His elevation brought
important improvements for the school of St. Victor. St. Victor's became a
royal monastery and was endowed with considerable properties, making
it economically independent.

The school's structure had changed considerably around the turn of
the twelfth century, in contrast to preceding periods. During the Carolingian age and even thereafter schools had served exclusively for educating
the clergy, in monasteries, for the monks. In the figure of Abelard, on the
other hand, we meet the wandering scholar who moves from school to
school, depending on the famous masters teaching there. The honorific
title "master" now came to refer to those whose chief occupation was
teaching, and later to officially licensed professors as well. In the cathedral
schools, under the oversight of the bishop, the cathedral chapter, to whom
the school's director (*scholasticus*) belonged, bore the responsibility for
instruction; similarly, in monasteries there was a school director entrusted
with this task. This director frequently rose to the rank of prior or abbot.
Herein can be seen how significant a monastery considered its school. In
fact, the fame of many monasteries was based on the significance of their
schools. Yet, unlike cathedral schools, the monastic and collegiate schools
were dedicated almost exclusively to educating their own up-coming
generation. This is evidently true also of the school of St. Victor after the
departure of its founder William of Champeaux. Even Hugh of St. Victor,
with whom we want to deal in detail, was a canon like his successors.

By the way, one must also distinguish between canons, hence secular
priests, and authentic orders of monks. There were many times considerable rivalries between them. Of the religious orders, the tradition-rich
Benedictines who lived purely contemplative lives were the most distinguished. But they likewise underwent multiple reforms, the Cluniac and
Cistercian being the most significant. The newer orders, such as the Franciscans and Dominicans, not only led a different way of life but cultivated
a different way of dealing with Scripture, too.

Hugh was born, probably between 1097 and 1099, at an unknown place. The tradition that he was of Saxon descent (from the area of Halberstadt) is not baseless but not conclusively demonstrable. He himself was silent about the matter. That young people from all around came to Paris, attracted by the fame of its schools, was so frequent that the report is believable. Hugh entered the monastery after 1114, when Gilduin became St. Victor's abbot. It is not known if he also received his education at St. Victor, but certainly he himself taught there. He must have taken up this activity before the appearance of his first writings arising from his teaching, which were written before 1125. Otherwise he seems, like Bede, to have spent a quiet, relatively uneventful life inside the monastery's walls. Only a few trips are reported. He died in 1141, still a young man by our conceptions, but the average life expectancy was low in that day.

As inconspicuous as was his life, so important is the role Hugh played in the history of biblical interpretation and scholastic theology as a whole. His writings cover the entire instructional program of his school. A special witness for this is Hugh's encyclopedic work, the *Didascalion de studio legendi* (*Textbook on the Study of Reading*). From its overall structure and presentation in details, it exhibits an important distinction as compared to the dialectical thinking of Abelard and his school. The secular sciences, the study of which is discussed in the first three books, are indeed necessary first steps along the way to complete knowledge, but they are not integrated into the study of theology per se, which the three last books deal with.

In his encyclopedic approach, Hugh stands in the scholastic tradition that can be traced back to Isidore of Seville, on whom he is dependent in various other respects. A student had to gain learning first in the liberal arts before advancing to *sacra pagina*, the study of Holy Scripture, that is, theology. In contrast to Abelard, who brought dialectics directly into the center of the treatment of theology, Hugh held to the older view according to which knowledge of the liberal arts is preparatory for the higher study of the Holy Scriptures but is in other respects distanced from it due to its special value. Thus, for example, he expressly says "that all the natural arts are of assistance to divine science, and lower wisdom leads in correct order to the higher" (*Sacr.* prol. 6, PL 176:185C). He was always critically disposed toward the dialecticians who sought to discover truth by their disputations.

Hugh took the content of the first books, which set out the knowledge of antiquity, from the tradition originating with ancient writers such as Cicero and Quintilian—and so also similar specialists for each branch of knowledge, such as Galen for medicine, Vitruvius for architecture, and so on—and transmitted by Boethius, Cassiodorus, Isidore of Seville, Bede, and Carolingian school leaders. Characteristic for him, however, is the overall conception of the significance of the sciences, the origin of which he explicitly discusses. The beginning of his book (after the foreword) is indeed still stamped by tradition, as when he says in connection with Boethius and the commentary tradition coming from him that wisdom consists of "the form of perfect Good" (*Did.* 1.1, 4,4–5 Buttimer). One must know this tradition in order to understand the sense of this statement; it is meant christologically: divine wisdom is incarnate in Christ (see John 1:14). But by coming to know wisdom, man comes to know himself, and indeed not by knowledge of external things but in and of itself, "for his immortal spirit, illumined by wisdom, knows its principle and understands how improper it would be to seek something outside himself when what he himself is can be sufficient" (4,7–9). "This is the dignity of the nature we all share, though we do not all know it to the same extent: … we are reconstructed by the teaching that we learn our own nature and that we learn to seek nothing outside ourselves that we can find within ourselves. For the study of wisdom is the highest consolation in life, because whoever finds it is happy, and whoever possesses it, blessed" (6,3–11).

These statements are noteworthy inasmuch as the ancient viewpoint according to which humanity itself is at the center of his thinking is taken up in a particular respect. Therein a way of thinking typical of the twelfth century shows itself. This age has been spoken of, not unjustly, as a "renaissance." Nevertheless, according to Hugh philosophical thinking is divine action, because wisdom comes from God, while human action exhausts itself in caring for the transitory body. Hugh speaks of this in chapter 8 of his first book (15,10ff.). Actions that contribute to the restoration of our nature are divine actions; those, on the other hand, that provide only what is necessary due to our weaknesses are human actions. Behind this is—and here Hugh remains a theologian—the idea that humans are the image of God. In this, Hugh distinguishes between insight (*intellegentia*) and knowledge (*scientia*): human actions give rise to knowledge, divine actions to insight. On this basis he drafts a system for the liberal arts in which special significance is ascribed to the trivium (the three arts of grammar, dialectic, rhetoric). Along with them the quadrivium also, with its fields of arithmetic, music, geometry, and astronomy, takes its traditional place. Added to this is yet a further schema of division into theory, practice, mechanics, and logic—in it, theology is placed in theory and ethics in practice, while a number of handwork skills, such as weaving, navigation, hunting, and medicine, are listed under mechanics (summarizing *Did.* 6.14; 130,15–132,3 Buttimer).

Hugh deals with the biblical sciences in the second part of his work, in books 4–6. He proceeds in textbook style here, too, so that in book 4 we first read all sorts of introductory scientific matters about the Bible's two Testaments: the names and division of the books of the Old and New Testaments (4.2); the authors of the Old Testament—here we find, as expected, the precritical view that regards Moses the author of the five books of Moses—(4.3) and those of the New (4.6); and the Apocrypha (4.7, 15). But we also read about the canons of the councils (4.11), the four main synods, ecumenical councils (4.12), and authentic (4.14) and inauthentic (4.15) writings of the fathers. For Hugh, Holy Scripture embraces not only the Bible but also works of the church fathers and decisions of the ecumenical councils; his concept of the canon extends into church history. On the other hand, he follows Jerome in limiting the Old Testament canon; he places the deuterocanonical books, unlike Isidore, not in the canon but in the Apocrypha. Moreover, we can gather from the presentation how many titles Hugh knew and presumably read for himself; he was evidently a highly educated man.

Of special interest are the hermeneutical principles Hugh develops in book 5. Here we find a chapter on the threefold sense of Scripture, which Hugh adopted in keeping with a schema common at its time (taken over from Gregory the Great, whereas Augustine and Bede distinguished a fourfold sense of Scripture), divided into historical, allegorical, and tropological (moral) senses. He took over (4.4) the seven rules of Tyconius (see above) literally, with minor changes from Isidore of Seville (*Etym.* 1.19.1–19). From these hermeneutical basic presuppositions, Hugh develops his overall understanding of the Bible: history means at the same time the literal meaning and the event that is expressed in it. Hugh explicitly stresses that, "in God's speech, not only the words but the things as well have something to say" (*Did.* 5.3, 96,24–25). Allegory and tropology are at the same time the main themes of Bible as well as methods of interpreting it. In a traditional way deriving finally from Origen, he understands the "fruit" of biblical reading on which, in his view, everything depends (see 5.6) as a path of the soul ascending in four steps. These four steps are reading (instruction = *doctrina*), meditation, prayer, and action (5.9, 109,15) and, somewhat apart, as the highest, fifth step, vision (*contemplatio*), "in which … already in this life is tasted in advance what will be the future wages of good works" (5.9, 109,17). All these ideas are familiar to us; they reflect the typically Western form of piety as it had developed in monasticism in particular. Hugh is a self-conscious guardian of tradition, even against the currents of other sorts of his time.

It is important, however—and in this respect Hugh's viewpoint gained special attention—that to his students he puts special value on an adequate consideration of the historical (= literal) sense. It is important "that you first learn history and the truth of events that take place, by repeating from the beginning to the end what has occurred, when it occurred, where it occurred, and by whom it occurred and entrust it to memory. That is, these are the four things especially required in history: person; action; time; and place (6.3, 113,24–114,2). Here the term "history" is to be understood in an extended sense: "When we use the meaning of this word in a wider sense, it is not at all unfitting that we call 'history' not only the narrative of events but that original sense of the narrative that is expressed in the truly literal sense" (6.3, 115–16). Hugh stresses the unconditional necessity of first setting philological and historical foundations over against those who "want to philosophize immediately" (114,8–9). Their so-called "science" is comparable to that of asses! Hugh evidently had reasons for such powerful expressions! His listeners were all too ready to skip over the laborious task of learning the literal sense and the details of history it contains. Now, of course, his listeners might well object; they evidently did so often: "I find much in historical things that seem of no use for anything. Why should I bother myself with things of such a sort?" (6.3, 115,11–12). Hugh first agreed with them but then immediately pointed out that such things are, of course, never important in themselves but viewed in a larger context and are unavoidable for understanding. It therefore holds, "learn everything (and) you will later see that nothing is superfluous!"

One can see already in these expressions that Hugh states his own views on which his special significance for the history of biblical interpretation is based. Incidentally, he repeated essentially the same statements about the Holy Scriptures once again in a somewhat later work, *De scripturis et scriptoribus sacris* (*On the Holy Scriptures and Their Authors*).

In order to assess them, we must look as well at his major systematic work, *De sacramentis christianae fidei* (*On the Mysteries of the Christian Faith*), which he wrote between 1130 and 1137 (PL 176:173–618). Central for this presentation is the basic distinction Hugh draws between the "work of foundation" (*opus conditionis*) and the "work of restoration" (*opus restaurationis*). He comes to speak of it already in the prologue. "There are two works containing everything that was made. The first is the work of foundation; the second is the work of restoration. The work of foundation is that by which that which did not exist became made. The work of restoration is that by which what became lost was made better. There the work of foundation is the creation of the world and all its elements. The work of restoration is the incarnation of the Word with all its mysteries" (*Sacr.* prol. 2, PL 176:183A–B.) Also with nearly the same wording in *Script.* 2 (PL 175:11A–B), the "work of restoration" also includes the "mystery of human salvation" especially. This basic dogmatic distinction between the two works influences the consideration of Scripture, too. In the chapter of *De sacramentis* that follows, the prologue speaks of how the Scripture deals with both works in sequence: first in the primeval history of the creation of the world, "which was made for humanity's sake; then "how man ... was led to the path of justice and obedience, then as man is fallen, [and] finally as he is restored" (PL 176:184B–C). It is important, as the first quotation makes immediately evident, that Hugh views the work of restoration as pivotally christological. This determines his entire interpretation of Scripture. Directly from it comes the threefold interpretation of Scripture, which he mentions immediately afterward (prol. 4, PL 176:184C–185A).

The overall schema of presentation in *De sacramentis* is therefore structured as an exegesis of the Holy Scriptures. The first book is, following the traditional model, a *hexaemeron*, an interpretation of the seven-day work of creation; the interpretation of the narrative of paradise and the fall of humanity (Gen 2–3) is then added. Book 2 begins with the age of grace, which according to John 1:17 came through Jesus Christ—in contrast to the time of the law given by Moses that Hugh does not mention! But the content of this entire book is then not biblical interpretation; it is a dogmatic treatise that speaks especially about the sacraments and orders of the church in which then-current, very practical questions are handled. For Hugh, then, the age of grace becomes a reality in the church, indeed in its quite concrete present form. He is a genuinely catholic thinker. In this part of his work he frequently cites Augustine and other church fathers, as he generally grants tradition wide scope. That he nevertheless remains bound to this time scheme can be seen in book 2, sections 17 and 18, where he speaks of the end of this age and of the future world. In other passages, to which we must still turn, he discusses the periodicization of the middle part of history in more detail.

Of particular interest here is the work *De arca Noe mystica* (*On the Mystical Ark of Noah*). It is the second part of a lecture on the ark that Hugh had begun with a longer first part of an allegorical interpretation of the ark's construction. After concluding this part of the lecture, Hugh had prepared a partially colored drawing of the ark in which a great deal of fantasy is in play, because the description in Gen 6:14–16 offers little information about the ark except its length, width, and height and the comment that it should have three stories—not all too many details. In any case, according to the biblical account, the ark is a rectangular box. Hugh adds that it is supported in the middle by a continuous column that represents at the same time the tree of life in paradise like Christ, "who according to the human form he assumed is planted in the middle of the church" (PL 176:684A). Since he stands in the middle and extends through all the stories, Christ supports his whole church, represented by the ark. The length of the ark stands for the (temporal) extension of the church, indeed from the beginning of creation to the end of the times, "since the holy church begins in its believers from the beginning on and will last until the end of the age of the world. We believe, namely, that there is no time from the beginning of the world to the end in which believers in Christ are not found" (PL 176:685B.) The upper half of the ark up to the column stands for the generations from Adam to Christ, the lower (half) for the periods from the incarnation to the end of times. In so doing it deals with his bodily line of descent from Adam to Christ, followed by the spiritual line from Peter and the other apostles and to the later church leaders, "who like spiritual sons followed the fathers in leadership of the church" (PL 176:685). Hugh later (ch. 4; PL 176:686B–687D) elucidates this in greater detail, taking up from Luke 3:23–38 the genealogy (in reverse sequence) running from Adam to the patriarchs and the Davidic line to Christ, and in the second part listing the popes, as Peter's successors, to the then-ruling Honorius II (1124–1130). Space is supposedly still left for those who follow, up to the end of the world! The result, then, is a continuous line of salvation history.

The three levels of the ark give occasion for a further subdivision (ch. 5, PL 176:688A–B). This is the division of salvation history into three periods: (1) the age of the natural law, from the beginning to the twelve patriarchs; (2) the age of the written law, from the twelve patriarchs to the incarnation of the word (Jesus Christ); and (3) the age of grace, from there to the end of the world. To these also correspond three sorts of humans: the humanity of natural law; the humanity of written law; and the humanity of grace (PL 176:688C). To be sure, only the most prevalent types of people are meant in each respective period: "When we pay careful attention, we find all these sorts of people in these distinct periods" (PL 176:688D). There are individual representatives of the type "people of the written law" and "people of grace" in the period of natural law, individuals of the "people of natural law" type are still found in the period of the written law, and individuals of the type "people of grace are already found at that time." All three types are found in the period of grace. But for each epoch the most prevalent sort are dominant, while each of the other two types lives in concealment, known to their closest associates alone. But there are also dislocations: in the age of the written law, many representatives of natural law hid themselves, concealing their errors in order to avoid the law's threats of punishment; in the age of grace after the revelation of the grace of God and the lifting of punishment, they again stepped forward into the light.

We see here before us the draft of a salvation-history schema that Hugh then expanded in what follows by additional, difficult distinctions. The designations of the individual components in the ark's three stories by terms and their interpretation permits the construction of a history of the development of virtues that constantly progresses. At its foundation is the statement found in connection with the overall division of ages. Accordingly, "the natural goodness of humanity may indeed be corrupted by sin but not completely extinguished, for there remains to this day a spark of natural reason within the human spirit, enabling everyone to distinguish between good and evil" (PL 176:689A–B). Here Hugh appeals to Paul's statements in Rom 2:14. Since the ark symbolizes the church, the growth of virtues certainly settles in its room. There Christians grow from their pride to fear (of punishment), then to pain (for sins), and then to love; from patience to compassion to repentance; from ignorance to knowledge to meditation and contemplation (PL 176:692C–D). Along 120 ascending steps—twelve stairs (the teaching of the apostles), each with ten steps corresponding to the Decalogue, which connect the three stories of the ark—sixty men and women climb upward to God. Thus the result is a consistent development of church history as a whole that is identical with salvation history. But at the same time the boundaries between church and world are fluid: what happens within the space of the church at the same time makes a mark on world history as a whole. The "work of restoration," as Hugh characterizes world history as a whole, is divided into three periods: the period of prevailing darkness, that is, the age before the incarnation of the Word; then the age of corporeality (efficacy in the visible sacraments of the church); and the age of the spiritual (which realizes itself invisibly through the sacraments; De arca Noe morali 4.9, PL 176:679).

Alongside such speculative-allegorizing interpretations, which certainly have a facet that illumines world history as a whole and in this respect also disclose Hugh's historical interest, in his exegetical lectures Hugh dealt with the literal sense more than was the custom at the time, offering annotations on it and the historical circumstances of statements in the biblical texts. It was evidently not Hugh himself but his students who collected annotations of this sort. Unfortunately, the printed edition in the Patrologia Latina is far from complete, as the sometimes variant materials in the surviving notes show. In addition, it has long seemed the case that not everything Hugh stated orally in lectures has been preserved in writing. Nevertheless, from what is available we can gain a good impression of the overall position Hugh set forth in his lectures. Itself noteworthy is what he says on the Septuagint at the beginning of his *Adnotationes elucidatoriae in pentateuchon* (*Explanatory Notes on the Pentateuch*, PL 175:29–86) as well as the corresponding notes on the books of Judges and Kings—his concern has to do with a collection of notes to the text and elucidations about word meanings, historical circumstances, and other factual problems necessary for understanding the literal sense. He does not shy away from explicitly stating there: "The seventy interpreters spoke from the human, not the divine, spirit, and therefore it is by no means unfitting when, as human beings, they err" (PL 175:32A). Instead, what is important is the *hebraica veritas*, the Hebrew truth: "For indeed the Septuagint edition, mentioned above, lacks a great deal of what is found in the Hebrew truth (the Hebrew original text)" (PL 175:30A). This is then shown by examples. Instead of following the Septuagint, one should prefer the original text, "the authentic books, that is, the Hebrew, in which the original authority and truth is contained" (PL 175:31A)

Although in this respect Hugh associated himself with a well-known demand of Jerome, his direct use of these books is hardly demonstrable. We can instead only surmise that Hugh had learned Hebrew himself, like his student Andrew of St. Victor (d. 1175) thereafter. This would have been an astonishing achievement for the time. Supporting this supposition is the fact that direct quotations from rabbinic commentaries are at times found in his *Adnotationes*, such as at Gen 49:12 (PL 175:59) from Rashi's Pentateuch commentary or at Exod 1:15 (PL 175:61) from that of Rashi's grandson Rashbam (Samuel ben Meïr), who was Hugh's contemporary. Another possibility would be that he had contacts with Jews in Paris, because the Jewish quarter was then in the city center, on the Ile de la Cité. In the details, then, we can read much that reminds us of modern methods of interpretation, with Hugh's interest in factual problems and historical questions. Of course, this does not mean that he was not also concerned with allegorical tropological exegesis. For him, as for others, it is undoubtedly this higher meaning that literal understanding was to serve. In his *Commentary on the Lamentations of Jeremiah* (PL 175:255–322), he undertakes threefold exegesis in exemplary fashion. It is remarkable, however, that he prefaced a foreword urging methodical care (PL 175:113C–115C) to his own handwritten copy of his sermon on the "Solomon the preacher" (PL 175:113–256) in which he had carried out a profoundly spiritual interpretation, There he emphasizes not only that a text is first opened up to correct understanding by an adequate consideration of the literal sense but also that those "who deny that mystical understanding and allegorical depth is to be sought when it is present in Holy Scripture" are just as blameworthy "as those who set about in abusive fashion to come up with one where none is present" (PL 175:115A). Nevertheless, in his personal piety Hugh was a deeply religious man who by contemplation and prayer worked for unity with God by considering God's works, above all the Scriptures. Yet he strongly urged students to work their way up methodically from philological and historical knowledge to the level of allegorical understanding. Dogmatic knowledge is also indispensable for this. As highly as the "mystical" sense is to be valued, beginners without solid basic knowledge should never dare venture there.

Hugh was the teacher of many students, and his pedagogical skills—as we can still clearly see in his writings—must have been quite unusual. Not only did the monastery of St. Victor enjoy an extraordinary upswing because of his activity; he also educated several very important students. Of the two most significant, Richard (d. 1173) developed the allegorical method of interpretation especially, whereas Andrew gave priority to explaining the literal meaning. In so doing, he also relied on the Hebrew original text of the Old Testament more strongly than his master and recommended knowledge of Hebrew to his students.

3.6. A Monk Expects the Age of the Spirit: Joachim of Fiore

Joachim was born around 1135 in Celico near Consenza, the capital of the province Calabria, which at the time belonged to the kingdom of the Normans ruling in Sicily and southern Italy. We do not know his precise birth date, but he is supposed to have been around sixty years old around 1195. His father, a notary at the Norman king's court in Palermo, wanted to gain this position for his oldest surviving son as well (two brothers had died early). Presumably Joachim was also active for a while in the chancery in Palermo, before (around 1166/1167) he made a trip to the Orient. That he was also in Byzantium is presumably a legend. Yet he is said to have traveled beyond Tripoli in Syria to Palestine. There he visited, among other things, monastic colonies at the Dead Sea (see *Conc.* 1.2.3a) and Jerusalem and, if we can believe the oldest autobiography, surviving in fragments, experienced a revelation about the two Testaments on Mount Tabor, the place of sacrifice of the prophet Elijah (1 Kgs 18). This experience led him to give up his worldly course of life and move through the country thereafter in a monk's cowl.

After returning from Palestine, he lived first as a hermit in the vicinity of Aetna but finally returned to Calabria, his homeland. Not even an encounter with his disappointed father there made him break his decision to live apart from the world from that point on. He spent some time first in Sambozina, a Cistercian monastery north of Cosenza, without entering there. Instead, after a while he left this abbey and, settling in a secluded hermitage, preached to the inhabitants of a nearby valley. Yet in time he came to doubt if this was permissible without ordination to the priesthood. Hence he went to the authorized bishop in Catanzaro in order to receive ordination. While on the way back, his encounter with a Greek monk who reminded him of the parable of the unfaithful servant (Matt 25:30) brought the decisive turn: he converted to monasticism, entering the nearby Curazzo monastery that had adopted the Cistercian rule. He soon advanced to become the prior there and, following the abbot's retirement, he was elected his successor. Unwilling to take on this office with its administrative tasks, he at first fled but was then persuaded to accept it nonetheless. He then administered the monastery for several years and long sought in vain to join it to a Cistercian monastery. He was able to do so only in 1188 through the intervention of Pope Clement III (1187–1191), whom he visited in Rome.

He already had contacts with popes prior to this, as shown by his 1184 meeting with Lucius III (1181–1185), who asked him to interpret an anonymous prophecy found shortly before. At the time Joachim was already reputed to be a prophet, though he himself certainly denied it. He is supposed to have once said he wanted to be nothing other than an interpreter of the Holy Scriptures, for which God had given him the "spirit of discernment" (*spiritum intelligentiae*). Lucius also granted him special permission (necessary in the Cistercian order) to write books. This permission was later confirmed by Clement III, with whom Joachim was friends. Clement asked him in 1188 to bring his works to their conclusion and present them to the papal chair; at Joachim's request, he also released him from his duties as abbot. Joachim intended now to devote his time entirely to the Scriptures, yet afterward he founded a monastery of his own in the secluded Sila Valley, naming it St. Giovanni in Fiore. It was at the same time the foundation of a new order to which Joachim gave a—regrettably, not preserved—revised Cistercian rule. It survived to the seventeenth century. Joachim did not live there either, cut off from the world. There are reports that he met with the English King Richard the Lionhearted, who, on crusade in 1190–1191, wintered in Sicily and asked for a prophecy about the crusade's outcome, as well as first in 1191 with Emperor Henry VI, who became his sovereign (d. 1197), and later with his widow Constance (who is said to have humbly prostrated herself on the floor before him to make confession), and with young Friedrich II, whom he went to see in Palermo regarding monastic affairs in the spring of 1200. Innocent III (1198–1216) was probably less well-disposed toward him. In Joachim's testamentary letter of 1200 to this pope, however, he expressed his complete loyalty to the holy chair, even in matters of faith. He wanted to be a faithful member of the church and remained one until his death on 30 March 1202.

This stands in contrast to his later effects among radical spiritualists such as Gerhard of Borgo San Donnino, whose radical new foreword (*Liber introductorius*) to the revised edition of Joachim's major work in 1254 sparked protest by the professors at Paris and led to a papal investigatory commission that met in Anagni in 1255 and carefully weighed the statements of Joachim and Gerardo against one another, as well as to the spiritual Franciscans who separated from their order after 1270. However, as we shall see, the roots of this radicalization that openly turned against the church in its present form are absolutely present in Joachim's writings.

With Rupert of Deutz, we have already come to know one important biblical interpreter who stemmed from the tradition of interpretation typical of monasticism. There was a way of living with Scripture in monasteries and convents different from that in the schools and upcoming universities. There the concern was not the mutual relationship of rational thinking and biblical contents but solely the spiritual content of Scripture. The method used for seeking out this spiritual content was collation (*collatio*), a continuous interpretation of a text by comparison with other biblical passages, by rhetorical and grammatical investigations, just as we have already encountered in the older tradition of interpretation. The goal of *lectio evangelica* was meditation on the text, leading to prayer and contemplation. It was at the center of life in the contemplative orders to which the Benedictines belonged. The life of the monks and nuns was shaped by it. From it, however, came the standards for all theological judgments as well, which were closely bound to scriptural statements. This, however, did not prevent there being quite original theological thinkers even among monks. One of them was Joachim of Fiore, whose memory remains to this day.

In the background of monastic biblical interpretation, as Joachim embodied it, stood at the end of the twelfth century both the confrontational stance against scholastic theology as conducted in the urban centers and the cathedral schools there and then in the thirteen century the universities emerging from them. Joachim underscored passionately the superiority of the eremitic life, "where there are not literary studies, not doctors of the church institution, where 'love from the heart and not hypocritical faith' rules in contrast to those who are puffed up 'by scholastic science'" (*Tract.* 294.25–26). Not only this, but the monastic form of life as such was carried out in a certain opposition to the established church with its clergy, its worldly possessions, and its many worldly forms of life. Within monasticism, then, there was still debate between the older orders, above all the Benedictines, who meanwhile became well-to-do and distinguished and—despite the reform movement of Citeaux arising from within the Benedictine establishment itself—had fallen into a crisis and the movement toward more radical forms of life. In Joachim this manifested itself at times in eremitism, which he, however, then gave up in favor of accepting a rule of order derived from the Cistercians, but above all in his basic judgments on the established church, which he of course did not state directly but were clearly the basis for his overall view of salvation history. To this extent he stood altogether within the context of the reform movements around the end of the twelfth and the start of the thirteenth century that launched a new initiative for reforming the institutional church after the effects of the older reform movement in the eleventh century had subsided. In Joachim's case, these trends combined with fervent expectations of the end time, which appeared at the time in apocalyptical currents within and outside the church.

To be sure, one must carefully distinguish, as we indicated, between Joachim's own statements and what later spiritualists made of them. The global theories of Joachim have been frequently discussed in broad outline in recent decades, especially because of the ideological implications many try to draw from them. But their exegetical roots are far less known than they deserve to be. A lack of critical editions stood in the way for a long time, too. In the meantime, at least the most important are available in reliable texts. Modern translations, however, are as good as nonexistent. This probably goes along with the fact that Joachim is by no means a thinker in tune with today's taste; the strict tie of all his thoughts to the interpretation of the Bible does not make reading his writings simple.

Joachim's three basic works are the *Liber concordiae Novi ac Veteris Testamenti* (*Book of the Harmonies of the Old and New Testaments*); *Expositio in Apocalypsim* (*Exposition of the Apocalypse of John*), and the *Psalterium decem chordarum* (*Psalter of Ten Strings*). Joachim began the first two before 1182 and completed the third in 1184. In his testimonial letter of 1200 all three are mentioned as a unified whole. Joachim later began a commentary on the Gospels, *Tractatus super quottuor Evangelia* (*Treatise on the Four Gospels*). An attempted harmony of the four Gospels, its completion was prevented by his death. Among his shorter writings are a handbook on the Apocalypse (*Enchiridion in Apocalypsim*); a treatise *Against the Jews* (*Contra Iudeos*), dealing with the valuing of the Old Testament; and a biography of Benedict of Nursia (ca. 480–547), which along with other of Joachim's statements attests to his high esteem for the founder of the order.

One interesting work, though its authenticity remains contested even today, we have available is the *Liber figurarum* (*Book of Figures*). In it Joachim's image of history is formed in symbolic signs, perhaps from the hand of his disciples but possibly even by Joachim himself. That this may be the case is not so improbable when we think of the example of Hugh of St. Victor. Illustrating the content of statements by symbols was part of the method of instruction current at the time. In fact, Joachim's theories are adapted in an outstanding way for pictorial presentation.

Compared to systematic works like the *summae* of the scholastics, the preparation of continuous commentaries, as monastic biblical interpreters presented them, is complicated for modern readers. Nowhere, not even in his more systematic work, the *Liber concordiae*, does Joachim develop his views in connected order; one can only find statements in the context of interpreting biblical statements. Nevertheless, Joachim, apart from certain instabilities that go along with differences between the traditions from which he draws, absolutely has an overall theological view. The *Liber concordiae* is certainly the most unified of his works, yet Joachim comes to speak of his favorite themes again and again in other places as well.

If one attends to Joachim's exegetical presuppositions, the first that comes into view is that he, like others, employs the basic methods passed down by tradition. He clearly knows the traditional exegetical methods and, in all, a fivefold sense of Scripture. (He sees the five senses—the literal, historical, moral, allegorical, and anagogical—symbolized by the five apostles who brought the Gospel to the Greeks: Peter, Andrew,

Paul, Barnabas, and John; *Tract.* 289.17–24). But Joachim also knows of a twelvefold unfolding of the sense of Scripture, which unfolds from the three sources of the "letter," the Old and New Testaments, and the writings of the church fathers (*Psalt.* 262d). They result when the five traditional senses are added to the seven other senses, which Joachim considers likewise spiritual but are to be ascribed to the domain of typology rather than allegory. Also basic is the use of typology, an inheritance Joachim took over from the ancient church; the only achievement of his own is based on the consistent execution of this method. His special interest lies in the harmony (*corcordia*) of the two parts of the Bible as well as—in the interpretation of the Apocalypse—in the symmetries of salvation history expressed in this book, often indicated by numbers. In a famous statement (*Exp. Apoc.* 39bc) Joachim once traced the receipt of his insight into this correspondence of the two Testaments and the full interpretation of the Apocalypse back to a direct illumination he received (between 1190–1195). Incidentally, Joachim considers even the two senses of the letter to be spiritual; for him, they would have no significance "unless we believed something spiritual was preproclaimed in them" (*Conc.* 1.12, 48,71a). For, "the historical letter of the two Testaments has been produced by the Holy Spirit in order to signify something by this [means] more than that the letter itself would be known on account of the events (described in it)" (*Conc.* 5.74, fol. 103a). Setting the two literal senses aside, the other ten correspond to the ten strings of the harp, a symbol for the Psalter (ibid.) that Joachim chose as the title of his Psalms book. In the introduction to this work Joachim presents the inner prehistory of the work's origin. According to this account, he had to pass through several stages of frustration and disappointment until, by singing the psalms, he came to a new balance of the soul that culminated in prayer. In addition to the harp (Psalter), the cithara is also of symbolic significance as the second chief-string-instrument.

It is typological understanding that he urges above all on the "pastors" of the church (*Exp.* 4.13.162b). It unfolds directly from the literal sense, but in it he can use all the images typical of allegorical interpretation of Scripture and point to a spiritual understanding. Thus Scripture is for him like a glassy sea, crystal hard, until the Spirit hovers over it (*Exp.* 106a–b). One must penetrate through the hard shell of the letter to the kernel (*Exp.* 39b and elsewhere). Typology, too, is therefore a "spiritual" form of Scriptural interpretation, only its goal is something different.

As his chief work shows by its very title, *Liber concordiae*, the relationship of the Testaments to one another, that is, the comparative aspect on a historical level, is Joachim's decisive starting point. The picture of this that he took over from the vision in Ezek 1:15–21, in which the two Testaments are inset within each other like a wheel (*Conc.* 2.1.1, 61,209ff.), has become famous. From this approach, then, one can speak of typology in the traditional sense. But this is only the one level. A second is immediately added to it: of great importance to Joachim is the viewpoint that the history of the church and the events occurring in it stand in a close factual relationship to events and figures in Scripture. The point of departure for this is the Pauline view of the church as the "body of Christ" (Rom 12; 1 Cor 12). From it Joachim concludes that the events and persons of church history continue and complete the history of Christ contained in Scripture: "These things [the events in the Old Testament] are all fulfilled in Christ and must still be fulfilled more completely in the body of Christ," he writes, for example, on Rev 3:7 (*Exp.* 5.1, fol. 89c). The two realms of the Old and New Testament are therefore to be supplemented by a third, the church. Joachim carried this principle out into individual details; he tries to prove "that the New, which corresponds to the Old, is fulfilled partly in kings, partly in the Roman bishops, but above all in the whole body of Christ, especially when something full of mystery [*mysticum*] occurs, because we believers are all one body in Christ" (*Conc.* 2.1.2, 14b).

Developed from this, as yet another level, is the division of salvation history into periods. This approach is in principle traditional. Augustine's division of the world into four ages became classical. Joachim takes it over but adds to the four ages of the world a fifth: (1) "before the law" (*ante legem*); (2) "under the law" (*sub lege*); (3) "under the gospel" (*sub evangelio* or *sub littera evangelii* and other terms); (4) "under spiritual understanding" (*sub spirituali intellectu*); and (5) "in the fatherland" (*in patria*), that is, "in the revealed vision of God" (*in manifesta visione Dei*). But if one considers that the first two ages are usually combined under the roof of the Old Testament and the fifth lies beyond time—as Joachim himself realizes (it is called an age figuratively, not literally; *Exp.* 5c)—actually only the three traditional epochs emerge. This without question forms the basic framework for the division of history into ages, as Joachim formulates them in the *Liber concordiae*: "Three stages of the world suggest the mysteries of divine Scripture to us: the first, when we were under the law; the second, when we were under grace; the third, which we expect as imminent, under more abundant grace" (*Conc.* 5.84, 112b).

But one does not yet do justice to the distinctiveness of Joachimite thinking with the mere division of history into periods. Distinctive for him is the symbolic understanding of certain biblical persons in biblical history. Of course, not even this understanding is altogether new, for a division of salvation history in terms of the persons who have introduced a respective period, for example, Adam and Christ (Rom 5:12–21; see also Hagar and Sarah, Gal 4:21–31), is already found in Paul. But the system is developed far more extensively in Joachim. The harmony of the two Testaments is based essentially on persons. We designate, he writes,

> as harmony in the strict sense the similarity of equal proportions of the Old and New Testaments. I say *equal* with respect to the number, not the worth, since person and person, class and class, war and war look upon one another mutually with their faces: like Abraham and Zechariah, Sarah and Elizabeth, Isaac, and John the Baptist, Jacob and the man Jesus, the twelve patriarchs and the apostles of the same number, and similar things, so that every (event), wherever it occurs, is certainly to be interpreted not according to allegorical understanding but with respect to the harmony of the two Testaments. For *one* really spiritual understanding emerges from the two. (*Conc.* 2.1.2, 62,1–8).

Moreover, to Joachim, figures for fixing and illustrating his ideas are evidently unavoidable: "But we can show this better if we choose figures as examples" (*Exp.* 15c).

Typology as a comparison of the two Testaments and the working out of their correspondences is certainly Joachim's presupposition from the history of interpretation, but he goes much further in relating it to all three periods of salvation history. "The harmony of which we have spoken is to be ascribed to the three classes of the elect [laity, priests, and monks] and the three stages of the world" (*Conc.* 2.1.27, 113,11–12). Joachim can carry the typologizing of persons from the Two testaments a whole distance further. In *Conc.* 5 (and *Psalt.* 265a), he sets out from the contrast of Hagar and Sarah as the two wives of Abraham in Gal 4:21–31 and distinguishes seven levels of typological understanding. Number symbolism plays a large role everywhere in his work, which dovetails not least with his affinity for apocalyptic. The three persons Abraham, Hagar, and Sarah can symbolize at the seven levels different stretches of salvation history, from the Old Testament groups and institutions to the historical synagogue and church and their officials and on to the heavenly Jerusalem of the end time and its inhabitants. But in it nothing more is left of the original intent of Paul, who had a christological goal in mind. Still, the schema is traditional in its basic approach.

But there is overlap between the one and the other, as the continuation of the above-quoted text expresses: "we believe in the one living God, that one is the Father to which the Old Testament spiritually refers, that one is the Son to which the New Testament spiritually refers, that one is the Spirit, who proceeds from the two: to whom the mystical understanding that proceeds, as stated, from both spiritually refers" (*Conc.* 2.1.2, 62,10–13). Historians of dogma will note that here Joachim adopts the teaching of the Western church, which in its dispute with the Eastern church had maintained in the *filioque* the procession of the Holy Spirit from the Father *and* the Son.

But the Trinitarian schema now leads Joachim one decisive step beyond what was customary in the employment of salvation history: from the relationship of the two Testaments and the periods of salvation history correlated to them comes a sequence of three periods. In so doing, the two of the former two (the periods of the Old and New Testaments) draw close to one another, while the third faces them antithetically: "Finally, just as the letter of the earlier Testaments preceded in time what is called the time of grace, so the letter of the New Testament precedes the time that will offer a greater grace, since it will give us grace upon grace [see John 1:16]" (*Tract.* 191.23–26) Thus even the New Testament becomes a "letter" (so also *Tract.* 21.26–22.2); the period marked by Christ becomes a transitional time for the time of the Spirit still to follow as that of greater worth! The Commission of Anagni put at the top of its critique as Joachim's first error precisely this, "that the 'eternal gospel' that is identical to Joachim's teaching supersedes the teaching of Christ and therefore the Old and New Testament." The contrast between letter and spirit is certainly Pauline (see esp. 2 Cor 3:6), but a conclusion is drawn from it that would have never come to Paul's mind: that the Holy Scripture and the Spirit are antitheses! But precisely this is the message of spiritualists of every age.

In carrying out this schema, Joachim again reaches back to the tradition of interpretation passed down to him when in book 5 of the *Liber concordiae* he divides the stages of history in terms of the seven days of the world's creation in Gen 1 (*hexaemeron*). Accordingly, the first interpretation (*Conc.* 5.3–9) offers an explanation of the seven days of creation as seven stages of Old Testament history from Adam to Christ; the second (5.10–19) as seven stages beginning still within the Old Testament but inclusive of the New Testament and earlier church history, from the Jewish King Azariah up to the present; the third (5.20–23, not carried to the end) as the "seven future ages" from the present to the end of the world; the fourth (5.24–40) as the seven ages of history as a whole, the sixth period of which begins with Christ but ends in the near future in order to usher in the seventh age, which will extend to the end of the world. Important in all this is the idea of development, expressed in the supersession of the various ages and the estates belonging to them. It extends from the figures of the Old Testament through the New Testament to the institutions and offices of the church (the bishops under the Roman bishop as their head and the priests) and then to the figures of the end time. In this process, the offices of each earlier period lose their significance in the period that follows.

The combination of various methods of calculation, which is again reflective of Joachim's preference for number speculation, certainly does not make an overview easy, yet one fact catches the eye: the periods of salvation history do not simply follow one other but overlap. While in the traditional model the period correlated with the first day of creation encompasses the Old Testament up to Christ, Joachim has the second period begin in the middle of the Old Testament with Azariah and extend up to the present. By this means two things are effected. First, for Joachim, the present becomes a turning point of great significance. The turn to a new age fundamentally different from the one before is expected in the near future. On the other hand, the shift of the beginning of Joachim's present age back to the Old Testament decisively reduces the role of Jesus Christ within salvation history, as we will see. Beyond this, however, the third age, the age of the Spirit, is also not only pure future: when Joachim can begin one of his schemas of division with Benedict of Nursia, the founder of the order, it already draws in the monastic form of life into his present.

The schema of history is found in other places even more developed and complicated. The table (*Lib. fig.* 18) in which several levels overlap is instructive, for example. According to the seven-day schema, the first five days extend from Adam to John the Baptist, who as the forerunner of Jesus concludes the Old Testament period and at the same time begins the new, sixth period, which lasts to the present day. According to Joachim (or his students), then, the seventh age characterized by the Holy Spirit breaks into the present. Yet another schema is the calculation of generations, which divides the periods in terms of ten generations (each at thirty years). Here the first period (*tempus*) extends from the beginning to Azariah, the second to Zerubbabel, the third to Christ, and then the following four to the present. Yet another schema is that already known to us in terms of the three *status* (stages), the third of which is identified with the age of the Holy Spirit. To this schema, however, yet another one is correlated, calculating the ten-generation schema differently. It produces seven *secula* (periods) from Adam to the priest Zechariah, the father of John the Baptist (Luke 1:55–66). He introduces one period, which—although identical to the second stage—is also equated with the seventh age (*septima etas*). But this is already characterized as the time of the coming of the Holy Spirit.

This multilayered schema of time (table 19 presents yet another, more complicated construct) suggests the multiplicity with which Joachim can periodicize salvation history by various numerical schemata. Number symbolism as such is likewise an ancient legacy. Hence the discrepancies between individual calculations as such should not be taken too seriously. What is certainly most important is the overarching schema of three ages, and in this schema the most decisive age is the third, the age of the Spirit, which is not identified with the present in any case, but still expected as at hand. It is to replace the present, which according to Joachim does not bring the spiritual salvation he hoped for anyway.

On the other hand, the transitions between the ages, which at first glance seem strange, are not chosen without consideration. The uninitiated reader will be surprised that one important age is begun precisely with King Azariah, about whom 2 Kgs 15:1–7 reports above all an illness of the skin. The explanation seems to lie in the fact that introduced within his domain is the name of the prophet Isaiah, who according to Isa 1:1 began his activity under this king. But Isaiah was long considered from the early church on the most important Old Testament prophet, whose proclamation directly related to Christ. This is confirmed by the interpretation of the trumpet in Rev 1:10, which Joachim viewed as an image of the harmony of the Old and New Testaments. It is divided in the middle by a knot, which according to Joachim divided the period of "Azariah and Isaiah up to John the Baptist" as the second age of the world (*Exp.* 40d). Yet further consideration must be given to Zechariah, the father of John the Baptist. Why does a new, evidently decisive, age begin with him?

Zechariah himself is not actually the decisive figure, but (as the citation above shows) his son John the Baptist. This becomes especially clear in Joachim's treatment of this person in the *Tractatus*. John the Baptist is one of the leading figures in characterizations of the epochs of salvation history. The *child* John characterizes the beginning of a new period, and indeed the time of the church, which still eats milk rather than solid food (see 1 Cor 3:2). This coincides with the interpretation of the infancy story in Luke, in which John plays such a large role alongside Jesus (Luke 1:5–25, 39–45, 57–66). In his commentary on the Gospels, Joachim treats the infancy history in Luke and Matthew at special length. Joachim also takes up the person of John the Baptist as a symbol. John is, on the one hand, as an adult, still an embodiment of the old order. On the other hand, his figure as a child points in advance prophetically to the growth of the church, extending from John up to the present. Incidentally, these statements appear in the famous passage (*Tract.* 6.29–7.18) in which Joachim characterizes the four Fospels and correlates four ages to them. Matthew belongs to the Old Testament, Luke to church history, Mark, who deals with the preaching of Jesus in his maturity, designates spiritual teaching (according to 1 Cor 2:6), and John the "inexpressible wisdom" that is to be expected with the coming of Elijah in the time of the Spirit. Here Joachim quotes 1 Cor 13:12a: "We see now through a mirror"; the chapter itself, 1 Cor 13, is one of his favorite texts. But he can also relate the multiplicity of the Gospels to the four animals in the vision of Ezekiel's calling (Ezek 1:5–14). This gives rise to the familiar symbols for the four Evangelists—man, lion, ox, and eagle—and from this in turn the four ages (*Tract.* 143.22–144.9; see also *Lib. fig.*, pl. XV). Further, the baptism of John the Baptist characterizes the present age of the church, "where we are"; the baptism of Jesus, on the other hand, the future, "where we will be" (*Tract.* 114.10–12). But the future is already breaking into the present: "The closer this world approaches the end, what John designates becomes all the more disdainful, and what is designated by Jesus, all the more clear and sublime" (*Tract.* 272.1–3)

It is striking that Jesus Christ is by no means the central figure. In the passage cited, the childhood of Jesus and his growth to maturity are mentioned, but the time of the childhood of Jesus is actually a preview of the expectation of the *Spirit*: his figure plays no role in the division of the times. As a man, Jesus is a "type of the Holy Spirit" (*Exp.* 23c)! The childhood and maturity of Jesus are symbolic of the maturation of the church from "milk" to "solid food." The "the bringing forth of the fruits" on the part of the church, however, is not counted from Jesus but from Zechariah (e.g., *Conc.* 4.2.1, 405,13–14), that is, actually from John the Baptist: "And since in the first stage of the world, which ... began with Moses but after the circumcision of Abraham, God the Father showed his glory, in the second stage, which began with John the Baptist, the Son made himself known to the Christian people, the completion of which coincides with the coming of Elijah" (*Tract.* 23.21–24.1) The small role Joachim ascribes to Jesus can also be seen in his treatment of the Paraclete (comforter) in the Gospel of John. In John the Paraclete remains strictly related to Jesus, representing him during his absence (John 16:14). But Joachim—who, by the way, never refers to the name Paraclete but only to the "spirit of truth"— cites John 16:13a (*Tract.* 9.19–20; 177.17–18; 199.3–4; 292.7–8) almost exclusively and relates the Spirit that Jesus brings either to a spiritual in contrast to a "fleshly" understanding of Scripture or to the fullness of the Spirit of the end time (on this, see also *Psalt.* 259d–260a).

Here the role of Elijah is especially emphasized: "Certainly the third stage, which begins with Elijah, relates to the Holy Spirit, because he will show in him his glory as the Father in the first, and the Son in the second" (*Tract.* 24.7–10) Joachim then explains that, although the Spirit will be poured out after the resurrection of Jesus "in accord with the literal sense" (Acts 2), he will come "in his fullness" only when he will be shown by the conversion of even the Jews (Rom 11:26, 31) by Elijah and his associates.

The return of Elijah is for Joachim, in connection with Matt 17:11 (but the verse is torn from its context, see v. 12!), the bringer of the new age of the Spirit: "As he once rebuilt with new stones the altar that had been torn down (1 Kgs 18:32), so the Holy Spirit, which he himself designates, ... will make the crooked ways straight and the uneven ways smooth" (*Tract.* 291.7–11). Elijah's sacrifice on Mount Carmel—we recall that Joachim himself was once there and possibly had his decisive spiritual experience there—is for him a symbolic event; at the beginning of his *Liber concordiae*, Joachim sees himself in the role of Elijah: "With Elijah we have to build an altar from the earth itself. The earth beneath is to be so arranged that water can be poured out, in that we expect fire from heaven that will consume the earth and water since—in that we expect a spiritual understanding that ... consumes this earthly superficiality of the letter, which is of the earth and speaks of terrestrial things" (*Conc.* 2.1.1, 60,198–202). For this new age Joachim expects (in keeping with 1 Cor 13:9–10) people to set aside their "zeal for the principles of that science that corresponds to patchwork"! They will instead "direct the eyes of the heart to that fullness of the Spirit that he (Jesus) promised in the Holy Spirit when he said, 'When the Spirit of truth comes, he will teach you all truth'" (John 16:13; *Tract.* 292.5–7). Here the spiritualist ideal at the core of Joachim's apocalyptic hope comes into view. He also expects for this imminent end time a fundamental transformation of humanity; those transformed by the Spirit will be given a "spiritual comprehension" (*Exp. Apoc.* 2.8, 64a). He shares with the apocalypticists the intense expectation of the imminence of the end time: he writes his *Liber concordiae* "because the predetermined time is there ... when anyone who is from the house of Lot hastens to get away from the borders of Sodom, when anyone who is of the family of Noah should join those who are saved in the ark" (*Conc.* 5.119, fol. 135b).

But for Joachim quite concrete hopes for the future of the church are tied up with this end time, "since that great Elijah, who will come in order to complete all things will introduce the monastic and eremitic way of religious life. And just as the literal sense of the earlier Testament corresponds in particular to the lay estate and the letter of the New to the clerical estate, so spiritual comprehension corresponds to the estate of the monks" (*Tract.* 195.18–22). He can also speak of the first period as that of the "marital estate," the second as the "clerical estate," and the third as the "spiritual estate" to which again the monks ("who are really monks") belong (*Tract.* 84.6). Joachim even includes the figure of Simeon (Luke 2:25–28, 29–32) into this exegesis by a similar interpretation: the young John the Baptist represents the clergy, and the young Jesus "signifies the gift of the Spirit with the estate of the monks (*Tract.* 86.3–4). On closer examination, then, his picture of the future is inspired completely by the ideals of his estate, of monasticism, that is, his eremitic variation of it. His description of his *ordo conventualium* (the estate of those belonging to monasticism) as "those who live simply, in solitude" (*Tract.* 85.3–4) is in agreement with this. What is visible here is not yet the later, open monastic revolt but indeed an inward turning away from the established church. This church as such is not repudiated—hence Joachim could constantly attest to his loyalty to each reigning pope. But it is a transitional appearance for the world epoch that is momentarily still continuing. But corresponding to this expectation is yet another, somewhat different, division of periods. In it, as it appears in the *Liber concordiae*, the age of the Spirit as the third period of salvation history begins with Benedict of Nursia and his "spiritual people," including the founder of the order to which Joachim belonged (in the variety of Cistercians and the order he founded; *Conc.* 2.1.4, 67,26–28; 4.2.1, 405,14–15; 5.21, fol. 70d). Actually, the role of Benedict—to whom, as we saw, Joachim dedicated a *Vita* of his own—was important for him.

From this monastic-stamped future, then, also comes Joachim's hope, which became famous, for a "spiritual church" (*ecclesia spiritalis*; *Tract.* 86.15) or even a "spiritual order" (*ordo spiritalis*; 87.27 and elsewhere), which would characterize the expected end time. A significant role is played in this regard by Dan 7:27, which tells that at the end time dominion is to be handed over to the "people of the saints of the Most High" (see, e.g., *Tract.* 25.9–11; 35.17–18). In like manner, Rev 14:6 is adduced in support of Joachimite talk of the "eternal gospel." Or he speaks of the "gospel of the Spirit" (*Tract.* 304.24–25). Though in this age not all of the external forms of the church will disintegrate completely, their structure, typified by monastic communal living, will no longer be comparable to the official, clerical church. "The clerical estate will cease at the end of the forty-second generation after the Lord's incarnation" (*Conc.* 4.2.2; 6–8 and elsewhere). In the age of the Spirit, those inspired by the Spirit (*spiritales*, *Conc.* 5.49, fol. 84c and elsewhere) will constitute the church. The term "spiritual men" (*homines spiritales*) is one of Joachim's core concepts; for it, 1 Cor 2:15 and Ps 82:6 are frequently quoted as prooftexts. Joachim can also call this the "little ones of the beginning of the Spirit, over which the Spirit of God is to be poured out" (according to Joel 2:28) or the "young ones" (*pueri*), who will have spiritual children (*Tract.* 90.26–91.1, 13). "Since in the first stage of the world the estate of the laity is glorified, in the second the estate of the clergy…, it is necessary that the estate of the monks is glorified, especially from Elijah's coming on" (*Tract.* 155.6–9). Typically enough, however, the institution of the papacy is to endure. Joachim's loyalty to the holy chair, as already mentioned, may express itself in this way. Perhaps, too, it is only caution when Joachim declares: "What be far off, the chair of Peter, which is the throne of Christ, will not therefore cease, … but transformed into higher glory it will endure into eternity" (*Conc.* 6.65, fol. 95d). Also to be mentioned here would be the expectation, later famous, of an "angelic pope" (*papa angelicus*), which had one of its starting points in Joachim because he once interpreted the angel of the Apocalypse (Rev 7:2) as referring to Christ *and* his vicar, the Roman pope (*Exp.* 120d).

The cessation of the old order will also mean—though Joachim does not express it very clearly—the end of the sacraments. At one point he speaks of the 1,260 years (= forty-two generations) "during which the sacraments of the New Testament continue" (*Conc.* 5.89, fol. 118a). The Commission of Anagni collected yet other of Joachim's statements along much the same lines. Joachim expected an age of the Spirit in which the truth will be known no longer in part but directly (quoting 1 Cor 13). When the Spirit "will teach all truth" to believers (John 16:13), the material signs, the sacraments, will no longer be necessary, for they will have done their service (*Conc.* 5.84, fol. 112a–c). Later readers of Joachim have again and again drawn upon his expectation of the beginning of a revolutionary new epoch, including revolutionaries up to our day, who, however, no longer able to understand Joachim's truly spiritual aims, have turned them inside out into their opposite. It was not the world but the forms of spiritual life that were to be changed, and the goal was not power but a meditative life with Scripture.

Thus Joachim holds a special place in the history of interpretation, but his figure is typical of a stance toward Scripture for which there were to be numerous other examples in later church history. Typical of this stance is an antithesis of the "letter" and the "spirit": the spirit is every-thing; the letter, nothing. Thus, as Joachim shows us, the external reality of the church is largely insignificant. It will disappear, and the priesthood and sacraments with it, in the period of the Spirit. Joachim's viewpoint is actually only a continuation of a tradition built into the monastic ideal of turning away from the world since the ancient church. Hence monasti-cism is the only institution he expects to survive at the end time. In this respect, however, he is no revolutionary but the representative of a specific conservatism. Later spiritualists have drawn from his descriptions of the end time conclusions he himself had definitely never intended.

3.7. The Bible and Aristotle: Thomas Aquinas

We take a further step into the thirteenth century, which in the history of theology can be called the period of high scholasticism, because in this era the enterprise of scholastic science had fully developed itself organi-zationally and also because the intellectual efforts to develop the content of theology with the help of philosophical categories and contents now reached its highest flowering, beyond which further development has never gone.

The situation in this epoch can be depicted in an exemplary way in the life and work of someone whose intellectual achievement surpassed all his contemporaries: Thomas Aquinas.

The exact birth year of Thomas is unknown; 1224 or 1225 are the most probable. Thomas came from a noble family of Lombard descent; he was born the son of the knight Landulf and his wife Donna Theodora at their ancestral castle Roccasecca in the kingdom of Sicily, midway between Rome and Naples. Nearby the castle ruins today is the little city of Aquino, from which Thomas received his name of origin. He was the youngest of numerous siblings, and in keeping with the custom of the times his parents placed him at the age of five as an oblate in the Benedic-tine monastery of Monte Cassino. They presumably hoped that, because of his lineage, he would rise to become the abbot of this distinguished monastery. But circumstances at the time were not favorable for the real-ization of this plan. The kingdom of Sicily was ruled (from 1198 to 1250) by Emperor Friedrich II, the Hohenstaufen, who periodically came into conflict with the pope over supremacy in Italy. In 1239 the conflict broke out again; the emperor's troops invaded the church's territories and drove away from the monastery of Monte Cassino all the monks who were not born in Friedrich's empire. Since only eight were able to remain, not even the oblates could be cared for any longer. At the abbot's advice, Landulf sent his son to Naples, the provincial capital, where in 1224 Friedrich II had founded a *studium generalis*, as it was then called, that is, a university, for study of the seven liberal arts in competition with the papal university of Bologna. Naples was, under Friedrich, a center of open-mindedness; especially outstanding were the emperor's relations toward the Oriental region, Byzantine Greek culture, and Islam in particular. He adorned his court with scholars who could transmit Arabic culture and the Islamic lifestyle. Aristotle in particular, by means of his Arabic interpreters such as Ibn Sinâ (Avicenna, 980–1037) and above all Ibn Rusd (Averroes, 1126–1198), who in Toledo had restored the unfalsified Aristotle to honor and translated his works into Latin, was once again and very forcefully transmitted to the West. Along with Arabic scholars, the philosopher Peter of Hibernia (Ireland) especially taught the original Aristotle. Hence in Naples young Thomas was able to learn Aristotelianism at first hand.

Naples was determinative for Thomas's career in still another respect: there he met the Dominicans. The order, then still young—founded in Toulouse by the Spaniard Dominicus Guzman (ca. 1175–1221) and confirmed in 1216 by Pope Honorius III—was, next to the Franciscans, one of the two mendicant orders that brought a new upswing into the monastic movement. The renewed ideal of apostolic poverty was one of the driving forces behind this. Its founder had set as the chief task preaching (first against the Albigensians or Cathars, a gnostic sect in south France), previously an exclusive but often neglected duty of the bishops (*ordo praedicatorum* = O.P.) Soon teaching was added, in connection with the newly founded universities. Convents were founded in Paris, Toulouse, and Naples as well as other places; the number of members of the order grew considerably. Thomas was so influenced by the Dominican way of life that he joined the order shortly after his father's death, presumably in 1255.

Since the Dominicans were in a quandary about what to do with the member from such a powerful noble family of the land in their convent, they sent him on a journey to Bologna with the order's General Johannes von Wildeshausen, then present in Naples. In fact, his family was evidently not in complete agreement with Thomas's decision, because the group was attacked along the way and Thomas was abducted by force to the ancestral castle Roccasecca, where he was held for over a year. He could not be dissuaded from his decision, however. When he was finally allowed to leave, his order sent him to Paris. There, little by little since the beginning of the century, a university had been constituted from the cathedral schools and teaching institutions on the left bank of the Seine—the grant of autonomy by statutes of Pope Innocent III in 1215 was a decisive step. Four faculties had been formed: theology; liberal arts; canon law; and medicine. In Paris, Thomas was apparently a student of Albert the Great (ca. 1193–1280), who taught (after 1246 as master of theology) at the Dominican study house there. By the statutes of 1231, the mendicant orders, including the Dominicans, had two teaching chairs within the theological faculty of the university. Thomas went with Albert to Cologne from 1248 to 1252. There Albert, recognizing Thomas's exceptional talent, made him his co-worker. As Bachelor of Bible (*Baccalaureus biblicus*) he had the task of the cursory overview reading of the Bible. This, as we learned in an earlier chapter, was done by brief glosses. He reached the second level of a scholar's career upon his return to Paris in 1252 as a Bachelor of the Sentences (*Baccalaureus sententarius*); as such, he read the sentences of Peter Lombard (see above). Not until 1256, after papal intervention, was he authorized for full teaching activity as a master. With this new office he turned again to the Bible, because the official duty of a theological master was to interpret the Holy Scriptures, but now on a new, deeper foundation.

In 1259, after an extremely successful teaching career in Paris, his order called Thomas back to Italy. He was active most of the time at the papal court, which in these years moved between various places in the environs of Rome, first Orvieto, then Viterbo, for a time as director of the Dominican study house in Rome (1265–1267). These were peaceful years during which Thomas was able to begin the most important of his works.

Then, however, the order saw it necessary to send him to Paris again. A fierce dispute over the role of Aristotle in theology had broken out there. Albert the Great and Thomas had gotten it accepted that Dominicans pursuing the study of theology study should make use of Aristotle's system as an aid in theological thinking. In Paris, however, after 1265 in the faculty of liberal arts, the philosopher Siger of Brabant (ca 1240?–1284) taught a radical Aristotelianism that affirmed the absolute authority of reason in its own realm—and therefore so, too, for example, the eternity of the world, an impersonal God (the "unmoved mover"), and a universal spirit (*nous*) instead of the individual spirit of each particular person. The postulate of double truth (truth of faith and truth of thinking) seemed near at hand. For this reason, the conservative party, which adhered without reservation to a plan of salvation history, considered Aristotelianism a basic enemy of theology. In Paris, its advocate was the Franciscan master Bonaventure (see below), who fought, for a time with great success, to keep Aristotle out of theological study entirely. The centrist position of the Dominican theologians, who wanted to draw Aristotle into the service of Scripture, had a difficult time of it.

At first the conflict went rather unfavorably for the Dominicans in that Bonaventure was successful; in 1272, Thomas was recalled to Naples, where during his final years of life he once again taught in his home study house. On 6 December 1273 he suffered a breakdown. Its causes are unclear. At any rate, he wrote no more from that time on. It is reported that he said that everything he had previously written was like straw to him. Shortly thereafter Pope Gregory X (1271–1276) ordered him to the ecumenical council he had called in Lyon. Thomas died while journeying there, on 7 March 1274.

Despite his quite short lifetime—Thomas was not yet fifty years old when he died—he left behind an uncommonly large body of work. It includes above all two *summae* (i.e., comprehensive accounts of Christian doctrine), *Summa contra Gentiles* (*Summa against the Heathens*) and, despite its enormous scope, the still incomplete *Summa theologiae*, Thomas's major theological work, as well as a commentary on the sentences (*Quaestiones disputatatae*; *Disputations on Questions of Hearers and with Other Masters*), commentaries on the works of Aristotle, and biblical commentaries. What an enormous workload Thomas managed from time to time can be judged by the report of his second sojourn in Paris, which says he dictated three different texts to three secretaries at the same time. The general uncertainty with respect to dating his individual works extends to his biblical commentaries as well; as a whole, they embrace his entire work career.

His biblical commentaries each differ in character according to the circumstances of their origin. His interpretations of each individual biblical work during his activities as a master at various places and over the series of periods of activity were originally presented orally in lecture and written down by his students or a copyist commissioned to do so. These lectures were interrupted by regular disputations and on occasion also by extraordinary, specifically arranged disputations on one theme or another at the request of other masters (*quodlibet*). In addition, on each such occasion there was preaching on the interpreted text. The copied lectures (*reportatio* or *lectura*) were later reviewed in part by Thomas himself and corrected. But there were also works the author composed in writing himself (*ordinatio*). The two *summae* are works of this sort. Most of the biblical commentaries are (partly corrected) lecture manuscripts. There are commentaries by Thomas on Isaiah, Jeremiah, Kings, Psalms, Job, Matthew, John, and the Epistles of Paul. A commentary on the Song of Songs, which Thomas is said to have dictated on his deathbed, is evidently not preserved. A gloss of the four Gospels with quotations from the church fathers (*Catena aurea*; *The Golden Chain*, officially *Glossa continua*, the continuous gloss) still follows the older model (see above pp. 135–39). It is distinguished, however, by the fact that Thomas includes Greek church fathers in his excerpts, although in Latin translation, and that he deals not only with Matthew but the four Gospels together.

We can form an adequate picture of the role of the Bible in the theology of Thomas only by keeping in view the above-described development of his work and its institutional presuppositions. Although the doctrinal works, the great *summae*, would seem to be at the center of his literary works in terms of scope and importance, they are nevertheless only a by-product of the master's teaching tasks. The official title of the master himself—master (or doctor) of *sacra pagina* (teacher of Holy Scripture)—shows the central role of biblical interpretation. The chief task of Thomas in the program of studies was, as ever, interpretation of the Bible. The morning hours of every workday, hence the best working times, were devoted to exegetical lectures. Disputation was secondary to it, and if the *summae* represent desk-written work—a working out of theological themes from systematic viewpoints— in terms of their origin and content, they still stood in connection with biblical interpretation. To recognize this is of central significance for understanding their contents. Even the *summa* was designed for nothing other than illuming the sense of biblical statements. This connection is still outwardly visible inasmuch as three supportive exegetical sections are taken up into the structure of the *summa*: (1) on creation (1.44–199); (2) on the law (2.1.90–108); and (3) on the person and work of Jesus (2.3.1–59). These are not add-ons. They represent a salvation-historical viewpoint that tracks the Bible. In addition, they point to the fact that, structurally, the systematics of the *summa* does not follow dogmatic principles alone but still takes the Bible as its starting point.

In the section on the law, Thomas distinguishes, on the one hand, the *lex aeterna*, the "eternal law," which is nothing other than the eternal wisdom of God with which he rules the world (2.1.93), the natural law (2.1.94), and the "human law" (positive law, 2.1.95–97) and, on the other hand, the biblical laws. He deals with the first of these at length. In so doing, characteristic is the distinction between the "old" and the "new" law. The old law is the law contained in the Old Testament (2.1.98–105). It applies to everyone, insofar as it corresponds to the natural (moral) law. A longer section (2.1.100) is then dedicated to the Decalogue, the laws of which are shown to correspond with the moral prescriptions of the natural law. To the extent the Old Testament laws are moral, they were even justifying laws, "that is, inasmuch as they prepared people for the justifying grace of Christ that they also proclaim" (2.1.100.12). Insofar as it is ceremonial law, the old law is not applicable universally but only to Jews. But it likewise had the quality of proclaiming Christ figuratively (2.1.102.2). To this extent, then, it was of salvific significance for the Jews!

Thomas next (2.1.106–108) deals with "the evangelical law, which is called the new law" (2.1.106, prooem.). To the new law applies, among other things, Gal 5:6; it is "the faith that works through love" (2.1.108.2.1). Then its contents are named: the sacraments (2.1.108.2), generally "in external things ... by which we are led into grace," as well as the moral prescriptions already available in the old law. To this applies in particular "the discourse that the Lord gave on the mountain [the Sermon on the Mount], [which] contains all the information about Christian life. In it the internal motivations of humans are ordered" (2.1.108.3). Thomas had earlier remarked that the commandments of the new law, being inward acts, are more difficult to keep than those of the old (2.1.107.4), but this is compensated for by stating that the new law is a law infused [in us] inwardly (2.1.106.1), or "the grace of the Holy Spirit itself as given inwardly" (2.1.106.2). From this emerges the answer to the question whether the new law justifies: as it is a grace infused in us inwardly, yes, but not as external command. The whole is a not unsuccessful attempt to delineate the theological content of biblical statements by scholastic distinctions.

According to many of his statements, Thomas clearly has no doubt that the Bible is the sole source of truth. This shows itself even at the beginning of his *summa*, where to the question—self-posed but surely raised by his students earlier—whether there must be another teaching in addition to the philosophical disciplines, he answers "that it was necessary for the salvation of humanity that there be a teaching according to divine revelation in addition to the philosophical disciplines that are undertaken by human reason" (1.1.2 sed contra). But according to Thomas it was also necessary "that people would be instructed by divine revelation about things that can be investigated by human reason" (ibid.). "Therefore nothing prevents dealing with the same things that the philosophical disciplines deal with in terms of the light of human reason by another science that deals with them in terms of what is known by the light of divine revelation." For, "the truth of God, when it is reasoned by reason, would be known by only few, and over a long time, and mixed with errors, where indeed the entire salvation of humanity depends on knowledge of his truth" (1.1.1) Here

Thomas can even speak of two theologies: "From there the theology that refers to holy (scriptural) doctrine is to be distinguished in kind from the other theology that is posited as part of philosophy" (1.1.2 ad 2). But what is meant by this are not two sciences but merely two aspects of the same philosophy. Double truth is simply incompatible with the standpoint of Thomas, who wants instead to place philosophy in the service of theology. But theology is *scriptural* theology; this becomes altogether clear in other statements. When in the articles that follow Thomas speaks of *sacra doctrina* (sacred doctrine), this term alternates with *sacra Scriptura* (Holy Scripture) and is obviously synonymous with it. Indeed, in one passage we find the explicit formulation *sacra scriptura seu doctrina*, "Holy Scripture, namely, doctrine" (1.1.2 ad 2) But this does not mean that Thomas equates Scripture and doctrine. Holy Scripture remains the object of faith; theological reflection always occurs on a foundation derived from it. It represents the attempt by means of reason, illumined by faith, to ground the truth contained in Scripture. One can also recognize that *sacra doctrina*, theological doctrine, remains closely related to Scripture in that for Thomas there are no division of theology into different fields: it is exclusively *biblical* theology.

At the same time, lacking in Thomas are statements that are characteristic of modern Roman Catholic theology. That Scripture is for him the *exclusive* source of truth is to be distinguished from the coexistence of Scripture and tradition, the prevailing doctrine especially after the Council of Trent (1545–1563), but the generally shared view in his day. This, of course, does not prevent Thomas, like his predecessors, from very frequently adducing quotations from the fathers, exclusively in the *catena aurea*, in support of his arguments in his other writings. They do not have the same authority as the Scripture, but their interpretations are completely valid, for the truth of Scripture is transmitted in the living tradition.

Another very influential doctrine of Roman as well as Protestant orthodoxy, that of the inspiration of Scripture, is not to be found in Thomas in this form (except for the quotation of 2 Tim 3:16 in 1.1.1). When he on occasion writes that "the Holy Spirit is the original author of the Holy Scripture" (*Quodl.* 7.6.14 ad 5), this is, given his Trinitarian starting point, equivalent to the statement "but the author of Holy Scripture is God." (*Summa theol.* 1.1.10). In addition to the divine original author (*auctor principalis*), there is also the human secondary author (*auctor secundarius*, viz., *instrumentalis;* see *Quodl.* 7.6.14 ad 5.).

There is an interesting section on prophecy in the *Summa* (2.2.171–174; see also *Ver.* 12). It is revealing for the entire understanding of the

Bible for Thomas. First, the intellectual approach here is characteristic. In article 1 Thomas answers the question "whether prophecy relates to knowledge" with a positive emphasis: "I answer, one must say that prophecy first and mainly consists in knowledge" (2.2.171.1). Revelation is "everything that ... cannot be recognized by humans apart from divine revelation" (2.2.171.3 ad 2). Prophets are people "who know things that are far beyond human knowledge" (2.2.171.1). Natural reason, of course, does not lead to this in the case of prophets, for their knowledge is of divine things, "namely, things beyond human knowledge revealed by God that cannot be confirmed by human reason, which they surpass" (2.2.171.1). There an "elevation by the Spirit" is necessary for prophecy, a form of inspiration, for which Thomas appeals to Ezra 2:1–2 and Job 32:8 (2.2.171.1 ad 4). Thomas can also call it a "divine light" that is characteristic of prophecy (2.2.171.3 ad 3) In other articles it is shown that prophecy is not a *habitus* but the result of each particular momentary experience (2.2.171.2) and—here Thomas is a child of his time—that it relates to the revelation of future things (2.2.171.4). One entire *quaestio* (173) is devoted to the problems of prophetic knowledge. Important here is the statement that the prophets have not seen the being of God himself but only images of it (2.2.173.1). Thomas also makes it clear that "the prophets did not know absolutely everything that the Holy Spirit intended (to reveal) in their visions or words or even deeds" (2.2.173.4). To this one should also compare the remark that "the prophecy is somewhat incomplete/imperfect in its sort of divine revelation" (2.2.171.4 ad 3). Thomas does not see all Scripture on one level but understands in it the witness to a historical revelation so that above all there is a qualitative distinction between the Old and the New Testament. About this: "The fullness of divine revelation will be available in the fatherland (the eternal home)" (ibid.) It has to do with a goal to which the church and each Christian are still on the way.

But there is already a vast difference between patriarchs and prophets, on the one side, and the apostles, on the other, with respect to the advance of revelation. "And though God revealed to the prophets what he would do for the salvation of the human race in a general way, the apostles knew with greater precision about things the prophets did not know....Even among the prophets themselves, the later knew what the earlier had not known.... And Gregory [the Great] says (*Hom. Ezek.* 16) that an increase of divine knowledge grew over the sequence of time" (1.57.5 ad 3). For Thomas, then, an increase of knowledge transmitted by revelation is an aspect in salvation history, which is in this way a history of knowledge, too. This means that as a quite general rule knowledge is more clear in the New Testament than in the Old (see *Ver.* 12.13 ad 5). This goes along with the fact that the apostles received knowledge directly from the Son of God (3.7. 7), while the patriarchs and prophets were taught by angels (*Lect. Eph.* 3.1.141). But Christ is the "first and chief teacher of the faith" (*Summa theol.* 3.7.7).

According to Thomas, however, the task of the theologian is fundamentally different from the situation of prophets and apostles. Supernatural truth is communicated to them only by immediate inspiration. Theology's mandate, by contrast, is to reconstruct by means of human reason that which is perfect truth in God and set down in the witness of the Bible (see 1.1.1.6. ad 3). This occurs by discursive thinking from principles to conclusions. In so doing one proceeds from the pregiven articles of faith in which this truth is laid down. Thus it depends on taking into account the increase of knowledge of faith through the ages; much that was contained in it only implicitly in more ancient times has been later unfolded and has led to increasing number of articles of faith (2.2.1.7). An up-to-date theology will have to consider this. On the other hand, the perfect knowledge of truth will be possible only in the eternal home.

The tool of Aristotelian logic seems to Thomas indispensable for theological intellectual work. In this regard he stands in a line with other theologians of his time. The significance of the rediscovery of Aristotle in the thirteenth century for the development of Christian theology, as became clear in recent years, cannot be appreciated highly enough. Radical Aristotelianism as Siger of Brabant advocated it was, of course, irreconcilable with Christianity, but Thomas was able to unite Aristotelian epistemology with biblical content in such a way that from it arose a special sort of Christian philosophy, which one today can rightly call "Thomist"—even though so-called Neo-Thomism, which for a long time represented the official doctrine in the modern Catholic doctrinal tradition, concealed more than illumined it. For Thomas, philosophy was never an end in and of itself; rather, he characterizes it (see also *1 Comm. sent.* prol. 1), along with the other sciences, in a statement that became famous (*Summa theol.* 1.1.5 ad 2), as "handmaiden" (*ancillae*) of theology. The most important thing about the Aristotelian image of humanity, as it was adapted by Thomas, was that it joins the soul and body far more intimately and ascribes a positive role to the body again, while the Platonic tradition, long dominant in theology, had negated what was bodily and inclined to a dualism that radically denied the worldliness of the world. But in adopting the holistic Aristotelian image of the human being, the biblical view could be rediscovered for the first time, because a model of thinking much more closely corresponding to it was available. The idea of creation, which during the epoch stamped by Neo-Platonist cosmology Christian exegesis adhered to only with difficulty, was now able to again more easily find an adequate equivalent in philosophical thinking. In the first part of his *summa* dealing with "On God" (*De Deo*), Thomas made use of the Aristotelian doctrine of the "unmoved mover" as the "efficient cause" (*causa efficiens*) in order to characterize in the third, concluding subsection the process of creation as "the emanation of creatures from the first cause, which is called creation" (1.45 prooem.). To be sure, the catch-word emanation (*emanatio*) takes up a basic idea of Neo-Platonism: that of the emanation from and return to original unity, which Thomas uses as the overall framework for his *summa*. But the Aristotelian starting point preserves the creatureliness of the world and prevents Platonic dualism between spirit and matter.

From the philosophical standpoint, however, very serious problems arise here. The relation of creator and creation cannot be integrated into the Aristotelian worldview, in which God is present only as first cause (*prima causa*), unmoved mover, and absolute being, but belongs at any case to the all-encompassing realm of being as well. That God created the world is purely a statement of belief that cannot be proved philosophi-cally-rationally. But when God is, on the one hand, the ultimate ground of possibility of all being prior to all beings and ,on the other hand, belongs to those beings himself, there emerges a tension that Thomas tries to resolve by the doctrine of an analogy of being (*analogia entis*). God's being is defined as "being by acting" (*esse actu*). But this remained problematic and was already criticized by Duns Scotus (ca. 1270–1308). Thomas combined it with the Neo-Platonist principle of the emanation and return of the world-all to the One in All, the "highest Ground," which ancient church tradition had already identified with the Christian God. Though this solution likewise was ultimately unsatisfactory, by combina-tions Thomas successfully constructed an impressive edifice of theological thought. It must be emphasized that in all this he was endeavoring to build all his thinking on biblical foundations, even though the rational criteria he applied were in the final analysis unable to match this intent.

With Aristotelian epistemology, which taught a knowledge gained by the senses, not innate ideas, the literal sense of Scripture also gained new significance. The fact that in Thomas, in contrast to previous devel-opment, the literal sense plays again an astonishingly significant role for exegesis is obviously due to Aristotle's influence. In addition, "Science is not concerned with individuals, but theology [*sacra doctrina*] deals with individuals. Consider Abraham, Isaac, Jacob, and so on. Therefore, theology is not a science" (1.1.2). This statement applies to only one specific aspect, for at other places Thomas expressly declares: "One must say that theology [*sacra doctrina*] is a science" (1.1.2 ad 2). The apparent contradiction is resolved by the distinction, encountered immediately thereafter, between two sorts of science: one that proceeds from things known by natural knowledge (e.g., geometry); and another that proceeds "from the light of a higher science" (1.1.2 ad 2). This statement shows that for Thomas exegesis means something other than the necessarily abstracting and generalizing natural sciences in that it is engaged in each case with concrete, historical existence. In addition, the worldview coming from Aristotle fundamentally transforms the exegete's view of Scripture as well. The theory of "first cause" and "secondary causes" can also be applied to the Bible. Thus, the authors of the individual books deserved consideration as "secondary authors," and the Bible as a whole was no longer merely a compendium of theological doctrines. This becomes clear as well in the equation of the literal sense with the historical sense. So Thomas can say of, for example, the paradise narrative: "The things Scripture says about paradise are set forth in the manner of historical narrative. But one must consider the truth of history as the foundation for everything Scripture transmits in this way" (1.102.1).

Thomas reflected thoroughly on his hermeneutical principles at the beginning of his *Summa* (1.1.10). There he presupposes the traditional teaching of the fourfold sense of Scripture as his theoretical foundation, but he has to defend it against the objection that the multiplicity of differing senses "in a work produces confusion and deception and cancels the certainty of the argumentation." "The Holy Scripture, however, must be so efficacious that it shows truth without any deception." Thomas copes with the difficulty by maintaining that, in distinction to all the sciences in which words have one meaning, this science (namely, the content of the Bible) has something special (because God is its author). Its uniqueness is "that the things that are identified by its words also themselves identify something." The first meaning, identified by words, is the literal sense; the second, that which is referred to by the things identified by words, is the "spiritual sense." (Thomas can also call it "mystical.") Thomas divides this spiritual sense, in turn, in the traditional way into allegorical, moral, and anagogical. But it is important that the literal or historical sense is fundamental, "because the senses are all based on the one, that is, the literal sense." This sense is also "the one the author intended"; for this very reason it deserves the most attention. That there are also other senses alongside it creates no confusion because—and this is an important statement—"there is nothing necessary for faith conveyed by the spiritual sense that Scripture does not convey openly by the literal sense elsewhere" (1.1.10 ad 1).

If already from the very start therefore the literal sense—with basic acknowledgement of the other possible levels of meaning also—is emphasized as the decisive, for Thomas there are also two other considerations that can support this. The first is that etiology and analogy actually belong to the literal sense (etiology gives the basis for a reported fact of history; analogy means that no one truth of Scripture contradicts another; ad 2). The second is that a parabolic or figurative sense is contained within the literal sense, because metaphorical speech (say, when one speaks of God's *arm*), is a customary means of style (ad 3). Here Thomas, working out of ancient rhetoric, is at the same time altogether modern, for ever-greater attention has been given to metaphor as an element of language in modern exegesis! All in all, then, the literal sense is of incomparably greater significance for Thomas than for many of his predecessors. This becomes clear also in that the literal sense alone can serve as a proof against heretics, not, say, the allegorical sense (1.1.10 ad 1). Therefore, in many of his commentaries, such as the Job commentary, Thomas attends to the literal sense in a hitherto quite unusual way.

A concrete example can make clear the practical execution of this principle. Unfortunately, however, the exegetical work of Thomas is still all too little examined because the primary official duties of a medieval master of *sacra pagina* as a biblical interpreter, described above, are too little known. One exception is the commentary on the Epistle to the Romans, which belongs in the context of his interpretation of the Pauline epistles and is to be considered among the fruits of the mature years of his activity as a master—in its final edition possibly from the last months of his teaching in Naples or shortly before his departure from Paris, therefore around 1272. The section that Thomas himself corrected concludes with 1 Cor 10. The rest of the commentary on the Pauline epistles up to Hebrews is a postscript to an earlier lecture.

The commentary on the Epistles to the Romans is well-suited to show the rational manner in which Thomas deals with Scripture. It is evident right off how Thomas evaluates Paul's epistolary corpus as a whole. We should of course not be surprised that he ascribes to the apostle all the letters ascribed to Paul, from Romans to Hebrews; historical criticism was unknown in his time and surroundings. In the prologue Thomas placed at the start of his collection of the lectures he had given on Paul's letters, he gives a systematic overview over them: "For he (Paul) wrote fourteen letters, nine of which instruct the church of the pagans; four the prelates and princes of the church, that is, the kings [by this Thomas means the so-called Pastoral Epistles]; and one the people of Israel, namely, that to the Hebrews" (no. 11). Paul, whom we know as the author of letters that were occasioned by current problems, becomes for Thomas something of a colleague, a master of theology, who plans and writes out his corpus of letters as a systematic work for instructing various sorts of church groups!

This view, however, corresponds perfectly to the characteristic way in which the exegesis of Thomas proceeds as a whole. There first emerges the exact plan with which Thomas divides Romans as a continuous whole before beginning the interpretation of each individual section. This love of order is altogether typical of high scholastic exegesis. One can also not mistake the progress that was aimed at by, for example, the chapter divisions of the Bible that were undertaken for the first time. (The chapter divisions of the Vulgate still in use today go back to the scholastic Stephan Langton, who died in 1228.) If the statements preceding the sections are gathered up, the result is a complete outline of the whole. Each point of the outline is headed by a sentence in which a basic statement about the section under concern is formulated and at the same time a look back at the sections handled before is given. So, for example, it states at Rom 5:1–5: "After the apostle showed the necessity of Christ's grace, because without it neither the knowledge of truth was of use to the pagans for salvation nor circumcision and the law to the Jews, he begins here to commend the power of grace." Similar expressions in other sections are constructed in quite parallel form. Not merely a loose connection is meant, but the interpreter seeks to discover an exact logical sequence of argument in the text. Divisions of the Epistle to the Romans were sought even before Thomas, but he now undertakes to ascertain in it a complete theological systematics. Grace is the overarching theme of the entire epistle. The first main part of the epistle speaks of its necessity (Rom 1:16b–4:25), its procurement (5:1–8:39), and its origin (9:1–11:36). The second part of the epistle (12:1–16:27) is joined to it, introduced by the formulation (at 12:1) "the use of grace."

Like earlier scholastic commentaries, Thomas's Romans commentary is made up of three forms: individual exegesis; questions; and excursuses. Here, too, the origin of these differing ways of proceeding can be explained by the course of an exegetical lecture: word-by-word explanation usually comes first. In the interpretation of Thomas, unlike early scholastic commentaries, one can recognize a strong formalization and rationalizing of this way of proceeding. In comparison with the *Summa,* many similarities come into view. These include, for example, the subdivision of the interpretation into sections numbered "first," "second," and so on. In this, principles of division of the highest degree of abstraction rule. Although the effect of a formalized procedure of this sort on today's readers is tiresome and monotonous, it leads to detailed and careful analysis. Grammatical and stylistic observations enter in, by which the means of classical exegetical science are handled with virtuosity.

Also characteristic for commenting is that mostly at the end of a small subdivision one or several biblical passages from various Old and New Testament writings are offered, which thematically touch on the interpretation presented in the interpretation. The system of prooftexting (*dicta probantia*) that became so popular in seventeenth-century orthodoxy is foreshadowed here. But there are also more complicated ways of proceeding. One is the so-called "distinction," which is used for clarifying the meaning of a term. So, for instance, with regard to Rom 13:11, "It is now already the time that we rise from sleep," an entire string of biblical passages unfolds, which are to illumine the sense of the statement: what is meant is not death, which is often called "sleep," as in 1 Thess 4:12, nor the natural sleep, as in John 11:12, nor the sleep of grace as in Ps 4:9, nor the sleep of contemplation, as in the Song 5:2. "Rather, by sleep is understood the sleep of guilt, as in Eph 5:14: 'Awake, those who sleep, rise from the dead'" (no 1062). For this sort of proof, medieval exegetes could draw from prepared collections of distinctions, like the *Summa Abel* of Alain of Lille.

The care in carrying out the formal construction of such an exegesis can be seen well in an example of the interpretation of a passage such as Rom 9:1–5. Thomas begins the interpretation with a systematic overview: "first, he (Paul) deals therefore with the election of the people; second, the fall of the Jews, in Rom 10. ... With respect to the first point, he does two sorts of things: first, he mentions the dignity of the Jews; second, he shows how the pagans were taken into this dignity, namely, 'but not that this has failed....' (9:6). ... With respect to the first point, he does two things: first, the apostle shows his attitude toward the Jewish people; second, he shows their worth, that is, 'who indeed are Israelites' (9:4). With respect to the first, he does two things: first, he confirms what he will say; second, he shows his attitude: 'That I have great sorrow....'" Thomas continues in this fashion. At the last-named phrase in verse 2 follows an elucidation fully in the style of a disputation over different possibilities of interpretation. "He stresses his pain, however, in a threefold way: first on account of its greatness." The scriptural proof for this is Lam 2:13: "Your pain is deep like the sea." To this, however, he adds a counterproof (*sed contra*): Sir 30:22: "Do not give your soul over to sorrow," "which seems to agree with the opinion of the Stoics, who keep away sorrow entirely from the soul of the wise." This, however, can be rejected on two grounds: (1) because it has to do with a bodily lack, "which nature detests"—and moreover because of the scriptural proof of Matt 27:38 (the sorrow of Jesus in Gethsemane); and (2) because grief over the sin of a neighbor for the sake of the commandment of love of neighbor is praiseworthy (scriptural proof: 1 Cor 12:21).

The commentaries of Thomas contain many sorts of more external explanations of the literal sense, as on grammatical, syntactic, and stylistic problems. The *determination* can be decisive in the question of why Paul (1:1), for example, calls himself a "servant of Jesus Christ." This term "servant" is, taken in itself, usually deprecatory. In connection with the determination "Jesus Christ," however, it has become a term of honor. A model of explanation popular from the time of Jerome is the etymology of names. Thomas used it in explaining the name Paul. This name can have three meanings: (1) in Hebrew (in which, however, the P at the beginning that is, according to Thomas, not given in Hebrew must be replaced by a corresponding letter), it can mean "wonderful" or "elect"; (2) in Greek it means "calm"; and (3) in Latin, "modest." These meanings all fit Paul, as Thomas then explains. Here again Thomas makes abundant use of "modern" forms of argumentation, particularly the syllogism, numerous examples of which are found in his works.

Thomas also utilizes Aristotle's philosophy as a matter of course, although it does not gain decisive influence on his understanding of content. Aristotelian categories such as cause, effect, form, content, purpose, nature, means, and goal are used readily. Ethical and anthropological statements of Aristotle are also repeatedly cited from his works, above all the *Nicomachean Ethics* and the *Metaphysics*, when they are consistent with biblical ideas. When they are not, as in the case of the eternality of matter (11.1.5 on Rom 11:36), they are rejected. Thus, on Rom 4:2, where Aristotle's opinion is cited as an objection to Paul's view that Abraham is not justified by works. Aristotle said a person's inner *habitus* is formed by the exercise of external works. Thomas grants this point, but in his view it relates only to human righteousness, while the righteousness that is valid before God exceeds human capacities. Hence a harmony between philosophical and theological theses results. Frequent recourse to Aristotle, whom Thomas can often label simply as "the philosopher," goes along with the general acknowledgement of Aristotle as authoritative in philosophical studies, which Thomas could presuppose among his auditors, and therefore has above all pedagogical reasons. To think and to formulate matters in terms of Aristotle had gained general currency at this time.

Nevertheless, a Neo-Platonist dualism remains in the works of Thomas, in the antithesis of the earthly and the heavenly. However, the use of the spiritual sense is relatively infrequent in his commentaries and limited chiefly to traditional themes of interpretation. In essentials these are the christological interpretation of the Old Testament, the Trinitarian interpretation of some passages of Romans, the church, which is fore-shadowed in some Old Testament themes, and the interpretation of the "mysteries" of the New Testament to the sacraments. Reflected here as well is the monastic background of Thomist exegesis, for life with the Eucharist marked the daily course of a Dominican monk such as Thomas.

In addition to word-by-word explanation, the commentary contains a larger number of questions (*quaestionen*), that is, sections in which par-ticular questions are elucidated in a somewhat lengthy discussion in the pro-and-con fashion of scholastic disputations. These questions may be of a historical-literary sort (e.g., where did Paul write the Epistle to the Romans?" [*Sup. Rom.* prol. 13]; who first brought the gospel to Rome?" [prol. 14]). But as a rule it had to do with basic theological problems, the answers to which break out of the framework of a purely contex-tual interpretation. For example, At Rom 8:17, "if we are children, then we are heirs," it can be objected that we can never inherit anything from God because God never dies. Presumably one of the auditors raised this question. The answer of Thomas is, "But one must say that this applies to temporal goods that cannot be possessed by several at the same time, and thus one must die so that another is the successor. But spiritual goods can be possessed by many at the same; therefore, it is not necessary that the father die so that the sons can be inheritors" (*Sup. Rom.* 648). In addition to this sort of rational explanation, there are other ways of answering a question, above all with the help of other scriptural passages or the juxta-position of various statements of the fathers between which Thomas then decides. Traditional and "modern" methods therefore run side by side throughout his works.

Excurses are even more extensive. Thomas turns to this form when a dogmatic problem requires a detailed explanation. An example is the lengthy expositions as regards Rom 1:4. Thomas devotes an entire lesson (ch. 1, lect. 3) to the lineage and nature of Jesus Christ as the Son of God. Here especially the christological errors emerging in the ancient church, such as adoptionism (the man Jesus was first adopted as Son of God at his baptism) are refuted. Here, then, it is not so much the exegete as the dogmatician who speaks. But a relevant biblical passage necessitates such a discussion.

The biblical interpretation of Thomas is certainly a premodern form of exegesis. Nevertheless, it is not without interest even to a contemporary reader. One way it is ahead of many purely historical-philological interested modern commentaries is that it always keeps the theological content of Scripture in view and is attentive to working this out by means of drawing together other viewpoints. There is no tension between exegesis and application. This goes along not only with the fact that a historical criticism, as has been customary since the Enlightenment, was not yet known. Thomas would never have understood that the Bible could be of significance apart from a theological understanding. The only reason for dealing with its statements is that it contains the divine truth from which alone the salvation of humanity proceeds. This is a position with which today's interpreters, if they aware of their responsibility, must struggle completely anew.

3.8. Understanding the World from the Bible: Bonaventure

At the same time as Thomas Aquinas worked, as we have already heard, Bonaventure (ca. 1217–1274) worked as a master at the University of Paris. Bonaventure, apparently the son of a physician in Bagnoregio near Orvieto and Viterbo in Tuscany, was born not far from Rome. His real name was Giovanni di Fidanza. Otherwise we know hardly anything certain about his youth except, as he himself reports, that he was once healed of a serious illness by the intercession of Francis of Assisi. Since Francis died in 1226, this must have been very early in Bonaventure's life, or it may be that his mother had called on Francis after his death. This is not impossible, given the customs of the time, and Francis enjoyed great respect among his followers already during his lifetime, more than ever after his death. Around 1235/1236 young Giovanni went to Paris to begin his study of the seven liberal arts with the arts faculty there. There he worked his way through the usual course of study of six or seven years, concluding around 1242. The crowning conclusion at the time was philosophy. Doubtless Aristotle was already taught at the Paris faculty of arts at the time and indeed not only the "organon" but the "physics" and the "metaphysics." But there had not yet been conflict over Averroists on the faculty. It was well-known that Aristotle was not a Christian philosopher and was in many respects irreconcilable with Christianity. This explains much of Bonaventure's later position regarding Aristotle's philosophy.

It did not mean, however, that he would not have known Aristotle well. In any case Bonaventure seems to have been a secular student. What led him to enter the Franciscan order in 1243, whether the old gratitude for Francis as a person passed along by his mother or the way of life of the Franciscans working in Paris, is uncertain. At any rate, it is certain that he began theology in the Franciscan study house. By the way, he was also accepted as a member of the Roman province in Paris, in accord with the statutes of the order.

We have already learned about the situation at the University of Paris in connection with the activity of Thomas Aquinas there. Just like the Dominicans, the Franciscans had their own study institute within the theological faculty. The first brothers had settled in Paris in 1219; in 1234 King Louis XII had given them a vast complex of buildings for their convent and the establishment of a theology study house. Pope Gregory IX confirmed this gift in 1236. At the same time, the Franciscan study house received a considerable upswing in that Alexander of Hales joined the order, bringing his teaching chair with him. Alexander, already famous, was a roughly fifty-year-old *magister regens* (holder of a teaching chair); he had already assumed this office around 1220. The protests of faculty colleagues belonging to the secular clergy, which led to a great conflict between the professors belonging to the secular clergy and the two mendicant orders, were unsuccessful because of papal support of the Franciscans. By this means the Franciscans held two theological chairs thereafter. Hence when Bonaventure took up his theological study there, he was able to hear Alexander of Hales and Johannes de la Rochelle. Thus presumably he also attended the lectures given at that time by the Dominican Hugh of Saint-Cher and Albert the Great, or at least knew their teachings. But he did not follow Albert's extensive acceptance of Aristotelianism—unlike Thomas Aquinas, working at the same time. After Alexander of Hales and John of Rochelle died in the same year, 1245, Eudes Rigaud (later archbishop of Rouen) and William of Middleton (from 1248) succeeded them. Bonaventure learned a great deal about Augustine from his teachers, particularly Alexander of Hales. A consistently strong Augustinianism was characteristic of Franciscanism. We find it again later in Bonaventure's own works. Otherwise he worked through the customary five years (1243–1248) of theological study and then the normal career of a theological teacher that we already know. He became a *baccalaureus biblicus*, responsible for summary lectures on the Bible in 1248, a *baccalaureus sententiarium* in 1250–1252, and hence had to read the *Sentences* of Peter Lombard (from which his own commentary on the *Sentences* emerged, later published). Finally, he began to prepare for his official teaching license (*licentia docendi*) and received it at the beginning of 1254. From then on he was *magister regens* at the Franciscan study house. After 1257 another task of importance was added: he was elected General Minister of the Franciscans. From then on he had to concern himself a great deal with the organization and internal problems of the order—especially to care for the conflict with the spiritualists (they appealed to the ideas of Joachim of Fiore for their extreme spiritualism) that broke out under his predecessor John of Parma (1247–1257). Yet he soon succeeded in calming the situation. He later (1265) warded off a call to become archbishop of York by a humble personal audience with Pope Clement IV. He was appointed cardinal bishop of Albano by Gregory XI (1272–1276) in 1273 and joined the curia. His episcopal ordination took place in Lyon, where Bonaventure accompanied the pope in preparation of the second council of Lyon. He was one of the influential theologians at this council, which was particularly dedicated to the idea of crusade and an attempted agreement with Byzantium, but he died during its sessions on 15 July 1274.

In order to understand the distinctiveness of Bonaventure's biblical theology adequately, it is important to keep its Franciscan stamp in view. It is not by accident that Bonaventure entered the minor brothers; their ideals were his, too. The Franciscan milieu was completely and decisively determined by the ideas of the order's founder, the charismatic Francis of Assisi (1181/1182–1226). His immediate relationship to the Bible was characteristic of him; he lived with it and in it and considered it obligatory without reservation. From constantly reading it, he knew it in large measure by heart. The revised *Regula bullata* (of 1223) first states at the top (rule 1) the demand on the brothers "to safeguard the gospel of our Lord Jesus Christ." In particular, the call addressed to himself and his followers to live in accord with the demands of Jesus in the Sermon on the Mount played a central role for Francis. In the Sermon on the Mount, Jesus summoned the disciples to follow him. Francis saw this as a call to the most rigorous asceticism, giving oneself no consideration, and absolute poverty. In addition, Jesus commanded the exercise of mercy. For Francis, this meant to be open for all, especially all the needy, to be applied to them without reservation. Likewise, he was devoted to the world in which he lived, conscious of himself as a part of God's creation. It is well known that in this he included also all the animals, which he could address openly as his brothers. Francis had also by nature constantly experienced the beauty of the cosmos; his famous hymn to "brother sun" is testimony to this. As a theologian, Francis was an autodidact. As the son of a well-to-do merchant, he had been trained for this career but was little educated in the broad sense of the term. His not infrequently profound theological thoughts are not based on academic study. Precisely for this reason, they affected in their immediacy all who encountered him.

Bonaventure had probably hardly known Francis personally, yet the order Franics founded evidently exerted a powerful attraction on him. Still, Bonaventure was a completely different fellow than Francis. Instead of rigorous bodily asceticism, the decisive impulse for him was concentration on scholarly work, which he pursued, however, in the spirit of Francis. A few rather skeptical remarks about theological study are passed down from Francis, although he apparently did not completely reject it. "The saint does not need to be led to knowledge by studies; it is God who teaches him wisdom from above. Thanks to the rays of eternal light he understands the Scriptures excellently," Francis is once supposed to have said. But his faithfulness to the church led him to honor—in addition to the priests, who serve at the table of the sacrament the body and blood of Christ—the theologians as well: "We must heed and respect even theologians and those who administer the most sacred word of God as those who serve us with the Spirit and life," we read in his testament. Nevertheless, charismatic-spiritualist dealings with Scripture were more than enough for him personally. The Franciscans themselves, of course, had already moved away from this position with the establishment of their study house in Paris. When Bonaventure entered there, he found a long-established program of study that led him along predesignated paths.

Still, the Franciscan spirit is unmistakable in Bonaventure's biblical interpretation. It is detectable everywhere in his works, but he also expresses it directly in the prooemium to his commentary on Luke, in which he discusses his role as a biblical interpreter at length. Bonaventure had, as it seems, cursorily lectured on the Gospel of Luke already as a *baccalaureus biblicus*, but then as a master (*magister*) these lectures were considerably revised. He chose as the motto of the prooemium the verse from Isa 61:1 that, according to Luke 4:18, Jesus read and interpreted in the synagogue in Nazareth: "The Spirit of the Lord is upon me, because he has anointed me. He has sent me to proclaim to the gentle ones, that I heal those oppressed of heart, preach release to the captives and release to the imprisoned (from their captivity)." He then interprets this motto at length with respect to the tasks of a doctor of the Holy Scriptures. Customary scholastic distinctions are by no means absent here. Thus Bonaventure introduces his elucidations with the remark that the Bible verse can be referred "by *general* understanding to a popular teacher of the Holy Scriptures, by *special* understanding to the blessed Evangelist Luke, [and] by *distinctive* [understanding] to Christ himself, who is the source of truth and grace" (*Comm. Luc.* prooem. 2, *Opera omnia* 7:3). Corresponding to this division, he then discusses "who and what sort of person the teacher [*doctor*] of this evangelical writing should be" (prooem. 3, 7:3). The attributes required of this person are drawn from interpreting the details of the verse: he must "be anointed with divine grace, installed in pure obedience, inflamed by brotherly inclination." The Old Testament prophets are the type for the first, the gift of the Spirit for the obedience, Moses for the brotherly affection of the apostle Paul (scriptural proofs: [1] 1 Kgs 19:16; 16:13; [2] Exod 3:10; [3] 1 Thess 2:7–8). For such a teacher there should also be a matching student: "He must have a humble, gentle, and believing hearer" (*Comm. Luc.* prooem. 6, 7:4). This is also demonstrated in detail for each of these concepts by prooftexts from the Scripture (e.g., Eccl 5:13; Ps 25[24]:9; Jas 1:21; Matt 11:29).

If we already here take a little glance at the position with which the Franciscan professors and their students entered into scriptural interpretation, the insight into the goal of such instruction is strengthened by the additional characterization of the Evangelist Luke as the author of the Gospel to be interpreted. Once again the scriptural statement of Luke 4:18 is the basis of the characterization. It is interesting that Bonaventure draws upon Aristotelian categories also to provide a framework for organizing his discussions: these are the terms "efficient cause" (*causa efficiens*) and "teleological cause" (*causa finalis*), which Bonaventure then distinguishes into external and internal causes and then to higher, lower, and middle efficient causes as well as first, middle, and final teleological causes. One can ascertain that Bonaventure also makes use of this terminology in his introductions to other biblical commentaries (on Ecclesiastes, the Wisdom of Solomon, the Gospel of John) from his years as a master.

On the other hand, it is absent from his late work, the *Collationes in Hexaemeron*. But these terms supply nothing more than a framework. Even here statements of content, again backed up by biblical passages, are decisive. Important in this regard is the gift of the Spirit promised to the Evangelist, developed from Luke 4:18 (in the context of which additional information is provided about the relationship between the Holy Spirit [above] and Luke [below] depicted in the extension from above to below). That the author of the biblical book is inspired is self-evident to Bonaventure. This is also explicated in detail with respect to the statement "has anointed." A certain proximity to Thomas is seen in the fact that Bonaventure is also concerned with doctrine: "The Holy Spirit taught the Evangelist by grace, and this, as instructed, taught, in that he wrote the church its evangelical doctrine" (*Comm. Luc.* prooem. 12, 7:5). This teaching is then first designated as "the making known of the truth" (*manifestatio veritatis*; 13, 7:5). A second designation refers to the statement in Luke 4:18 "that I healed those who are broken-hearted" and defines the "healing of our weakness" as an effect of the gospel (15, 7:5). A reference to Wis 16:12 and a Jerome-citation that Luke was a physician support this statement. The prooemium then comes to its crowning conclusion in a new transition (16–24) that now offers a christological interpretation of the verses. Revealing in this regard is the concluding paragraph, which provides the interpretation of the four faces in the vision of Ezek 1 to the four Fvangelists, as we encountered before in Joachim of Fiore.

This example shows us the wide extent to which the old traditions of interpretation played a role in Bonaventure's interpretation. That Bonaventure certainly knew Joachim's writings is certain, but he makes use of the literature available to him to a much greater extent. His interpretation in large measure embodied the tradition as regards the materials as well as the methods, as they were customarily dealt with in the monastic teaching system. His originality lies in the overall framework he gives his theology and the weight he attaches to the areas of theological study.

The *Breviloquium*, which Bonaventure composed at the request of his audience for a brief summary of his theological teaching, is of special significance in this regard. The prologue of this essay in particular deserves our attention, because it can be considered the most important high-scholastic biblical hermeneutics (theory of understanding). Although a *summa* of theology with a Trinitarian outline is really the main part of the *Breviloquium*, its actual purpose is to show his professorial colleagues (masters) that all decisive theological statements are contained in the Bible. Seeking the center of theological work in biblical theology is the specific concern of Franciscan theologians, in contrast to the temptations of systematic-philosophical theologizing that he sees to be the center among his colleagues, even Dominicans such as Thomas Aquinas. The prologue is directed not to his colleagues but to students, for whom Bonaventure wants to teach the love for the Holy Scripture and remove the anxiety they feel because of its apparent inscrutability—it seems like an impenetrable forest to them (see *Opera omnia* 5:208b). By presenting the goals and methods of biblical interpretation to them, he wants to introduce them to work on the Scripture and deter them from switching to the apparently easier way of disputing about sentences. That he mastered this art, too, he had demon-strated by his *baccalaureus sententiarius*.

Also in the prologue to the *Breviloquium* (5:201–291), we again find Bonaventure's custom of introducing his discussions with a scriptural passage from which the external and internal division of the subsequent discussions then emerge. This time it is Eph 3:14–19 (5:201a); by the way, it is used yet again, for a different purpose entirely, in the prologue to his treatise *Sololoquium* (*Opera omnia* 8:28a). From it, one realizes that the interpretation of a scriptural passage is not fixed once and for all; it can definitely be adapted to a context. The same holds for individual terms as well; in Bonaventure, they represent a variety of possible aspects that can vary almost playfully. It is precisely here, in the richness of the Scriptures, not in its conceptual clarity, that its value lies for him.

Bonaventure first precedes his further discussion with an organiza-tional principle in that he draws a number three from the introductory text: "The great teacher of the people (Paul) opens in this word the starting point [*ortum*], the progress [*progressum*], and the resting point [*statum*] of Holy Scripture" (*Brev.* 5:201a). This threefold raster of terms creates a framework for a movement that, proceeding from the Trinity, leads along the way of humanity to salvation to the final resting point of the fullness of eternal blessedness back to the Father, Son, and Holy Spirit. "The progress of the Holy Scripture, however, is not adapted to the laws of arguments, definitions, and divisions in keeping with the way of other sciences, but in keeping with that which is useful for salvation, it describes partly by simple words and partly by mystical words (to be interpreted spiritually) the entire content of the universe in as it were one *summa*" (5:201b). This is first interpreted cosmologically-soteriologically in deal-ing with the fourness of breadth, length, height, and depth, which in Eph 3:18 already carried a figurative meaning. Thus it describes "the entire content of the universe as it were in one *summa*, in which the *breadth* is thought. It describes the (historical) course, in which the *length* is thought. It describes the preeminent position of those who are saved at the end, in which the *height* is thought. It describes the misery of those who are to be damned, in which the *depth* not only of the *universum* itself but that of the divine judgment is constituted" (5:201b). Alongside this statement can be set another, which follows toward the end of the prologue. According to this, Scripture deals "with the entire *universum* with regard to the highest and the lowest, the first and the last, and with regard to the intermediary course (of history)" (5:208a). Cosmology and salvation history, according to Bonaventure, are displayed in a synopsis together in the Scripture.

From this first process in which Scripture is set in a world-comprehensive framework, "as far as it is of help for salvation to have knowledge of it (the universe)" (5:201b–202a), there emerges another, which now lets a number four follow upon the number three. It is also developed from the Ephesians quotation stated at the beginning. The breadth (§1, 5:202b–203b) means accordingly the composition of the Scripture from the Old and New Testaments. Here Bonaventure likewise ascertains a harmony in which the groups of the books of the Old and New Testaments correspond to one another: the Old Testament "has legal, historical wisdom, and prophetic books; the New Testament has similar books, which correspond to this in fourfold fashion. For to the books of Law correspond the Gospels, to the historical [books], the history of the Apostles, the wisdom, the letters of the apostles, especially Paul, [and] to the prophetical corresponds the book of the Revelation, so that the correspondence between the Old and New Testaments is thus wondrous" (5:202b–203a). Like the number three, the number four is also a symbol of harmony. This Bonaventure knows to be underscored with the sequence of the books and groups of books of the Old Testament and New Testament, which to him represents at the same time a consistent unfolding of the truth in which he compares Scripture with "a wide river that swells more and more from the confluence of many waters." "For after first the legal books were available in Scripture, then later the water of wisdom was added to the historical books, and as third in addition was added the teaching of wise Solomon, then also the teaching of the holy prophets, and finally evangelical teaching was revealed, which was presented by the mouth of Christ, written down by the Evangelists, [and] disseminated by the holy apostles" (5:203b).

The *length* of Scripture (§2, 5:203b–204b) refers to that of the world history described in Scripture, "that is, from the beginning of the world to the day of judgment" (5:203). In particular, it has here to deal with the (traditional) division into three ages of the world (*tempora*), which is overlapped by a further schema of division into seven epochs (*aetates*), five of which strikingly fall into the Old Testament periods, while the sixth ("from Christ to the end of the world") and the seventh run simultaneously. This seventh, which is calculated "from the rest of Christ in the grave to the universal resurrection," seems to stand in associative connection with the seven-day schema of the creation account, God's rest on the seventh day in particular. Here, and in the related idea that to this seventh epoch an eighth of resurrection will be connected, the dependence on Augustine, who essentially founded the periodicization of salvation history as such, is quite evident (see Augustine, *Gen. litt.* 4.11.21). The number seven is brought into connection with the seven-day work of creation already in Augustine. Although not here, in other passages in Bonaventure (*Coll. hex.* 16; see below) is also added the thought that the "greater world" (*major mundus*), that is to say, creation as a whole, corresponds to the "smaller world" (*minor mundus*), to humanity, for whom the number seven is also characteristic.

In Bonaventure's subsequent discussions of the height (*sublimitas*, §3, 5:204b–205b) of Scripture, he is strongly dependent on this, and indeed on (Pseudo-)Dionysius the Areopagite, much read at the time, and hence on a Neo-Platonist worldview. Included here are the ideas of a cosmic hierarchy that extends from the church below over the world of angels divided into various levels in the middle and to the divine spheres above (5:204b) as well as that of a corresponding hierarchy in the human soul. Bonaventure crosses from here over into theology, the tasks of which he compares to the ladder to heaven of Gen 28 and sees analogous to the structure of the soul, for, while philosophy deals with things in nature "or in the soul according to the knowledge implanted by nature," theology deals "with the things relating to the grace and glory (of God) as well as eternal wisdom" (5:205a). What is distinctive is the connecting idea that theology's effort to rise on the ladder is therefore successful only because it is met by Christ approaching from above, who on the basis of assuming human nature is not only the hierarch in the heavenly hierarchy but—in the framework of the Trinity—also mediator in the spheres of angels and the earthly world. Therefore—here Bonaventure appeals to Ps 133 (132)— the oil of unction streams down from him "not only on the beard, but the hemline of the robe, that is, not only in the heavenly Jerusalem but also up to the still struggling church" (5:205a).

The *depth* of Scripture (§4, 5:205b–206b) refers to the various senses of Scripture, which Bonaventure holds in the traditional way. Here there is nothing distinctive, because the theory of the various senses of Scripture had uncontested validity throughout the Middle Ages. Besides the literal sense, Bonaventure recognizes three spiritual (mystical) senses, which he calls (5:205b) the *allegorical* ("when one event is indicated by another event, regarding what is to be believed"), *tropological* ("when by that which occurred, something that is to be done is indicated"), and *anagogical* ("when that which is adumbrated is what is to be hoped"). Similarly in the *Hexaemeron* (2.13, 5:338b). The *Reductio artium ad theologiam* distinguishes between one literal sense and a three-part mystical, that is, spiritual, sense (5:321b). The same teaching is built again in another way in *Coll. hex.* 13.9–11 (5:389a–b). In addition to the one literal sense, then, come three figurative senses. They correspond to the three ways God reveals himself in each creature: "According to substance, power, and effect." "And each creature represents God, who is triune, and how humans come to him." But one comes to God by faith, hope, and love. As a consequence, each creature must consider "what is to be believed, what is to be hoped for, and what is to be done." From this the well-known three senses of Scripture emerge. But in this section is encountered also the interpretation of the four faces from Ezek 1:5–14 as the four senses of Scripture, in which Bonaventure appeals to the example of Gregory the Great (*Hom. Ezech.* 6.12ff.): the human face designates the natural face (literal sense); the lion, because of its magnificence, the allegory; the ox, which pulls the plow and makes the land fruitful, the tropological (moral) sense; the eagle, which flies to the heights, the anagogical. Of interest still is especially the statement in *Coll. hex.* 13.3 (5:388a), where in connection with Ps 33 (32):7 it is stated that God set the spiritual senses of Scripture within the husk of the literal sense like the water of the sea in a tunnel. Accordingly, the spiritual senses are not really additional senses but signify figurative aspects that in Bonaventure's view are contained in the literal sense by its very nature.

From the last won observation emerges also the emphasis with which Bonaventure refers his hearers to the necessity of a thorough study of the literal sense. No one can reach the deeper meanings, "if he is not familiar by memory by the custom of the reading of the text and the letters of the Bible; otherwise, he will never be competent in scriptural interpretation." It is as in knowing language: "Just as someone who disdains learning the first basics from which language is built can never learn the meaning of the manners of speech or the correct law of their constructions, so someone who disdains the wording of the Holy Scripture never raises himself up to their spiritual meanings" (5:207a; see also *Coll. hex.* 19.7, 5:421a–b). He formulates the express rule: "Interpreters must take heed that an allegory is not to be sought everywhere and that not everything is to be explained mystically" (5:207a). It would therefore do Bonaventure an injustice to equate his efforts for the spiritual meanings of Scripture with superficiality or with disdain for the literal sense. It is nevertheless obvious that the literal sense as such has no independent meaning for him; it is merely the "husk" in which the spiritual senses are enclosed. Also to this there are unambiguous expressions, among those *Coll. hex.* 19.7 (5:421b), worth noting that one ought not remain with the a, b, c, of the literal sense "like the Jew, who always gravitates toward the literal sense." Bonaventure disdains the high achievements of Jewish exegesis for the explanation of the literal sense; he lacks any understanding of it. This shows itself in the immediately following resumption in 19.9, to which Bonaventure adds the example of a Jew who read the passage Isa 53:1–12: "And reading it according to the literal sense, he could find neither congruence [*concordantiam*] nor sense (5:421b). For Bonaventure, this had to happen, for only a christological understanding gave sense to the passage.

One other basic idea important to Bonaventure is that Scripture contains all the knowledge necessary for salvation. A typical statement on this is found in *Coll. hex.* 19.7: "Whoever, therefore, wants to learn may seek knowledge at the source, that is, in the Holy Scripture, because among the philosophers there is no knowledge *of the forgiveness of sins*, not even in the *summa* of the teachers, because these have been scooped from the original texts, the original text, however, from the Holy Scripture." One is reminded of Pascal's statement, much later: "Not the God of the philosophers....." The Franciscan teacher has a strong aversion to all knowledge distancing itself from the Bible. Several times in his use of 1 Cor 1:20 one finds the statement about the foolishness of faith that brings the wisdom of the world to nothing (see, e.g., *Comm. Luc.* 12.30, 7:318b; 8.93, 7:215a). On the other hand, he does not reject philosophy entirely but assigns it the role of a servant: "the work of theology sets philosophical knowledge under itself and accepts as much of the nature of things as is necessary for the fabrication of the mirror by which divine things are shown (represented)" (*Brev.* prol. §3, 5:205a).

There is therefore no fundamental rejection of philosophy in Bonaventure. In the case of Aristotle, he specifically rejects his teaching of the eternity of the world and that he sought happiness only in earthly things, but he excuses him at the same time, because he gained these views by natural knowledge alone (*Coll. hex.* 7.2, 5:365a–b). He values Plotinus, whom he calls "noble," more highly and Cicero ("Tullius"), because they taught the cardinal virtues (7.3, 5:365b), which by this means also has come to our knowledge (7.4, 5:366a). "So they seemed enlightened and by themselves were able to possess blessedness" (7.3, 5:365b). Yet this must be decisively repudiated: "But still they remain in darkness; they did not have the light of faith, but we have the light of faith" (7.3, 5:365b–366a). The reason is that the philosophers knew nothing of original sin. They were sick without knowing it: "They did not know the sickness because they did not know its cause" (7.9, 5:367a). Therefore their virtues were also useless: "They therefore did not know faith, without which the virtues are of no use" (7.6, 5:366b). The repudiation of the philosophers is thus not a repudiation of their ethical principles, which Bonaventure values; he distances himself from them on the basis of their disregard of original sin and because of their lack of faith. In this he stands in the succession of Augustine, to whom he expressly appeals (7.6, in connection with the citation above).

Of course, in the eyes of philosophers the Bible cannot be ascribed any convincing power because it only tells individual events: "Since, indeed, this narrative mode could not occur in the way of a certainty of reasons, because (according to Aristotle) individual events cannot be proven, God provided instead of the certainty of reason for this Scripture the certainty of authority" (*Brev.* prol., 5:201a). Therefore, Bonaventure was already aware of what was to represent a problem for Lessing much later, but he brushes it aside with the proof of authority! From this results, on the other hand, the postulate that the Scripture contains everything necessary, "for the Holy Spirit, its perfect author, could not say anything false, anything superfluous, but also not too little" (5:201a).

Therefore he also seeks in the Bible itself the explanation of all the phenomena of the world worth knowing "for salvation." That there is a progress, a temporal sequence in the origin of the biblical books, goes together with the gradually increasing human knowledge to which the development of Scripture was adapted, "since it required as its condition the human ability to understand such that the progress of Holy Scripture should be awaited in correspondence with the human power of under-standing" (*Brev.* prol., 5:202a). But herein, too, lies a reference to what is necessary for human salvation: "that is, because the Holy Scripture, respectively, theology, is a learning that gives sufficient knowledge of first principles, in keeping with the condition of pilgrimage, insofar as it is nec-essary for salvation" (*Brev.* 1.1, 5:210a; see also 5:201b–202a).

Bonaventure, however, by no means considers the human ability to gain knowledge the origin for finding the truth by means of the Scripture: "That is, it has not arisen by human investigation but by divine revelation" (5:201a). In his understanding, faith is also necessary—stemming from the divine Trinity, sent by God: "This is the knowledge of Jesus Christ, from whom the certainty and understanding of the whole of Holy Scrip-ture originally derives. It is therefore impossible for anyone to advance in understanding it unless he has infused faith in Christ into himself before-hand, as so to speak the lamp, the gateway, and indeed the fundament of all Scripture" (5:201a–b). How this is to be understood can be learned more precisely from another of Bonaventure's statements at another place in the *Breviloquium* (5.7, 5:260b–261a). Necessary in this is, first, infused faith (*fides infusa*), which comes about by the irradiation of truth that elevates the soul. Then comes the conviction of authority that strengthens the soul. This occurs through the Holy Scripture. "Both occur by Jesus Christ, who is Glory and Word [see Heb 1:3; John 1:1], and by the Holy Spirit, who shows and teaches the truth and many believed it." The faith instituted by Christ is therefore the prerequisite for scriptural understanding, the content of the Scripture the confirmation and securing in faith. This thought is developed in the prooemium to the John commentary as well. There Bonaventure speaks of the "certainty of authority," which stands in contrast to the "certainty of demonstration," which would only empty faith instead of producing it. Thus Scripture follows another way of proceeding, the way of narrating: "And this is the reason why all the books of Scripture are rendered in the form of narrative and not that of reasoning, because they are to produce faith that occurs by free consent" (*Comm. Joh.* prooem. 2 ad 1.2, *Opera omnia* 6:243b).

On the other hand, there are throughout also rules of method with which the interpreter can exhaust the content of Scripture. In §6 of the prologue to the *Breviloquium*, Bonaventure sets out such principles. The first of these rules is sanctified by a long tradition: first, obscure scriptural passages should be explained by other passages that are clearer. The example Bonaventure gives of this reminds us of numerous similar examples from the history of interpretation: in Ps 35 (34):2, "weapon and shield" mean "truth and goodwill," for Ps 5:13 reads "The shield of your favor" and Ps 91 (90):7 "like a shield surrounds yourself your truth" (5:207a). That Bonaventure applied the method of innerbiblical association is to a large extent an indication of how firmly rooted it was in tradition. He compares the Scripture to a zither in this respect: the deep string does not produce harmony by itself, only in unison with many others: "Thus one passage of Scripture depends on another, constantly relates to one passage a thousand others" (19.7, 5:421b). He also reaches back to tradition for the understanding of the literal sense by expressly appealing to Augustine's *De doctrina christiana* (3.10.14ff.; *Brev.* 5:207b–208a). According to this, there are three possible levels of understanding. When the original meaning of the words expresses faith or love, one must remain with it. Where the words designate something from the created realm, or from specifically Israelite ways of speaking, such as "the sheep bear twins" (Song 4:2), they are to be understood as figurative: it seems to Bonaventure clear "that the *sheep* stands for people, the *twins* doubled love." The third rule is that the interpreter, if a literal as well as a spiritual understanding seems evident, must first discuss whether a literal or figurative understanding is suitable, if both together are not possible. This applies, for example, to all the Old Testaments laws, which indeed had originally a historical sense but which have lost this meaning for Christian understanding. But if both are possible, one must accept both. Here also the tendency is not to aim at univocity but to mine the riches of Scripture from every side possible.

According to Bonaventure, the Holy Scripture is also placed in a specific way in the history of the world, which is a history of God with humanity. God so fashioned the world in creation "that by it, like by a mirror and a trace, humanity would be led to love and to praise God the creator. After this there is a doubled book, namely, one written from within that is God's eternal art and wisdom and another described from outside, that is to say, the visible world." Since there is only one creature that unites the external sense (like the animals) and an inner sense (like the angels), humans should come "to knowledge of the inner and external described book that is the wisdom and its work. Since in Christ eternal wisdom and its work coincide in one person at the same time, he is called the book described inward and external (Ezek 2:9) for the restoration of the world" (*Brev.* 2.11, 5:229a). Behind this christological reference, introduced somewhat abruptly, there seems still to shine through Bonaventure's basic view of salvation history: accordingly, the world that was in the beginning thought of as a mirror of God for humans in the primeval state is no longer in its original condition; it requires a restoration in order to be able again to fulfill this function. God created the world for the sake of the *minor mundus*, the smaller cosmos, that is, for the sake of humanity, who should be the mediator between God and world (see *Brev.* 7.4, 5:284b). This relationship was destroyed by the fall, but God does not give up on the world; he wants to restore it—which can occur only in congruence with the restoration of humanity. "When man was in good condition, this world would have to be arranged in a good and restful condition; with the fallen man this world would have to be made worse also; with the confused, likewise confused; with the purified man, it would likewise be purified; with the renewed, likewise renewed; and with the perfected man, it likewise comes to rest" (7.4, 5:2851). How salvation history moves toward this restoration of humanity by vast turns, and creation with it, according to Bonaventure's sketch of salvation history—in which Christ is the decisive figure of mediation—space is lacking here to present. The strong influence of Augustine and his image of history in this is immense. What interests us is the role the Bible plays for the Franciscan theologians.

We have brought before our eyes the image of the constantly swelling stream that Bonaventure used in the prologue of the *Breviloquium* for the

Holy Scripture. In this gradual increase the Scripture itself is inserted into salvation history. In *Coll. hex.* 13.8, the image is deepened and (in interpreting a word in the book of Esther) more precisely taken up once again: "The Scripture was a small source in law-giving, since the book of the regulations of the law is short, but it grew larger thereafter in the books of Joshua, Judges, Kings, Ezra, Judith, Tobit, Esther, Maccabees. Therefore it was transformed into light, namely, the prophets, for prophecy is light. Then into the Son, that is to say, the gospel." From this emerges a step-by-step growth of knowledge already in the Old Testament, which is, however, completely put in the shade by the gospel in the New. However, this is also balanced in another way: the many typological references between the Old and New Testament that Bonaventure points out in the traditional way are for him conclusive proof of the harmony that governs in the Bible as a whole.

Now, of course this salvation-history view of Bonaventure would be misunderstood by conceiving history and the Bible that unfolds within it in the sense of a development. For the noetically defined approach of the theologian, concern has to do instead with a process of knowledge in which what matters is the fact that man—we would use in its place a collective term such as humanity—regains the perfect insight destroyed through the fall into the world and so his creator. It has to do with a return to origin, and this return we could understand altogether intellectually, although it is tied with faith. Neo-Platonist influences (via Pseudo-Dionysius) play a role. In this context, Bonaventure speaks of several books. The first is the book of the world in which, as we already heard, God wanted to make himself known as creator. Christ, as was said in the same context, is the book of the restoration of the world, which itself has been confused by the confusion of humanity introduced by the fall. Since humans lost by the fall both the knowledge of the creator as well as the traces of him remaining in creation, "this book of the world was, so to speak, dead and extinguished, and another book was necessary by which this would be illumined to receive the sense of things. But this is the book of Scripture" (*Coll. hex.* 13.12, 5:390a). Finally, therefore, it is not creation itself that is destroyed by the fall, but humans in their knowledge of God as the creator. The restoration comes about in that Scripture leads humans back to this knowledge. The return to the origin is to be understood not cosmologically but spiritually.

One thus, of course, must immediately again restrict this statement if it is misunderstood intellectualistically. The spiritual hermeneutics expressed in the threefold spiritual sense of Scripture to which Bonaventure adheres with tradition prevents such a false interpretation that would overlook the holistic character of living with Bible as Bonaventure demands it and actualizes it himself. It has to do not with mere understanding but with an existential relatedness. Nevertheless, knowledge is meant. Of course, Bonaventure's explicit dissociation from profane philosophy, which does not know of a "knowledge of forgiveness of sins," shows how he understands the task of theological thinking as of another kind. Theology is for him the understanding of faith, and, as we have seen, this faith, which can only be bestowed by the illumination of the Spirit, is a prerequisite for understanding the Bible.

Near the end of his life, Bonaventure wrote yet another large work, which remained incomplete; we have already quoted from it many times. It was, as were so many others before, an overall view of salvation history in terms of the account of the seven day creation of Gen 1, a *hexaemeron*. We can see in this large-scale work a final witness that for Bonaventure theology could have its place only as interpretation of the Bible. But the concern in this work was not that of a biblical commentary in the strict sense. Rather, we have before us addresses (under the title *Collationes* = *Contributions*), which Bonaventure delivered before a large public audience in Paris in April/May of 1273. In this, his intent in the broadest sense is to show once again within the comprehensive framework of the traditional schema of the seven days of creation a correspondence between creation and salvation, the world and humanity. Only with respect to salvation does he speak of creation, and he understands the way of humanity in a traditional way as the way of meditation, which is not to be understood in the sense of speculative vision but in the spirit of monasticism as the advance to God's daily commissioning of people to service. Unfortunately, the work remained incomplete, coming to its end with the vision of the fourth day of creation. Thus we do not know how it would have rounded out as a whole. Its intent and audience distinguishes the *Hexaemeron* from the class-writing *Breviloquium*; nevertheless, many themes are repeated in spite of an inner development of Bonaventure that can also be observed. Especially important for our theme is the vision of the third day of creation (*Coll. hex.* 13–19), which has to do with the testimony of the Holy Scripture. Once again in comparison to the simpler form of the *Breviloquium*, we encounter here a yet heightened effort of Bonaventure to exhaust the manifold possibilities of spiritual scriptural interpretation in an ever more refined subdividing of the threefold spiritual sense of Scripture.

The relationship between the "book" of creation and the "book" of Scripture is more clearly formulated in the *Hexaemeron*:

It is certain that man, so long as he stood (upright), had the knowledge of created things. But when man fell, when he lost the knowledge, there was no one to lead him back to God. Therefore this book of the world was, so to speak, dead and extinguished, and another book was necessary by which this would be illumined to receive the sense of things. But this is the book of Scripture, which restores the similarities, the peculiarities, and the sense of things that are written in the book of the world. For the book of Scripture restores the entire work again to know God, to praise, and to love God. (13.12, 5:390a).

There, too, it applies: "If you do not know the order and the origin of restoration, you will not know the Scripture" (3.1.1, 5:345a). Even the historical scheme of history is altered in contrast to the *Breviloquium*: in *Coll. hex.* 16 is introduced, instead of a simple schema, a doubled schema of sevens, in which the first seven periods of world creation extends to Christ, the second from Christ to the end of the world, and a exact parallelization between the two periods of history is possible. That this schema was taken over from Joachim of Fiore is probable, as is the fact that its modification in Bonaventure is to serve to ward off Joachimite influences among the Franciscans.

One other thing becomes clear in the *Hexaemeron*: the true center of Scripture is Christ. Bonaventure places this statement right at the beginning. After establishing (likewise important for him) that the Spirit teaches those to whom it is spoken, only for the church (for what is holy should not be cast to hounds, nor pearls to swine; see Matt 7:6) the sentence immediately follows, "For he [the Spirit] teaches where one must begin, that is, from the center. This is Christ. If this center is scorned, then one has nothing" (1.1, 5:329a). To this belongs also that Bonaventure grants traditional typology (by the term *figurae sacramentales* [mystery-filled prefigurations]; 14.1, 6:393a) a central place. It is specified that the prefigures of Christ dealt with here are found in not only the Old Testament but also the New Testament. The division into four ages, each with three mysteries, which again can be interpreted as twelvefold, yields the number of 144 possibilities of interpretation corresponding to the secret number of Rev 7:4 (14.8–16, 5:394b–396a). But then not all these, but only forty-eight figures, are referred to Christ (14.17–30, 5:396a–398b). Twelve types for the antichrist are then named (14.1–9, 5:398a–399b). Bonaventure's main intention in *Collationes* 1 is to set forth Christ's absolute mediatorial position in seven steps. It is also the key to the Scripture. The well known passage Luke 24:45 serves Bonaventure as the point of contact for this statement, which he relates to John 1:14, Rev 19:13, and others (3.10–11, 5:344a). From this, then, follows the important statement: "If you do not know the order and origin of the restoration, you cannot know the Scripture" (3.11, 5:345a) The central role Christ plays as the center of Scripture for Bonaventure is certainly a legacy from Francis and hence a distinctive characteristic of Franciscan theology. This implies also—as always, the relationship might be judged differently—a proximity to Luther and the Reformation. This, too, is surely tied to Bonaventure's formation as an Augustinian. The fact that the theology of the cross plays an important role in his case can be added, but it is less evident in his biblical interpretation.

There is no question that, within the framework of traditional scriptural interpretation, the *Hexaemeron* marks a high point that could hardly be surpassed. That the future should belong nevertheless not to Bonaventure but Thomas Aquinas is perhaps no accident. The consistent innerbiblical theology, as Bonaventure pursued it, no longer had any possibilities of development over time. However, it was not so limited that during his lifetime Bonaventure could not exercise an extraordinary influence in his order and, beyond that, his church.

4
JEWISH INTERPRETERS OF THE MIDDLE AGES

The significance of medieval Jewish interpreters for the modern under-standing of the Bible should not be underestimated. The influences of Diaspora Judaism on the cultures of the various European lands where Jews lived from the time of the Roman Empire on were considerable, in spite of many, ever-intensifying persecutions culminating in expulsions from entire lands. Memories of these pogroms endure and weigh heavily like shadows over the history of Christian-Jewish relations. Nonetheless, there were times of friendly coexistence between the two groups of people, when there was no lack of contact between Christian and Jew. One espe-cially favorable situation for friendly coexistence arose under the caliphate of Cordova in Spain, because Islam granted minority-status protections to both religions of the book. Yet Jewish communities were frequently tol-erated, indeed, enjoyed certain privileges, in lands under Christians rule as well. Thus there were long intervals when cultural exchange as well as economic relations (Jews frequently dominated trade and banking) could develop. Not until the eleventh century did the situation come to a mounting crisis in many areas, at the end of which (1096) the first crusade began. This development went along with the consolidation of the church through reform movements and its all-dominating role in the public they brought about. With ever-increasing intensity, state and church felt Judaism's outsider position as a religious minority that stubbornly resisted Christianization. Efforts were therefore made to convert Jews, first by argument, then later by other means as well, including force.

Nevertheless, careful investigations, such as about the social situation of the Jews in northern France in the twelfth and thirteenth centuries, have shown that at that time they lived together with Christians in full assimilation. Rashi, for instance, working in northern France during the first crusade, lived there, as it seems, completely undisturbed, while at the same time radicalized masses of Christians in the Rhineland overran Jewish communities. For most of the eleventh century, however, Jews had lived in Mainz and Worms undisturbed, some being granted episcopal and imperial privileges. Only later was the situation to change drastically for the French Jews, with their expulsion from the kingdom in 1307. (They were expelled from England earlier, in 1291.) In light of the role the Bible played in the two religions, it is no wonder that disputes developed between Christianity and Judaism over understanding the Bible—for Christians the Old Testament, for Jews the Torah—and that Christian exegetes wanted to learn about the Old Testament from Jewish interpreters. Hebrew was no longer a living language even in early Christian times, and, due to the predominance of the Babylonian Talmud, traditional Jewish literature was written mainly in Aramaic. Even so, Jewish interpreters had an invaluable advantage of direct linguistic access to the Bible because of their knowledge of the original language of the Old Testament. Christian exegetes with few exceptions were unfamiliar with Hebrew, and when they tried to gain such knowledge or at least information about the original meaning of biblical expressions, they could receive it only from Jews.

Although frequently such exchanges were officially forbidden, there were definitely ways of gaining such information, since Jews and Christians lived in such close proximity to one another. What Jerome had already sought in antiquity—contact with Jewish people in the vicinity for information and possibly instruction in Hebrew—some Christian interpreters of the Middle Ages undertook, too. This certainly happened only rarely; upon closer examination, most of the knowledge about the meaning of the names and words of the Bible one encounters in Christian exegetes goes back to information from Jerome. In addition, official Christian-Jewish public disputes were frequent, particularly in the eleventh century, the period of Rashi's activity, and were concerned especially with their differing understandings of the Bible. On such occasions, Christian theologians tried to persuade their Jewish disputation partners of the correctness of the christological understanding of the Old Testament. Conversely, it was the intention of the Jewish biblical interpreters first to convince their associates in faith, and if possible also Christians, that they alone had the correct understanding of the Hebrew Bible and then to show that Christian views were misinterpretations. Neither of the two confessional groups, however, went at this task without bias; each was in large measure determined by its own tradition of interpretation.

Jewish exegesis of the Middle Ages was as strongly bound to tradition as Christian exegesis was. The Jewish traditional literature, which had

already formed in the early post-Christian centuries and developed further throughout the Middle Ages, was an essential part of interpretation
of the Bible, although certainly in a sense other than the Christian. Rabbinic Judaism, surviving defeat by the Romans and final expulsion from
Palestine as the sole ruling way in the Diaspora, understood itself above
all as the true guardian of the Torah, which one had to develop as a comprehensive life order and to adapt it to new circumstances. The Bible was
indeed not the sole source of these rules, because the rabbis also made
decisions on their own authority or later adapted them to the Bible. In
principle, however, the entire order rested on biblical bases. From this
emerged the rule work of the halakah, which was first developed in the
tractates of the Mishnah. Later the Gemara was added, first in Palestine
(the Palestinian Talmud, third–fourth century), then in Mesopotamia,
which, with the talmudic academies of Sura and Pumbedita, had become
more and more the center of Diaspora Judaism. There also was found,
during the Abassid caliphate of Baghdad, a center of the Islamic world.
The Mishnah and Gemara were joined to the Talmud. They contained,
in addition to halakah, moral-edificatory narratives (haggadah) that
served the pious instruction of the Diaspora communities. Both forms of
midrash (= interpretation) were tightly interwoven in the Mishnah and
Babylonian Talmud. The Babylonian Talmud, in essentials closed at the
time of the flowering of the Babylonian academies in the eighth century,
became its authoritative form in the West as well, by which—after the end
of the school of Jerusalem in the eleventh century even in Palestine—it
gained acceptance, particularly in Spain (where the exilarch Natronai ben
Zabinai, deposed in 771 and expelled from Bagdad, had fled). Learned
rabbis throughout the centuries have considered imparting the talmudic
tractates and commenting on them to be their most important task.

Because the Talmud was at its core an interpretation of the Bible and
communities encountered this biblical order of life chiefly in this mediated form, work with the Bible itself receded to second place in Judaism.
The most powerful protest movement against this was the sect of the
Karaites, founded at the start of the eighth century, who recognized the
biblical Torah as sole authority and denied the talmudic tradition as a
whole. It has indeed been able to maintain itself as a limited movement to
the present, above all in Byzantine and Eastern Europe. Adherents of the
Babylonian Talmud, however, successfully averted its frontal attack on the
literature of tradition for Judaism as a whole.

Nevertheless, the debate with the Karaites became the germ cell
of a new form of dealing with the Bible. It was no one less than Saadia

ben Josef (882–942), the leader (the title Gaon = "the sublime one") of the most important Babylonian academy of Sura, who had led the fight against the sect, who helped bring about the breakthrough to a methodological approach with the Bible. His Arabic translation of Scripture and his commentary on it laid the basis for a new approach: rational criteria and considerations of grammar and lexicography were put to use in ascertaining the "natural" meaning of the wording of any biblical statement, which was worthy of attention on its own, alongside that of the figurative sense. His model was of such great influence on later Jewish exegetes, in Arabic lands especially, that a new era can be said to have begun with him. This literal sense was named by the term *peshat* by a group of Talmudists who followed his initiative, while the edifying-figurative sense was called *derash*.

A distinctive biblical exegesis developed somewhat later in French-German Judaism than in Arabic Spain and from independent roots. The presumed origins of this population group point in the direction of Italy and from there beyond, toward Byzantium, so that lines of connection to the original land of the Karaites but also to the Babylonian tradition are to be assumed for them. We will first turn to their most important representative.

4.1. Biblical Literal Sense and Talmudic Tradition: Rashi

The medieval tradition took little interest in the dates of a scholar's personal life, thus all the more exclusively on his works. Hence our reports on the dates of Rashi's birth and death are uncertain and secondhand. He was born, it seems, in the year 4800 by Jewish time-reckoning (i.e., 1039/1040 c.e.) and died in 4865 (1104/1105 c.e.). He is said to have been sixty-five years old. Solomon bar Isaac (Rabbi Schelomoh Yitshaqi; shortened: Rashi) came into the world about 120 kilometers southeast of Paris at Troyes, the historical capital of Champagne, at the time a flourishing commercial city at the intersection of two major routes to Italy and the Near East, and died there. He was the offspring of a prominent family of scholars tracing its line of descent from Rabbi Johanan the Sandalmaker, a student of Rabbi Akiba. Of course, since such a tradition cannot be proven, the family's actual ancestry lies in darkness. Although he himself had no sons, he was the father-in-law and grandfather of other scholars. Perhaps the best known is his grandson, Rabbi Samuel ben Meir (Rashbam; ca. 1085–1174.) As customary in Judaism, the rabbis engaged in their scholarly activity as an additional occupation.

Rashi seems to have lived from the proceeds of a vineyard, as occasional references disclose.

In the eleventh century and even thereafter, Jews in northern France and the Rhineland lived in close symbiosis with their Christian neighbors. Their deportation into ghettos, closed-off living areas, was still unknown. Thus a lively exchange of culture followed, and economic and business relations were quite close between followers of the two confessions. Jews were not restricted to certain occupations. As Rashi's example shows, it was quite usual for Jews to own vineyards and gain their livelihood from them. To do so, Christian day workers were employed, or one had Christian employees in the wine trade. Economic factors evidently played a role: thus Christians plowed the fields of Jewish landowners or built houses for them on the Sabbath and vice versa, Christians might have Jewish co-workers for Sunday work. The churches were also tolerant toward the Jews. No attempt was made to exclude them from, say, the markets. This era of toleration came to its end only at the outbreak of the first crusade around the year 1096. The pogroms erupting in the Rhineland and elsewhere and carried out by the authorities, as well as the measures of economic oppression in particular, are reflected in Rashi's correspondence from this period.

Rashi could not receive his education in Troyes. He went, instead, to the center of Jewish scholarly education for his studies: in the Rhineland (at the time called Lotharingia.) One of the largest Jewish communities in the Rhineland was in Mainz as long ago as the ninth century. Talmudic research was pursued there possibly as early as the days of Charlemagne, for which the migration of a famous family of scholars from Babylon, the Kalonomides family, gave stimulus. At the start of the eleventh century at the latest, a talmudic academic was founded. At the time of Rashi's stay, its director was the famous teacher Rabbi Jacob ben Yakar (d. 1064). He introduced Rashi into talmudic study in particular. Another of Rashi's teachers in Mainz was Rabbi Isaac ben Judah. After Rabbi Jacob's death, Rashi left Mainz and went to Worms, where likewise an old Jewish community and an academy existed. There his teacher was Rabbi Isaac ben Eleazar ha-Levi. It is reported that Rashi completed his studies in spite of severe financial difficulties, for he had already started a family. How long he stayed in Worms (presumably a few years) is not known in any detail. At the end of his study he returned to Troyes, where he remained for the rest of his life. There he founded a scholarly academy around 1070 and apparently wrote all his commentaries—on the Talmud, Pentateuch, and other biblical books. By the way, we can picture the origin

of these commentaries as quite similar to the way Christian biblical commentaries were produced: Rashi presented his interpretation orally in
his teaching hours, and his students wrote down his commentary. Afterwards the master looked it over and revised it, in some circumstances
several times over the course of the year. Rashi is said to have revised his
Talmud commentary three times over the course of his lifetime. The final
version—not in every case complete—is preserved. From what we know
of Christian biblical interpreters of the time, Joachim of Fiore, among
others, it is not surprising to learn that Rashi also illustrated difficult biblical facts by drawings. Unfortunately, these have been omitted in later
printings of his commentary.

Due to Rashi's activity, Troyes and its academy became so famous
that it served as the center of French talmudic and biblical interpretation
thereafter, well into the thirteenth century. Rashi was able to reconcile the
up-to-then divergent theories and practices of the various Jewish schools
that derived from Gershom ben Judah, and he thus united Jewish research
in Europe. Rashi personally gained standing within Judaism as an uncontested authority: his Talmud commentary in particular became standard
reading in all talmudic schools. This role extended so far that later printed
editions of the Talmud included Rashi's commentary along with the texts.
Beyond this, Rashi (and his students after him) were called upon to decide
current legal conflicts to which talmudic law applied. He did not live as a
scholar closed off from the world but engaged in a lively correspondence
on questions of law and other everyday affairs. A vast collection of such
decisions is preserved in which Rashi's authority evidently ended the
debate that arose. His influence extended throughout European Judaism
and contributed greatly to uniting it under an obligatory form of life.

This high estimate of Rashi's Talmud commentary was evidently in
keeping with his own view as well, for he composed this work apparently
before he turned to commenting on the Bible. This is an important fact to
know, because it shows that Rashi by no means understood his involve-
ment with the Bible and its literal sense in particular as an alternative
to the Talmud. His basic stance in this regard was, as we will still see in
detail, thoroughly conservative. Nevertheless, his biblical commentaries
have gained far greater attention in later exegesis. Modern biblical interpreters who see Rashi as one of their most significant precursors are in
large measure justified. In fact, he can be considered in certain respects a
pioneer of a new direction in biblical understanding. On the other hand,
the fact that he was a pioneer means that much in him was still immature,
that he had not gained full clarity about the full significance of his new

approach to the Bible and its relationship to traditional forms of interpretation. Precisely for this reason, however, it is especially fascinating to deal with his commentaries.

When we select for closer examination Rashi's Pentateuch commentary from his commentary works (which encompass the Pentateuch, the Prophets, and the Writings; he was the first Jewish interpreter to elucidate the entire Bible), there are both material and practical reasons. Rashi evidently began his biblical interpretation with the Pentateuch commentary because the five books of Moses formed the central part of Scripture for Judaism. As the most important task of biblical instruction, the interpretation of the Torah had therefore to come at the lecture cycle by necessity. For these reasons also, when in the previous century and at the start of this century the German science of Judaism introduced a new way of dealing with the history of Jewish biblical interpretation in the Middle Ages, Rashi's Pentateuch commentary was considered of greatest importance and was the first to appear in modern translations. Hence there is a relatively easily accessible English-language edition also available to English readers.

The first thing to be said about Rashi's Pentateuch commentary is that we find ourselves dealing with, although in selection, a verse-by-verse interpretation. This corresponds perfectly with what we observe in Christian commentaries of the same period. The dislike of systematizing of any sort, however, is considerably greater among Jewish interpreters—apart from the system that the order of life obligatory for all Jews materializes from all sorts of textual comparisons between statements of the various biblical books, but within the Pentateuch particularly through the legal structure of halakah. As Rashi had shown in his Talmud commentary, he mastered this traditional material completely. Even in his Pentateuch commentary he grants an important place to traditional interpretation. He would have had to do so in order to avoid the suspicion that he wanted to ignore the halakah. But he draws from the vast abundance of tradition only a limited selection of halakic and haggadic explanations. These are drawn in part from early traditional material, the Tannaitic midrashim, and in part from the Talmud. On the other hand, he lets it be known at various places that his special interest lies elsewhere. The first statement of this sort we find at Gen 3:8, where it is said that Adam and Eve heard "the voice of the LORD" who walked through the garden of Eden. Here Rashi says, "There are many haggadic midrashim, and our rabbis have already collected them in their position in Bereshit Rabbah [the talmudic tractate on Genesis]. But I come only to bring the simple sense [peshat] of the verse, and such haggadot that explain the words of the text in a way appropriate for its context." There then follows the simple notice that the two would have heard God's voice as it came through the garden. This "But I come" or "I came" is a formula recurring many times with which Rashi introduces his own explanation that apparently first occurred to him and relates to the literal sense (*peshat*) of the statement under concern. But various other formulations are to be adduced by which Rashi introduces the explanation of his own that is to render this "text-appropriate" sense. Thus Rashi first remarks on the statement in Exod 23:2, "Do not follow a majority into evil": "For this verse there are explanations (midrash) by the wise of Israel (the rabbis), but they do not fit the statement's wording very well." He then quotes a whole host of halakic interpretations, such as the rabbis who tried to find in the sentence the legal advisory that a judgment is legitimate only if it is decided not by a majority of not one but at least two judges or that one should not reach a judgment against the voice of the presiding judge, because the youngest member of the judicial tribunal is always asked for his opinion first. Mentioned as well is the paraphrase of the Targum that sees in the text an advisory against being evasive in answering court inquiries. In the end, he states: "But to explain it (the verse) in terms of its simple sense [*peschat*], I would say that the interpretation is, 'Do not follow the majority into doing evil. If you see the evil bend the law, I do not say I will go along with them because they are in the majority.'" In returning to the verse's original sense, Rashi causes the entire artificial structure of halakic tradition to collapse.

In this explanation, and others like it for which examples can be given, it becomes clear that Rashi's intention is to bring the original sense of the biblical statements to life again among his students, who are completely buried in rabbinic traditional exegesis. Overall about one third of his commentary is devoted to interpreting the literal sense. In the numerous phrases "But I say," "but I interpret this verse," and the like, the interpreter's love of discovery emerges, which again brought to light a long-forgotten truth. The significance of the rediscovery of the literal sense can be visualized today only by realizing how far the traditional model of rabbinic halakic and haggadic interpretation had pushed the biblical foundations into the background. The parallel to Christian allegorical biblical interpretation is obvious, all the differences of method and content notwithstanding. In both cases the biblical text is merely the foil for the formal canonical foundation of a system that had over time distanced itself far from the Bible. To put an end to this development,

however, Jewish biblical interpreters such as Rashi and his successors
had a decisive advantage: they were able to read the Old Testament Bible
in its original Hebrew. This knowledge enabled them to penetrate to the
original sense of the biblical statements by investigating word meanings,
grammar, and syntax.

One other aspect remains to be mentioned, which modern Jewish
authors like to highlight with respect to Rashi's word exegesis: his anti-
Christian apologetics. It should not be overstated, however. On the
contrary, its relatively rare appearance seems to mean that Rashi was little
disposed toward polemics of this sort. In cases when Christian interpreters
tried to interpret an Old Testament statement in messianic or Trinitarian terms, he set the literal sense over against them. But this is actually
done rather indirectly. So, at Gen 1:26, where Christian interpretation was
accustomed to refer the phrase "Let us make man" to the Trinity, Rashi
explains altogether unpolemically that God deigned to consult with his
angels, to which a reference to Dan 4:14 is attached. As a Jewish interpreter, Rashi naturally held firm to the customary interpretation, as, for
example, on Gen 3:15. But at the word "seed," to which Christian allegorical view attached as *protoevangelium*, he does not comment at all. In
many passages outside the Pentateuch for which Christian exegesis put
special stress on a christological interpretation, Rashi's restatement of the
Jewish standpoint may have been consciously formulated in opposition to
the Christian, as, for example, when for the suffering servant of God in Isa
53 he presents the traditional Jewish collective understanding of "servant"
as Israel, or when at Ps 2:2 he rejects any reference to the Messiah (presented by rabbis as well) and remarks in the sense of *peshat*: "It would be
more correct to refer the statement to David himself." In these instances,
however, explicit polemics are conspicuously absent. If we add Rashi's
statement, found elsewhere, that Christianity is not to be considered an
idolatrous religion, we recognize the attitude of toleration behind it. On
Num 24:17–19, the fourth Balaam prophecy, a messianic view was also
alive in the Jewish tradition. Rashi follows the messianic interpretation
of verse 19 in the Targum and midrash (Pesiq. Rab. 13) with reference to
Ps 72:8 and Obad 18, while in verse 17 he finds an allusion to David, with
reference to 2 Sam 8:2. But this is relatively seldom the case. Christian
interpretation goes unmentioned. Actually, one can recognize that traditional Christian interpretation of the Old Testament and Jewish midrashic
interpretation pay no attention to each other with respect to content. The
two were first again able to enter into conversation together on the basis
of the literal sense.

In Rashi's commentaries explicit references are found to the fact that he used the Hebrew-Aramaic lexica of Menahem ben Jacob ben Saruq (ca. 910–970) and Dunasch ibn Labrat (ca. 920–980). Ben Saruq's work, the *Machberet* (grouping) arranges the words in the order of their roots, while ibn Labrat wrote the *Teshuvot* with the addition of views. Here was laid a lexical foundation on which a literal interpretation of biblical statements could be built. But Rashi did not follow these two lexicographers in every case; divergent accounts of roots can be found in his works too. Grammar and etymology play a significant role in Rashi. A nearly complete Hebrew grammar can be compiled from his commentaries. For example, he knew—more than his predecessors ben Saruq and ibn Labrat—complete stem-forms of verbs. He quite often sought to recapture adequately the meaning of a Hebrew term in his native language, Old French (incidentally, in Hebrew letters), so that his commentaries are a treasure house for research in the history of the French language. Nearly one thousand such French glosses (*loazim*) have been counted in his Bible commentaries, over two thousand in his interpretations of the Talmud.

These references become more understandable when we realize that there was a Jewish Old French biblical translation to which Rashi referred. Hebrew and Aramaic (the language of the Babylonian Talmud and the Targums) were indeed only scholarly languages or familiar only from synagogue readings from the Bible, much as Latin was used in Christian worship and among scholars. (Whether Rashi knew Latin, at least to some extent, is uncertain.) In any case, in his youth Rashi himself, like his audience, had learned the Bible in their native Old French language. The aim of Rashi's Old French rendering of Hebrew words was to contribute to correcting the French edition on the basis of the original text. Manuscripts of native-language editions, corrected in keeping with his specifications, were then prepared later. Rashi was intensively concerned with word meanings. For him, lexicography and etymology were closely connected. But his efforts to define the sense of a word from its original meaning, limited by the still incomplete knowledge of the time and the weakness of its method, often seem arbitrary to today's observers. But in many respects pioneering work in Hebrew lexicography was accomplished already at the time. In so doing, however, Rashi still used methods originating in antiquity. Rules such as assonance (paronomasia) as the bases of comparison between two words distant from one other with respect to content, but also ambiguity of a term (polysemy) and the equivalence of meaning of various words (synonymy), are all methodological approaches to word explanations that are also found frequently in Rashi. In addition to inner-Hebrew parallels, he also referred to Greek words, among other things. At the basis of this seems to be recourse to the ancient interpretive traditions of Greek biblical translations, with which—it is recently said to be shown—Rashi remains in unbroken continuity. In this respect he is oriented toward the past rather than the future. He also liked to draw on the Aramaic of the Babylonian Targum in order to explain the meaning of Hebrew words. On the other hand, however, he can also occupy himself in detail with the various nuances of meaning of Hebrew prepositions, refer to the meaning of accents in the traditional text, offer suggestions for rearranging words in the text—and thus do text-critical work nearly in the modern sense.

Based on his efforts for the simple sense of the text, Rashi arrived at some remarkable explanations. One example is his interpretation of Gen 1:1. Rashi understands the first sentence of the Bible—after he had first mentioned the talmudic interpretation (Genesis Rabbah), in which the world was created for the sake of the Torah and Israel—in its literal meaning as follows: "At the beginning of the creation of heaven and earth, when the earth was still formless and void and darkness, God said: 'Let there be light!'" (i.e., verses 1 and 2 are subordinated to verse 3.) The creation of the light is therefore the *first* work of creation. As the basis for this, Rashi cites language usage: the Hebrew word *bereshit* "is linked in scripture with the words that follow" (e.g., Jer 26:1: "At the beginning of the reign of Jehoiakim"; Gen 10:10; Deut 18:4; Hos 1:2). "Therefore you must say here also, in the beginning, when God created, as if it was existing at the beginning of creation." "The verse is not intended to teach the sequence of creation in order to say that these (heaven and earth) were created first. If this were its intention, the term *berishona* would have been used." But Rashi has a substantive objection as well. Verse 2 states that "the Spirit of God hovered over the waters." From this, one might "surmise that the water was already created before the earth." This contradiction leads Rashi to the conclusion "that the verse does not teach us anything about a sequence of what was earlier and what was later." The construction of Gen 1:1 and its meaning have been disputed again and again in later research. Rashi's explanation represents an important contribution to the discussion. His knowledge of Hebrew language usage particularly makes his explanation superior to those of other contemporaries. In cases when a term's meaning is in doubt, however, reference back to the Targum, which offers a mainly literal translation of the text into Aramaic, is also of assistance. Thus, for example, with regard to the first verb form in Gen 27:33, where the Targum that Rashi explicitly names as his source had correctly rendered the word's meaning as "trembled," while the midrash that Rashi mentioned had imaginative elaborations as well: "He saw hell [gehenna] open up beneath himself."

One characteristic trait of Rashi's biblical interpretation that is observable throughout his commentaries, however, is its two tracks. Instances when he rejects the traditional exegesis of a verse as unsuitable and substitutes his own "text-adequate" interpretation are relatively few. We find far more frequently a procedure of another sort: *peshat*, the understanding related to the original sense and *derash*, traditional interpretation from the Mishnah and Talmud, are simply placed side by side. But to be distinguished here is the halakic midrashim, that is, rabbinic rules for daily living, law, and court decisions that had developed over the centuries from the biblical law books and now formed a firmly established system, on the one hand, and the haggadic midrashim, which represented nothing more than edifying-homiletic developments from narrative material and thus was far less obligatory. As for the halakah, Rashi considered himself highly bound to tradition, which in most cases he reproduces. Nonetheless, examples are also found where he added a *peshat* interpretation to the approved halakah, though it could be harmonized with the halakah. Thus on Exod 12:2, which speaks of a month in which the Passover festival should be celebrated, there was a halakic explanation already given in Mekilta stating that the new moon should be described as the beginning of the month. Rashi gives this but adds as a textual explanation that the month referred to is Nisan, which is considered the first in the sequence of the months. In an era when the original sense of a biblical statement received hardly any attention, this was important information. Such cases, however, did not give rise to any conflict with traditional interpretation, which was interested here in a more precise dating of the Passover. However, there are also cases in which Rashi certainly must have faced contradictions between the tradition and the original sense of a biblical statement. He seems, as a rule, to have avoided going into these matters more closely in order to avoid a conflict. One example is his explanation of the regulation in Exod 21:6. The rabbis had softened its original sense, that the slave whose the ear was bored through should voluntarily remain the lord's slave "forever," by harmonizing the regulation with that of Num 25:10 from the Jubilee Year law, which stipulates that every slave should be set free after a term of fifty years. Rashi adopts this harmonization with the comment that *le'olam* could also mean "for a long time," that is, fifty years. But he was presumably aware of the regulation's original meaning.

But also in numerous cases having to do with a haggadic explanation, Rashi was ready to acknowledge this alongside the literal sense. For example, Gen 35:8 reports that Deborah, Rebekah's nurse, had died and been buried below Bethel and, as Rashi interprets the term, "below the plain." (Actually, an oak tree is meant.) Here the rabbis themselves had already debated the problem why Jacob received news of the death of the nurse but not of the death of his mother Rebekah, of whom nothing is said. The midrash Genesis Rabbah resolves the difficulty by stating that Rebekah died on the same day but that the news was kept secret. Rashi adopts this haggadah and supports it by rendering the word 'alon ("oak") by "another," that is, "another grief," by which he appeals to the Greek word allos. Thus the honor of the patriarchs, a rabbinic concern, is preserved.

Another example of combining two modes of interpretation with one another is Rashi's explanation of Gen 11:28. There it is reported—in a Priestly written text, according to modern scholarship, but distinctions of sources were completely outside the horizon of Rashi's time—that Haran (the brother of Abraham and the father of Lot) died before his father Terah. Rashi gives the explanation according to the statement's literal sense: "at the lifetime of his father." But at the same time, he cites a haggadic midrash (Genesis Rabbah) that renders the Hebrew expression 'al-pene as "by the guilt" and appends a lengthy story to it. In this story, Terah complained to King Nimrod (Gen 10:8) about his son Abraham for destroying his idols. Nimrod thereupon cast Abraham into a red-hot oven (a recollection of Dan 3). Abraham emerged from it unscathed. Haran, however, was unable to decide and made his judgment dependent on the outcome of the trial. Only when Abraham stepped forth from the fire unharmed did he declare himself for him. Thereupon Haran was thrown into the oven and burned. He died, then, by the guilt of his father Terah. The midrash also explains Ur Kasdim, the place named in connection with this story, as "the fire of the Chaldeans." Rashi also cites this information and adds another explanation of Ur as "well," that is, as "valley." This, as Rashi explicitly states, is the interpretation of Menahem (ben Saruq) and therefore stemmed from the Machberet. He again seems to find no contradiction between derash and peshat.

Another case is Rashi's explanation of the covenant God made with Abraham in Gen 15. Here Rashi brings to the statement in verse 10 that Abraham had divided the sacrificial heifer, goat, and ram in preparation for the covenant enactment, but not the birds, the peshat explanation that in making a covenant it was customary to divide an animal and to walk between the pieces. In one breath, however, he refers to the rabbinic interpretation that cattle, rams, and goats (according to Ps 22:13; Dan 8:20) mean the peoples of the world, and Israel (in Song 2:14) would be compared with young doves: "Therefore, he divided those animals as indicating that the peoples of the world would pass away. But he did not divide the birds, thereby indicating that Israel would last eternally." Rashi does not seem to have noticed the contradiction in the method.

As a final example, the episode from the flood narrative is to be mentioned, namely, the remark in Gen 7:16, "And God shut him in." What is meant is that God closed the ark behind Noah when the great rains set in, and the ark was left to the waters. Here Rashi proposes, as the simple sense of the statement: "He shut before him because of the waters." Thus, he explains the word meaning of the Hebrew *ba'ad* as "before" (with additional passage citations). Prior to this, however, he referred to the midrash in Genesis Rabbah stating that, when Noah and his family and the animals entered the ark, God protected it from the furious attacks of the other people who, having become guilty, wanted to kill Noah, by encircling them with bears and lions who ripped some of them to pieces. He mentioned this story only briefly, as was his custom, but he obviously assumed his students were familiar with it.

In cases of obvious contradictions, the presupposition that the entire Pentateuch had to come from Moses, self-evident for Rashi, often necessitated quite artificial interpretations. Thus Rashi explained the statement in Gen 1:6, "Let there be a firmament," not as the creation of heaven; rather, since the creation of heaven and earth was already spoken of in verse 1, he translated, "Let the heaven be made firm." Another example is the contradiction, which likewise Rashi noticed, between the reports of the creation of woman in Gen 1 and 2. Whereas later interpreters concluded from this that there were two different sources, Rashi explained the finding by referring back to a traditional rule of interpretation (*kelal* and *perat*) stating that the Torah often first makes a general statement and then specifies it more precisely. Thus the creation of man and woman is first spoken of in Gen 1, and the matter is then set forth in greater detail in Gen 2. The contradiction between the two descriptions in the flood narrative—according to Gen 6:19, two specimens, a male and a female, of each sort of all the animals enter the ark; in Gen 7:2, on the other hand, clean and unclean animals are distinguished, and seven pairs each of the clean animals as well as the birds are said to be brought in—is resolved in a similar fashion. Here again the general statement is presented first; the more detailed description follows.

In cases of anthropomorphic statements about God, Rashi can save himself with rationalist interpretations of another sort. Thus in the famous statement in Gen 1:26 where God says, "Let us make humankind in our own image." The idea that an image of God could be made seems to him impossible. Instead of this, "in our own image" means in the casting mold that, as Rashi explains, God prepared for the creation of humans. Following this, "in our likeness" means nothing other than that God possesses understanding and reason and that humans should have the same, by which it is maintained that God's understanding and reason cannot be compared to human attributes.

Also striking is Rashi's reverence for the patriarchs, whom he consequently defends against every possible moral reproach. For example, according to Rashi, when Rachel steals her father's household gods (*teraphim*; Gen 31:19), she did it only in order to save him from idolatry.

All in all, today's reader of Rashi's commentaries comes away with a completely contradictory impression. In many of his word explanations and interpretations of the simple sense (*peshat*), Rashi seems very modern. When he makes room for midrash, even in its often imaginative haggadic form, as he does in numerous cases, he seems to be an adherent and transmitter of traditional rabbinic interpretation. He was evidently not yet able to move beyond this in-between stance, had not yet decided for the one or the other of these two modes of interpretation, or rather could not yet see the contradiction in which further pursuit into the original sense of the biblical statements would turn into the midrashim proliferating over the course of centuries, edifying moralizing or even halakic harmonizing and supplementary (expanding) rules.

Some of his students went on to take a further decisive step. To be mentioned here in particular is Rashi's grandson, Samuel ben Meier (Rashbam). He programmatically called for separating the literal sense from all the midrashic exegesis, explaining in his commentary on the Pentateuch on Gen 1:26: "Moses wrote nothing (about) angels, purgatory, or mystical speculation, but only about things (such as those) we see in the world." Over the course of time, the rationalist outlook that had entered Sephardic Judaism of Spain earlier under Arabic influence won more room in Ashkenazic Judaism in middle Europe as well. Another representative living at the same time to be mentioned is Joseph Kara and his biblical commentaries. Incidentally, it must be added that this rationalist-philological direction of exegesis was anything but universally approved by rabbinic interpreters of the Middle Ages. Moreover, during the period Rashi was active, the Hassidic (Jewish-mystical) movement emerged, possibly in his immediate vicinity (in the Rhineland during his stay there), but he took no notice of it at all. Thus his exegesis of the literal sense is merely one of various lines alive at the time. Nevertheless, it has been of central significance for the development of modern biblical understanding. This is not least because Nicholas of Lyra, the great Franciscan exegete (of whom we will hear in the next chapter), used Rashi's commentaries in such large measure. Martin Luther, in turn, was greatly influenced by Nicholas. He also made use of Jewish exegesis, including Rashi's works, among others, in his great undertaking of a German translation of the Bible from the original languages (see volume 3). Rashi's commentary on the Pentateuch was the first Hebrew book ever printed, in 1475.

4.2. Under the Influence of Arabic Culture: Abraham ibn Ezra

Abraham ben Meier ibn Ezra was probably born in 1089 in Tudela in northeast Spain; the earlier view that his birthplace was the city of Toledo is incorrect. When Ibn Ezra (he is usually referred to by his family name) came into the world, Tudela was still in Moorish hands. Yet the *reconquista*, the Christian reconquest of Spain, had already begun. It went from the Pyrenees and led first to the formation in the north of the peninsula of small frontier states, which gradually extended to the south. Toledo, the major cultural center of Castile, had already been reconquered in 1085 by the Castilian King Alfonso VI (1065/1072–1109). Tudela, the city of Ezra's birth, was incorporated into his empire by Alfonso I of Aragon (1104–1134), the victorious conqueror. We do not know whether Ibn Ezra lived under Christian rule: Cordova, where he stayed for a while, remained in Muslim possession for a long time (until 1236). The further extension of the Christian monarchies and their unification into a Spanish empire overall belong to a later period. The last Moorish bastion, Granada, did not fall until 1492. In a Christian-ruled area, Ibn Ezra would presumably have had tolerably good living conditions for a Jewish scholar, because the Christian governments were at first tolerant of Muslims and Jews; the era of compulsory conversions and the inquisition falls largely in the fifteenth and sixteenth centuries. On the other hand, the cultural flowering made possible by religious toleration in Islamic areas was unable to continue. The fanatical Almoravides, called into the land from North Africa in 1086 by King Al-Mu'tamid ibn Abbad of Seville (whom they soon pushed out themselves), tried to bring about a radical Islamization of the Spaniards under their rule. After all this, their pressure later eased, and Jewish life was able also to recover somewhat. But the old flowering was probably not again reached. At the least, Ibn Ezra's personal life situation could not have been good. The precise reasons for his poverty, which he speaks of with self irony in a well-known poem, are not known.

> Sphere of heaven, hosts of stars, have conspired against me
> When I was born.
> Therefore nothing brings me profit, whatever I might start with.
> Were I to conduct business with candles, sunshine would continue always.
> If I bought clothes for the dead, everybody would remain alive.

Legends have in part grown around his life and his relationship to his famous contemporary Judah Halevi (ca. 1075–1141), who is said to have given his daughter to be Ibn Ezra's wife under romantic circumstances. It can be confirmed that Ibn Ezra knew the poet and philosopher personally in Cordova, where he also lived, but their theological outlooks were, as we will see, greatly opposed. Overall, we have to guess at details of his life from incidental notices in his works. It is certain that he was married and that he had four sons, although only one is known by name, Isaac. He was a gifted poet, living first in Baghdad, where he possibly converted to Islam—surely an occasion of deep distress to his father. Persecutions, which Ibn Ezra mentions, may have been the reason for his emigration around 1138–1139, like a flight "with terrified soul." He lived the life of a wanderer thereafter, until his death in 1164. The changing places where he stayed are known primarily because he names the places where he wrote each of his books. He first traveled to Rome but soon came into conflict with the Jewish community there. In 1145 he was in Lucca, then Mantua and Verona. In 1147 he left Italy and traveled first through Provençe, where he visited Narbonne and Béziers, then to northern France (Rouen and Dreux). A brief stay in London (after 1158) was presumably ended by his return to Narbonne, where we meet him in 1161. Presumably he died there. That he traveled to the Holy Land in advanced age and died in Rome are among the legends built up about his life.

Ibn Ezra was a man of many talents. Among other things, he occupied himself as poet, writing secular, liturgical-spiritual, and philosophical poems that are strewn throughout his many printed works and manuscripts. In so doing, he followed a widespread custom, for a whole series of learned rabbis known to us wrote sacred and liturgical poetry; serving in this capacity, they were called *paitanim* (bards). Since the Bible was the basis of such poetry, this custom contributed a good deal to knowledge of the Bible and the Hebrew language.

He also wrote scientific works on mathematics, astronomy, and astrology. His interest in philosophy is shown in his writings on the philosophy of religion, which are preserved in the form of epigrams. The most significant is the poem "Chaj ben Meqîz," in which the ascent of the soul from the realm of the earthly-material world into the realm of the intelligible one is described in keeping with the Neo-Platonic system.

Such a clear expression of his philosophical standpoint—we recognize in his Neoplatonist-Aristotelian views his dependence particularly on the Arabic philosopher Avicenna (980–1037)—is of course not to be found in his commentaries. But even there his affiliation with the Spanish school of rationalist biblical interpretation clearly emerges, as it, founded by Saadia Gaon, was trained especially in the Arabic thinkers who had transplanted forms of ancient thinking into their culture and transmitted them to Spanish Judaism. He is to this extent a representative of the twelfth-century "Enlightenment" in the realm of Judaism. This becomes especially clear in his relationship to Judah Halevi, who had written in his *Kuzari* a great apologetic work defending the historically conditioned faith of Israel against the "faith of the philosophers." For Ibn Ezra, on the other hand, it is knowledge that holds first place: insight and understanding are true worship of God, or at any rate they precede true worship of God as a condition.

This shows itself in the method he employs in his biblical exegesis. In it, grammar and lexicography play an important role as the first preconditions for interpreting the Hebrew text. In the field of grammar, Ibn Ezra's merit consists above all in that he critically revised the results of the grammatical and linguistic works of his predecessors Judah Hajjug, Menahem ben Saruq, and Dunash ben Labrat and enlarged them by his own observations. He adopted the system of the three-radicality of Hebrew verbs from Hajjug. His own handbooks—*Moznei Leschon Haq-quodesh* (*Scales of Sacred Speech*; frequently cited as *Moznei*), *Sefer Zahot* (*Book of Elegant Style*), and *Safa Berura* (*Pure Speech*)—were much used.

The great respect his commentaries enjoyed in the age of humanism, the Reformation, and on into modernity is explained by the careful linguistic and historical exegesis we encounter in them, in which he anticipated much knowledge of historical-critical research.

Ibn Ezra wrote all his biblical commentaries during the second half of his life, while staying in different places of exile. It is uncertain whether, as many maintain, he actually commented on all the biblical books. Apparently his earliest transmitters did not know of commentaries he wrote on all the Scriptures. Interpretations of the Former Prophets (the historical books), Chronicles, Proverbs, Jeremiah, Ezekiel, and Ezra–Nehemiah are unavailable, as are many earlier editions and parts of his surviving commentaries. Ibn Ezra also commented multiple times on many biblical books or revised older commentaries. Most of his commentaries are also available in more recent printings, predominantly from the nineteenth century, some with German or English translations. His commentaries on the five books of the Pentateuch were the last to be translated into English. This edition was not completed until recently (2004).

Ibn Ezra's principles of interpretation (which he elucidates in the introduction to his commentary on the Pentateuch) are essentially the same in all his commentaries. With respect to the halakah (the legal sections in the Pentateuch), he follows the interpretation of the Talmudists and repeatedly confesses that he wishes humbly to bow to their judgments because their knowledge surpasses his own. But when the Torah is not the concern, he feels himself free in a completely different way. Here he rests the decisive value on the literal sense. He thanks the Masoretes for caring so greatly for the preservation of the wording of the Bible, but he opposes those who try to defend the text in every detail. Typical is his statement (on Exod 17:3; 18:21): "The Hebrews do not care about the words but the sense." Nevertheless, he held with few exceptions to the traditional Hebrew wording. The emphasis falls on etymological and grammatical explanations, for which his schooling in the works of the Spanish linguists as well as his fine feeling for the Hebrew language put him in good stead. In order to clarify factual problems in biblical statements, he liked to draw upon experiences from his numerous travels, along with his familiarity with the way of life, morals, and customs of foreign peoples. In this, a clear rationalistic trait is unmistakable. Ibn Ezra loves to comment on the opinions of earlier interpreters, and when he rejects them, he frequently does so with biting satire. Precisely this—along with his concise style that pleasantly distinguishes him from many contemporary commentaries, in which many statements are tersely, almost elliptically, formulated and therefore are not easy to interpret—contributed to the popularity of his commentaries. He constantly rejects the views of the Karaites with special severity, but the opinions of other believers (Muslims and Christians) are only rarely cited. He evidently considers inner-Jewish differences of greatest danger.

One reason especially for selecting Ibn Ezra's Isaiah commentary here as an example of his interpretation is that an edition (by M. Friedländer) with an English translation is readily available, although it is quite free and not always reliable. Indeed, it omits the frequent excurses on special problems in other commentaries with which Ibn Ezra follows the style of interpretation customary in his time. On the other hand, precisely this facilitates an overview of this commentary. The Isaiah commentary is one of Ibn Ezra's earlier commentaries. He wrote it in Lucca in 1145. Despite its early origin, it already displays the exegetical mastery that made Ibn Ezra so famous.

Opening Ibn Ezra's Isaiah commentary, one encounters an entirely different atmosphere than the typical medieval commentaries we have learned of in the course of our investigations. Concentration on problems of literal meaning, the concise style of formulation, the austerity of expression—all this makes this commentary seem in many ways very modern. Ibn Ezra, however, shares with other medieval commentators the system of word-for-word explanation. At the end of the foreword to his Pentateuch commentary, he had explained that he wanted first to explain each word individually, then the sense and context of the whole. Yet the elucidation of individual words predominates in the Isaiah commentary.

The heading of the book of Isaiah (Isa 1:1) speaks of Isaiah as the "son of Amoz." To this, Ibn Ezra cites the opinions of earlier interpreters, one group of rabbis, that when the father of a prophet is named, he is also a prophet, and some other rabbis, that Isaiah was a member of the royal family, his father Amoz being a brother of King Amaziah (801–773 B.C.E.). To this, Ibn Ezra states that, while in many cases the father of a prophet was himself a man of significance or even a prophet, in many others he was not. For example, "David, the son of Jesse" (2 Sam 23:1): David was "a man of God" (2 Chr 8:14); Jesse was not. It is the same with prophecy as with royalty, as in the case of Jehu, king of Israel, the son of Nimshi (1 Kgs 19:16); Nimshi was not a king. Ibn Ezra then deals with the problem of the ambiguity of the sentence: "In the vision of Isaiah, the son of Amoz, the prophet" (2 Chr 32:32), where the term "the prophet" can refer to Amoz as well as to Isaiah. "But from the words 'to Isaiah the prophet, the son of Amoz' (2 Kings 19:2) we learn that Isaiah was 'the prophet.'" The method Ibn Ezra used was in one respect not new: from the beginning it was the custom of the rabbis to argue on the basis of comparing biblical passages. But Ibn Ezra's interest in clarifying a grammatical-historical question about the literal meaning is somewhat unusual nevertheless. In Isa 1:1 the information follows: "In the days of Uzziah, Jotham, Ahaz, and Hezekiah, kings of Judah." To this, Ibn Ezra remarks "Isaiah probably began his prophetic career in the last year of King Uzziah, as will be shown below [at Isa 6:1]. And in accord with this form of wording [*peshat*], (it holds) that he died in the days of Hezekiah. For if his days had extended into those of

Manasseh, this is what would have been written." In this regard, Ibn Ezra refers back to a talmudic legend (b. Yebam. 49b; y. Sanh. 10:2), according to which King Manasseh killed Isaiah for saying "my eyes have seen the King, the Lord of hosts" (Isa 6:5, which according to Exod 33:20 is a death threat). Ibn Ezra adds, "When the statement is based on tradition, it ought to be true." His own view is clear, but he has to cover himself!

Ibn Ezra then moves on to the explanation of the Hebrew wording that follows and in doing so shows his care in considering the Masoretic Text. Thus he remarks on Isa 1:9, where the Masoretes put a sentence separator (*athnach*) after the first half-sentence: "If the Lord of hosts had not left us a small remnant." Ibn Ezra writes: "Connect 'a small' with 'remnant' because of the separator accent, because it is an important rule that the accent marks have to be considered as carefully as possible." Modern interpretation is often far less strict in this regard, because in this case the sense of the second half-sentence seems to become much clearer if it is rendered as "well nigh we would have been like Sodom," especially since this also seems to match the word form better. This variant lets us take a look at the discussions of contemporary grammarians and text-linguists, whose observations are by no means lacking in precision. But even Ibn Ezra is not always consistent in following his own rules.

Ibn Ezra is careful in giving attention to Hebrew roots. He does not acknowledge that consonants can be exchanged (except for some "soft" letters, in which he considers it possible). He is also familiar with the method of comparative philology; thus he can refer to terms in the Syriac of the Targums, the language of the Talmud, and Arabic, as parallels for explaining a Hebrew expression. For example, for the word "tripping" (*taphoph*) in Isa 3:16 describing the demeanor of the distinguished daughters of Jerusalem, Ibn Ezra restates the opinion of "some," who render the word by "speaking" and refer to *wehatteph* "and speak prophetically" (Ezek 21:2) as a parallel. To this, Ibn Ezra remarks: "But this is incorrect in terms of grammar." According to other commentators (who again are not mentioned by name), it means "affected, stilted," to which reference is made to the Aramaic equivalent *a'tiph*, "to move slowly, like someone who swims along the surface of the water." "Others think it is derived from *taph* (child), and I incline to this view: to go slowly like a child." Thus possible derivations of a word are investigated with great precision. It is worth noting that the derivation Ibn Ezra offers for the term *taph* ("child") in Isa 3:16 is found in modern lexica as well. But Ibn Ezra's precise knowledge of postbiblical Hebrew also stands him in good stead. Thus, for example, he writes on *hetas* ("tears off") in Isa 18:5, that it means the same as "cut; it is found in old rabbinic language also." Considering that there were so few preparatory works in the field of lexicography on which Ibn Ezra could rely, his achievement in this area should not be underestimated.

Another problem Ibn Ezra is well aware of is the distinction between the Hebrew kinds of actions of verbs and the tenses representing stages of time in modern European languages. He stresses (e.g., on Isa 1:21; 6:4) the necessity of rendering the prefixed and suffixed conjunctions of the biblical Hebrew by the present, imperfect, future, or pluperfect tenses. Even today, anyone who tries to learn biblical Hebrew or translates a biblical text struggles with these difficulties. In fact, in the case of the living language, there is no return to the old system, since Modern Hebrew has adopted the European system of tenses. As a grammarian, Ibn Ezra is already familiar with terms for present, future, and so on and therefore stands at the transition to modern culture, which his European setting made familiar to him.

In explaining a difficult expression, Ibn Ezra frequently has recourse to the assumption that it is an elliptical mode of expression. Thus on Isa 10:21, the symbolic name of Isaiah's son Shear-jashub (= "the remnant returns," he writes, "Add 'Jacob' after the first 'remnant': the remnant of Jacob, that is, Judah, will return. In like manner, repeat 'return' before 'to': 'the remnant of Jacob will return to the mighty God.'" Similarly at verse 34: "The thickets of the forest will be hacked down with an axe." The second half-verse reads: "The Lebanon falls by a mighty one." On this Ibn Ezra states: "'by a mighty axe'; 'axe' is to be expanded by the preceding 'by an axe.'" Even modern interpreters have difficulties in understanding the second half-verse, in which for "mighty" (which could refer to Yahweh or the Assyrian king) many other suggestions are proposed, even equivalents for "axe." Ibn Ezra's proposal remains altogether worthy of consideration. Another example is Isa 43:25, which poses problems for interpreters to this day. Here it reads "from my mouth comes righteousness, a word that does not turn back." The difficulty is due to the fact that "word" in the second half of the verse seems suspended in air. Therefore a host of alternative proposals about this passage has been made in recent times. Ibn Ezra suggests repeating "a word" before "truth," which because of the elliptical mode of expression is missing in the text, and thereby hits the presumable meaning. He likewise suggests, in the second half-verse of the final line, of thinking once again of the "to me" of the next-to-last half-verse, which is likewise correct. In passages where there is an adjective alone, Ibn Ezra inserts an equivalent noun, as in Isa 15:9, "For I bring upon Dibon [= Dibon in Moab] even more disaster" or 28:2, where he suggests expanding the two adjectives "a stronger and more powerful" by adding "day" or "host." A modern alternative suggestion is the occasionally encountered alteration of the words themselves by the change of vocalization into substantives, because adjectives standing alone are indeed unusual. But here again Ibn Ezra's adherence to the Masoretic Text, including its vocalization, forces him to the conclusion that we have to do with an elliptical statement. When grammatically impossible formulations appear, for example, a *status constructus* that stands alone (a form to which a *status absolutus*, corresponding to the genitive, must be added), Ibn Ezra likewise assumes a deliberate ellipsis, for the idea that a word in sacred text could be left out by mere carelessness is inconceivable to him. In passages where the subject and predicate do not agree, he likewise prefers assuming an elliptical mode of speaking, for example, Isa 2:11: "The haughty looks (eyes) of people drop." Modern interpretation reckons with a scribal error here. Ibn Ezra, however, remarks that "the looks" is the same as "each of the looks," so the subject and predicate again agree. While he seems a very modern exegete in many respects, he is a completely orthodox Bible believer in his adherence to the Masoretic wording. A similar outlook is still found in many modern Jewish interpreters as well.

From these and other examples it emerges that Ibn Ezra's etymological, grammatical, and stylistic explanations of the literal sense still deserve attention and are not without significance even for modern interpreters. The high esteem Ibn Ezra has always enjoyed in this area is justified in full measure.

Ibn Ezra's remarks on Isa 1:11 lay on another level: "I have had enough of burnt sacrifices." The wording is an anthropomorphic phrase. In truth, it applies Ps 50:12: "If I were hungry, I would not tell you." With regard to God's speaking, Ibn Ezra thinks in a completely orthodox Jewish way. Likewise in verse 14, with regard to "I am weary of it" he offers the brief remark: "A figural phrase [*maschal*]." For figural designations of God, which are frequently found in the Bible, Ibn Ezra likes to turn back to the explanation that one has to add the praeposition "like" (*ke*). This applies to people as well, such as "watcher" in Isa 21:8 (by which the prophet himself is meant), which reads "lion" in the Masoretic Text (and modern interpreters correctly explain as a scribal error for "watcher"). But since Ibn Ezra does not question the Masoretic wording, explaining the language as pictorial is the only option remaining to him: "I think a *ke* (like) must be added, as in 'like a devouring fire' (Deut 4:24). The watcher calls with a loud voice like a lion." More appropriate, it seems to me, is the understanding of the expression of Isa 22:23 "like a peg" in the proclamation about Shebna, where Ibn Ezra likewise proposes "like" as a supplement. Incidentally, in adopting a basic talmudic rule as a matter of principle ("the language of the Torah corresponds to human language"), Ibn Ezra stresses the necessity of pictorial language in the Bible.

Of special interest, of course, are Ibn Ezra's remarks on the chapters of the book of Isaiah that play a special role in traditional Christian interpretation. On Isa 7, the narrative of the prophet's meeting with King Ahaz during the so-called Syro-Ephraimite war, we find the customary word-for-word explanation for most statements. Thus Ibn Ezra remarks on Isa 7:2, "Because the first king of the twelve tribes, Jeroboam, came from the tribe of Ephraim, his kingdom is named accordingly." It therefore has to do with the interpretation of a historical fact. Whether the explanation is correct may be set aside here. On verse 6, the question discussed is whether, as some commentators maintain, the "son of Tabeel" is the same person as the "son of Remaliah" (presumed by this is a continuous exchange of consonants between the two names). On this, Ibn Ezra explains: "This is nonsense, because the son of Remaliah is previously mentioned, and he says together with Aram: 'Let us place a king in their midst, the son of Tabeel.'" While these explanations are all brief, Ibn Ezra is more expansive with regard to the famous statement of the Immanuel sign in Isa 7:14. Here we find one of the few passages in which he cautiously goes into the Christian interpretation. Ibn Ezra remarks: "I am surprised at those who say that (this) is said about Jesus, because Ahaz was given the sign, and he (Jesus) was born many years later. In addition, it is said: 'For before the boy is able to understand about rejecting evil and choosing good, the land will be abandoned' (7:16), and the lands of Ephraim and Damascus were desolated in the fifth year of Hezekiah." In this connection he then goes into the interpretation that equates Immanuel with King Hezekiah (a view still advocated in recent times!). This, he claims, is chronologically impossible. "This is incorrect, even if we say that this had been prophesied at the start of the rule of Ahaz. See, his entire (time of) rule lasted sixteen years, and when he died, Hezekiah was twenty-five years old." Ibn Ezra then comes to the conclusion: "It seems to me, Immanuel is the son of Isaiah. This was also Maher-shalal. The latter is confirmed by the phrase, 'and I went to the prophetess'" (8:3). Ibn Ezra adds, Shear-jashub is also a son of Isaiah (7:3), and all three sons would have received symbolic names pointing to the future. The question of Immanuel's identity is not finally resolved even to this day, and Ibn Ezra's answer is still rightly given attention.

Ibn Ezra also offers some chronological reflections on the phrase in 7:16, "before the child is able to understand about rejecting the evil and choosing the good." "There are some who say this is at the age of twenty, because of the words of Moses (Exod 30:14): 'From twenty years on' (everyone is to pay a tax). If [this was] so, the prophecy must have been proclaimed after the second year of King Ahaz. Beyond this stands the calculation: Ahaz ruled for sixteen years, the exile of the northern kingdom took place in the sixth year of the King Hezekiah (722 B.C.E.). Hence there are twenty years from the second year of Ahaz to the deportations from the northern kingdom." Again, it can be seen that comparisons between the various biblical passages are typically rabbinic; on the other hand, the interest in chronology, that is, history, is Ibn Ezra's own.

The interpretation of Isa 11 is an example of Ibn Ezra leaving the decision between two possible overall interpretations open. Here is the view shared by most interpreters that the chapter deals with the Messiah and over against it the opinion of Rabbi Moses Ha-Kohen, who advocates the interpretation with respect to King Hezekiah. Ibn Ezra offers a few words about each of the individual verses, speaking for the one attribution or the other, but does not give a clear-cut judgment of his own.

Also of special interest to the modern interpreter is how Ibn Ezra with his historically sharpened view expressed his view on the relationship between the two parts of the book. It is not to be expected at the outset that Ibn Ezra anticipated the discovery that was not clearly expressed until in the eighteenth century, that chapters 40–66 of Isaiah stem from another prophet who lived at the time of the Babylonian exile. Yet he seems to come quite close to this realization. In any case, it did not escape him—or others before him—that the Babylonian exile is what is spoken of here. Yet he first examined—by strictly contextual exegesis—only the transition from chapter 39 to chapter 40. In chapter 39 (which, by the way, contains an Isaiah narrative taken from 2 Kgs 20:12–19), the prophet announced to King Hezekiah that the treasures he had shown the legation from Babylon, and even some of his own sons, would be carried away to Babylon. Ibn Ezra remarks on this that this sad announcement was followed quite appropriately by the words of consolation in chapter 40. He then takes into account the view of Rabbi Moses Ha-Kohen, in which these words of consolation refer to the Second Temple (its rebuilding by Zerubbabel; see Haggai and Zechariah). "But to my knowledge the whole (refers) to our exile. Only in the middle of the book are there words to remember the Babylonian exile (the end of the Jewish Diaspora to be expected for the messianic age), and in the final part of the book there are words that refer to the future, as I will explain." Unfortunately Ibn Ezra does not give his readers the explanation.

We find here that Ibn Ezra was familiar with aspects of interpretation that are altogether related to typology customary in Christian exegesis. The idea that the Babylonian exile reflected the Diaspora of the time and therefore the announcement of its end can be read figuratively as a foretelling of the time of the Diaspora's end is absolutely related to this hermeneutical approach. In addition, however, he pursues considerations pointing in an altogether different direction as well. Thus he then gives some hints letting it be known that he perhaps had doubt about the prophet Isaiah's authorship of the second part of his book, but he did not dare express them openly. That is to say, he adds: "But know the orthodox say that the book of Samuel was written by Samuel and that this is correct up to (the words) 'and Samuel died' (1 Sam 25:1). Further, see that the books of the Chronicles confirm that which brings the names of David's descendants in genealogical sequence down to the offspring of Zerubbabel (1 Chr 3). The words 'kings will see it and stand up, princes, and will pray' (Isa 49:7) support this view. There is also the possibility of interpreting, when they hear the name of the prophet, although he is no longer living." Although Ibn Ezra moves here in hints, his view clearly seems to be that those parts of the books of Samuel narrating events after Samuel's death could not have been written by him. The same would then have to apply as well to those parts of the book of Isaiah that are set in a period long after the prophet's death. In Ibn Ezra's view, the song of God's servant in Isa 49 has to do with the prophet. The kings and princes spoken of in 49:7 would therefore have to be contemporaries of the servant of God, that is, the prophet. But is it Isaiah? Even the books of Chronicles permit the time of their origin to be recognized by the generations of the descendants of David, which they present as last in their genealogical list. Ibn Ezra concludes with a remark typical of him: "But the wise will understand" (the translator paraphrases the statement in a way that rather veils its meaning). The conclusion is obvious that he had in all probability come to the judgment that Isaiah 40–66 could not derived from Isaiah; however, out of regard for his readers, he wants to leave it to them to draw their own conclusions.

While Ibn Ezra referred the songs of God's servant—he himself, of course, did not know this label—in chapters 42, 49, and 50 to the prophet himself, he has a different opinion on 52:13–53:12. On 52:13 he remarks at the outset, "this section is very difficult." "Some regard the statement, 'See, my servant will be clever' as a reference to Jesus and interpret 'my servant' as the body. This has no validity; the body cannot be clever, even though a man is living." Ibn Ezra then comes to the judgment that only Israel could be meant here. This he concludes from the context: a statement about Israel ("the Lord is going before you," etc.) precedes the section in 53:12, and a similar one ("Rejoice, you who are barren") follows it in 54:1. This is interesting in terms of method, because it presupposes a continuous textual context. One at first gets the impression that an exceptional position of the servant of God poems did not occur to Ibn Ezra. For chapter 53 he then apparently leaves two possible interpretations open: what is meant is either once again an individual Israelite (the prophet?) or Israel as a whole. But his true opinion then emerges at the conclusion of this section: "See, I have interpreted the entire section for you by presupposing that Israel is 'my servant.' But my opinion is that the one to whom the prophet says 'See, my servant, on whom I will rely' (42:1) as well as 'and he said to me, you are my servant' (49:3), and of whom it is written 'My servant, the righteous one, shall make many righteous' (53:11), this one is the same as the one of whom it is said 'I gave my back to those who struck' (50:6). As I indicated in this half of this book (on 40:1), these interpretations all depend on one another." Here again it becomes clear that, while Ibn Ezra indeed accepted the official view outwardly, he makes what his real opinion is unmistakably clear to anyone who can read between the lines.

The great attention given to Ibn Ezra's commentaries is shown, among other places, in the fact that many commentaries were later written on his commentaries. Rashi alone is his equal in popularity; indeed, Rashi even surpassed him in some respects, because he was in many ways more versatile. Ibn Ezra became important, especially from humanism on, because of his rational outlook, his predominant occupation with philological and historical problems of the literal sense, for in his works one could find numerous observations of assistance in understanding the original text on which such great emphasis was placed starting at this time. In addition, his basic stance matched in many respects what moderns found of concern to them as well. But above all it was his intimate familiarity with the Hebrew language, its grammar and forms of expressions, and the rabbinic tradition of interpretation that, precisely because he had critically adapted it, was later of great value to non-Jewish interpreters of the Old Testament. What had been the case for Jerome was the case as well in this much later time: Christian exegetes—especially if they tried to understand the original text of the Old Testament—could not do without the help of Jewish biblical experts. The first Christian Hebraists, Johannes Reuchlin in particular, rendered incomparable service in that they preserved the Jewish tradition of interpretation to which Ibn Ezras's commentaries belonged as central elements and reproduced it in Christian exegesis. On this matter, more will have to be said later.

5
Late Medieval Exegetes

5.1. Learning from the Jews: Nicholas of Lyra

Rashi's influence extended not only to Jewish biblical interpreters following him. It was of still greater significance for the development of modern
biblical understanding that he found among Christian theologians a follower who had acquired a knowledge of the Hebrew language sufficient
to be able to read Rashi's commentaries and was intensively interested in
his interpretation of the literal sense. This was the Franciscan Nicholas of
Lyra (ca. 1270–1349).

Nicholas was born in the village of Lyra, not far from Evreux in Normandy. His precise date of birth is unknown; we have to uncover it, like
most other dates of his life, indirectly from scattered references. As we
have already seen time and again, the Middle Ages took little interest in
the personal fates of individuals, whether kings or saints. This applies all
the more to a Franciscan monk who, despite the prominent positions he
held and apart from his scientific achievements and the fame they brought
him even during his lifetime, spent his life in Christian humility. Around
the turn of the century Nicholas entered the Franciscan monastery of Ver-
neuil in the vicinity of his birthplace. But evidently he was sent to Paris
after only a few years, apparently because of his outstanding scholarly
achievements. In 1309 he was already counted among the best known
theologians there, engaging in, among other things, a public disputation
"On the Jews."

We have already become acquainted with the Franciscan study house
in Paris because of Bonaventura's activity there. When Nicholas passed
through the customary scholarly course there, he would have first been
baccalaueus biblicus or at least *baccalaureus sententiarium*, although we
lack direct reports on this. Nonetheless, there are references to a commentary on the sentences (which is not preserved), and two handwritten

(manuscripts) of *Quaestionen* (*On the Incarnation of Christ*; *On the Jews*) that he himself edited are handed down. Nicholas then evidently became a *magister biblicus* and received as well the official assignment of delivering lectures on the Bible, which he did with great success. His main work, the *Postilla litteralis super totam Bibliam*, arose from this, as did the *Postilla moralis* in which Nicholas sets forth a moral interpretation of the Bible.

Nicholas also held high offices in his order for a time. He was a provincial minister of the Franciscans, first from 1319 to 1324, in the provincial order of France (embracing Paris, northern France, and Flanders), then from 1324 to 1330 in the province of Burgundy. He then evidently withdrew from his offices. His main work was already completed, but he was tirelessly active until his death in October of 1349. Nicholas was buried in the Franciscan chapter hall of the Parisian convent. Unfortunately, a fire destroyed the grave site in 1580, with the loss of the epitaph. Hence the outward traces of his life are erased.

While only a few copies of most of the other writings of Nicholas are preserved, hundreds of manuscripts of the *Postilla literalis* are found in European libraries. This shows how popular his commentary must have been. Already during the author's lifetime exemplars were traded among prominent public figures; numerous printed editions were prepared after the invention of printing. The first printing, in five folio volumes, was made in 1471; numerous others came thereafter, up to the last (Antwerp) edition of 1634. Unfortunately, there is no modern critical edition at all, which may account for the relatively scant interest in Nicholas in recent research. In earlier times one knew to appreciate his role more highly. This is confirmed also by the traditional popular verse highlighting Nicholas of Lyra's significance for Martin Luther: "If Lyra had not the lyre played, Luther his dance would not have made" ("Si Lyra non lyrasset, Lutherus non saltasset"). Actually, Luther had drawn heavily from Lyra's *Postilla literalis* for his own lectures on the Bible. He found there what was so important to him: an interpretation of the literal sense of the Scripture, free of the allegorical interpretations that Luther was convinced falsified the clear Word of God with which he dealt above all else. But on closer examination of the intellectual presuppositions by which Nicholas carried out his literal exegesis, it becomes clear that they also are in a quite specific way time-bound. One observation, which would be worth closer investigation (though it cannot be developed here), is the Aristotelian conceptuality that emerges in Nicholas. Such a philosophical, though unreflective, approach would also account for his special interest in the realities in the Bible.

Postilla, the title of Nicholas's commentary like that of numerous similar works, points quite directly to the descent of such interpretations from teaching activity. This commentary, again in keeping with the custom of the time, is a verse-by-verse explication. A docent was accustomed to announce the transition of one biblical statement to the next with "after this" (*post illa*). From this is derived the catchword for the title. One peculiarity of his *postilla* is, among other things, that Nicholas interpreted the entire Bible of both Testaments, indeed the canonical books from Genesis to the Apocalypse of John (part 1) and the noncanonical books (part 2). That is a magnificent achievement, one that could not replicated by an exegete living today because of the massive growth of secondary literature and the differentiations of modern methodology. That Nicholas was a very careful worker is also evident from the dates he occasionally slips in; from them we can tell precisely how long he labored on his work. He began in 1322 and concluded it (with a supplement on Ezek 40–48) in 1332.

Nicholas introduced his commentary with two prologues. In the first, "De commendatione sacrae Scripturae in generali" ("On the Recommendation of the Holy Scripture Generally," PL 113:25–30), we can already recognize from its traditional content the *principium*, that is, the celebratory address a medieval university theologian had to deliver when he received the doctoral degree and from then on no longer interpreted the Bible in merely cursory fashion with quotations from church teachings but was permitted to present his own teaching. Among the other traditional statements of the newly minted doctor of theology was praise of the incomparably higher worth of the Bible over the writings of the secular sciences and philosophy, in that these relate solely to this-worldly life, while the Holy Scripture, on the other hand, "to the blessedness of the life to come." This does not deny that he, like all students, learned the "liberal arts" very well and understood as well how to use them for theological work. This is shown in the following section, in which he speaks of the knowledge of God of the philosophers. Here he proceeds, by reference back to Aristotle's theory of principles, from the fact that the basic principles of human knowledge are "known by nature." The philosophers have all erred only with respect to the implications for the first cause. Since God is the first cause—here again the Aristotelian definition is striking—and Scripture has God for its author, complete knowledge of God can be gained from it alone. Nicholas absolutely attributes a knowledge of God to the philosophers, "insofar as it extends to the attributes that can be derived from it by research into the knowledge that proceeds from the creatures, as the philosopher (Aristotle) (says) in chapter 12 of the

Metaphysics." "But the prophets and holy apostles who passed down to us this Scripture by the revelation of the Holy Spirit, had a knowledge of the divine attributes that transcends an investigation by reason."

In these statements we encounter at first a typical scholastic theologian who, like Thomas Aquinas, by whom he was greatly influenced, has been educated in the Aristotelian spirit. For him the rational-speculative knowledge of God seems to be a central goal that his biblical interpretation serves. But when he says the goal of this knowledge of God is that the interpreter "in that he speculates, that is, meditates, on love is brought to the love of this so-known object, namely, God," the Franciscan ideal peaks through the philosophical conceptuality. It is also to be noticed that theology and biblical interpretation are seen completely as in the old manner. A distinction between them is not considered at all; for the Franciscan exegete, the system of *sacra pagina* is still taken for granted.

Traditional also are the discussions that then follow. In them, Nicholas stresses that Scripture, in distinction to other books, has more than one sense: "It is distinctive to this book that the things designated by words refer to something other." What is meant is the fourfold sense of Scripture (literal sense, "mystical" sense, "tropological" or moral sense, anagogic sense), which Nicholas also knows and will not deny—indeed, he himself later offered an extensive moral interpretation of the Bible (*Postilla moralis*). In Rev 5:1 is mentioned a book in the hand of the one who sits on the throne (Christ the world ruler) written on from inside and outside. This doubled inscription symbolizes for Nicholas the multiple (external and internal) sense of Scripture.

All the more interesting for us, then, is the second prologue that Nicholas sets in advance of his *Postilla*: "De intentione auctoris et modo procedendi" ("On the Intention of the Author and the Way of Proceeding"). He comes here to the concern that moves him in an altogether special way. The figurative meanings of Holy Scripture presuppose "the literal sense as, so to speak, the foundation. There, just as a building that is tilting on its foundation is inclined to collapse, so also a mystical interpretation that deviates from the literal sense is to be judged inappropriate and inadequate." Therefore the literal sense is to be ascertained first, especially because it alone removes doubt. But the biblical text may be falsified by mistakes of copyists "who because of the similarity of letters in many passages wrote something other than the text actually reads, who made points at various passages where they ought not to be made, and who began or ended verses that ought not be begun or ended," by the inexperience of correctors, and by errors of tradition. In addition, "our translation" (the

Vulgate) frequently deviates from the Hebrew wording of the Old Testament. According to Jerome, it is thereafter necessary in such cases to refer back to the Hebrew text. Therefore, he intends to draw upon not only the writings of the Catholic doctors but also the Hebrew, "Rabbi Solomon (Rashi) in particular, who is especially revered among Hebrew doctors."

Here we find a program for text-critical work that was revolutionary for its time and has rightly made Nicholas famous. But in referring back to Jewish traditions he pays tribute to theological controversy in that he explicitly adds that care is to be taken here, because in his opinion the Jews cannot resist the temptation of altering passages that clearly spoke of Christ's divinity and foretold his coming. Thus the old polemical tradition that the Jews falsified the text is accepted.

It has often been discussed how extensive Nicholas's knowledge of Hebrew was. He doubtless penetrated into the mysteries of this language more deeply than nearly any other Christian theologian; it has even been conjectured that he was of Jewish descent himself or went to a Jewish school in the vicinity of his home place. These rumors, arising early on, cannot be confirmed, however. He evidently learned Hebrew from at least one Jewish teacher, with whom he, as was the case time and again since Jerome, could gain closer contacts. He himself once speaks of the fact that in his works, especially the *Postilla*, he "accepted nothing from his own brain, but (only) under the direction, in consultation with, and on the advice of people who were expert in Hebrew." Modern Jewish researchers certify that he reproduced Rashi's exegetical remarks correctly throughout, although for theological reasons he had to take issue with him at some places. The extent of such polemics is contested. While modern Jewish researchers place emphasis more heavily on the passages in Nicholas where traditional christological exegesis emerges in contrast to Jewish views, one must beware of an anachronistic judgment. For a Christian exegete of the day, such a stance was taken as a matter of course. If Nicholas is evaluated in light of his own time, his efforts on behalf of the literal sense are seen to be significant.

Nicholas was not even the first medieval Christian theologian who learned Hebrew. Andrew of St. Victor, mentioned above, and Herbert of Bosham (d. 1190) are only two of the well-known Christian experts in Hebrew. In addition, the Oxford and Parisian master Robert Grosseteste (ca. 1165–1253), his famous student Roger Bacon (ca. 1214–1292), and his student Guillaume de la Mare are to be mentioned, all reputable Hebraists. Nicholas of Lyra, however, was the first to introduce the results of Jewish exegesis in the form of Rashi's *peshat* interpretation into Christian commentaries on the Old Testament. He mentions Rashi's name on almost every page. In the second prologue of his *Postilla* can be seen also a changed view of Nicholas with reference to the figurative ("mystical") sense of Scripture. He now has strong reservations about representatives of this view: "Although they said many good things, they have nevertheless uncovered the literal sense too little and increased the mystical sense in a way that the literal sense, buried under so many mystical interpretations, is nearly smothered." Therefore, "I intended with God's help to insist on the literal sense and occasionally insert a few, brief mystical explanations, that is, seldom." It is also striking that in connection with this discussion Nicholas still elucidates the seven rules of Isidore of Seville (actually, they are derived from Tyconius). Here his comments on the third rule, "On God and Letters," are of special interest. The usual view of the matter is that the same wording ("letter") has a historical as well as a "mystical" sense. But the rule could also be understood otherwise, as relating likewise to the literal sense. "In this respect it is to be ventured that on occasion the same wording has a double literal meaning." For example, in 1 Chr 17:13, God speaks to David about Solomon: "I will be a father to him, and he shall be a son to me" (2 Sam 7:14). This is said in the first literal sense about Solomon. But since the same word is stated about Christ in Heb 1:5, it must have a second sense as well. But this second sense cannot be a mystical sense, because a figurative sense cannot demonstrate (so Augustine) what the apostle wants to demonstrate in this epistle, that Christ is higher than the angel(s). It must therefore have to do with a second literal sense. "This (scriptural) authority was fulfilled in Solomon in the literal sense, but less than perfectly, because he was God's son only by grace, but in Christ more perfectly, because he is the Son of God by nature." It is disputed to what extent the doctrine of a double literal sense can already be found in Thomas Aquinas, who likewise represented the elsewhere popular medieval view of the double author of Scripture, but for Thomas it was still, in keeping with tradition, the figurative (allegorical) meaning in which the divine author's intention was made evident.

What is here merely suggested, later theologians carried out further in discussing the question of the different authors of the Bible—the human authors of various texts and the divine author of the whole Bible—and over the intentions of both: the individual author and the "author of the whole," which each come into play in the wording.

A few examples from primeval and patriarchal history may illuminate how Nicholas of Lyra carries out the interpretation of the Bible's literal sense.

On the first word of the Bible, "in the beginning" (Gen 1:1), Nicholas remarks: "Thus is described what is made before any day. But this (word) 'before' is, according to this presentation, not used for the (idea of) duration but only (for the idea of) nature, just as the tone (the possibility of the sound) precedes the voice (the realization of the sound). Therefore, (Scripture) says: 'in the beginning,' that is, the time or the production of things." It is worth noting that in this interpretation Nicholas does not adopt Rashi's solution, although he must have known it, but understands Gen 1:1 as an independent main clause. He nevertheless struggles with the same problem as Rashi, in that he seeks to solve the riddle of time— which could not have been before creation, even though the formulation in the creation account gives this impression. His starting point, unlike the Jewish exegete's, is a "realist" approach: the idea of a thing is there *before* its realization; thus the possibility of time is there before it becomes reality in the first work of creation. On this matter, incidentally, it is to be noted that these considerations have to do with the fact that Nicholas had to debate with pagan Aristotelianism, which was not unknown to him at the University of Paris—as we have heard—according to which matter was eternal. A creation from nothing was the decisive counterposition that Nicholas, as a self-conscious Christian, wanted to defend. Nevertheless he, like other theologians of his time, put Aristotelian conceptuality to full use.

Another example of how Nicholas expressly calls on the witness of Rashi is his explanation of Gen 1:7, "And God made the firmament." "This (word) *to be made* is not to be understood with respect to a substantial form. Rather, it is to be understood according to an attribute [*qualitas*] of the firmament itself. But the text does not state what this attribute is. Yet Rabbi Solomon the Hebrew says that it is a firmness, of which Job (37:18) says, 'Have you perhaps created the heaven with him?' which is cast firm, as if it were in ore." We again note how Nicholas works with Aristotelian conceptuality (form and quality) in order to provide an exact description of what the statement meant. These statements, by the way, are dependent on Rashi's considerations on Gen 1:6, which reads, "And God said, 'Let there be a firmness,'" even though it was already said in verse 1 that God had created heaven and earth. Rashi had solved the problem by maintaining that God's work on the second day was not the creation of the heaven as such but the hardening of its previously pliable consistency. This argument, revived afresh by an Aristotelian conceptuality, is again underpinned by an investigation of the term "to make," in which Nicholas once again refers back to Rashi: "But that in the Holy Scripture is said

of a thing that it is 'made' with respect to the acquisition of an accidental attribute, the same Rabbi Solomon shows from what is found in Deut
21:10–14 about the Gentile women who is enslaved by a Hebrew man. It
is said of her there that when he wants to have her for a wife, 'she shall cut
her hair and trim her nails,' according to our translation. The Hebrew text
has 'she shall do her nails'. It obviously follows from this that 'to do the
nails' refers to one of their accidental attributes."

At verse 8, Nicholas deals, like Rashi before him, with the old problem of why the formula "And God saw that it was good," which is used
for all the other days, is missing in the second day of creation. To this
Nicholas first advances the opinion of "some" (it is found in Jerome and
Hrabanus Maurus but ultimately derives from the midrash Gen. Rab.
4:6) that the number "two" has an evil ring to it, because it signifies the
division of unity. This view is rejected by appeal to Luke 10:1, in which
the sending of the disciples two by two proves that the number two, is on
the contrary, to be evaluated very positively, because it designates mystical "love" (according to Gregory the Great). We see here that Nicholas
can actually fall back into allegorical methods of interpretation, evidently because he wants to ward off the view he is rejecting on the same
level. He also rejects the view "of others" that the second day was not
good because the angels fell on this day, for, thus Nicholas notes, nothing of this is in Scripture. The derivation of this apocryphal opinion is
unknown. What is more important is that here Nicholas formulates a
basic principle: he can acknowledge only what is attested in the Bible.
For a satisfactory answer, he then refers back to Rashi's judgment:

> Therefore Rabbi Solomon answers, and more, as it seems, in accord with
> the intention of the wording [secundum intentionem literae], in that he
> says, and it is true that this word "And God saw that it was good, etc." is
> said on other days as confirmation of the work on this day—but a con-
> firmation presupposes an actually completed work. On the second day,
> however, though the distinction of the heavenly bodies takes place in
> particular, the separation of the groundwater is nevertheless also men-
> tioned, and since this division is not completed before the third day,
> when the waters are gathered in one place, is the mentioned word on
> the second day left out, and he says it twice on the third day, as is clear
> in the wording, once for the work of the second day, once for the work
> of the third day.

With respect to the classical problem of the plural in Gen 1:26 "let
us make humankind," Nicholas follows the Christian tradition in that he

interprets it as Trinitarian. He polemicizes against Rashi's (midrashic) view that God consulted with angels in this act of creation. The fact that the singular is continued in verse 27, "and God created humankind in his image," means according to Nicholas the unity of the triune God.

Another difficulty surfaces soon afterward: "Male and female he created them." To this Nicholas debates extensively with Rashi's discussion of this passage and evidently also draws upon a midrashic collection:

> On the basis of this text, some Hebrews (in the midrashim) state that in the first form human nature had been created bisexual. That is to say, the bodies of the man and the woman were joined at the side in such a way that they formed a continuous body, but they were later separated by divine power. But because what is said later—"he took one of his ribs and made from it a woman ... and he closed up the place with flesh" (Gen 2:21–22)—seems (to speak) against this, such a filling in would have been unnecessary if the bodies were merely separated. For this reason they answer by saying that the word *sela'* that is understood here as "rib" is equivocal in Hebrew, because it means "rib" and "side"—for this there are many examples in the Hebrew Bible, which I pass over— and it is similar in French, where "rib" and "side" are written the same (*coste*) but differ somewhat in their pronunciation. Proponents of this view maintain that the translation would have to be "he took one of the sides," when he separated the bodies of the man and the woman. With respect to the second statement, "And he filled the place with flesh" (Vulgate on Gen 2:21), they say, and it is true, that the Hebrew text has, "and he closed the flesh over it"—that is, he drew the skin over the flesh at the point of the separation.

Here Nicholas mentions what was in his day a "monster": Siamese twins who were born in 1322. But such things occur in nature by accident, and it is not to be assumed that the creator of all things would have created such a "monster" in the beginning of the creation of the human race. Further, it is previously (2:20) said that God had brought all the animals before man so that he might find a companion among them, but that this was not successful, so he had been compelled to create the woman from the rib. This he would not have been necessary if the man and woman had already existed as a hermaphrodite.

From this Nicholas agrees with Rashi's opinion that the man was created first only as a man and that the woman was formed later from the man's rib. The fact that Gen 1:26 nevertheless already speaks of the creation of man *and* woman occurs by way of anticipation, because Scripture wanted to mention immediately thereafter God's order, "be fruitful and multiply," for which the mention of the man and woman was necessary. Specifically how the creation of the woman took place is then depicted at length in Gen 2.

It must be once again noted that the idea of possibly distinct sources— such that Gen 1 would be interpreted independently of Gen 2—was inconceivable in those times. A context-related exegesis, which Nicholas carried it out much as Rashi did, would thus have to attempt to overcome the obvious contradictions between the two reports of creation by a harmonizing outlook. In the way it works out, however, one can ascertain in the case of Nicholas of Lyra a careful attention to the findings in the text, especially those of the Hebrew original.

Differences between Rashi and Nicholas of Lyra arise by the nature of the case, particularly where they have differing doctrinal views. This is the case, for example, in the interpretation of Gen 4:1: "Adam knew his wife." In Rashi's view, this took place even before the first human couple was expelled from the garden of Eden, for according to the prevailing Jewish view, Adam and Even already led a married life while in paradise. For Rashi, the verb form in Gen 4:1 (where the suffix form *yada'* is used) is decisive: if it were meant that Adam first had sexual relations with his wife only after the expulsion, the prefix form would have had to be used. Apart from the fact that here even Rashi's grammatical knowledge of ancient Hebrew is evidently limited, Lyra's divergent opinion, however, also depends on basic prejudices. From the monastic-Christian viewpoint, celibacy is to be valued more highly than married life. Nicholas therefore first criticizes the correctly stated Jewish interpretation and appeals instead to that of the "Catholic doctors," Augustine particularly, according to which the first people lived in paradise as virgins and had sexual relations together only after their expulsion from it. Nicholas sweeps aside the objection that the first humans had already been summoned in Gen 1:26 to "be fruitful and multiply" with the remark that this was meant only in the general sense and would still have required a specific command of God for its execution at the appropriate time. Hence all the children of Adam and Eve were produced after the expulsion.

An intensive search for the literal sense in close dialogue with Rashi's view is found in Nicholas's treatment of the history of the patriarchs, in which he is of course bound to traditional Christian guidelines in his theological interpretations. Thus he wonders, along with Rashi, why Abraham is told in Gen 11:31, "Go forth from your homeland," even though according to Gen 11:42 he had already set out from his home. Here Nicholas accepts Rashi's explanation that what is meant is the departure from Haran, where Abraham had already arrived. The interpretation "by some" that what is meant is that Abraham indeed already moved bodily, but not yet in spirit, because he planned to return, Nicholas dismisses with the comment: "It seems unlikely that Abraham wanted to return to the tyranny of Nimrod. Therefore, it is better to say, *Go forth from your land*; that is, distance yourself further from him." But there are also passages that are important for Christian interpretation. This applies, for example, for Gen 12:3. To this Nicholas remarks, "*And in you shall all peoples* (literally, *relatives*) *be blessed.* The Hebrews interpret this as follows: when someone wished another something good, he used to say, 'May God bless you, as He blessed Abraham.' Christians relate it to Christ, and better, as it seems. In you shall be blessed, etc., that is, in the seed (descendant) who will be born from you, who is Christ. For there are some Christians among every people, and therefore the blessing of Christ extends to every generation on earth. This, however, cannot be said of the person of Abraham." Here traditional typological interpretation is carried out at the expense of the literal. It is contested in modern exegesis, as ever, whether the verb form used here is to be understood as a passive ("to be blessed") or reflexively; the direct christological interpretation, however, is no longer discussed.

By today's standards, then, it would have to be said that, in the case of Nicholas, exegesis of the historical sense is not the sole method, but he nevertheless grants it an important place, particularly in the core and memorable passages of traditional Christian exegesis. His theory about a possible double literal sense, as mentioned above, enables him to do this. It would be an anachronistic demand, however, to expect him to have completely rejected it.

How Nicholas justified his interpretation of the literal sense on the basis of the Aristotelian presuppositions of his thought, one can learn well in his prologue to the interpretation of the Psalter (*Postilla*, 1492/1971 edition, vol. 3). Here he proceeds from the four Aristotelian categories of causality: efficient, material, formal, and final causes. There are two efficient causes: God is the first cause; David, the instrumental. While according to Augustine David was the author of all the psalms, Jerome, Hilary, and all the Hebrew doctors believed that he did not compose them all, only most of them. The titles of the psalms show that some of them were composed by Moses, Solomon, and others. Ezra, however, had probably compiled the book of Psalms itself. For Nicholas, then, the combination of divine and human authors poses no problem, because the human and the divine Spirit worked together in the composition.

The formal cause consists, according to Nicholas, in the "form of the tractates" (i.e., the organization of the psalms) and the "form of using them," in this case the intent of the Psalms, praise of God. The final (cause) consists in that the praise sung by the whole church is directed to the hope of future blessedness.

In addition to these formal hermeneutical rules, however, Nicholas can also come to insights that seem quite current, such as that the sequence of the psalms does not correspond at all to their origin in time and that an older psalm can often come after a more recent one, because the origin of the Psalms collection extended over a long time (in the interpretation of Ps 1).

A special comment is still to be made about Nicholas's interpretation of the New Testament. Already in his prooemium to the Gospel of Matthew (1492/1971 edition, vol. 4), it is clearly expressed how he understands the Gospels. He does not stand alone in this in his time but with the view current at the time, as represented especially by the monastic orders. For Nicolas, the content of the Gospels is above all law. Although there are four Gospels, "yet the law, or evangelical teaching, is one." In its fourfold form, "it surpasses every other law given, human and divine." "The real meaning of the law is to eradicate offenses, to order the customs or actions of people, to lead to blessedness, and to pass on the truth in a clearer and simpler way." Then follows a lengthy catalogue of vices against which the law is directed. The civil law allows many things and lets much go unpunished. The Mosaic law, although given by God, still allows a great deal of evil, such as the grant of a letter of divorce (Deut 24:1). Therefore the human and the Mosaic laws are imperfect. "But the evangelical law, being the most perfect, allows no evil," since Jesus himself is the lawgiver. The truth, which is still veiled in the Old Testament, is visible in the New. A sign for this is the passion of Jesus, tied to the tearing of the curtain in the temple (Luke 23:45). In the case of Nicholas, however, the atoning power of the death of Jesus is not in view. The *way* of Jesus, even his passion, is for him rather an exemplar that serves to be imitated. This imitation of Jesus (see the title of the widely disseminated tract of Thomas à Kempis, 1380–1471) is the medieval-monastic mode of pious theological and practical dealings with the passion. In the case of Nicholas, we are also a long way from the Reformation. Likewise, already well-known to us is the interpretation of the four faces of Ezek 1 as the four Evangelists, which surfaces in Nicholas in the prologue to Matthew and occupies a wide space in it.

Nevertheless, his interpretation had epoch-making effects, in that he put incomparably greater importance on understanding the literal sense than was the custom before him. That in so doing, above all by his use of Rashi's commentary work, he utilized the revival of Jewish biblical interpretation of around two hundred years earlier had an influence on the advance of interpretive scholarship, which because of its isolation would not have come about apart from his intermediary activity. Hence the high esteem that Nicholas has long enjoyed is justified in full measure, despite the inconsistencies we can observe in him.

5.2. The Bible, God's Eternal Book: John Wyclif

At the conclusion of our tour of medieval biblical interpretation we must still mention a man who, because of his extraordinary influence on the Reformation epoch, ranks among the best known figures of the later Middle Ages, although he never advanced in his social position beyond the status of an Oxford Doctor of Theology: John Wyclif. There were times when this man was given effusive praise, by Protestants especially. Titles such as "morning star of the Reformation" were heaped upon him, and a German-English society for the dissemination of his works, the Wyclif Society, saw to it before World War I that most of his numerous writings were published in modern editions. One of his biblical commentaries, the *Postilla super totam Bibliam*, the notes of his exegetical lectures in Oxford between 1372 and 1378, remained unpublished and partly missing.

The career of John Wyclif resembles in many respects that of other university theologians we have already met. Like a good many contemporaries, his precise ancestry and birth year are unknown. That he came from North England, where there was a family by his name, is a mere supposition, and even his birth year, about 1330, is estimated by approximation from later dates of his life. Since he pursued the career of a secular priest, he should have come to Oxford, according to the custom of the time, at about fourteen or fifteen years of age, without entering an order. Like every student, he first had to study three years for his *baccalaureus artium* (B.A.) and three years more for his *magister artium* (M.A.). As a master he had to teach for two years and fulfill administrative tasks of various sorts. We know almost nothing about all these early years of Wyclif, except that in 1356 he was still a baccalaureate (*baccalaureus*), a fellow (endowed member) of Merton College, which granted needy students lodging and a small stipend. In 1360 we meet him in neighboring Balliol College as a master of arts (the liberal arts, that is, especially philosophy). The length of time in these first levels of education had made young Wyclif a profound authority on contemporary philosophical debates, in which he himself took part with his philosophical works. Wyclif must have played a prominent role in Balliol, where he was the third master, for already in 1361 he was awarded the largest prebend the college had, that of Filling-ham in Lincolnshire. With this award, he withdrew from the college itself but remained—perhaps after a temporary stay in Fillingham, although this is uncertain—in Oxford, where he took rooms in Queen's College. He lived there until his banishment from Oxford in 1381. Queen's was a financially poor college that rented some of its rooms to foreign scholars. Wyclif was able to live there many years without being a fellow. That he did not over time move to Fillingham, nor to any of the other benefices he received, goes along with the system of so-called absenteeism (the absence of the office holder), widespread at the time: posts as canon and pastoral offices were given to theologians active at universities, but also to deserv-ing crown dignitaries, co-workers of bishops, and, indeed, even members of the papal curia in Avignon, without requiring them in fact to occupy them personally. Officially, it sufficed to have the position administered by a representative (*vicarius*), a member of the lower clergy, and many times not even this was done. One must consider in this regard that a regular salary system is an invention of recent times. In the Middle Ages one's livelihood could be secured only if it was based on material revenue. Although Wyclif later fiercely criticized the excesses of this practice, he himself profited from it to no small degree.

Talented students could add to their education in the "liberal arts" similarly lengthy specialized studies. One could gain the rank of bach-elor (*baccalaureus*) of theology (B.D.) after five years; at least about two years more were necessary for the doctoral degree (D.D.). Wyclif had by no means hurried in this regard, for he did not receive his doctorate in theology until 1372. In the meantime, he experienced a disappoint-ment that may partly account for his highly negative stance toward the established church later on. In 1365, Archbishop Islip of Canterbury appointed Wyclif the warden of his recently founded Canterbury Col-lege, after Islip had previously removed the first warden, Wood, who came from the monks, because of dissension between the monastic and secular members of the college. After the archbishop's death, however, his successor reinstated the earlier rector as early as 1367. Not even a protracted appeal to the pope was of any avail; finally (1371 at the latest), Wyclif had to vacate the post and return to Queen's. Nevertheless, the reputation Wyclif enjoyed in Oxford and beyond around 1371 on the basis of his philosophical works, even before his theological promotion, was considerable.

This reputation was perhaps also the basis for his political activity, which began around this time. The background is to be seen in the system of taxation that was long a point of conflict between the English church and the king and the pope. The crown's financial needs had increased because of the devastating Hundred Years' War with France (with interruptions, 1338–1461), that of the pope because of the expenses of the curia—also extraordinary, as was that of Gregory XI's (1370–1378) war with Florence. Both parties and the English Parliament disputed over the taxes the clergy were to pay, for the assets of the church (by far the largest property owner) were immense. It had to do as well with the tithes to be gained from the filling of benefices, for which bishops, landed nobility, the king, and the pope competed with one another.

To resolve the issues in conflict, a delegation was sent in 1374 to Brussels, where it met with the pope's emissaries. Wyclif was one of the delegates. We do not know how this confidence in his diplomatic abilities came about. By 1371, however, he seems to have come to enjoy the protection of John of Ghent (John of Gaunt)—the younger son of King Edward III (1327–1377) and later king (as Henry IV, 1399–1413)—who protected him against attacks afterward as well. The attacks came from, among others, William Courtenay, at the time (1375–1381) the bishop of London, who in 1377, certainly with a negative outcome, ordered Wyclif to St. Paul's Cathedral to answer personally for his support of John of Ghent's attacks against William Wickham, the bishop of Winchester (1367–1404). In the same year Gregory XI condemned eighteen out of a list of fifty statements of Wyclif's, which his opponents had presumably forwarded to Rome. Even his appearance before the bishops assembled in Lambeth Palace in 1378 ended with only a mild admonition.

These events fall already in the period when Wyclif had made himself unpopular in Oxford and beyond because of his views on the precedence of secular rule in the church, collected in his three-volume work *De civili dominio* (*On Civil Lordship*, 1376–1378). This work was part of a *Summa theologiae* growing to fourteen volumes, which Wyclif had begun in 1373 by concentrating first on legal and political questions. In the process he judged the current condition of the church ever more critically. Much like other opponents before him, he held a model of decline for the history of the church. The turning point, in his view, was the pontificate of Pope Innocent III (1198–1216), particularly the Fourth Lateran Council (1215), with the doctrine of transubstantiation (the change of the elements of the Eucharist), defined for the first time there. He viewed church history up to Innocent positively; thereafter, the church took a turn for the worse. It was therefore necessary to return to the faith and practice of the early church. A less significant turn, according to Wyclif, had already occurred under the emperor Constantine. The so-called "donation of Constantine" (which was later disclosed as a forgery) had established a division of state and church power. Wyclif viewed the subsequent period as still positive over-all and advocated returning to it. How much his increasing opposition toward the church during this time was due to personal disappointments is disputed. Added to his painful experience with Cambridge College came the embitterment that he received nothing more in payment for his diplomatic service than the rural pastorate of Lutterworth. Other promo-tions he had hoped for, even from the pope, failed to come. Later, when Wyclif became known as an advocate of heretical views, such hopes were no longer to be thought of anyway. Still, he was spared serious threats against him on the part of the curia because the great schism followed the death of Gregory XI. Since France supported the antipope Clement VII (1378–1394), England adhered to the pope residing in Rome, Urban VI (1378–1389); even so, the papacy was disabled for a long time.

From 1378 on Wyclif issued his writings at an ever-faster pace. In that year, after *De civili dominio*, came *De veritate sacre scripture* (*On the Truth of the Holy Scriptures*) and *De officio regis* (*On the Office of King*); now Wyclif granted the king the right to rule and reform the church; he demanded that the clergy renounce all worldly goods except those nec-essary for life. Appearing as well was *De ecclesia* (*On the Church*). In this work Wyclif advocated double election (to salvation and judgment) and maintained that the elect alone constituted the church, not its vis-ible members, including the pope. His denial of the established hierarchy reached its climax in *De potestate pape* (*On the Power of the Pope*, 1379). Finally, Wyclif denied in two writings, *De apostasia* (*On Apostasy*) and *De eucharistia* (*On the Eucharist*), both in 1379, a central affirmation of Catholic teaching: the transubstantiation (change) of the elements in the Eucharist. The other writings Wyclif published up to the time of his death (31 December 1384) added hardly anything new in content but became ever sharper in tone. New, however, was the fact that Wyclif finally turned against the mendicant orders as well, which were at first his allies.

Oxford University ultimately took official action against him. A com-mission appointed by Chancellor Bartin in 1381 condemned Wyclif's teachings. He appealed in vain to the—still minority-aged—king (Richard II, 1377–1399) and published a *Confessio* but then withdrew to his pastor-ate at Lutterworth, where he lived in seclusion until his death. During his last years, despite soon suffering his first stroke, he still launched into a hectic writing activity. A second stroke then ended his life. He was not bothered personally during his lifetime, although William Courtenay, who became archbishop of Canterbury in the spring of 1382, convened in May of that year a conference at the House of the Black Mendicants (Blackfriars = Dominicans) in London, which condemned twenty-four of Wyclif's statements. The church's later measures against his teaching were all posthumous, directed against the so-called Lollards, his followers in Oxford and later the wider environs, from 1382 on. Also posthumous was the final measure against him, ordered by the Council of Constance in 1415 but not carried out until 1428: his grave in Lutterworth was opened and his bodily remains thrown into a nearby river. We find this quite repulsive, but it was a typically medieval way of dealing with heretics.

In order adequately to understand Wyclif's characteristic view of the Bible, we must first take a look at his philosophical ideas. In the background was the so-called dispute over universals, which runs throughout the Middle Ages but gained new intensity in the second half of the thirteenth century because of the Aristotle renaissance. At its origin was the opposition between Plato and Aristotle, which, also by way of Neo-Platonist speculation, had influenced Christian thinking and introduced particulars into theological thinking on the open question of the relationship between universals and particulars. For the Platonic tradition, the universals (the ideas) are the real, and individual things are merely their embodiments. In the Aristotelian line, it is held that each concrete particular is conceived as the real and the universal term as merely a generalization abstracted from the particulars (nominalism). Christian-Platonist thought—transmitted by Augustine above all—added to "realism" the tendency to equate the ultimate universal with God, in whom all ideas have their place and reality in its totality is united. A powerful countermovement against this had formed toward the end of thirteenth century; foremost among its representatives were the Franciscans Duns Scotus (ca. 1265/1266–1308) and William of Ockham (ca. 1285–1349). Despite all the differences between them, they agreed in calling for the separation of theology and philosophy, while Thomas Aquinas still considered a synthesis of the two to be possible. In particular, they were critical of reason's capacity to arrive at an idea of God and the possibility of a universal building of the world constructed on the idea of God. Only faith can provide access to God. Anyway, God is strictly transcendent (beyond all created reality), his will is decisive, and all divine and human actions are contingent, underived.

But there was also a reactive movement by those who wanted to hold firm to the philosophical-theological synthesis and the Augustinian (= realist) tradition against the "moderns" (*moderni*). Among those with greatest influence on Wyclif were Robert Grosseteste (before 1168–1253), chancellor of Oxford University and later bishop of Lincoln, and Thomas Bradwardine (ca. 1290–1349), archbishop of Canterbury. In the case of Grosseteste, it was not only his opposition to papal abuses and his emphasis on the Holy Scriptures but above all his metaphysics of light (in his main work *De luce* [*On Light*]) that made the greatest impression on Wyclif. From the creation of light (Gen 1:3), Grosseteste speculated about God as the light by which the entire creation is formed and penetrated and therefore connected to its creator. Whereas Grosseteste's activity came before the nominalist dispute of the late thirteenth century, in Bradwardine's *De causa Dei* (*On God as First Cause*, written in 1344) we have a direct reaction to the current discussion. Bradwardine joins together a strict Augustinianism that stressed (against the modern "Pelagians") God's grace as prior to all good works in time and nature as well as an equally radical doctrine of predestination (doctrine of God's predetermination). It led nearly to the implication of viewing God as the author even of sin. That in so doing Bradwardine also stressed the will of God in a one-sided way shifted him closer to Ockham, whom he had planned to oppose. Wyclif also valued Bradwardine particularly because he, too, had studied in Merton College, where his memory was still alive. That we can have firm certainty about divine truths was what drew Wyclif to the "profound doctor" above all.

According to his own statements, Wyclif was, it seems, originally a follower of the nominalist school. Exactly when he converted to realism is unknown. In retrospect, however, he received this insight as a salvation: "It took a long time before I learned to understand this sense of the theory of ideas from the statements of the Scripture. After I had discovered it, illumined by God, first in a superficial way, I gave thanks full of joy to God, together with his servant Augustine and others whom God chose in eternity to be of aid to me as his servants" (*Dom. div.* 1.9, 63 Poole). Wyclif can recognize that his earlier philosophical views had seduced him to the judgment "Scripture is false" (*Ver.* 2.5). He now joyfully recants this and confesses that it was blasphemous. Not until his philosophical thinking changed was he able to acknowledge the truth of Scripture.

Another basic principle in Wyclif's philosophical viewpoint was his dualism. His entire system was oriented to the idea of double substances. It is not only that substance and accident are to be distinguished; it has to do also with the opposition between God and humanity, the divine and the natural, Holy Scripture and human tradition, faith and reason,

Christian and secular community. This dualism expressed itself directly in Wyclif's Christology: he repeatedly stresses that Christ is God *and* human. Wyclif drew this dualism from Greek thought by way of Augustine; its direct source was Augustine's *City of God*. But Wyclif pursued this principle also to its ultimate conclusion.

The actual debates about his philosophical views did not erupt until 1371–1373, when Wyclif was already on the theological faculty. He formulated them in *Summa de ente* (*On Being*) and two tractates, *De universalibus* (*On Universals*, first published in 1985!) and *De tempore* (*On Time*). We also find them summarized in his apologetic work against John Kenningham, a Carmelite who had fought Wyclif's metaphysical views in several writings during these years, evidently because of their consequences for understanding the Bible (see these, and Wyclif's replies, in *Fasciculi zizaniorum* (*Booklet about Weed*); see Matt 13:24–30, the title coming from the Carmelite Thomas Netter Waldenis [d. 1430], its presumed author).

At the basis of Wyclif's metaphysical system was his view that the archetypes of every being (human beings, dog beings, tree beings, each and every created being itself) have an eternal existence in God and are part of his eternal being. Wyclif called the being of these archetypes *intelligible* being and took the view that it, and so God, is demonstrable by human reason. Differentiated within this intelligible being is both the *universal created* being, the *potential* being of secondary causes, and the *actual* being—the being realized in and every individual, that is, an individual person, dog, or tree. While this tripartite division goes back to Augustine and belongs to the standard ideas of Platonizing theology, the coinherence of intelligible being with God and God's attributes of necessity and eternality was a previously unusual realization. It led to the result that indeed not the created individual but its archetype coincided with God's existence and was therefore necessarily existent and indestructible. The being of God was ultimately identical with the being of creation itself. Therefore all being was eternal. Every possibility is at the same time actual, for since God foresees it as possible and God cannot possibly know something that is not, it also must be. Another aspect was the de-limitation (according to Wyclif, "expansion," *amplicacio*) of time, deduced from the eternality and omniscience of God, namely, its absolute predetermination. According to Wyclif, past, present, and future coincide for God, because "God knows everything present, past, and future intuitively" (*Fasc. ziz.* 463). Time is for him eternal presence. Thus there is nothing God does not foreknow and predetermine. The absolute predestination of the destiny of each and every person, one's predetermination for good or evil, corresponding to salvation or judgment, was the implication Wyclif drew up overall to its ultimate exaggeration. Everything future is already present to God as well. Kenningham's objection to this was, among other things, that then even the antichrist (announced for the end times) must already be here now (*Fasc. ziz.* 35). But in practice Wyclif recognized a certain distinction. In God, according to Wyclif, there is a double will: the formal that is unchangeable; and the changeable in his activity. The parable of the potter in Jer 18 (see Benrath, 73, text 74, n. 172) offers him the occasion to distinguish also two correspondingly different sorts of prophetic statement: that which announces the predetermined disaster as inevitable; and that which threatens disaster but may or may not come about, depending on human conduct. Nevertheless, the predetermined destiny to salvation or damnation is not to be reversed even by contrary conduct for a while. Even if persons destined for salvation find themselves for a while in mortal sin, their ultimate salvation is certain, while, vice versa, occasionally doing right cannot save those destined for damnation. Wyclif's doctrine of the true church is likewise derived from his metaphysical approach, together with its practical consequences that only the truly elect should have any say in it.

The Platonic-Aristotelian system at the basis of his thought affected also his position in the eucharistic dispute. Since no substance that is grounded in the particular archetype of its being in God can vanish from the world, the substances in the Eucharist, bread and wine, cannot possibly be changed. They remain bread and wine and are not changed into the body and blood of Christ, as the Catholic doctrine of transubstantiation says. It is also impossible, as attempted by Aristotelian thinking, to separate substance and accidents in such a way that, say, bread and wine remain as mere accidents, while their spiritual substances change into the body and blood of Christ. Based on his dualistic view, Wyclif came to a solution that has been called "consubstantiation": materially, the bread and wine remain, while the spiritual substance is changed into the body and blood of Christ (see also his *Confessio*; *Fasc. ziz.* 115–132). But it can also be noted that Wyclif came to this judgment because he did not find the doctrine of transubstantiation in the Bible. His philosophical standpoint could be harmonized with his biblicism.

Wyclif had already developed this self-consistent but extremist system of thought during the period of his activity as a philosophy teacher, adding to it applications to various theological and church-political matters only later. Only his tone and the consistency of the conclusions he drew intensified in his later years.

His view of the Bible likewise followed from this overall approach. Here we must recall first that earlier theologians also had emphasized the Bible's role as source of revelation. We highlighted the exclusivist view of its significance as it was straightforwardly stated by several Franciscan theologians (e.g., Bonaventure). For a long time, Wyclif considered himself closely tied with the Franciscans and other mendicant orders, until in his later years he included them in his sweeping condemnations of the present form of the church. But his approach was in fact far from theirs, because philosophical metaphysics, not the Bible, was the starting point for his thought. The Scripture as a whole is the one word of God, coming from God's mouth. It is "the law of Christ, the testament of God, and the faith of the church" (*Ver.* 1.5, 1:100 Buddensieg). It is inspired word for word and is true in its wording—here Wyclif follows the trend of his times. But he went further by grounding this truth metaphysically: the Bible as a book composed in writing is the material form of the eternal Word of God, which as such existed and exists before its written version in historical time. Wyclif identifies five grades of the Holy Scripture:

> It is first the book of life. Second, the truths written in it are in accord with its intelligible being. These are both absolutely necessary in Scripture; they are not distinguished in essence but only by reason. Third, Scripture can be taken as the truths one must believe in terms of the way they are inscribed in terms of existence or effect in the book of life. Fourth, Scripture is taken for the truth to be believed, which is inscribed in the human soul by nature. In the fifth way, the Holy Scripture is understood as manuscripts, words, and other signs that are aids for preserving the above-named truths. (*Ver.* 1.6, 1:108–9)

But for Wyclif the Holy Scripture is not to be equated with the biblical manuscripts: "That materially graspable [*sensibilis*] text in words or manuscripts is not Holy Scripture, just as a painted or imagined man is called man because of his similarity with a true man" (*Ver.* 1.6, 1:111). Wyclif mentions in his writing against Kenningham three "nests" in which he is raised with other chickens of Christ (*Fasc. ziz.* 453); these discussions are quoted once again by Kenningham (*Fasc. ziz.* 14). The third, and highest, is metaphysical, that from the eternity of God, "and therefore all that is, was, or will be is present to God. And we resolve disputed questions by this truth and affirm that the Holy Scripture is true with respect to its intention of speaking [*de vi sermonis*]." Because the truth of the Bible is anchored in the eternity of God, it is unchangeable; therefore, it is conceived fundamentalistically: the Bible cannot contain anything false; each and every individual word is equally true. This has to be so, because each word is present in God in eternity. From the start of his discussions with Kenningham on, Wyclif affirmed the timelessness and literal truth of the Bible. Repeatedly (*Ver.* 1.2, 1:28–29; 1.3 1:50, 53; 1.9, 1:195), Wyclif can speak of the "logic of Scripture," which transcends all human logic. He stresses the "humility" of this "heavenly logic," which excludes all arrogant disputes (*Ver.* 1.2, 1:29). For Wyclif, the Scripture is not only the mirror of truth but is itself the original truth; as the book of life, it contains all truths. Indeed, it is itself the Logos, the Word. Wyclif frequently bases this statement on the (presumably faulty) Vulgate text of John 10:35: "Non potest solvi scriptura, quem pater sanctificavit et misit in mundum" ("the Scripture cannot be annulled, whom the Father sanctified and sent into the world"). From this follows the principle: the Scripture is Christ, Christ is the Scripture.

This same metaphysical foundation could lead him to diametrically different conclusions in his judgment of the Bible and that of the church. The church was also eternal in its idea contained in God, but because its present form deviates from the idea, it must be radically changed. The form of the Bible, by contrast, corresponded to its ideal and was just as eternal and perfect as it. Wyclif repeats this claim time and again, among other places in his extensive work, *On the Truth of the Holy Scriptures*, but in much more concise form in his late work, *Trialogus* (*Trialogue*, 1382). As the first of Wyclif's works published in Basel, as early as 1525, the *Trialogus* was able to be used by the continental Reformers. In it they could rediscover their own views inasmuch as Wyclif claimed that existing church institutions would all have to be evaluated by whether or not they are mentioned in Holy Scripture and that only those found there are legitimate. Since he could find neither popes nor cardinals nor bishops in the Bible, the hierarchy was a falsification of the true church,

Of the statements about the Bible in the *Trialogus* (3.31, 238–43 Lechler), three are to be emphasized: (1) the Scripture is true because it is the book about the life of Christ in which all truth is contained; (2) it is the book of the eternal and temporal truths it contains; and (3) it is the book in which God's laws are given. Because the Bible contains the words of Jesus, it can never be false, for Christ would never deceive. Hence Wyclif stresses, among other things—here in complete contrast to Nicholas of Lyra—that differences among translations of the Bible do not even matter; the truth is not changed by this (commentary on Ps 44:1). Seeming discrepancies within the Bible must be smoothed over. One popular way to do so is the assumption of "equivocations" (ambiguities of

words), of which Wyclif frequently makes use. Not even biblical chronology can display any error—a problem hotly disputed in later centuries.
Of course—and here Wyclif follows Augustine—one must distinguish
between the Bible's implicit and explicit meanings. Some truths were not
evident and had to be found with the help of reason. Its rules should be
applied to the Bible throughout. Wyclif also reckons throughout with a
multiple sense of Scripture and the possibility of differing interpretations.
In this sense one can hardly speak of *sola scriptura* ("Scripture alone") in
his case, since in interpreting it he can often appeal to teachers of the early
church, especially Augustine and Jerome, but to more recent theologians
as well, such as Bernard of Clairvaux, Hugo of St. Victor, or Robert Grosseteste. He can also say that, for example, Solomon's instruction in Eccl
12:12, "study no more, my son," cannot mean that the writings of Augustine and other church fathers are to be excluded, even though they do not
have the same authority as the Bible itself (text in Benrath, 22 n. 38). He
expressly stresses (*Dom. div.* prol. 1–2): "For greater assurance in discov-
ering their insights, I will rely mainly on two leaders, philosophy and the
commentaries of the fathers who have been approved by the church." But
the following also applies: the teaching of the four great fathers, Augustine included, is to be accepted only to the extent it corresponds with
Scripture or reason (*De eucharistia* 277 Loserth). This presupposed, for
Wyclif there can be no logically irreconcilable statements in the Bible. He
also has no objection to the use of Aristotelian logic, when its function
remains that of a servant: "I do not deny that Aristotle was a great philosopher whose books are justly read and deservedly studied." "Therefore,
Christians learn philosophy, which is learned in a pious way from the
books of Aristotle, not because they come from Aristotle but because it is
the (philosophy) of the authors of the Holy Scripture and hence as it were
their own philosophy, which is correctly taught in books of theology"
(*Ver.* 1.2, 1:29). Wyclif also maintains that the Bible is in itself a logical
book even in the sense of universally valid logic according to Aristotle's
standard, and it must be judged according to logical principles. Reason
therefore plays a decisive role for him.

This, of course, confronts Wyclif with the task of demonstrating—in
reply to contemporary critics of the Bible who thought they discovered imperfections and contradictions in it by logical reasoning—that
the Bible is without errors or contradictions. Some of these discussion
points had already emerged in the debate with Kenningham, and Wyclif
takes them up in his biblical commentary as well. One passage that still
provokes discussion today is Amos 7:14, where Amos seems to say, "I am

no prophet, nor a prophet's son, but I am a herdsman who dresses syca-more trees." On this, the *Glossa ordinaria* offers the information (which came from Gregory the Great and was similarly attested by Thomas Aquinas [*Summa theol.* 2.2.71] and to a certain extent by Kenningham) that Amos did not have prophetic inspiration at the time he confronted Amaziah, but certainly at a later point of time, and therefore he was not at that moment a prophet in the actual sense. In his Bible commentary (Benrath, 77–78, text n. 180), Wyclif applies here his theory of expansion (*amplicatio*) to the tense to his passage: Amos expands the present and includes the past in it: "Before God called me I was not a prophet, but a cowherd!" Unfortunately, Wyclif lacked the knowledge of Hebrew to document the ambiguity of the statement's tenses from the structure of the Hebrew nominal sentence!

Another biblical passage for which Wyclif had to demonstrate the timelessness of all biblical statements was Lam 5:7, because Kenningham had questioned it: "Our fathers have sinned and are no more." At this, Kenningham triumphed: "Some things were and are no longer. Therefore not everything that was still is. Therefore there is a consistent advance from what is first, what precedes, to what is last. There are not all the things that were" (*Fasc. ziz.* 25; see also 29). Such an argument is in Ken-ningham's case the result of his nominalist starting point: the only thing that can be known to be "present" is what can be found as existent at some certain point in time. Wyclif, however, cannot agree at all with this logic. In his commentary he gives his position on the problem in an excursus (Benrath, 63; text 62–63, n. 144). Here Wyclif, who understands the term "are" (*sunt*), like Kenningham, metaphysically, comments: "they have no being" cannot be meant in this passage. Rather, "the fathers" are not par-ticipants in the sentence of punishment during the Babylonian captivity, although they participated in the sin. That they are fathers applies also for no particular moment but only according to the expanded understanding of time (*in magno tempore*), in which all humans are sons of Adam and the Jews sons of Abraham (John 8:33, 37, 40). In interpreting this passage, then, Wyclif remains within the framework of his metaphysics. This logic can also be applied to the genealogy of Jesus. Thus, say, at Matt 1:1, where Wyclif explains that the simultaneous designation of Jesus as the son of Abraham and the son of David is possible because the terms "father" and "son" cannot be understood narrowly as a single generation but in a wider sense (text in Benrath, 104, n. 51). Wyclif applied other biblical passages as well, such as John 8:58: "For before Abraham was, I am." To this Wyclif says, "Christ shows the Jews the divine nature according to which he preceded Abraham. That is to say, there is neither future nor past in eternity" (Benrath, 211, n. 512). The statement in Exod 3:6, cited by Jesus in Matt 22:32, "I am the God of Abraham and the God of Isaac and the God of Jacob," is formulated in the present tense, but it applies to the future, because all things are equally present to God. The resurrection of the dead will indeed come chronologically first.

Wyclif also had to address the objection of his opponents that biblical statements were in places contradictory or false. In this case, Kenningham with his criticism had already forced him to backtrack a bit. Wyclif had originally claimed that the Bible is true word for word. But Kenningham's contention, that then, for example, the crowd's statement about Jesus, "you have an evil spirit" (John 7:20; see *Fasc. ziz.* 6–7), would have to be true had led him from the "word for word" (*de vi verbi*) to a somewhat more flexible viewpoint that this truth applies with respect to the particular intent of a statement (*de virtute sermonis*). Thus he now comments on Mark 3:39, "he has an unclean spirit": "But it does not follow from this that I must admit that Christ has an evil spirit but that the Pharisees said it" (commentary, excursus on Luke 9; Benrath, 364–65; see also 224). Yet he also had to explain evident contradictions, like that between the word of Jesus in John 7:8, "Go up to this festival, but I am not going up," and his presence at the Festival of Booths in Jerusalem shortly after (John 7:14). Wyclif's explanation corresponds to his understanding of time. That is, the statement was not meant absolutely but only relatively: Jesus did not want to go up together openly with the disciples, but he did not mean he did not want to do so at all. Wyclif explains this by an analogy: if someone asks me if I have said Mass, and I answer no, this does not mean that I have never said Mass, but the answer refers only to the current day (commentary, excursus on Luke 9:3; Benrath, 362–63).

Wyclif's understanding of faith (see the excursus on faith, commentary on Mark 5:34, Benrath 205, nn. 488–89; also Benrath, 204–6) is similar to the legal view as we already encountered it in Nicholas of Lyra. False views of faith, which Wyclif enumerates, do not in his view make clear the seriousness of God's command: "Therefore, when we know that God demands humility and that his law is observed under penalty of an immensely greater damnation, it is certain that every one of us who commits an act it forbids is lacking in faith" (Benrath, n. 488). The genuine believer must always be mindful that God is indeed patient and slow to punish, but ultimately it will indeed be imposed. "Thus in the case of the true fathers who constantly lived in fear of the Son, it was as if the supreme taskmaster constantly held the rod over their heads." To this, Wyclif also adduces Prov 28:14: "Happy is the one who is never without fear" (Benrath, 206 n. 490). Scripture does not merely contain the law of God; it really *is* God's law. Natural law (*lex nature*), the Mosaic law (*lex mosaica*), and the law of the gospel (*lex evangelica*) agree and supplement one another; they are not antithetical. But the evangelical law is more clear, more concise, more important, and more useful than the other two forms of the law (commentary, prologue to Matthew; in Benrath, 98 n. 29). But nothing about this position is peculiar to Wyclif; on the contrary, here he is a typical late medieval theologian, as the example of Nicholas of Lyra shows. Going along with it is the fact that the last-mentioned remarks about the evangelical law are taken directly from Nicholas's foreword to the New Testament!

Wyclif's sermons, which are all legalistic in character, confirm this impression. But he takes one decisive step beyond Nicholas and other predecessors in setting the "law of God" over against "human law" and from this antithesis deriving a starting point for his critique of the contemporary church. As in Nicholas, so in Wyclif there is a summons to discipleship of Christ and with it a threefold foundation of the demand for humility. In a lengthy excursus of his commentary on Matt 11:28–30 (text in Benrath, 354–62; see also 236–42 [an academic speech?]; also, on the treatment of the theme in the passion history, 179–97), he sets forth his understanding of what is evidently for him most essential in the gospel. In understanding the "Savior's call" as a call of Christ to the teacher of virtue and lawgiver (*legifer*), he gains from the demand of humility the standard for his negative judgment on all his contemporaries, above all the influential circles of the church who resist this demand by their behavior.

Hence it comes as no surprise that Wyclif cannot understand even the Pauline letters otherwise. Despite his knowledge of Augustine, he does not take into account the Pauline doctrine of justification but instead stresses the instructions that can be applied to the life of the church. It squares with this that in his *principium* (his theological inaugural as a newly promoted doctor, which now appears as a prologue to the interpretation of Job but was evidently not connected with it originally), Wyclif elucidates— still in a conservative way, however—the presuppositions for understanding the Bible itself (this text and others in Benrath, 338–46), with knowledge of Aristotle's moral philosophy given an important place. In keeping with this also is the fact that he establishes the proposition that a student of Holy Scripture would have to bring along for his understanding that he is morally good. Further, he requires "experience in the study of philosophy and the practice of virtue." This is more important than the talent for rational speculation. He interprets especially the Sermon on the Mount in a completely Aristotelian sense.

At any rate, Wyclif can understand the Evangelists' statements about Jesus in a classically messianic fashion—as he stresses by referring to the fulfillment of the twenty-two preconditions for the Messiah prophesied in the Old Testament—(commentary on Matt 1:1; see Benrath, 102–3). He is therefore in this respect altogether orthodox.

All in all, one must say that, viewed objectively, there is not much left of Wyclif's reputation as "the morning star of the Reformation." It by no means applies in any case to the starting point of his thought and the consequences drawn from it for his understanding of the Bible. His thinking is deeply rooted in the Middle Ages, although with his church-critical implications he had in view consequences extreme for his time. If there is any truth to his reputation, then it is due more to his historical influence than to his teachings. His high esteem of the Bible, above all as a book of law important for simple people, was one reason that he promoted the production of an English translation or at least advocated such an undertaking, though not himself leading the way. His followers produced this translation, which has become known as the Lollard Bible. An older, awkward version appeared during Wyclif's own lifetime, a more elegant one later. The official church wanted to prevent vernacular translations of the Bible in order to protect the clergy's monopoly on its interpretation. This accounts for the struggle that such translations occasioned. Wyclif first gained a following among academicians in Oxford. After Archbishop Courtenay suppressed the movement by severe interrogations in 1381, it dispersed into the surroundings, toward Leicestershire especially, but Northampton as well. In the early decades, until it was dealt a decisive blow by the failure of a rebellion led by the knight Sir John Oldcastle in 1414, a good many nobles evidently belonged to it; sympathizers were suspected even at the court of Richard II. The care with which biblical manuscripts and the manuscripts of sermons and collections of writings (*floretum* and *rosarium*) were produced indicates at least a well-equipped copyist workshop in which costly materials and corresponding experts were available. On the other hand, it is unlikely that Wyclif himself sent out a group of itinerant preachers. There is no evidence he did so, and it seems difficult to square with the academic character of his way of working. It is his writings especially that have been influential. But he taught theoretically a good deal about the imitation of Christ and how it is to be spread by the preaching of simple disciples of Jesus. His listeners were the first to draw the practical implications from this. This teaching was at first altogether official and indeed similar in many respects to views prevalent among the mendicant monks. Only after the failure of Oldcastle's revolt were his followers driven completely underground and recruited thereafter only among handworkers and simple people. But this movement, which soon turned the tag Lollards ("murmurers"), originally meant as a term of derision, into a name of honor, was never completely rooted out, managing to maintain itself up into the age of the sixteenth-century English Reformation.

In addition, Wyclif had an influence in faraway Bohemia. Here it was the young master Jan Hus (ca. 1371–1415) who was prompted by his academic teachers at the University of Prague (especially Stanislaus of Znaim and Stephan of Kolin), who had concerned themselves intensively with Wyclif's philosophical realism, to copy for himself in his own hand several of Wyclif's tractates in 1398. Later (shortly after 1400), Wyclif's theological writings became known in Prague, his view of the Eucharist in particular becoming a matter of controversial discussion. Though Hus himself never adopted Wyclif's doctrine of the Eucharist, he was accused of doing so nevertheless at the Council of Constance (1415), which ended by condemning him and burning him at the stake. On the other hand, his doctrine of the church (De ecclesia), with its distinction between the elect and the reprobate, his specific criticisms of the church, and his ideas of reform were often based on Wyclif's writings. The great interest Wyclif's writings on church and state found in Czech circles can be seen in the journey of the two Czechs Mikulás Faulfis and Jiri von Knenice in search of exemplars in England in 1407. They obtained a copy of De dominio divino. The issue of nationality also played a role among the Czechs. This was true even with respect to philosophical foundations: the German professors at Prague University mostly advocated nominalist views; the Czechs, realist. Hus himself was not so much a thinker as a practical church reformer. The Hussite movement aimed at a Czech national church, even against the curia in Rome. This influence on history certainly worked out differently than Wyclif himself could have imagined it. Nevertheless, it contributed to his later reputation far more than his own teachings would have themselves.

CONCLUDING WORD

Our way has led us through a thousand years of the history of interpretation. At the place in history where we began this way, the world of classical antiquity still seemed to continue unbroken, even though Roman citizens could not overlook the dangers arising from the onslaught of new peoples from every side during the second half of the fourth century and more than ever at the turn of the fifth. The plundering of Rome by the Visigoths under Alaric in 410 marked a turning point that made the end of the *pax Romana* dramatically clear to every inhabitant of the Roman Empire. Nevertheless, a thousand years later the cultural rays of Greco-Roman antiquity were still as lively as ever in the scholarly activity of the schools and universities and from there into the thought and feeling of the cultured classes of Europe—as made possible by the Latin language as the medium for border-crossing dialogue. But the *artes liberales* (liberal arts) were still merely the substructure of the pyramid of courses of study and faculties upon which theology as the crown of science arose. Church theologians, lay clergy, and monks are by far the well-known theologians who gave theological science its rank and name. But no less important is the work of countless contributors: preachers and teachers who, working in silence, conscientiously administered the theological heritage.

But theology, in accord with the understanding prevailing to the end of the Middle Ages, was *sacra pagina*, the study of the Holy Scripture. Interpretation of the Bible remained its basis, despite the logical-dialectical method that arose and gradually developed from John Scotus Eriugena on, which called medieval theology as a whole to a scholasticism using largely rational argumentation. We saw that this label is false: it was attached to the medieval theologians later by their humanistic opponents, who from the fifteenth century on sought to distance themselves from their predecessors by similar reproaches. Hence we will return to this matter in the next volume. The dialectical forms of resolving the problems of theology go along with the construction of courses of study at the universities and their effects of the ancient forms of thought at their foundation as ever.

But they were never able to gain dominance in the field of theology. That the Bible remained the central source of theology also hindered the distancing of theological theory building from church piety. The preaching of famous bishops such as Ambrose of Milan and Gregory of Rome and their literary works are closely interrelated.

The monastery also played an important role in dealings with the Bible. In the daily course of their liturgical celebrations, in Bible reading and psalm singing, in the copying activity of their monks, but above all in their biblically based spirituality, there developed an intensity of living with the Bible as would hardly be conceivable outside its walls. On the negative side of the ledger, however, ordinary church people, the laity and the simple, uneducated members of the community, were largely cut off from closer familiarity with the Bible. At most, they got to hear the texts that played a role in the sermon; translations of Holy Scripture in the vernacular languages were officially forbidden. From this unfilled need, a movement such as the Lollards could emerge in later medieval England, which disseminated its own translation of the Bible.

A large part of medieval theological literature thus consisted of writings about the Bible, commentaries, and occasionally hermeneutics and other resource works of benefit for biblical study. Even systematic theological works such as the large *summae*—the most famous being that of Thomas Aquinas—systematized by means of philosophical-logic theological statements that as such were derived from the Bible. Their biblical foundations were therefore not to be lacking. In Thomas they were of completely equal rank alongside the philosophical presuppositions of thought.

Overall it can be said that the tie to Holy Scripture had kept Christian theology from disintegrating into directions completely separate from one another. Oppositions and debates between various schools and currents—which, of course, did not disappear—were never able to lead to a complete separation and abandonment of a common foundation, because this was given by the biblical tradition. Differing points of view had to prove themselves again and again by appeal to the Bible.

Biblical commentaries, however, were the main object of our investigations, and on this basis we traced the sorts of dealings with the Holy Scripture among prominent exegetes over the centuries. We had to limit ourselves, by necessity, to exemplary descriptions. Although we met with the titles of numerous works by Christian and Jewish authors and could even consider a representative selection more closely, the size of the editions preserved and prepared by recent editors (e.g., the well-known

Migne and his colleagues) as well as in significant part printed sources as well is considerably larger than could be expressed in this presentation.

I hope nonetheless to have drawn an adequate overall picture. As we saw, medieval commentary literature is by its very nature the literature of tradition. Originality was less important to its writers than the true restatement of the testimonies of the fathers, whose reliable knowledge cast its light on the Holy Scriptures. What was individual could largely recede. But that this yielded no uniformity went along with the writers' differing circumstances of life, their personal distinctiveness, their membership in different theological schools, secular or monastic traditions. Differing philosophical presuppositions of thought, whether of Platonic, Aristotelian, or Stoic character, could also influence exegesis. Such interrelationships shaped traditional exegesis as well as medieval biblical interpretation in various ways and make attention to it instructive.

Essential presuppositions of exegesis retaining validity even in later times were already set down in late antiquity. The effect of many interpreters on posterity was limited, of course, because the dissemination and recognition of their exegetical achievements were hampered by condemnations of their teaching. Such, for example, is the case with the Antiochenes, such as Theodore of Mopsuetia, whose services for interpreting the literal sense of Holy Scripture first received full recognition only in modern times. However, it also applies to a certain extent to Origen as well, on the other side of the methodological spectrum. His spiritual exegesis, however, had struck such deep roots in church consciousness that it could live on in exegetical practice even without explicit appeal to him. This becomes all too clear, for example, in the pastoral work of Bishop Ambrose of Milan, for whose preaching the return to the "spiritual" sense of Scripture was unavoidable. Somewhat later the Roman Gregory the Great set out along similar paths, although due to his circumstances he was active in a far more literary way and put the emphasis on the Bible's topological, that is, moral, meaning.

Also important for the history of interpretation are the theologians who made more fundamental thoughts on the Holy Scripture. In so doing it came down to their linguistic form. To be highlighted here especially would be Jerome, who dealt with the *hebraica veritas*, that is, the Hebraic original of the Bible, and produced a Latin translation of the Old Testament that, as the Vulgate, became authoritative for the entire West and eclipsed older, unreliable forms of the texts. He was also the first Christian biblical theologian who sought out contact with Jews of his surroundings for the sake of their knowledge of Hebrew. Only much later, in the High

Middle Ages, was the Jewish tradition of interpretation in his prominent representatives noticed even by some Christian exegetes. In the
case of Augustine, who wrote the first important biblical hermeneutics,
the valuation of Holy Scripture as a testimony to God's activity in history is important, and it takes its own, although not first, place alongside
the others in his theological thinking, greatly shaped by Platonic influences. But Augustine was also influential because of the methodical rules
for scriptural interpretation that he developed—or from Tyconius and
others.

We learned about monastic living with the Bible from John Cassian and, based on his report, of its origins in Egypt. But the profound
familiarity of monks with the Bible, extending to its verbal knowledge
by heart, and the wide room it occupied in their course of daily worship,
stamped by prayer and song, and also in their everyday tasks, already
came clearly into view in the oldest of the Egyptian monastic rules. Also
the later theological activity of monastic theologians—of whom we have
learned an entire series, Venerable Bede, Rupert of Deutz, Hugh of St.
Victor, Joachim of Fiore, Bonaventure, and Nicholas of Lyra—is inseparable from this presupposition. Their relationship to the Bible was never
determined purely intellectually but was stamped by a close relationship
to life, which included "mystical" piety, meditation, and ascetic morality. From this it is understandable that the tropological and analogical
senses of Scripture would play an especially large role in their work. In
individual monks such as Joachim of Fiore, an awareness of the end time
could even gain exceptional significance. On the other hand, the fact that
a monk, Nicholas of Lyra, put such heavy emphasis on the literal sense
shows the wide band of the speculative interests possible in monastic
exegesis. Indeed, here, as we saw, the special influence of Jewish biblical
interpretation makes itself evident.

Biblical interpretation as tradition—this characteristic of medieval
exegesis becomes especially clear in the places where the transmission
of inherited interpretation becomes the true aim of literary activity. We
pointed this out in regard to the specific forms of catena formation and
above all glosses of the Bible. The biblical text, framed round about by
glosses (i.e., quotations from the fathers' commentaries), as it was long
passed on in biblical manuscripts and in the end even in printed form,
becomes a special means of passing on tradition. This is the origin of the
explanatory statements by individual authors, though the important thing
is not naming the author by name but its diversity—and internal correspondence—maintaining the once formulated exegetical knowledge of

certain biblical verses and sections, which serves to safeguard them and make them accessible to later readers. Hence the formation of tradition is continued, especially since the possibility of adding more recent inter-pretations is not fundamentally limited except by the space available for it. Something similar is known in the field of Judaism as well, such as in the publication of an edition of the Talmud with Rashi's commentary encircl-ing the text.

One chapter was also devoted to Jewish interpreters of the Middle Ages. This, too, is a selection from a much wider field, from which a series of well-known names might still be mentioned. The selection of Rashi and Abraham ibn Ezra as examples here was especially because of their influ-ence on history, which was such that their special sort of interpretation developed up to contemporary exegesis. In both cases the advantage that Jewish interpreters had over nearly every Christian came fully into play: their intimacy with the Hebrew language of the Bible (and the Aramaic), which prompted them to give special consideration to the literal sense and reference works on its interpretation, grammar, and lexicography. Jewish specialists played a pioneering role in both fields. In addition, contact with Arabic culture and the rationalism of the Aristotelian stamp alive in it led to a rational sort of biblical understanding in these exegetes, as it first returned in the age of the Enlightenment. That a good many of their judgments strike us at the first glance as "modern" shows the intellectual proximity of present historical-critical exegesis to their approach.

Standing apart, however, is the biblical understanding of John Wyclif, with whom we concluded our passage through the medieval history of interpretation of the Bible. Once greeted as "the morning star of the Ref-ormation" and thus still much-considered in recent times, upon closer investigation of his thought he seems rather odd. The oddity is prompted above all by the metaphysical approach (of Platonic-Aristotelian stamp) of his thought, with which he seeks to dissolve all of the Bible's contents into a universally valid truth and a supra-temporal system. To be sure, this gives the impression that he wanted to confirm the Bible's universal validity, allowing it to be applied as supra-temporal truth, but in reality he subordinates it in the process to an abstract thinking that has its own value. That just such a historical effect could develop, from Wyclif and on beyond John Hus up to the Reformation, is one of the absurdities of his-tory, from which it is, as is well known, not free.

With Wyclif we near the time of the end of the Middle Ages, which like all transitions between periods cannot really be dated with precision. I will deal with the subsequent section of the history of interpretation in the third volume in this series. Humanism and the Reformation above all will be at its center. In so doing we come to a decisive epoch that altered relations to Scripture in various ways and that is, today as before, of central significance for biblical understanding. The abundance of sources available for this period and the breadth of discussion about it will necessitate dedicating to it a volume of its own.

Selected Resources and Readings

Suggestions for additional readings are arranged by chapters. Commentaries on individual biblical books are not listed.

General

Ackroyd, Peter R., and Christopher F. Evans, eds. *From the Beginnings to Jerome*. Vol. 1 of *The Cambridge History of the Bible*. Cambridge: Cambridge University Press, 1970.

Brinkmann, Henning. *Mittelalterliche Hermeneutik*. Tübingen: Niemeyer, 1980.

Brunhölzl, Franz. "Bibel." Columns 39–75 in vol. 2 of *Lexikon des Mittelalters*. Edited by Robert Auty et al. 10 vols. Munich, Artemis-Verlag, 1977–1999.

Classen, Peter. "Die hohen Schulen und die Gesellschaft im 12. Jahrhundert." *Archiv für Kulturgeschichte* 48 (1966): 155–80.

Dobschütz, Ernst von. "Vom vierfachen Schriftsinn: Die Geschichte einer Theorie." Pages 1–13 in *Harnack-Ehrung: Beiträge zur Kirchengeschichte*. Leipzig: Hinrichs, 1921.

Ebeling, Gerhard. *Kirchengeschichte als Auslegung der Heiligen Schrift*. Sammlung gemeinverständlicher Vorträge und Schriften aus dem Gebiet der Theologie und Religionsgeschichte 189. Tübingen: Mohr Siebeck, 1947.

Margerie, Bertrand de. *Introduction à l'histoire de l'exégèse*. Vol. 1: *Les Pères grecs et orientaux*; vol. 2: *Les prèmiers grands exégètes latins*. Paris: Cerf, 1980–1983.

Riché, Pièrre, and Guy Lobrichon, eds. *Le Moyen Age et la Bible*. La Bible de tous les temps 4. Paris: Beauchesne, 1984.

Rost, Hans. *Die Bibel im Mittelalter: Beiträge zur Geschichte und Bibliographie der Bibel*. Augsburg: Kommissions-Verlag M. Seitz, 1939.

Smalley, Beryl. *The Study of the Bible in the Middle Ages*. Oxford: Basil Blackwell, 1952.

1. Famous Interpreters of Late Antiquity

1.1. Theodore of Mopsuetia

Works

Theodore of Mopsuestia: Commentary on Psalms 1–81. Translated by Robert C. Hill. SBLWGRW 5. Atlanta: Society of Biblical Literature, 2006.

Theodore of Mopsuestia. Commentary on the Minor Pauline Epistles. Translated by Rowan A. Greer. SBLWGRW 26. Atlanta: Society of Biblical Literature, forthcoming.

Theodori Mopsuesteni commentarius in XII prophetas. Edited by Hans N. Sprenger. Biblica et Patristica. Wiesbaden: Harrassowitz, 1977.

Literature

Bultmann, Rudolf. Die Exegese des Theodor von Mopsuestia. Stuttgart: Kohlhammer, 1984.

Downey, Glanville. A History of Antioch in Syria from Seleucus to the Arab Conquest. Princeton: Princeton University Press, 1961.

Greer, Rowan A. Theodore of Mopsuestia: Exegete and Theologian. London: Faith Press, 1961.

Raddatz, Alfred. "Theodor von Mopsuestia." Pages 167–77 in vol. 2 of Gestalten der Kirchengeschichte. Edited by Martin Greschat. 12 vols. Stuttgart: Kohlhammer, 1981–1986.

Wickert, Ulrich. Studien zu den Pauluskommentaren Theodors von Mopsuestia. Berlin: Töpelmann, 1962.

Zaharopoulos, Dimitri Z. Theodore of Mopsuestia on the Bible: A Study of His Old Testament Exegesis. New York: Paulist, 1989.

1.2. Didymus the Blind

Works

Commentary on Zechariah. Translated by Robert C. Hill. FC 111. Washington, D.C.: Catholic University of America Press, 2006.

Kommentar zu Hiob (Tura-Papyrus). 4 vols. PTA 1–3, 33. Bonn: Habelt, 1968–1985.

Vol. 1: Kommentar zu Hiob Kapitel 1–4. Edited and translated by Albert Henrichs. PTA 1. Bonn: Habelt, 1968.

Vol. 2: Kommentar zu Hiob Kapitel 5,1–6,29. Edited and translated by Albert Henrichs. PTA 2. Bonn: Habelt, 1968.

Vol. 3: *Kommentar zu Hiob Kapitel 7,20C–11*. Edited and translated by Ursula Hagedorn, Dieter Hagedorn, and Ludwig Koenen. PTA 3. Bonn: Habelt, 1968.

Vol. 4: *Kommentar zu Hiob Kapitel 12,1–16,8a*. Edited and translated by Ursula Hagedorn, Dieter Hagedorn, and Ludwig Koenen. PTA 33. Bonn: Habelt, 1985.

Kommentar zum Ecclesiastes. 6 vols. PTA 9, 13, 16, 22, 24–26. Bonn: Habelt, 1969–1983.

Vol. 1: *Kommentar zu Ecclesiastes Kapitel 1,1–2,14*. Edited and translated by Gerhard Binder and Leo Liesenborghs. 2 parts. PTA 25–26. Bonn: Habelt, 1979–1983.

Vol. 2: *Kommentar zu Ecclesiastes Kapitel 3–4,12*. Edited and translated by Michael Gronewald. PTA 22. Bonn: Habelt, 1977.

Vol. 3: *Kommentar zu Ecclesiastes Kapitel 5–6*. Edited and translated by Johannes Kramer. PTA 13. Bonn: Habelt, 1970.

Vol. 4: *Kommentar zu Ecclesiastes Kapitel 7–8,8*. Edited and translated by Johannes Kramer and Bärbel Krebber. PTA 16. Bonn: Habelt, 1972.

Vol. 5: *Kommentar zu Ecclesiastes Kapitel 9,8–10,20*. Edited and translated by Michael Gronewald. PTA 24. Bonn: Habelt, 1979.

Vol. 6: *Kommentar zu Ecclesiastes Kapitel 11–12*. Edited and translated by Gerhard Binder. PTA 9. Bonn: Habelt, 1969.

Psalmenkommentar. 5 vols. PTA 4, 7–9, 12. Bonn: Habelt, 1969–1983.

Vol. 1: *Kommentar zu Psalm 20–21*. Edited and translated by Louis Doutreleau. PTA 7. Bonn: Habelt, 1969.

Vol. 2: *Kommentar zu Psalm 22–26,10*. Edited and translated by Michael Gronewald. PTA 4. Bonn: Habelt, 1968.

Vol. 3: *Kommentar zu Psalm 29–34*. Edited and translated by Michael Gronewald. PTA 8. Bonn: Habelt, 1969.

Vol. 4: *Kommentar zu Psalm 35–39*. Edited and translated by Michael Gronewald. PTA 9. Bonn: Habelt, 1969.

Vol. 5: *Kommentar zu Psalm 40–44*. Edited and translated by Michael Gronewald. PTA 12. Bonn: Habelt, 1970.

Sur la Genèse: Texte inédit d'après un papyrus de Tours. Edited and translated by Pierre Nautin, with Louis Doutreleau. 2 vols. SC 233, 244. Paris: Cerf, 1976–1978.

Sur Zacharie: Texte inédit d'après un papyrus de Toura. Edited and translated by Louis Doutreleau. SC 83–85. Paris: Cerf, 1962.

LITERATURE

Bienert, Wolfgang A. *Allegoria und Anagoge bei Didymos dem Blinden von Alexandria*. PTS 13. Berlin: de Gruyter, 1972.

Gauche, William J. *Didymus the Blind: An Educator of the Fourth Century*. Washington, D.C.: Catholic University of America, 1934.

Kramer, Bärbel. "Didymus von Alexandrien." *TRE* 8:741–46.

Layton, Richard A. *Didymus the Blind and His Circle in Late-Antique Alexandria: Virtue and Narrative in Biblical Scholarship*. Urbana: University of Illinois Press; Bristol: Bristol University Press 2003.

Tigcheler, Jo. *Didyme l'Aveugle et l'exégèse allégorique: Étude sémantique de quelques termes exégétiques importants de son commentaire sur Zacharie*. Graecitas Christianorum Primaeva 6. Nijmegen: Dekker & van de Vegt, 1977.

1.3. JEROME

WORKS

Commentaire sur Jonas. Edited and translated by Yves-Marie Duval. SC 323. Paris: Cerf, 1985.

Commentaire sur S. Matthieu. Edited and translated by Émile Bonnard. SC 242, 259. Vol. 1: books 1–2; vol. 2: books 3–4. Paris: Cerf, 1977–1979.

Commentarioli in Psalmos: Tractus sive homiliae in Psalmos. Edited by Germain Morin. Anecdota Maredsolana 3. Oxford: Parker, 1895–1903.

Commentarioli in Psalmos. In *Hebraicae quaestiones in libro Geneseos; Liber interpretationis hebraicorum nominum; Commentarioli in Psalmos; Commentarius in Ecclesiasten*. Edited by Claudio Moreschini. CCSL 78. Turnhout: Brepols, 1958.

In Hieremiam libri VI. Edited by Siegfried Reiter. CSEL 74. Turnhout: Brepols, 1960.

Sancti Eusebii Hieronymi Epistulae. Edited by Isidorus Hilberg. 4 vols. in 3. CSEL 54–56. Vienna: Verlag der Österreichischen Akademie der Wissenschaften, 1996.

LITERATURE

Barr, James. "St. Jerome's Appreciation of Hebrew." *BJRL* 49 (1966/1967): 281–302.

Bartelink, G. J. M. "Hieronymus." Pages 145–65 in vol. 2 of *Gestalten der Kirchengeschichte*. Edited by Martin Greschat. 12 vols. Stuttgart: Kohlhammer, 1981–1986.

Cain, Andrew. *The Letters of Jerome: Asceticism, Biblical Exegesis, and the Construction of Christian Authority in Late Antiquity*. Oxford: Oxford University Press, 2009.

Grützmacher, Georg. *Hieronymus: Eine biographische Studie zur alten Kirchengeschichte*. 3 vols. Leipzig: Dieterich, 1901–8. Repr., Aalen: Scienta, 1969.

Hagemann, Wilfried. *Wort als Begegnung mit Christus: Die christozentrische Schriftauslegung des Kirchenvaters Hieronymus*. TThSt 23. Trier: Paulinus-Verlag, 1970.

Jay, Pierre. *L'exégèse de Saint Jérôme d'après son commentaire sur Isaie*. Paris: Études augustiniennes, 1985.

Kelly, John N. D. *Jerome: His Life, Writings and Controversies*. London: Duckworth, 1975.

Nautin, Pierre. "Hieronymus." *TRE* 15:304–15.

1.4. AMBROSE OF MILAN

WORKS

Commentary of Saint Ambrose on the Gospel according to Saint Luke. Translated by Íde M. Ní Riain. Dublin: Halcyon, 2001.

Sancti Ambrosii Mediolanensis Expositio Evangelii secundum Lucam; Fragmenta in Esaiam. Edited by Marcus Adriaen and Paolo Angelo Ballerini. CCSL 14. Turnhout: Brepols, 1957.

Sancti Ambrosii Mediolanensis Episcopi Opera Omnia. Edited by Jacques-Paul Migne. PL 16. Paris: Migne, 1845.

Sancti Ambrosii Opera. Edited by Karl Schenkl, Henricus Schenkl, Michael Petschenig, Otto Faller, and Michaela Zelzer. CSEL 32, 62, 64, 73, 78, 79, 82. Vienna: Tempsky; Leipzig: Freytag, 1897–1996.

Traité sur l'Evangile de saint Luc. Edited by Gabriel Tissot. 2 vols. SC 45, 52. Paris: Cerf, 1956–1958.

LITERATURE

Dassmann. Ernst. "Ambrosius von Mailand." *TRE* 2:362–68.

Dudden, F. Homes. *The Life and Times of St. Ambrose*. 2 vols. Oxford: Clarendon, 1935.

Duval, Yves-Marie. *Ambroise de Milan: XVIe Centenaire de son élection épiscopale: Dix études rassemblées par*. Paris: Études augustiniennes, 1974.

Maur, Hans Jörg auf der. *Das Psalmenverständnis des Ambrosius von Mailand*. Leiden: Brill, 1977.

Pizzolato, Luigi Franco. *La dottrina esegetica di Sant'Ambrogio.* Milan: Vita e pensiero, 1978.

Ramsey, Boniface. *Ambrose.* The Early Church Fathers. London: Routledge, 1997.

Savon, Herve. *Saint Ambroise devant l'exégèse de Philon le Juif.* 2 vols. Paris: Études augustiniennes, 1977.

1.5. JOHN CASSIAN

WORKS

Collationes. Edited by Eugène Pichery. SC 42, 54, 64. Paris: Cerf, 1955–1959.

De Institutis. Edited by Jean-Claude Guy. SC 109. Paris: Cerf, 1965.

Opera. Edited by Michael Petschenig. CSEL 13, 17, 18. Vienna, Tempsky, 1886–1888.

Pachomius. *S. Pachomii Abbatis Tabennensis Regvlae monasticae: Accedit S. Orsiesii eiusdem Pachomii discipuli Doctrina de institvtione monachorvm.* Edited by Bruno Alders. Florilegium Patristicum 16. Bonn: Hanstein, 1923.

LITERATURE

Chadwick, Owen. "Cassianus." *TRE* 7:650–57.

———. *John Cassian: A Study in Primitive Monasticism.* Cambridge: Cambridge University Press, 1950; 2nd ed., 1968.

Frank, Karl Suso, ed. *Askese und Mönchtum in der alten Kirche.* WdF 409. Darmstadt: Wissenschaftliche Buchgesellschaft, 1975.

Lorenz, Rudolf: "Die Anfänge des Abendlandischen Monchstums im 4. Jahrhundert." *ZKG* 77 (1966): 1–61.

Merton, Thomas. *Cassian and the Fathers: Initiation into the Monastic Tradition.* Edited by Patrick F. O'Connell. Monastic Wisdom. Kalamazoo, Mich.: Alban, 2005.

Prinz, Friedrich. *Frühes Mönchtum im Frankenreich : Kultur und Gesellschaft in Gallien, den Rheinlanden und Bayern am Beispiel der monastischen Entwicklung (4. bis 8. Jahrhundert).* 2nd ed. Munich: Oldenbourg, 1988.

1.6. AUGUSTINE

WORKS

De doctrina christiana libri quattuor. Edited by William M. Green. CSEL

80. Vienna: Hoelder-Pichler-Tempsky, 1963 = pages 1–167 in CCSL 32. Turnhout: Brepols, 1962.

De spiritu et littera liber unus. In *De peccatorum meritis et remissione et de baptismo parvulorum ad Marcellinum libri tres; De spiritu et littera liber unus; De natura et origine animae libri quattuor.* Edited by Carl Franz Vrba and Joseph Zycha. CSEL 60. Vienna: Tempsky, 1913.

Enarrationes in Psalmos. Edited by Eligius Dekkers and Johannes Fraipont. 3 vols. CCSL 38–40. Turnhout: Brepols, 1956.

LITERATURE

Matron, Henri. *Saint Augustin et la fin de la culture antique.* Paris: de Boccard, 1958.

Pontet, Maurice. *L'exégèse de Saint Augustin, prédicateur.* Paris: Aubier, 1945.

Schindler, Alfred. "Augustin/Augustinismus I." *TRE* 4:646–98.

Strauss, Gerhard. *Schriftgebrauch, Schriftauslegung und Schriftbeweis bei Augustin.* BGBH 1. Tübingen: Mohr Siebeck, 1959.

Wieland, Wolfgang. *Offenbarung bei Augustinus.* TTS 12. Mainz: Matthias-Grünewald-Verlag, 1978.

2. Mediators between Antiquity and Middle Ages

2.1. Gregory the Great

WORKS

Homiliae in Hiezechihelem prophetam. Edited by Marcus Adriaen. CCSL 142. Turnhout: Brepols, 1971.

Moralia in Iob. Edited by Marcus Adriaen. 3 vols. CCSL 143–143B. Turnhout: Brepols, 1979–1985.

LITERATURE

Evans, Gillian R. *The Thought of Gregory the Great.* Cambridge: Cambridge University Press, 1986.

Gillet, Robert. "Gregoire le Grand." Cols. 872–910 in vol. 6 of *Dictionnaire de spiritualité, ascétique et mystique.* Edited by Marcel Viller et al. 17 vols. Paris: Beauchesne, 1932–1995.

Fontaine, Jacques, Robert Gillet, and Stan Pellistrandi, eds. *Gregoire le Grand.* Paris: Éditions du Centre national de la recherche scientifique, 1986.

Manselli, Raoul. "Gregorio Magno e la Bibbia." Pages 67–101 in *La Bibbia nell'alto medioevo: 26 aprile–2 maggio, 1962.* Settimane di Studio del Centro Italiano sull'alto medioevo 10. Spoleto: Centro italiano di studi sull'alti medioevo, 1963.

Markus, Robert Austin. "Gregor I." *TRE* 14:135–45.

Richards, Jeffrey. *Consul of God: The Life and Times of Gregory the Great.* London: Routledge & Kegan Paul, 1980.

Wasselynck, René. "L'influence de l'exégèse de S. Grégoire Ie Grand sur les commentaires bibliques médiévaux (VIIe-XIIe siècle)." *RThAM* 12 (1965): 157–204.

2.2. Isidore of Seville

Works

Etimologías: Edicion bilingüe. Edited by José Oroz Reta. 2 vols. Madrid: Editorial Católica, 1982.

Opera omnia. Edited by Jacques-Paul Migne. PL 81–83. Paris: Migne, 1862.

Literature

Brehaut, Ernest. *An Encyclopedist of the Dark Ages, Isidore of Seville.* New York: Franklin, 1964.

Collins, Roger John Howard. "Isidor von Sevilla." *TRE* 16:310–15.

Díaz y Díaz, Manuel C., ed. *Isidoriana: Colección de estudios sobre Isidoro de Sevilla.* Centro de Estudios "San Isidoro," 1961.

Diesner, Hans-Joachim. *Isidor von Sevilla und das westgotische Spanien.* Trier: Spee, 1978.

———. *Isidor von Sevilla und seine Zeit.* Stuttgart: Calwer, 1973.

Fontaine, Jacques. "Isidore de Séville." Cols. 2104–16 in vol. 7.2 of *Dictionnaire de spiritualité, ascétique et mystique.* Edited by Marcel Viller et al. 17 vols. Paris: Beauchesne, 1932–1995.

———. *Isidore de Séville et la culture classique dans l'Espagne wisigothique.* 2 vols. Paris: Études augustiniennes, 1959.

———. *Tradition et actualité chez Isidore de Seville.* London: Variorum, 1988.

Pérez de Urbel, Justo. *Isidor von Sevilla: Sein Leben, sein Werk und seine Zeit.* Cologne: Bachem, 1962.

2.3. Venerable Bede

Works

Expositio actuum apostolorum et retractatio. Edited by M. L. W. Laistner. Cambridge: Mediaeval Academy of America, 1930.

Opera exegetica. Edited by Charles Williams Jones et al. CCSL 118a, 119a, 119b, 120, 121. Turnhout: Brepols, 1967–1983.

Literature

Blair, Peter Hunter. *The World of Bede.* London: Secker & Warburg, 1970.

Browne, George F. *The Venerable Bede: His Life and Writings*: Studies in Church History. London: SPCK, 1930.

Kottje, Raymund. "Beda Venerabilis." Pages 58–68 in vol. 3 of *Gestalten der Kirchengeschichte.* Edited by Martin Greschat. 12 vols. Stuttgart: Kohlhammer, 1981–1986.

Loyn, Henry Royston, and Knut Schäferdiek. "Beda Venerabilis." *TRE* 5:397–402.

Mayr-Harting, Henry. *The Coming of Christianity to Anglo-Saxon England.* New York: Schocken, 1972.

Meyvaert, Paul. *Benedict, Gregory, Bede and Others.* London: Variorum, 1977.

Thompson, A. Hamilton, ed. *Bede: His Life, Times and Writings.* 2nd ed. Oxford: Clarendon, 1969.

Willmes, Ansgar. "Bedas Bibelauslegung." *Archiv für Kulturgeschichte* 44 (1962): 281–314.

2.4. Alcuin

Works

Epistolae Karolini aevi. Edited by Ernst Dümmler, MGH, Epistulae 4. Berlin: Weidmann, 1895.

B. Flacci Albini seu Alcuini opera omnia. Edited by Jacques-Paul Migne. 2 vols. PL 100–101. Paris: Migne, 1851–1863.

Literature

Duckett, Eleanor Shipley. *Alcuin, Friend of Charlemagne: His World and His Work.* Hamden, Conn.: Archon, 1965.

Edelstein, Wolfgang. *Eruditio und sapientia: Weltbild und Erziehung in der Karolingerzeit. Untersuchungen zu Alkuins Briefen.* Freiburg im Breisgau: Rombach, 1965.

Gaskoin, C. J. B. *Alcuin: His Life and His Work*. London: Clay, 1904. Repr., New York: Russell & Russell, 1966.

Heil, Wilhelm. "Alkuin." *TRE* 2:266–76.

Michel, Paul, and Schwarz, Alexander. *Unz in obanentig: Aus der Werkstatt der karolingischen Exegeten Alcuin, Erkanbert und Otfrid von Weissenburg*. Studien zur Germanistik, Anglistik und Komparatistik 79. Bonn: Bouvier, 1978.

Riché, Pièrre. *The Carolingians: A Family Who Forged Europe*. Translated by Michael Idomir Allen. Philadelphia: University of Pennsylvania Press, 1993.

Wallach, Luitpold. *Alcuin and Charlemagne*. Studies in Carolingian History and Literature, Cornell Studies in Classical Philology 32. Ithaca, N.Y.: Cornell University Press, 1959.

2.5 JOHN SCOTUS ERIUGENA

WORKS

Commentum in S. Evangelium sec. Johannem. Edited by Edouard Jeauneau. SC 180. Paris: Cerf, 1972.

De divina praedestinatione. Edited by Gulven Madec. CCCM 50. Turnhout: Brepols, 1978.

Homélie sur le prologue de Jean. Edited by Edouard Jeauneau. SC 151. Paris: Cerf, 1969.

LITERATURE

Allard, Guy H., et al., eds. *Jean Scot, écrivain: Actes du IVe colloque international de la SPES*. Montréal: Bellarmin; Paris: Vrin, 1986.

Beierwaltes, Werner, ed. *Eriugena. Studien zu seinen Quellen*. Vorträge des III. internationalen Eriugena-Colloquiums Freiburg i. Br., 27.–30. August, 1979. Abhandlungen der Heidelberger Akademie der Wissenschaften, Phil.Hist. Kl., 3. Heidelberg: Winter, 1980.

Otten, Willemien. *The Anthropology of Johannes Scottus Eriugena*. Brill Studies in Intellectual History 20. Leiden: Brill, 1991.

Schrimpf, Gangolf. *Das Werk des Johannes Scottus Eriugena im Rahmen des Wissenschaftsverständnisses seiner Zeit: Eine Hinführung zu Periphyseon*. Münster: Aschendorff, 1982.

3. The Bible and Theology in the Middle Ages

3.1. Catena and Glosses

Froehlich, Karlfried, and Margaret T. Gibson, eds. *Biblia Latina cum Glossa Ordinaria: Facsimile Reprint of the Editio Princeps by Adolf Rusch von Strassburg.* Turnhout: Brepols, 1993.
Mühlenberg, Ekkehard. "Katenen." *TRE* 18:14–21.
Smalley, Beryl. "Glossa Ordinaria." *TRE* 13:452–57.
Weigand, Rudolf. "Glossen, kanonische." *TRE* 13:457–59.

3.2. Sentences and Questions

Baltzer, Otto. *Die Sentenzen des Petrus Lombardus: Ihre Quellen und ihre dogmengeschichtliche Bedeutung.* Studien zur Geschichte der Theologie und der Kirche 8.3. Leipzig: Dieterich, 1902. Repr., Aalen: Scientia, 1972.
Beumer, Johannes. "Biblische Grundlage und dialektische Methode im Widerstreit innerhalb der mittelalterlichen Scholastik." *Franziskanische Studien* 48 (1966): 233–42
Hödl, Ludwig. "Die dialektische Theologie des 12. Jahrhunderts." Pages 137–47 in *Arts liberaux et philosophie au Moyen Age: Actes du quatrième Congrès international de philosophie médiévale, Université de Montréal, Montréal, Canada, 27 août-2 sept. 1967.* Edited by Ludwig Hödl. Montréal: Institut d'études médiévales; Paris: Vrin, 1969.
Paré, Gérard, A. Brunet, and P. Tremblay. *La renaissance du XIIe siècle. Les écoles et l'enseignement.* Paris: Vrin, 1933.
Riché, Pièrre. *Ecoles et enseignement dans le Haut Moyen Age: Fin du Ve siècle-milieu du XIe siècle.* Paris: Picard, 1979.
Stegmüller, Friedrich. "Sentenzenwerke." *RGG* 5:1701–3.

3.3. Abelard

WORKS
Historia calamitatum. Edited by Jacques Monfrin. 3rd ed. Paris: Vrin, 1967.
Petri Abaelardi Opera Theologica. Edited by Eligius M. Buytaert. CCCM 11–15. Turnhout: Brepols, 1969–2004.

LITERATURE

Angenendt, Arnold. "Peter Abaelard." Pages 148–60 in vol. 3 of *Gestalten der Kirchengeschichte*. Edited by Martin Greschat. 12 vols. Stuttgart: Kohlhammer, 1981–1986.

Buytaert, E. M., ed. *Peter Abelard: Proceedings of the International Conference, Louvain, May 10–12, 1971*. Medievalia Lovanensia Series 1/2. Leuven: Leuven University Press, 1973.

Centre national de la recherche scientifique, and Association Française pour les Célébrations Nationales. *Abelard et son temps: Actes du colloque international organisé a l'occasion du 9e centenaire de la naissance de Pierre Abélard (14–19 mai 1979)*. Paris: Belles Lettres, 1981.

Cluny. *Pierre Abélard, Pierre le Vénérable: Les courants philosophiques, littéraires et artistiques en Occident au milieu du XIIe siècle: Abbaye de Cluny, 2 au 9 juillet 1972*. Colloques Internationaux du Centre Nationale de la Réchèrche Scientifique 546. Paris: Éditions du Centre national de la recherche scientifique, 1975.

Grane, Leif. *Peter Abelard: Philosophy and Christianity in the Middle Ages*. Translated by Frederick and Christine Crowley. New York: Harcourt, Brace & World, 1970.

Peppermüller, Rolf. *Abaelards Auslegung des Römerbriefes*. BGPhMA NS 10. Münster: Aschendorff, 1972.

3.4. RUPERT OF DEUTZ

WORKS

Commentaria in Canticum Canticorum. Edited by Rhaban Haacke. CCCM 26. Turnhout: Brepols, 1974.

Commentaria in evangelium sancti Johannis. Edited by Rhaban Haacke. CCCM 9. Turnhout: Brepols, 1979.

De divinis officiis. Edited by Rhaban Haacke. CCCM 7. Turnhout: Brepols, 1967.

De gloria et honore filii hominis super Mattheum. Edited by Rhaban Haacke. CCCM 29. Turnhout: Brepols, 1979.

De sancta trinitate et operibus eius. Edited by Rhaban Haacke. 4 vols. CCCM 21–24. Turnhout: Brepols, 1971–1974.

De victoria verbi dei. Edited by Rhaban Haacke. MGH, QG 5. Berlin: Böhlau, 1970.

Lesungen über Johannes: Der geistige Sinn seines Evangeliums. Translated by Ferdinand Edmunds and Rhaban Haacke. 2 vols. Trier: Spee-Verlag, 1977.

Os meum aperui. Die Autobiographie des Rupert von Deutz. Edited by Walter Berschin. Cologne: Luthe-Verlag, 1985.

Oehl, Wilhelm, ed. *Deutsche Mystikerbriefe des Mittelalters.* Munich: Müller, 1931.

LITERATURE

Arduini, Maria Ludovica. *Rupert von Deutz (1076–1129) und der Status Christianitatis seiner Zeit: Symbolisch-prophetische Deutung der Geschichte.* Cologne: Böhlau, 1987.

Holze, Heinrich. "Schriftauslegung aus monastischer Theologie bei Rupert von Deutz." Pages 229–39 in *Scriptura: Das reformatorische Schriftprinzip in der säkularen Welt.* Edited by Hans Heinrich Schmidt and Joachim Mehlhausen. Gütersloh: Mohn, 1991.

Van Engen, John H. *Rupert of Deutz.* Berkeley and Los Angeles: University of California Press, 1983.

3.5. HUGO OF ST. VICTOR

WORKS

The Didascalicon of Hugh of St. Victor: A Medieval Guide to the Arts. Translated with an introduction and notes by Jerome Taylor. Records of Civilization: Sources and Studies 64. New York: Columbia University Press, 1961.

Hugonis de Sancto Victore Didascalion de studio legendi. Edited by Charles H. Buttimer. SMRL 10. Washington, D.C.: Catholic University of America, 1939.

Ioachim abbas Florensis Psalterium decem cordarum. Edited by Kurt-Victor Selge. Fonti per la storia dell'Italia medievale, Antiquitates 34. Rome: Istituto storico italiano per il Medioevo, 2009.

Tractatus in expositionem vite et regule beati Benedicti: Cum appendice fragmenti (I) de duobus prophetis in novissimis diebus praedicaturis. Edited by Alexander Patschovsky. Fonti per la storia dell'Italia medievale, Antiquitates 29. Rome: Istituto storico italiano per il Medioevo, 2008.

LITERATURE

Baron, Roger. *Études sur Hugues de Saint-Victor.* Paris: Desclée, De Brouwer, 1963.

Ehlers, Joachim. *Hugo von St. Viktor: Studien zum Geschichtsdenken und zur Geschichtsschreibung des 12. Jahrhunderts.* 7th ed. Wiesbaden: Steiner, 1973.

———. "Hugo von St. Viktor und die Viktoriner." Pages 192–204 in vol. 3 of *Gestalten der Kirchengeschichte*. Edited by Martin Greschat. 12 vols. Stuttgart: Kohlhammer, 1981–1986.

Sicard, Patrice. *Hugues de Saint-Victeur et son école: Introduction, choix de texte, traduction et commentaries*. Turnhout: Brepols, 1991.

Taylor, Jerome. *The Didascalion of Hugh of St. Victor*. New York: Columbia University Press, 1961.

3.6. JOACHIM OF FIORE

WORKS

Concordia Novi ac Veteris Testamenti. Venice, 1519. Repr., Frankfurt am Main: Minerva, 1964

Enchiridion super Apocalypsim. Edited by Edward Kilian Burger. Toronto: Pontifical Institute of Mediaeval Studies, 1986.

Expositio in Apocalypsim. Venice, 1527. Repr., Frankfurt am Main: Minerva, 1964.

Liber de concordia Novi ac Veteris Testamenti. Edited by E. Randolph Daniel. TAPS 73.8. Philadelphia: American Philosophical Society, 1983.

Das Reich des Heiligen Geistes. Translated from the Latin by Rose Birchler. Munich-Planegg: Barth, 1955.

Psalterium decem chordarum. Venice, 1527. Repr., Frankfurt am Main: Minerva, 1964.

Tractatus super quattuor evangelia. Edited by Ernesto Buonaiuti. Fonti per la Storia d'Italia 67; Scrittori seculo 12. Rome: Tipografia del Senato, 1930.

Tondelli, Leone, Majorie Reeves, and Beatrice Hirsch-Reich. *Il Libro delle Figure, dell' Abbato Gioachino da Fiore*. 2 vols. 2nd ed. Turin: Societa editrice internazionale, 1953.

LITERATURE

Benz, Ernst. "Joachim-Studien I: Die Kategorien der religiösen Geschichtsdeutung Joachims." *ZKG* 50 (1931): 24–111

———. "Joachim-Studien II: Die Exzerptsätze der Pariser Professoren aus dem Evangelium Aetemum," *ZKG* 51 (1932): 415–55.

———. "Joachim-Studien III: Thomas von Aquin und Joachim von Fiore. Die katholische Antwort auf die spiritualistische Kirchen- und Geschichtsanschauung." *ZKG* 53 (1934): 52–116.

Denifle, Heinrich. "Das Evangelium Aetemum und die Commission zu Anagni." *ALKG* I (1885): 49–142.

Grundmann, Herbert. *Neue Forschungen über Joachim von Fiore*. Münstersche Forschungen 1. Marburg: Simons, 1950.

———. *Studien über Joachim von Floris: Beiträge zur Kulturgeschichte des Mittelalters und der Neuzeit*. Leipzig, 1927; Repr.,: Darmstadt: Wissenschaftliche Buchgesellschaft, 1966.

Lerner, Robert E. "Joachim von Fiore." *TRE* 17:84–88.

Mottu, Henry. "Joachim von Fiore." Pages 249–66 in vol. 3 of *Gestalten der Kirchengeschichte*. Edited by Martin Greschat. 12 vols. Stuttgart: Kohlhammer, 1981–1986.

———. *La manifestation de l'Esprit selon Joachim de Fiore: Herméneutique et théologie de l'histoire d'après le "Traité sur les quatre évangiles."* Neuchatel: Delachaux, 1977.

Reeves, Marjorie. *The Influence of Prophecy in the Later Middle Ages: A Study in Joachimism*. Oxford: Clarendon, 1969.

———. *Joachim of Fiore and the Prophetic Future*. New York: Harper & Row, 1976.

Reeves, Marjorie, and Beatrice Hirsch-Reich. *The Figurae of Joachim of Fiore*. Oxford: Clarendon, 1972.

Töpfer, Bernhard. *Das kommende Reich des Friedens: Zur Entwicklung chiliastischer Zukunftshoffnungen im Hochmittelalter*. Berlin: Akademie-Verlag, 1964.

West, Delno C., and Sandra Zimdar-Swarz. *Joachim of Fiore: A Study in Spiritual Perception and History*. Bloomington: Indiana University Press, 1983.

3.7. THOMAS AQUINAS

Des heiligen Thomas von Aquin Kommentar zum Römerbrief. Translated by Helmut Fahsel. Freiburg im Breisgau: Herder, 1927.

Lectures on the Letters to the Romans. Translated by Fabian Larcher. Edited by Jeremy Holmes, with the support of the Aquinas Center for Theological Renewal. Online: http://www.aquinas.avemaria.edu/Aquinas_on_Romans.pdf.

Summa contra gentiles. Edited by Petrus Marc. 2 vols. Turin: Marietti, 1961–1967.

Summa theologiae. Edited by Petri Caramello. 3 vols. in 4. Turin: Marietti, 1952–1956.

Super epistolas S. Pauli Lectura. Edited by Raphaelis Cai. 8th ed. 2 vols. Turin: Marietti, 1953.

LITERATURE

Arias-Reyero, Maximino. *Thomas von Aquin als Exeget: Die Prinzipien seiner Schriftdeutung und seine Lehre von den Schriftsinnen.* Einsiedeln: Johannes Verlag, 1971.

Chenu, Marie-Dominique. *Toward Understanding Saint Thomas.* Translated by A.-M. Landry and D. Hugues. Chicago: Regnery, 1964.

Domanyi, Thomas. *Der Römerbriefkommentar des Thomas von Aquin: Ein Beitrag zur Untersuchung seiner Auslegungsmethoden.* Basler und Berner Studien zur historischen und systematischen Theologie 39. Bern: Lang, 1979.

Kühn, Ulrich: "Thomas von Aquin." Pages 212–25 in vol. 1 of *Klassiker der Theologie.* Edited by Heinrich Fries und Georg Kretschmar. Munich: Beck, 1981.

Pesch, Otto Hermann. *Thomas von Aquin: Grenze und Größe mittelalterlicher Theologie.* Mainz: Matthias-Grünewald-Verlag, 1988.

Seckler, Max. *Das Heil in der Geschichte: Geschichtstheologisches Denken bei Thomas von Aquin.* Munich: Kösel-Verlag, 1964.

Weissheipl, James A. *Friar Thomas D'Aquino: His Life, Thought, and Works.* Oxford: Blackwell, 1975.

3.8. BONAVENTURA

WORKS

Collationes in Hexameron et Bonaventuriana quaedam selecta. Edited by Ferdinand M. Delorme. Bibliotheca Franciscana Scholastica Medii Aevi 8. Quaracchi: Collegio San Bonaventura, 1934.

Collations on the Six Days. Translated by José de Vinck. Vol. 5 of *Works of St. Bonaventure.* Patterson, N.J.: St. Anthony Guild Press, 1969. Repr., Quincy, Ill.: Franciscan Press, 2000.

Opera Omnia. Edited by R. P. Bernardini et al. 10 vols. Quaracchi: Collegio San Bonaventura, 1882–1902.

LITERATURE

Bougerol, Jacques Guy. *Introduction to the Works of Bonaventure.* Translated by José de Vinck. Paterson, N.J.: St. Anthony Guild Press, 1963.

———, ed. *S. Bonaventura 1274–1974/5, Bibliographia Bonaventuriana (c.1850–1973).* 5 vols. Rome: Collegio San Bonaventura, 1974.

Detloff, Werner. "Bonaventura." *TRE* 7:48–55.

———. "Bonaventura." Pages 198–211 in *Klassiker der Theologie*. Edited by Heinrich Fries und Georg Kretschmar. Munich: Beck, 1981.

Gilson, Etienne. *The Philosophy of St. Bonaventure*. Translated by Illtyd Trethowan and Frank J. Sheed. Paterson, N.J.: St. Anthony Guild Press, 1960.

Mercker, Hans. *Schriftauslegung als Weltauslegung: Untersuchungen zur Stellung der Schrift in der Theologie Bonaventuras*. Veröffentlichungen des Grabmann-Institutes NS 15. Munich: Schöningh, 1971.

Ratzinger, Joseph. *The theology of history in St. Bonaventure*. Translated by Zachary Hayes. Chicago: Franciscan Herald Press, 1971.

4. Jewish Interpreters of the Middle Ages

General

Bacher, Wilhelm. *Die Bibelexegese der jüdischen Religionsphilosophen des Mittelalters vor Maimûni*. Strassburg: Trübner, 1892.

Greenberg, Moshe, ed. *Jewish Bible Exegesis: An Introduction* [Hebrew]. Jerusalem: Mosad Bialik, 1983.

Greive, Hermann. *Die Juden: Grundzüge ihrer Geschichte im mittelalterlichen und neuzeitlichen Europa*. Darmstadt: Wissenschaftliche Buchgesellschaft, 1982.

Schubert, Kurt. *Judentum im Mittelalter*. Vol. 2 of *Die Kultur der Juden*. Wiesbaden: Akademische Verlagsgesellschaft Athenaion, 1979.

Vajda, Georges. *Introduction à la pensée juive du Moyen Age*. Paris: Vrin, 1947.

Winter, Jacob, and August Wünsche. eds. *Geschichte der rabbinischen Literatur während des Mittelalters und ihrer Nachblüte in der neueren Zeit*. Trier: Mayer, 1894. Repr., Hildesheim: Olms, 1965.

4.1. Rashi

Works

Berliner, Abraham. *Der Kommentar des Solomon ben Isaak über den Pentateuch*. Frankfurt am Main: Kauffmann, 1905.

Herczeg, Yisrael, trans. *The Torah with Rashi's Commentary, Translated, Annotated and Elucidated*. 2 vols. Brooklyn, N.Y.: Mesorah Publications, 1995.

Widmer, Gottfried. *Die Kommentare von Raschi, Ibn Esra, Radaq zu Joel, Text, Übersetzung und Erläuterung: Eine Einführung in die rabbinische Exegese.* Basel: Lewin, 1945.

LITERATURE

Banitt, Menahem. *Rashi, Interpreter of the Biblical Letter.* Tel Aviv: Chaim Rosenberg School of Jewish Studies, Tel Aviv University, 1985.

Federbusch, Simon, ed. *Rashi: His Teachings and Personality.* New York: World Jewish Congress, 1958.

Gelles, Benjamin J. *Peshat and Derash in the Exegesis of Rashi.* Leiden: Brill, 1981.

Shereshevsky, Esra. *Rashi, the Man and his World.* New York: Sepher-Hermon Press, 1982.

4.2. IBN EZRA

WORKS

Lipshitz, Abraham, ed. *The Commentary of Rabbi Abraham Ibn Ezra on Hosea: Edited from Six Manuscripts and Translated with an Introduction and Notes.* New York: Sepher-Hermon Press, 1988.

Shachter, Jay F. *Leviticus.* Vol. 3 of *The Commentary of Abraham Ibn Ezra on the Pentateuch.* Hoboken, N.J.: Ktav, 1986.

LITERATURE

Friedländer, Michael. *Essays on the Writings of Abraham ibn Ezra.* Society of Hebrew Literature, Publications Series 2. London: Trübner, 1877.

Greive, Hermann. *Studien zum jüdischen Neuplatonismus: Die Religionsphilosophie des Abraham Ibn Ezra.* Berlin: de Gruyter, 1973.

Rosin, David. "Die religionsphilosophie Abraham ibn Esras." *MGWJ* 42 (1898): 17–33, 58, 73, 108–15, 154–61, 200–214, 241–52, 305–15, 345–62, 394–407, 444–57, 481–505; 43 (1899): 22–31, 75–91, 125–33, 168–84, 231–40.

5. LATE MEDIEVAL EXEGETES

5.1. NICHOLAS OF LYRA

WORKS

The Postilla of Nicholas of Lyra on the Song of Songs. Edited and translated by James George Kiecker. Milwaukee: Marquette University Press, 1998.

Postilla super totam Bibliam. 4 vols. Strassburg, 1492. Repr., Frankfurt am Main: Minerva, 1971.

Prologus (in *Postillam litteralem*); *Prologus secundus; De intentione auctoris et mode procendendi; Prologus in moralitates Bibliorum.* Edited by Jacques-Paul Migne. PL 112. Paris: Migne, 1879 (pp. 26–36).

LITERATURE

Deeana Copeland Klepper. *The Insight of Unbelievers: Nicholas of Lyra and Christian Reading of Jewish Text in the Later Middle Ages.* Jewish Culture and Contexts. Philadelphia: University of Pennsylvania Press, 2007.

Hazard, Mark. *The Literal Sense and the Gospel of John in Late-Medieval Commentary and Literature.* Studies in Medieval History and Culture 12. New York: Routledge, 2002.

Langlois, Charles. "Nicolas de Lyre, Frere Minéur." *Histoire littéraire de la France* 36 (1924): 355–400.

5.2. JOHN WYCLIF

WORKS

De civili dominio. Edited by Johann Loserth. 3 vols. London: Trübner, 1885–1902. Repr., New York: Johnson Reprint, 1966.

De dominio divino libri tres: To Which Are Added the First Four Books of the Treatise De pauperie Salvatoris. Edited by Lane Poole. London: Trübner, 1890. Repr., New York: Johnson Reprint, 1966.

De eucharistia tractatus major. Edited by Johann Loserth. London: Trübner, 1892. Repr., New York: Johnson Reprint, 1966.

De veritate sacrae scripturae. Edited by Rudolf Buddensieg. 3 vols. London: Trübner, 1905–1907. Repr., New York: Johnson Reprint, 1966.

Fasciculi Zizanorum Magistri Johannis Wyclif cum tritico. Ascribed to Thomas Netter of Walden. Edited by Walter Waddington Shirley. Rerum Britannicarum medii aevi scriptores 5. London: Longman, Brown, Green, Longmans, & Roberts, 1858.

Johannis Wiclif trialogus cum supplemento trialogi. Edited by Gotthard Victor Lechler. Oxford: Oxford University Press, 1869.

Opus evangelicum. Edited by Johann Loserth. 4 vols. in 2. London: Trübner, 1895–1896. Repr., New York: Johnson Reprint, 1966.

Tractatus de mandatis divinis accedit tractatus de statu innocencie. Edited by Johann Loserth and F. D. Matthew. London: C. K. Paul, 1922. Repr., New York: Johnson Reprint, 1966.

Tractatus de officio regis. Edited by Alfred W. Pollard and Charles Sayle. London: Trübner for the Wyclif Societ, 1887. Repr., New York: Johnson Reprint, 1966.

LITERATURE

Benrath, Gustav Adolf. *Wyclifs Bibelkommentar.* Arbeiten zur Kirchengeschichte 36. Berlin: de Gruyter, 1966.

Hurley, Michael. "Scriptura Sola: Wyclif and His Critics." *Traditio* 16 (1960): 275–352.

Kenny, Anthony, ed. *Wyclif in His Times.* Oxford: Oxford University Press, 1986.

Lahey, Stephen E. *John Wyclif.* Great Medieval Thinkers. New York: Oxford University Press, 2009.

McFarlane, K. B. *Wycliffe and English Nonconformity.* Harmondsworth: Penguin, 1972.

Robson, John Adam. *Wyclif and the Oxford Schools.* Cambridge: Cambridge University Press, 1961.

Smalley, Beryl. "Wyclif's Postilla on the Old Testament and His Principium." Pages 253–96 in *Oxford Studies Presented to Daniel Callus.* Oxford: Clarendon, 1964.

Workman, Herbert B. *John Wyclif: A Study of the English Medieval Church.* Oxford: Clarendon, 1926. Repr., Hamden, Conn.: Archon, 1966.

Index of Names and Places

INDEX OF SUBJECTS

Index of Biblical References

CPSIA information can be obtained at www.ICGtesting.com

230872LV00006B/7/P